The book accomplishes a great fact-finding mission describing the consequences of right-wing populists in government for party competition. It begins the hunt for theory and finds new puzzles: the effects of radical right-wing government involvement are more complicated than anticipated. The book is an indispensable building block for any scholar dealing with this subject.

Herbert Kitschelt, George V. Allen Professor of International Relations,
Duke University, USA

In 2000 Hainsworth *et al.* noted that the extreme right was moving "from the margins to the mainstream." Fifteen years later, in a long-overdue but worthy 'successor' to Hainsworth's seminal volume, Akkerman *et al.* observe that radical right-wing populist parties have now solidly moved "into the mainstream".

Cas Mudde, Associate Professor, Department of International Affairs,
University of Georgia, USA

This book offers an updated and in depth analysis of case studies of right-wing populism and extremism, alongside the validation of a crucial hypothesis: have these parties conquered more of the political space of the moderate mainstream right? Thanks to an empirically grounded comparative survey examining the phenomenon, the authors demonstrate that, contrary to shared wisdom, the populist far right is still secure in its extreme position, and remains quite distant from other mainstream parties all over Europe. Moreover, underlining the fact that the gap between extreme and mainstream parties has only been narrowed where a critique of the European Union is concerned, the authors offer further hints to the sensitive topic of euro-scepticism.

Piero Ignazi, Professor of Comparative Politics, University of Bologna, Italy

Radical Right-Wing Populist Parties in Western Europe

Radical right-wing populist parties, such as Geert Wilders' Party for Freedom, Marine Le Pen's National Front or Nigel Farage's UKIP, are becoming increasingly influential in Western European democracies. Their electoral support is growing, their impact on policy-making is substantial, and in recent years several radical right-wing populist parties have assumed office or supported minority governments.

Are these developments the cause and/or consequence of the mainstreaming of radical right-wing populist parties? Have radical right-wing populist parties expanded their issue profiles, moderated their policy positions, toned down their anti-establishment rhetoric and shed their extreme right reputations to attract more voters and/or become coalition partners? This timely book answers these questions on the basis of both comparative research and a wide range of case studies, covering Austria, Belgium, Denmark, Finland, France, the Netherlands, Norway, Switzerland, and the United Kingdom.

Analysing the extent to which radical right-wing populist parties have become part of mainstream politics, as well as the factors and conditions which facilitate this trend, this book is essential reading for students and scholars working in European politics, in addition to anyone interested in party politics and current affairs more generally.

Tjitske Akkerman is Assistant Professor in the Department of Political Science at the University of Amsterdam, the Netherlands.

Sarah L. de Lange is Associate Professor in the Department of Political Science at the University of Amsterdam, the Netherlands.

Matthijs Rooduijn is a Post-doctoral Researcher and Lecturer in the Department of Political Science at the University of Amsterdam, the Netherlands.

Extremism and Democracy

Series Editors: Roger Eatwell, University of Bath, and Matthew Goodwin, University of Kent.

Founding Series Editors: Roger Eatwell, University of Bath and Cas Mudde, University of Antwerp-UFSIA.

This new series encompasses academic studies within the broad fields of 'extremism' and 'democracy'. These topics have traditionally been considered largely in isolation by academics. A key focus of the series, therefore, is the (inter-)relation between extremism and democracy. Works will seek to answer questions such as to what extent 'extremist' groups pose a major threat to democratic parties, or how democracy can respond to extremism without undermining its own democratic credentials.

The books encompass two strands:

Routledge Studies in Extremism and Democracy includes books with an introductory and broad focus which are aimed at students and teachers. These books will be available in hardback and paperback. Titles include:

Understanding Terrorism in America
From the Klan to al Qaeda
Christopher Hewitt

Fascism and the Extreme Right
Roger Eatwell

Racist Extremism in Central and Eastern Europe
Edited by Cas Mudde

Political Parties and Terrorist Groups (2nd Edition)
Leonard Weinberg, Ami Pedahzur and Arie Perliger

The New Extremism in 21st Century Britain
Edited by Roger Eatwell and Matthew Goodwin

New British Fascism
Rise of the British National Party
Matthew Goodwin

The End of Terrorism?
Leonard Weinberg

Mapping the Extreme Right in Contemporary Europe
From local to transnational
Edited by Andrea Mammone, Emmanuel Godin and Brian Jenkins

Varieties of Right-Wing Extremism in Europe
Edited by Andrea Mammone, Emmanuel Godin and Brian Jenkins

Right-Wing Radicalism Today
Perspectives from Europe
and the US
Edited by Sabine von Mering and
Timothy Wyman McCarty

Revolt on the Right
Explaining support for the radical
right in Britain
Robert Ford and Matthew Goodwin

The Politicisation of Migration
Edited by Wouter van der Brug,
Gianni D'Amato, Joost Berkhout
and Didier Ruedin

Radical Right-Wing Populist
Parties in Western Europe
Into the mainstream?
Edited by Tjitske Akkerman,
Sarah L. de Lange and
Matthijs Rooduijn

Routledge Research in Extremism and Democracy offers a forum for innovative new research intended for a more specialist readership. These books will be in hardback only. Titles include:

Radical Right-Wing Populist Parties in Western Europe

Into the mainstream?

Edited by
Tjitske Akkerman, Sarah L. de Lange
and Matthijs Rooduijn

LONDON AND NEW YORK

First published 2016
by Routledge
2 Park Square, Milton Park, Abingdon, Oxon OX14 4RN

and by Routledge
711 Third Avenue, New York, NY 10017

Routledge is an imprint of the Taylor & Francis Group, an informa business

British Library Cataloguing in Publication Data
A catalogue record for this book is available from the British Library

Library of Congress Cataloging in Publication Data
Names: Akkerman, Tjitske, editor. | Lange, Sarah L. de, editor. |
    Rooduijn, Matthijs, editor.
Title: Radical right-wing populist parties in Western Europe : into the
    mainstream? / edited by Tjitske Akkerman, Sarah L. de Lange,
    Matthijs Rooduijn.
Description: New York, NY : Routledge, 2016. | Series: Routledge studies
    in extremism and democracy | Includes bibliographical references.
Identifiers: LCCN 2015032846| ISBN 9781138914834 (hardback) |
    ISBN 9781138914988 (pbk.) | ISBN 9781315687988 (e-book)
Subjects: LCSH: Right-wing extremists–Europe, Western. |
    Populism–Europe, Western. | Political parties–Europe, Western. |
    Europe, Western–Politics and government–1989-
Classification: LCC JC573.2.E85 R34 2016 | DDC 324.2/13094–dc23
LC record available at http://lccn.loc.gov/2015032846

ISBN: 978-1-138-91483-4 (hbk)
ISBN: 978-1-138-91498-8 (pbk)
ISBN: 978-1-315-68798-8 (ebk)

Typeset in Bembo
by Taylor & Francis Books

Contents

List of illustrations

Figures

Tables

List of contributors

Tjitske Akkerman is Assistant Professor at the Department of Political Science, University of Amsterdam.

Flemming Juul Christiansen is an Associate Professor at Roskilde University.

Kristina Hauser, MA is a doctoral fellow at the University of Salzburg at the Chair of Austrian Politics in Comparative European Perspective.

Reinhard Heinisch, PhD is Professor of Austrian Politics in Comparative European Perspective at the University of Salzburg.

Gilles Ivaldi is Researcher in Political Science, CNRS-University of Nice.

Ann-Cathrine Jungar is a Senior Lecturer in political science at the School of Social Sciences at Södertörn University, Stockholm.

Anders Ravik Jupskås is currently lecturer at the Department of Political Science, University of Oslo.

Sarah L. de Lange is Associate Professor at the Department of Political Science, University of Amsterdam.

Paul Lucardie is officially retired but continues to work as a researcher on a voluntary basis. He has been affiliated to the Documentation Centre on Dutch Political Parties (DNPP) at the University of Groningen.

Oscar Mazzoleni is Professor at the Institute of Political, Historical and International Studies, University of Lausanne.

Teun Pauwels is Policy Analyst at the Flemish Ministry of Education and Training.

Matthijs Rooduijn is Postdoctoral Researcher at the Amsterdam Institute for Inequality Studies (AMCIS), University of Amsterdam.

Simon Usherwood is Associate Dean of the Faculty of Arts & Social Sciences at the University of Surrey.

Acknowledgement

This book started with the conference 'Into the mainstream? Radical right-wing populist parties in the new millennium', University of Amsterdam, 19/20 June 2014. We would like to thank the Amsterdam Institute for Social Science Research and the Department of Political Science for their joint support. We would like to thank all the participants/authors and Wouter van der Brug, Matthew Goodwin, Simon Otjes, and Joost van Spanje for their contributions.

1 Inclusion and mainstreaming?

Radical right-wing populist parties in the new millennium

Tjitske Akkerman, Sarah L. de Lange and Matthijs Rooduijn

Introduction

The West European radical right-wing populist party family has gone through various transitions during the past three decades. In the 1990s, the adoption of anti-immigration and populist master-frames opened up an escape route from the margins for many radical right-wing populist parties. As a result, they gained increasing support from voters, with parties like the French National Front (Front National; FN), the Austrian Freedom Party (Freiheitliche Partei Österreichs; FPÖ), the Norwegian Progress Party (Fremskrittspartiet; FrP), and the Swiss People's Party (Schweizerische Volkspartei; SVP) supported by more than 10 per cent of the electorate (see Table 1.1).

After the turn of the millennium, the upward trend continued for most radical right-wing populist parties, with the Danish People's Party (Dansk Folkeparti; DF) and the Flemish Interest (Vlaams Blok/Belang; VB) also crossing the 10 per cent mark. Moreover, a number of new, electorally successful radical right-wing populist parties emerged on the scene, such as the Alliance for the Future of Austria (Bündnis Zukunft Österreich; BZÖ), the Greek Popular Orthodox Rally (Laikós Orthódoxos Synagermós; LAOS), the Dutch List Pim Fortuyn (Lijst Pim Fortuyn; LPF), the Dutch Party for Freedom (Partij voor de Vrijheid; PVV), the Swedish Democrats (Sverigedemokraterna; SD) and the Finns Party (Perussuomalaiset; PS). As Table 1.1 shows, the average radical right-wing populist party vote share in national elections has increased from 8.0 per cent in the 1990s to 12.5 per cent in recent years (see also Mudde 2013; Zaslove 2011).

As a consequence of increased support, various radical right-wing populist parties have entered governments, either as cabinet members or as support parties of minority governments (Akkerman and De Lange 2012; De Lange 2012a, 2012b). In Austria, Finland, Italy, the Netherlands, Norway and Switzerland, radical right-wing populist parties took up the responsibilities that come with holding office, while in Denmark and the Netherlands, the DF and the PVV agreed to support minority governments without formally joining them (see Table 1.2). Many of these parties participated in multiple coalitions, leading to the formation of 17 governments including, or being supported by, radical right-wing populist parties between 1990 and 2015.

Table 1.1 Average percentage of radical right-wing populist parties' vote share in national elections in Western Europe

Country	Party	1990–1999	2000–2009	2010–2015
Austria	BZÖ		7.4	3.5
	FPÖ	22.0	12.8	20.5
Belgium	FNb	1.6	2.0	
	VB	8.1	11.8	5.8
Denmark	DF	7.4	13.2	16.7
	FrP	5.1	0.6	
Finland	PS	2.4	2.9	18.3
France	FN	13.7	7.8	13.6
	MNR★		1.1	
Germany	REP★	1.9	0.6	
Greece	LAOS		3.9	1.8
Italy	LN	9.1	5.6	4.1
Netherlands	CD	1.6		
	LPF		11.4	
	PVV		5.9	12.8
Norway	FRP	10.8	19.9	16.3
Sweden	NyD	4.0		
	SD		3.3	12.9
Switzerland	SVP	16.4	27.8	28.9
United Kingdom	BNP★		1.9	
	UKIP★		1.9	7.9
Average		8.0	7.5	12.5

Note: ★ Party only elected to the European Parliament.
Source: data from www.parlgov.org.

At the same time, the strength of the party family should not be overstated. Radical right-wing populist parties have also experienced electoral decline during the past decade (e.g., the VB) and some have disappeared from the political stage altogether (e.g., the LPF and the Swedish New Democracy [Ny Demokrati; NyD]). Not all Western European countries have electorally successful radical right-wing populist parties. Moreover, participation in national government is not always an option for successful parties. In Belgium, France, Sweden and the United Kingdom, radical right-wing populist parties have not had any opportunity yet to enter national office (Mudde 2013). Nevertheless, for most parties the trend seems to be upward. The electoral growth of the radical right-wing populist party

Table 1.2 Radical right-wing populist parties in office

Country	Party	Cabinet	Composition	Period
Austria	FPÖ	Schüssel I	ÖVP-FPÖ	2000–2005
	BZÖ	Schüssel I	ÖVP-BZÖ	2005–2006
Denmark	DF	A.F.Rasmussen I	V-KF-(DF)	2001–2005
	DF	A.F.Rasmussen II	V-KF-(DF)	2005–2007
	DF	A.F.Rasmussen III	V-KF-(DF)	2007–2009
	DF	L.L.Rasmussen I	V-KF-(DF)	2009–2011
	DF	L.L.Rasmussen II	V-(DF)	2015–
Finland	PS	Sipila II	KESK-KOK-PS	2015–
Italy	LN	Berlusconi I	FI-AN-LN-CCD-UCD	1994–1994
	LN	Berlusconi II/III	FI-AN-LN	2001–2006
	LN	Berlusconi IV	PdL-LN-MpA	2008–2011
Netherlands	LPF	Balkenende I	CDA-LPF-VVD	2003–2003
	PVV	Rutte I	VVD-CDA-(PVV)	2010–2012
Norway	FrP	Solberg I	H-FrP	2013–
Switzerland	SVP	–	–	2003–2007
	SVP	–	–	2007–2011
	SVP	–	–	2011–

family, as well as its recent participation in government coalitions, provide important clues that the parties belonging to this family have become a force to be reckoned with.

This book aims to assess whether the described developments have induced radical right-wing populist parties to move into the mainstream. The starting point for this assumption is the inclusion-moderation thesis, which holds that participation in democratic institutions and procedures will amend the radical nature and ideology of political parties. According to Berman (2008), there are two explanations for the moderating effects of inclusion. First, inclusion into the electoral game will have a moderating effect according to the Downsian logic of the median-voter theorem. Downs (1957) argues that parties will appeal to the median voter in order to attract a majority of votes, provided these are normally distributed along the dimension on which they compete. Over time, this vote-seeking logic will force parties to abandon the narrow or sectarian profiles on the basis of which they were first founded. If West European voters were to be normally distributed and if radical right-wing populist parties strive to obtain an electoral majority, the Downsian logic should also apply to these parties. It is questionable, however, whether radical right-wing populist parties in West European democracies have adopted this as their main objective (see below). A second explanation focuses on inclusion into office. Assuming office is supposed to have a moderating effect, because in West European democracies it requires the formation of coalitions. In coalition governments, policy and ideological distances that exist between coalition partners have to be bridged. For radical right-wing populist parties this implies that they have to adjust their agendas and positions to those of mainstream right-wing parties, because cooperation with these parties is their most likely ticket into office. Moreover, parties that enter office must be able to convince voters that they can deliver the goods; when they are busy filling potholes and fixing sewage systems they cannot devote their energy to ideological radicalism (Berman 2008: 6; MacMillan 2006).

The inclusion-moderation thesis is mainly focused on (orthodox) religious parties, (e.g., Brocker and Künkler 2013; Elman 2014; Gurses 2014; Kalyvas and Van Kersbergen 2010; Somer 2014; Schwedler 2011, 2013; Tepe 2012; see also Karakaya and Yildrim 2013 on communist parties; Przeworski and Sprague 1986 on socialist parties). Research on the radical right-wing populist party family that systematically tests the inclusion-moderation thesis is scarce. On the basis of case studies it has been claimed that entrance into office need not imply that radical right parties de-radicalise (Albertazzi 2009; Minkenberg 2013). Moreover, a few case studies have indicated that some radical right parties manage quite well to uphold a radical profile while in office (Albertazzi and McDonnell 2005; Frölich-Steffen and Rensmann 2007). Thus, it might be the case that inclusion into office is not sufficient to pressure radical right-wing populist parties to moderate.

The inclusion-moderation thesis is mirrored by the exclusion-radicalisation thesis, which stipulates that parties that are excluded from the party and political system will radicalise their stances. The exclusion of political parties often occurs through legal bans (Downs 2001, 2002). Such bans are, however, exceptional in Western Europe, and the number of radical right-wing populist parties affected by bans is minimal (Bale 2007). Legal prosecution of radical right-wing populist politicians for breaching discrimination or hate speech legislation is more common. In addition to legal measures, radical right-wing populist parties sometimes suffer political exclusion in the form of a refusal of other parties to cooperate with them (e.g., by means of a *cordon sanitaire*) (Downs 2001, 2002). Some studies have indicated that the exclusion of radical right-wing populist parties by means of a *cordon sanitaire* indeed results in political rigidity or radicalisation (Downs 2002; Minkenberg 2006; Van Spanje and Van der Brug 2007). However, other studies present the opposite evidence and there is, therefore, no consensus that isolation leads to the radicalisation of radical right-wing populist parties (Akkerman and Rooduijn 2014).

In this introduction, we will first clarify how we define and operationalise the radical right-wing populist party family. Next, we will discuss the concept of mainstreaming. What does it mean to move into the mainstream? Programmatic and behavioural changes of non-mainstream parties in the direction of the mainstream have to be specified and carefully operationalised in order to get comparable results. We will then outline our explanatory framework. Central to our approach is that parties are actors that set goals and make choices in response to external conditions like inclusion and exclusion. The ways in which parties react to internal or external changing circumstances may vary substantially. It is important, therefore, to assess the strategies that are generally available to radical right-wing populist parties, and to contextualise how strategies are adapted in reaction to external or internal constraints and opportunities. Moreover, external conditions such as inclusion and exclusion need to be explored further. In the final part of this introduction, we will discuss the contextual variables that may be constraints or incentives for radical right-wing populist parties to go into the mainstream. The inclusion/moderation and exclusion/radicalisation literatures provide a good starting point for making an inventory of contextual variables, but radical right-wing populist parties may face specific opportunities and constraints that need to be taken into account.

Defining radical right-wing populism

The term 'radical right-wing populism' describes a group of parties that are right-wing in their rejection of individual and social equality. The parties take radical, non-centrist positions on issues that are central to their ideology, and they are populist 'in their appeal to the common man and his allegedly superior common sense' (Betz 1994: 4). In more substantive terms, the parties adhere to an ideology that includes authoritarian, nativist and populist elements (Mudde 2007). Central to their ideology is nativism, a combination of nationalism and xenophobia. According to Mudde (2007: 19), nativism is 'an ideology, which holds that states should be inhabited exclusively by members of the native group ("the nation") and that non-native elements (persons and ideas) are fundamentally threatening to the homogeneous nation-state'. When translated into programmatic positions, nativism leads to anti-immigration stances, and in recent years, to anti–European Union and anti-Islam stances. Since the early 2000s, the focus has shifted to Islam as a non-native religion in Western Europe. The nativist critique on Islam stems from the observation that Islamic values are at odds with liberal democratic values, such as the autonomy of the individual, democracy, emancipation of homosexuals and women, equality of men and women, freedom of expression, and separation of church and state (Akkerman 2005, 2015; Betz 2007; Betz and Meret 2009; Zúquete 2008).

On the basis of existing studies of radical right-wing populism, we have identified 21 radical right-wing populist parties that have gained representation in the European Parliament or in national parliaments. Most of these parties – such as the Austrian FPÖ, Danish DF, Dutch PVV, Flemish VB and French FN – are the usual suspects. Their membership of the family of radical right-wing populist parties is undisputed since authoritarianism, nativism and populism are clearly present in their programmes, and nativism forms the core of their ideology. The same goes for many smaller radical right-wing populist parties, such as the British National Party (BNP), Austrian BZÖ, Dutch Centre Democrats (Centrum Democraten, CD), Belgian National Front (Front National; FNb), Greek LAOS and German Republicans (Republikaner; REP) (e.g., Carter 2005; Mudde 2007).

However, we have also included parties that originally started out as agrarian populist parties, regionalist parties, and the like, and later converted to radical right-wing populism. These parties include the Finnish PS, the Italian Northern League (Lega Nord; LN) and the Swiss SVP. Some parties have been included that are border cases. These are cases for which there is no consensus about their membership of the radical right-wing populist party family. The Dutch LPF, the Norwegian FrP and the UK Independence Party (UKIP) belong to this group (e.g., Mudde 2007). We have included these parties because country experts tend to describe them as radical right-wing populist parties (e.g., Akkerman and Hagelund 2007; De Lange 2007; Meret and Siim 2012). Although anti-immigration positions were occasionally de-emphasised by the FrP (Valen and Narud 2007) and were relatively moderate on the LPF platforms, immigration has been important – if not key – to the electoral successes of these parties (Evans and Ivaldi 2010; Jupskås 2013; Van der Brug 2003; Van Praag 2003). Thus, they are in many ways functional equivalents to 'genuine' radical right-wing populist parties, taking similar positions in the political space and attracting voters with similar backgrounds (e.g., De Lange and Rooduijn 2015; Rydgren and Van Holsteyn 2005). Another reason to include these borderline cases is that they could potentially represent archetypes of evolution among radical right-wing populist parties. In other words, radical right-wing populist parties might have developed in different directions over time, with some parties mainstreaming and other radicalising. Thus, knowledge about the variation in these parties' backgrounds and evolutionary paths helps us to assess why some parties eventually move into the mainstream while others do not.

Dimensions of mainstreaming

Research is scarce on the subject of 'mainstreaming'. The term 'mainstreaming' has been used to indicate a process of convergence between mainstream parties, on the one hand, and radical parties, on the other hand. Green parties, for instance, have become more like the mainstream left, and vice versa; the former moderated their programmatic stances and adjusted their party organisation, and the latter embraced environmental issues (Bomberg 2002; Mair 2001). As a result of these changes, green parties have become coalitionable (or *Koalitionsfähig*) and have governed with left-wing mainstream parties (Müller-Rommel and Poguntke 2002). Convergence between radical right-wing populist parties and mainstream parties of the right, especially on immigration and integration issues, has also been observed, and has been associated with these parties' government participation in the early 2000s (Bale 2003, 2008; Bale *et al.* 2010; Curran 2004; Green-Pedersen and Krogstrup 2008; Norris 2005; Van Spanje 2010).

However, when used this way, the concept of mainstreaming lacks clarity. It is used to describe a process that takes place in two opposite directions, referring to both changes of mainstream parties towards radical parties – a process that might more aptly be called 'radicalisation' – and changes of radical parties towards mainstream parties.

The term is defined here more strictly as a process in which radical parties change to become more like mainstream parties. To accurately describe this process, we should define more precisely what is meant by the term 'mainstream'. The term is widely used in political science studies, but definitions are generally lacking. It is an umbrella term that has at least two different meanings. First, 'mainstream' refers most often to centre left and centre right parties – that is, to Christian democratic, conservative, liberal and social democratic parties. In other words, it denotes parties that have a centrist position on the classic left-right scale and that attribute importance to socioeconomic issues (Adams *et al.* 2006; Marks *et al.* 2002; Meguid 2005). Kitschelt (1989) has referred to these parties as 'conventional' parties. In this sense, the term 'mainstream parties' is often used in contrast to 'radical parties' (i.e., parties that take relatively radical positions on issues) and 'niche parties' (i.e. parties that exploit programmatic niches, including green parties, left-libertarian parties, regionalist parties and radical right-wing populist parties).

Second, the term 'mainstream parties' is also used to describe established parties. Established parties are defined on the basis of their loyalty to the political system (Abedi 2004; Capoccia 2002; Sartori 1976). In this sense, mainstream parties are contrasted to those that are anti-establishment, anti–political establishment and anti-system – that is, parties that seek to reform or overthrow the existing political system, and the norms and values on which it is based. In sum, the term 'mainstream' can encompass programmatic and positional centrism, the high salience of socioeconomic issues, and behaviour and stances that show commitment to the principles of liberal democracy and to the formal and informal rules of the political game.

On the basis of these characteristics of mainstream parties, the non-mainstream features of radical right-wing populist parties can be identified. In contrast to mainstream parties, radical right-wing populist parties have (1) programmatic profiles that are non-centrist, (2) programmatic profiles that evolve around sociocultural rather than socioeconomic issues and (3) an anti-establishment outlook on politics (see Table 1.3). In other words, radical right-wing populist parties are at once radical parties, niche parties and anti-establishment parties. Let us briefly describe each of these elements.

First of all, radical right-wing populist parties take radical, non-centrist positions on issues that are central to their ideology, such as European integration, immigration and integration, and law and order. Their radicalism is relative, in the sense that they take positions that are more outspoken than their mainstream competitors. These parties are therefore situated at the far end of the political spectrum. In other words, the term 'radical' points to radical right-wing populist parties' spatial location (e.g., Ignazi 2003; Van Spanje 2011b). Keeping in mind that the usage of the term 'radical' is relative, the substantive stances taken by radical parties remain open. A party could be non-centrist in its socioeconomic or sociocultural positioning, or because of its position on other particular issues. In the case of radical right-wing populist parties, it is their positioning on sociocultural issues that is radical, whereas their positioning on socioeconomic issues is often more centrist (e.g., Mudde 2007; Rovny 2013).

Second, radical right-wing populist parties are niche parties because they primarily campaign on issues that do not belong to the traditional, socioeconomic left-right dimension. Characteristic for niche parties is their specific programmatic offer. They compete on a small number of issues, which are not defined in socioeconomic terms (Bischof forthcoming; Meguid 2005, 2008; Miller and Meyer 2010; Wagner 2012). Radical right-wing populist parties first and foremost compete on issues that belong to the sociocultural dimension, such as the European Union, crime and security, and the influx of immigrants and their subsequent societal integration. Socioeconomic issues are secondary to their programmes (Mudde 2007).

Third, radical right-wing populist parties are characterised by their disloyalty to the political establishment. In contrast to mainstream parties, which are committed to the status quo, radical right-wing populist parties display anti-establishment attitudes and behaviour (Abedi 2004; Rooduijn 2014; Schedler 1996). They have transformative aspirations regarding not only policies but also meta-politics – that is, the informal and formal rules of the game. These aspirations have their origins in the populist ideas of radical right-wing populist parties. As has already been noted, populism is one of three key elements in the ideology of radical right-wing populist parties. Populists claim that the elites are unable or unwilling to represent the ordinary people and therefore propagate the empowerment of the people at the cost of elites. They target elitist features of the democratic system but do not criticise the democratic system as such. Apart from holding populist ideas, anti-establishment parties also exhibit behaviour that challenges the rules of the game, whether in parliament, in office or in the media (Deschouwer 2008; Kenney 1998; Krouwel and Lucardie 2008; Otjes 2012). They can, for example, walk away from plenary debates, turn their backs to the presidium or use unparliamentary language in debates. They may also demonstrate their anti-establishment character while in national office by refusing to take responsibility for government policies or by criticising backroom politics.

Finally, in addition to these factors, which follow from the three dimensions of 'mainstreamness', a fourth factor should be considered – a party's reputation. The move away from classic extreme right subjects such as anti-Semitism, racism and references to Nazism or fascism, which started in the late 1980s in some of the older radical right-wing populist parties, is not yet a closed chapter for all of them. Some parties have made the described changes half-heartedly to avoid internal strife or to remain appealing to pockets of voters. Consequently, some radical right-wing populist parties, such as the BNP, the FN, or the SD, are still associated with (neo-)fascism or (neo-)Nazism. These parties do not easily gain a reputation as legitimate democratic competitors because of the ideas that linger on in their programmes, unofficial party documents or the statements of their representatives, often in lower ranking, local bodies. Moreover, their organisations sometimes still have ties to nationalist milieux or to explicitly extremist organisations. Mainstream parties often 'demonise' radical right-wing populist parties on the basis of their ideological and organisational reputation (Van Heerden 2014). Although not all members of the radical right-wing populist party family have extreme right origins (see, e.g., the mainstream roots of the PS, PVV or SVP), they are all vulnerable to demonisation owing to the principle of 'guilt by association'. In the run-up to the 2014 elections to the European Parliament, for example, the public debates and political outcries about the formation of various alliances of radical right-wing populist parties made it clear that history does matter. The refusal of Nigel Farage, the leader of UKIP, to cooperate with the FN, FPÖ, LN, PVV and VB was phrased in terms that set UKIP apart as an acceptable, mainstream, moderate party. At the same time, the willingness of Wilders, the leader of the PVV, to forge an alliance with the FN came as a surprise and was heavily criticised because in the past he used to distance himself from the FN on the grounds that it had a reputation of being anti-Semitic and racist (NRC 14-09-2013; *Vrij Nederland* 21-05-2014). In the Netherlands, his choice of 'friends' was used by rivalling parties to portray the PVV as an extreme right party (*Nu.nl* 07-05-2014; *Vrij Nederland* 11-11-2013). In a similar vein, the choice of the DF and the PS to join the European Conservatives and Reformists (ECR), the faction led by the British Conservatives, is (partly) motivated by their desire to distance themselves from parties that are perceived as beyond the pale. These considerations and debates demonstrate that the reputations of radical right-wing populist parties as legitimate democratic parties are still contested and should be included in an assessment of whether these parties are heading towards the mainstream.

Explanations for mainstreaming

After the turn of the millennium, radical right-wing populist parties gained opportunities to enter national office in various countries, which according to the inclusion-moderation thesis, is an incentive for parties to move into the mainstream. Yet, we do not simply hypothesise that parties with these opportunities will move into the mainstream while those without them will not. We argue that changes in opportunities cannot adequately explain party change. Parties play a crucial role as actors that react to changing circumstances (Harmel and Janda 1994). They have to be aware of new opportunities, and they have to decide whether they wish to adapt their goals and strategies accordingly. Radical right-wing populist parties may have good reasons to be careful about entering office. Entrance into office potentially has high costs in terms of policy and votes. To understand party behaviour generally and to assess more specifically the behaviour of radical right-wing populist parties, the first step is to assess how parties perceive new opportunities, which goals they prioritise and how they handle trade-offs between these goals.

Therefore, we will first look at party behaviour, in general, and that of radical right-wing populist parties, in particular. We will then look more closely at the changes in social and political circumstances that were relevant for radical right-wing populist parties before and after the turn of the millennium.

Table 1.3 Dimensions of mainstreaming

Dimensions of non-mainstreamness	Evidenced by	Indicators for mainstreaming
Radical party	Core positions are radical	Core positions are moderated
Niche party	Issue agenda is limited Sociocultural issues are emphasized	Issue agenda is expanded and socioeconomic issues are emphasized more strongly
Anti-establishment party	1) Anti-establishment positions 2) Rules of the game are challenged	Anti-establishment positions are moderated Rules of the game are respected
Extreme right reputation	1) Anti-Semitic/racist expressions 2) Ties with extremists	Anti-Semitic/racist expressions are suppressed Ties with extremists are severed

Party goals

The scholarly literature attributes one or more of three objectives to political parties. They seek to maximise office, policy or votes, or a combination of these objectives (e.g., Müller and Strøm 1999; Strøm 1990a). As Strøm (1990a: 570–571) argues 'we can fruitfully think of vote-seeking, office-seeking, and policy-seeking as three independent and mutually conflicting forms of behaviour in which political parties can engage'. Office, policy and votes correspond closely to the three arenas in which parties compete: the executive arena, the legislative arena and the electoral arena.

The office-seeking party seeks to win control over the executive in order to maximise its access to the spoils of office, which are the 'private goods bestowed on recipients of politically discretionary governmental and sub-governmental appointments' (Strøm 1990a: 567). These private goods usually take the form of cabinet portfolios but can also entail patronage appointments within the legislature and elsewhere (e.g. in the judiciary, the civil service, parastatal agencies, and sub- and supranational government institutions). The spoils of office can be less tangible and may, for example, take the form of public recognition and media exposure. Importantly, parties supporting a minority government can also share in such spoils of office.

The model of policy-oriented parties assumes that 'the parliamentary game is, in fact, about the determination of major government policy' (De Swaan 1973: 88). Parties are expected to have policy positions on which they campaign in elections and which they seek to realise in the legislative and executive. Although an important way to realise policy objectives is to assume office, it is also possible for parties to bring about policy changes through legislative procedures (Laver and Schofield 1998: 53–54). The ways in which policy-seeking parties can achieve their goals are thus manifold.

The model of the vote-seeking party is derived from the work of Downs (1957: 28), who claims that 'parties formulate policies in order to win elections, rather than win elections in order to formulate policies'. Generally speaking, vote-seeking behaviour is qualified as a means to achieve either office or policy influence.

In more recent years the idea that *the* office-seeking party, *the* policy-seeking party, or *the* vote-seeking party does not exist has become widespread. The vast majority of political parties seek to satisfy more than one goal simultaneously, which has led to attempts at an integrative theory of competitive party behaviour (Budge and Laver 1986; Laver 1989; Müller and Strøm 1999; Narud 1996; Sened 1996; Sjöblom 1968; Strøm 1990a). These theories take into account that parties (1) compete in different arenas, (2) have to reconcile short- and long-term interests and (3) can pursue goals for both intrinsic and instrumental reasons. As Sjöblom (1968: 31) argues, to the extent 'that the actor at the same time strives towards several goals that are interdependent, so that all goals cannot at the same time be optimized, a weighing of one against the other must be made'.

To give only one example in which these elements surface, policy realisation requires parties to please voters and to form and maintain agreements with other parties over a sustained period (Lupia and Strøm 2008). In the legislative arena, however, parties are forced to water down their positions in order to make policy compromise possible, while in the electoral arena, parties have to mark policy distances to maintain a distinguishable profile for the voter. To satisfy the two conditions that are necessary for policy realisation is thus not an easy task since competition in different arenas can require different strategies, and strategies employed in one arena can have a contradictory effect on the realisation of objectives in another (Narud 1996).

In a similar fashion, government participation also involves substantial trade-offs. Government participation is attractive to parties for at least two reasons. First, through government participation, parties obtain a share of the spoils of office, most notably portfolios. Second, through their control of these portfolios, they are able to influence government policy – an objective that they also realise on a more general level through their contribution to the coalition agreement, which constitutes the cornerstone of government policy. However, government participation can also involve negative consequences. For one, the potential coalition agreement can entail policy compromises that a party is unwilling to make, either on principle or because the party fears electoral punishment if it does not keep its electoral promises. Retrospective voting is an important determinant of electoral behaviour, and it has been demonstrated that incumbency effects are often negative because voters judge that the discrepancy between promises and performance is too large. Consequently, parties lose reliability and hence support (Mackie and Rose 1983; Müller and Strøm 1999; Strøm 1990b).

Radical right-wing populist parties, party goals and party change

Radical right-wing populist parties pursue office, policy or votes, and they face trade-offs between these goals. Some of these trade-offs are similar to those faced by mainstream parties, whereas others are specific to the radical right-wing populist party family because of its distinct electoral, ideological and organisational features.

Three observations can be made suggesting that at least a number of radical right-wing populist parties are office-seekers. First, radical right-wing populist parties have rarely declined offers to participate in government coalitions. Although this claim is not easily substantiated given that coalition negotiations are usually surrounded by secrecy, it appears that when invited, most radical right-wing populist parties have entered government at the national level. The notable exception to this rule is the PS, which declined to govern after the 2011 elections in Finland. Bale (2003: 69) therefore concludes that 'far right party leaders over the past decade have deliberately (and not always without difficulty) sought to achieve a place in national government'. Second, radical right-wing populist parties have rarely voluntarily left government coalitions. Certainly, many of the government coalitions in which these parties have participated have been short-lived, but the coalitions' tenure has usually been terminated by the mainstream parties involved in the government coalitions. The only radical right-wing populist parties that have actively brought down the governments in which they participated or which they supported were the LN in 1995 and the PVV in 2012 (see Chapter 7 on the Netherlands). Lastly, the majority of radical right-wing populist parties has extensive experience in subnational executive coalitions. This experience usually precedes participation in national governments by several years, if not several decades. The subnational experiences of radical right-wing populist parties testify to these parties' willingness to take up responsibility in executive coalitions. Even some of the radical right-wing populist parties that have not participated in national governments have secured executive positions at the subnational level. The FN, for example, has provided several mayors and has taken part in numerous regional executive coalitions.

Although these observations suggest that radical right-wing populist parties are office-seeking, conventional wisdom has it that these parties are less interested in government participation than mainstream parties. While mainstream parties are often characterised as primarily or exclusively office-seeking, radical right-wing populist parties are often described as being more concerned with vote maximisation than with government participation (De Swaan 1973: 166). Even though government participation is often a distant goal of radical parties, it nevertheless remains one of the objectives that they try to realise. According to Pedersen (1982: 8), 'the goal of any minor party is to pass the threshold of relevance, and, to become an influential, at best a ruling party'. This rule includes radical right-wing populist parties. Unlike mainstream parties, it is far less clear that these parties can be characterised as *exclusively* or *primarily* office-seeking parties. Radical right-wing populist parties sometimes put policy and votes before office, a point discussed further below. Moreover, the populist rhetoric of radical right-wing populist parties might cloud observations. They are generally highly critical of coalition governance, which supposedly interferes with the direct translation of voters' preferences into policy outcomes. This condemnation does not imply, however, that they reject government participation on a priori grounds. On the contrary, as the true representatives of the people, radical right-wing populist parties might feel that they are more entitled to govern than other parties.

In addition to being office-seekers, the majority of radical right-wing populist parties are also policy-seekers. Again, several observations back this claim. First, these parties have a clearly circumscribed and coherent ideological programme, which they seek to implement. Second, they actively promote this programme in elections. Third, they try to influence policy-making directly and indirectly. They actively take part in the legislative process (e.g. Minkenberg 2001) and try to spread their ideology through a 'strategy of contamination' (Bale 2003; Curran 2004; Bale 2008; Bale *et al.* 2010; Norris 2005; Van Spanje 2010). This way, radical right-wing populist parties can exercise electoral pressure on mainstream parties and 'force' these parties to co-opt their issues and policy positions, even when they cannot influence policy-making directly. This 'strategy of contamination' is widely practised by parties that are located on the fringes of the political space (e.g., Dumont and Bäck 2006). Some scholars even contend that radical right-wing populist parties are policy-seeking above all. They are less likely, for example, to respond to changes in public opinion than mainstream parties (Ezrow *et al.* 2011). This is especially the case when parties are mostly ideologically driven. Radical right-wing populist parties tend to prioritise policy purity above policy influence. They are policy *purifiers* rather than policy *influencers* (Helboe Pedersen 2012). Therefore, they will have difficulty accepting compromises in exchange for office. Even when coalition agreements move particular policies closer to their preferred positions, these small gains may not be acceptable to parties that see themselves as purifiers (see also Lucardie 2000). Radical right-wing populist parties are therefore likely to cherish their ideological purity and resent policy compromises.

In addition to office- and policy-seekers, radical right-wing populist parties are also, and perhaps above all, vote-seekers. Electoral studies show that a substantial portion of voters who support radical right-wing populist parties do so on the basis of their policy agendas. In other words, the vote for a radical right-wing populist party is first and foremost an ideological vote (e.g., Van der Brug *et al.* 2000). This implies that issue agendas and policy positions are an important part of radical right-wing populist parties' vote-seeking strategies. Voting for these parties is also motivated by political discontent and cynicism, albeit to a lesser extent. Anti-establishment attitudes and behaviour can therefore also be part of a vote-seeking strategy.

How radical right-wing populist parties prioritise their goals remains a question that has yet to be answered on the basis of empirical evidence. There are some indications that initially they attached greater importance to votes than office or policy (e.g., De Lange 2012a, 2012b). In the 1990s and early 2000s, most radical right-wing populist parties seemed to focus primarily on votes; they could be described as short-term vote-seekers and long-term office- and policy-seekers. A potential explanation why these parties initially tended to give votes a more prominent position is that they used to be smaller than most mainstream parties and hence ran a greater risk of falling below the threshold of representation (Bolleyer 2007). Thus, the pursuit of votes was vital to the survival of these parties as parliamentary forces. In the long run, however, radical right-wing populist parties may continue to have good reasons to prioritise vote-seeking. These parties have fewer options than mainstream parties to join coalitions because they are situated on the fringes of the political space (cf. Smith 1997). To compensate for this handicap, they are likely to strengthen their bargaining position through electoral growth (cf. Schofield and Sened 2006: 3). Moreover, if radical right-wing populist parties have to rely on a strategy of contamination to influence policy outcomes, this strategy will only be effective if they put electoral pressure on mainstream parties by making inroads in other parties' electorates – hence the espousal of vote-seeking strategies.

Finally, radical right-wing populist parties run greater risks when they pursue office-seeking strategies and seek to control these risks through the creation of an electoral buffer. The trade-offs between office, policy and votes that radical right-wing populist parties face differ from those of many other parties. More than other parties, they face a trade-off between office, on the one hand, and policy and votes, on the other. The reason for the trade-off difference is that government participation entails a series of challenges that affect radical right-wing populist parties' capacities to realise their policy objectives and to max-imise future voter support. More specifically, in government, radical right-wing populist parties have to make serious policy concessions and abandon some of their policy promises. This situation is difficult because the voters and activists supporting radical right-wing populist parties tend to value policy purity. As a result, radical right-wing populist parties are electorally often strongly bound to their electoral promises. When they adjust their policy positions, they normally face a decrease in electoral popularity (Adams *et al.* 2006). And, although negative incumbency effects are registered by most parties that assume office (Müller and Strøm 2000), government participation by a radical right-wing populist may be especially detrimental to the attainment of its policy and vote-seeking goals (Buelens and Hino 2008; Van Spanje 2011a).

Mainstreaming and the pursuit of party goals

We conceive of mainstreaming as a party strategy, a strategy that is designed to promote the pursuit of office, policy or votes, or a combination of these goals. The strategy can consist of one of the dimensions of mainstreaming described above (Table 1.3) or it can be a mix of these dimensions. Radical right-wing populist parties can moderate their positions on core issues, expand their issue agenda, show more respect for the rules of the game or try to overcome their extremist reputation.

First of all, the mainstreaming of radical right-wing populist parties can be a consequence of the pursuit of office. It is possible that the increased opportunities to join government coalitions at the national level in the 2000s have pushed these parties to the mainstream. Since assuming office in Western Europe tends to involve joining a government coalition, it is required that policy distances between parties are bridged and that compromises are reached. For radical right-wing populist parties, this requirement could mean that they orient their agendas and policy positions to those of mainstream right parties (e.g., Christian democrats, conservatives and liberals) because they are most likely to join forces with these parties (e.g., De Lange 2012a, 2012b). Moreover, radical right-wing populist parties that are interested in office also have incentives to demonstrate to their potential partners that they are reliable and credible allies – for example, by toning down their anti-establishment rhetoric, obeying the parliamentary rules and 'sanitising' their party.

However, mainstreaming need not occur only as a consequence of office-seeking behaviour. It can also be the consequence of *experience in* office. Being in office can have strong socialising effects, especially when parties join a government coalition. Being a coalition member implies a commitment to a policy agreement, which is based on policy compromise. Compromise necessitates the justification of policy positions that are different from radical right-wing populist parties' ideal positions. The impact that these parties have on any policy agreement is limited since they are normally 'merely' junior members in government coalitions. As a result, government participation can have a moderating effect on radical right-wing populist parties' stances. Vote-seeking while in government can also have a moderating effect. It has been argued that parties in office must be able to convince voters that they can deliver the goods. However, when they are busy filling potholes and fixing sewage systems, they cannot devote their energy to ideological radicalism (Berman 2008: 6; MacMillan 2006). In office, parties have to legislate in many policy domains, forcing them to widen the scope of their policy agendas. Thus, when they are in office, radical right-wing populist parties cannot devote their entire attention to immigration and integration or to law and order policies; they must take a stance on socioeconomic issues as well. Lastly, in office, it is difficult to maintain an anti-establishment profile since governing parties are in many ways part of the establishment. For the same reason, it is difficult not to play by the rules of the game. However, radical right-wing populist parties supporting a minority government might have more opportunities to maintain an anti-establishment profile than radical right-wing populist parties that are members of a majority government. Moreover, radical right-wing populist parties' mainstreaming as a result of participation in government can be a short-lived phenomenon when it is only a result of their partners in the coalition forcing them into the mainstream. When back in opposition, the parties may radicalise again. In such cases, mainstreaming is not the result of internal change and may therefore be merely ephemeral and cosmetic. When office-seeking is a strategy, however, mainstreaming should already be apparent before the entrance into office. Office-seeking parties will, for instance, signal their willingness to negotiate and compromise to potential partners during election campaigns through media statements. When the choice for office-seeking is internally supported by party elites and activists alike, mainstreaming may prove to be a successful and enduring strategy for the party.

As has been noted above, radical right-wing populist parties potentially face high costs when they join the mainstream. While a radical profile, a niche party profile, and anti-establishment attitudes and behaviour tend to be barriers to entering office, they can be rewarding electorally. A vote-seeking strategy may therefore be a disincentive for radical right-wing populist parties to move into the mainstream. Differentiating themselves programmatically from mainstream parties rather than competing for the median voter tends to be a successful vote-seeking strategy for radical right-wing populist parties – provided that the distinctive niche issues have high salience (Adams *et al.* 2006; Ezrow 2008; Lynch *et al.* 2012; Meguid 2005, 2008). In other words, electoral competition on niche issues like immigration and integration may incite centrifugal rather than centripetal tendencies. Research indicates centrifugal tendencies in the competition on these niche issues. It shows that mainstream right parties have radicalised under pressure from the electoral success of radical right-wing populist parties (Akkerman 2012; Alonso and da Fonseca 2012; Bale 2008; Curran 2004; Van Kersbergen and Krouwel 2008; Van Spanje 2010). As a consequence, radical right-wing populist parties may fear losing voters and issue ownership when they do not clearly differentiate themselves from their mainstream competitors. Vote-seeking in such cases may therefore even lead to radicalisation. With regard to their anti-establishment profiles, radical right-wing populist parties may also have to reckon with electoral costs when opting for office. Cynical voters and party members may deplore entrance into office as renouncing the fundamental opposition to an elitist political system. The dilemma of how to combine a populist stance with office tends to remain relevant for these parties after entering office (McDonnell and Newell 2011). Voters may be disappointed when radical right-wing populist parties soften their anti-establishment stance once they are in office (Albertazzi and McDonnell 2007; Van Spanje 2011a).

To sum up, the choices that parties make about goals and strategies are generally important in explaining party change, particularly in the case of radical right-wing populist parties. When pursuing office, they tend to face relatively high trade-offs in terms of votes and policy. Change is therefore a risky and delicate process for radical right-wing populist parties. Opportunities to enter office tend to imply hard choices and to require high internal flexibility. But the hard choices can sometimes be softened. When opting for office, it is likely that radical right-wing populist parties will try to find strategies that enable them to minimise the costs of trade-offs between a radical policy profile and entrance into office. For instance, the parties may minimise policy costs by pursuing a strategy of logrolling (Akkerman and De Lange 2012; De Lange 2012b). Rather than compromising on core issues like immigration and integration in negotiations with coalition partners, they will try to shift the main policy costs to socio-economic issues (cf. Afonso 2015). Radical right-wing populist parties may also try to maintain anti-establishment positions or behaviour while they are in office by pursuing a strategy of 'one foot in and one foot out' (Albertazzi and McDonnell 2005). Whether this strategy is successful depends on the coalition partners' willingness to accept it and on the opportunities that the political systems provide for challengers. Under favourable conditions, an outsider status can be partly maintained by radical right-wing populist parties when in national office (Albertazzi and McDonnell 2010; Fröhlich-Steffen and Rensmann 2007). Such strategies are perhaps essential for radical right-wing populist parties to successfully adapt to changing environments.

Internal and external conditions influencing mainstreaming

Parties are actors that set goals and make strategic choices, but their array of choices is defined by external and internal factors (e.g., Brocker and Künkler 2013; Harmel and Janda 1994; Harmel *et al.* 1995). Two types of external factors can be distinguished: changes in the societal environment and changes in the political environment. The first type includes changes in cleavages, electoral markets and in media agendas as well as socioeconomic change and the emergence of new policy problems in society. The second type includes changes in the political systems in which radical right-wing populist parties operate, in the structure of party competition resulting from party system change and in the ways in which main competitors react. Characteristics of the political system, such as the existence of an electoral threshold, gerrymandering and regulations for party finance, as well as characteristics of the party system, such as the degree of fragmentation and polarization, the dimensionality of the political space, and the positions that parties take in that space, impact on opportunities for radical right-wing populist parties to grow electorally, influence policy agendas and outcomes, and participate in government coalitions. Together these factors make up the Political Opportunity Structure (POS).

In addition to these external conditions, which are discussed extensively in the literature on the inclusion-moderation thesis, party change is also shaped by internal conditions (e.g., Harmel and Janda 1994; Harmel *et al.* 1995). These conditions include, but are not limited to, party organisation, leadership and factionalism, and experiences in local and regional political arenas. In other words, party change is not only a consequence of changes in the environment, it is also the result of party agency, that is, the extent to which a party is able and willing to seize opportunities. We therefore present the following explanatory model for mainstreaming (see Figure 1.1).

Societal environment

Several societal trends have created a favourable environment for the emergence and growth of radical right-wing populist parties. First, the emergence of new policy problems as a result of globalisation has made citizens more concerned about sociocultural questions, most notably immigration and integration and law and order. Changes in media systems and media coverage were important in bringing attention to these new issues in the political arena (Walgrave and Van Aelst 2006). Political parties have incorporated these issues in the political agenda, which has led to the development of a two-dimensional political space, structured by a socioeconomic and a sociocultural dimension, and new patterns of party competition. In this political space, a clear electoral niche for radical right-wing populist parties is present. This niche is primarily defined by these parties' positions on the sociocultural dimension (i.e., a distinctly authoritarian-nationalist position) (Kitschelt 1995; Kriesi *et al.* 2008). Second, due to the emancipation of voters as a result of secularisation, individualisation and increasing levels of education, public opinion has become more critical of the functioning of political parties and politicians and voters have become more volatile, deciding only shortly before the elections on their vote choice and frequently changing party preferences between elections (e.g., Dalton 2013; Kitschelt 2002; Pharr and Putnam 2000). These developments have created a favourable environment for new parties in general, and parties with anti-establishment attitudes in particular.

However, in recent years the financial and economic crisis has reshaped the political agenda, altering citizens' concerns and preferences and potentially providing radical right-wing populist parties with incentives to mainstream. Since socioeconomic issues have become more prominent again, it could be electorally rewarding for radical right-wing populist parties to abandon their niche party profile by de-emphasising sociocultural issues and emphasising socioeconomic issues.

Political environment

The inclusion-moderation literature puts great emphasis on the way in which institutions form constraints and incentives for mainstreaming. The electoral system, for example, determines whether parties are likely to convert their electoral support into parliamentary seats and thus whether they have the opportunity to influence policy or assume office. Opportunities to enter office are conditioned by political system characteristics. For instance, in countries with majority systems, such as Britain and France, entrance into office is highly dependent on gaining electoral dominance. As these countries have majority or plurality electoral systems, radical right-wing populist parties experience great difficulties entering the national parliaments. Moreover, the state structure determines how many access points there are for parties and whether they can use regional assemblies to influence national politics. And constitutional and legal provisions can influence parties' electoral potential, for example through regulation of party finance and media access. Particularly important for radical right-wing populist parties are also legal provisions regarding the prosecution of politicians and party bans, as these might influence these parties strategic choices and behaviour. The (threat of) prosecution or dissolution can be an important incentive for moderation (Bale 2007).

However, most institutional factors are rather static and therefore cannot always explain changes in party goals and behaviour. For this reason, party system variables, which vary from one election to the next, might be equally or more relevant than political system variables when explaining mainstreaming. Changes in the composition of the party system, as well as decreases or increases in the level of polarisation and fragmentation affect electoral opportunities and thereby the opportunities for office. It has been noted, for example, that the 'swing to the right' around the turn of the century has created important opportunities for radical right-wing populist parties. The combination of electoral growth of mainstream right and radical right-wing populist parties on the one and changes in party positions on the other hand, mean that opportunities to enter national office increased substantially after 2000 (Bale 2003; De Lange 2012a, 2012b). Other parties' decisions influence the opportunities of radical right-wing populist parties and hence their choices and agendas. For instance, the willingness of mainstream parties to accept radical right-wing populist parties as electoral allies or coalition partners varies considerably. Some coalitions are unlikely to form because policy or personal differences between parties are simply too large, and parties exclude cooperation on a priori grounds (cf. Strøm *et al.* 1994). In the case of radical right-wing populist parties, these a priori grounds are often related to the illiberal character of their programmes. As a consequence, these parties are subjected to an informal or formal *cordon sanitaire*. In Belgium, for example, the refusal of mainstream parties to cooperate with the VB has effectively deprived the party from any opportunity to enter local or national office (Damen 2001).

Internal factors

In addition to factors external to radical right-wing populist parties, a number of internal factors influence these parties' capacities to make strategic choices, to pursue their goals and to seize opportunities. These factors include party organisation and factionalism, party leadership and relevant learning experiences at the local and regional levels.

It is important to look at the internal conditions that shape party goals. Even when leading elites within a party see opportunities to maximise votes or assume office, they may face insurmountable resistance from party members and factions (Harmel and Janda 1994: 261). Resistance of activists within the party, who are usually more ideologically driven and more radical in their stances than party leaders (May 1973), can prevent party leaders from seizing perceived opportunities. Particularly in bottom-up, decentralised and democratically organised parties this may be the case since party members have great influence on the strategic and ideological courses in such parties. In some parties, platforms can be amended by party members, and decisions to join government coalitions can be challenged, or even vetoed. It has, for example, been demonstrated that democratically organised parties are less likely to change party positions for strategic reasons (Ignacio 2004; Schumacher *et al.* 2013). Intraparty democracy can thus be an impediment to office- or vote-seeking behaviour.

Internal adaptation to environmental incentives is therefore an important condition for strategic and programmatic change. Democratically organised parties may need to streamline their decision-making procedures in order to achieve their goals. However, highly institutionalised parties are less flexible and therefore can adjust their organisation less easily to changes in the environment. Besides the degree of democratisation and centralisation, the level of institutionalisation is also an important factor that constrains strategic behaviour and party change. In sum, radical right-wing populist parties' internal conditions are important to explain why they react differently to similar changes in the environment (see also Art 2011).

The variety of social and political conditions in which radical right-wing populist parties operate influence their goals and strategies (see Figure 1.1 for a summary). Internal conditions can limit these parties' flexibility to change their goals and strategies. In the end, the ways in which radical right-wing populist parties perceive environmental changes and adapt their goals and strategies are decisive in explaining whether and how far they move into the mainstream.

Outline of the book

The first chapter by Tjitske Akkerman, Sarah de Lange and Matthijs Rooduijn addresses in a general and comparative way the question whether and in what ways radical right-wing populist parties have moved into the mainstream. Making use of expert surveys, comparative manifesto data and their own measurements, they assess whether radical right-wing populist parties have mellowed program-matic positions, broadened their scope of issues or toned down populist stances. Yet, mainstreaming need not only be apparent in party agendas; it can also take place at the level of public opinion. In the next chapter, Matthijs Rooduijn assesses whether voters of radical right-wing populist parties and mainstream parties have become more alike. These comparative analyses are the prelude to the main part of the book, which consists of case studies.

An approach focusing on party behaviour requires case studies in order to assess whether and to what extent radical right-wing populist parties have moved into the mainstream. First, it enables refined assessments of changes in party agendas based on country-specific data and of positions and behaviour in public debates, parliament or local and national office. Questions that are best answered by using a variety of country-specific data include the following: has a radical right-wing populist party changed its policy profile (radical, niche or populist)? Has it mellowed its positions on immigration and integration, on European integration or on law and order? And has it extended its attention to socio-economic issues, toned down its anti-establishment stance or succeeded in building up a respectable reputation? Second, case studies are required to explain party behaviour. The opportunity to enter national office or to experience being in office may be important incitements to move into the mainstream, but these conditions are far from sufficient to explain why some radical right-wing populist parties make this move while others do not. Goals and strategies need to be assessed by using not only official statements but also non-official statements such as internal documents or interviews. Which goals are prioritised? Have parties (successfully) developed strategies to minimise trade-offs? Have they managed to prevent internal conflicts? And even if opportunities for office are highly uncer-tain, does this uncertainty imply that parties will not move into the mainstream? Such questions can only be answered on the basis of an in-depth approach.

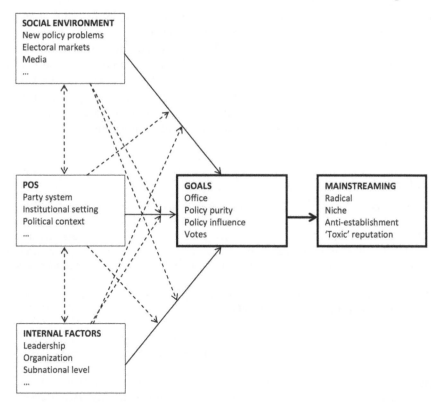

Figure 1.1 Explanations for mainstreaming

The cases assessed in this book cover most countries in Western Europe and focus on electorally successful radical right-wing populist parties with stable party organisations. Some of the radical right-wing populist parties have been in national office in the past, whereas others are in office at the moment of writing. Radical right-wing populist parties without office experience have also been included. However, we have selected only those parties that have already gained an electoral breakthrough and for whom national office is, at least in the longer term, a realistic option. The case studies focusing on parties with past experience in office as formal coalition partners or, as in the case of the PVV and the DF, as formal support parties, include the following: Reinhard Heinisch and Kristina Hauser study the FPÖ in *Austria*, a party in office from 2000 to 2005; Flemming Juul Christiansen assesses the evolvement of the DF in *Denmark*, a party which supported a minority government from 2011 to 2011 and is in office as a support party again at the time of writing; the PS in *Finland*, central in the case study of Ann-Cathrine Jungar, entered government for the first time in 2015; Tjitske Akkerman writes about the PVV in the *Netherlands*, a party that supported a minority government from 2010–2012; the FrP in *Norway*, central in the contribution by Anders Jupskås, entered government for the first time in 2013; Oscar Mazzoleni writes about the SVP in *Switzerland*, a party that has been incumbent with a short interruption in 2008. Other contributions focus on parties without experience in office as of yet: Gilles Ivaldi writes about the FN in *France*; Paul Lucardie, Tjitske Akkerman and Teun Pauwels focus on the VB in *Belgium*; and Simon Usherwood studies UKIP in the United Kingdom. Finally, Tjitske Akkerman assesses whether the findings in these case studies legitimate the conclusion that radical right-wing populist parties are moving into the mainstream.

References

Abedi, A. (2004) *Anti-Political Establishment Parties: A Comparative Analysis*, New York: Routledge.

Adams, J., Clark, M., Ezrow, L. and Glasgow, G. (2006) 'Are niche parties fundamentally different from mainstream parties? The causes and the electoral consequences of Western European parties' policy shifts, 1976–1998', *American Journal of Political Science* 50, 3: 513–529.

Afonso, A. (2015) 'Choosing whom to betray: Populist right-wing parties, welfare state reforms and the trade-off between office and votes', *European Political Science Review* 7, 2: 271–292.

Akkerman, T. (2005) 'Anti-immigration parties and the defence of liberal values: The exceptional case of the List Pim Fortuyn', *Journal of Political Ideologies* 10, 3: 337–354.

Akkerman, T. (2015) 'Immigration policy and electoral competition in Western Europe: A fine-grained analysis of party positions over the past two decades', *Party Politics* 21, 1: 54–67.

Akkerman, T. and de Lange, S. L. (2012) 'Radical right parties in office: Incumbency records and the electoral cost of governing', *Government and Opposition* 47, 4: 574–596.

Akkerman, T. and Hagelund, A. (2007) '"Women and children first!" Anti–immigration parties and gender in Norway and the Netherlands', *Patterns of Prejudice* 41, 2: 197–214.

Akkerman, T. and Rooduijn, M. (2014) 'Pariahs or partners? Inclusion and exclusion of radical right parties and the effects on their policy positions', *Political Studies*. Article first published online, 30 June 2014. Doi: 10.1111/1467-9248.12146.

Albertazzi, D. (2009) 'Reconciling "voice and exit": Swiss and Italian populists in power', *Politics* 29, 1: 1–10.

Albertazzi, D. and McDonnell, D. (2005) 'The Lega Nord in the second Berlusconi government: In a league of its own', *West European Politics* 28, 5: 952–972.

Albertazzi, D. and McDonnell, D. (2007) *Twenty-First Century Populism: The Spectre of Western European Democracy*, New York: Palgrave Macmillan.

Albertazzi, D. and McDonnell, D. (2010) 'The Lega Nord back in government', *West European Politics* 33, 6: 1318–1340.

Alonso, S. and da Fonseca, S. C. (2012) 'Immigration, left and right', *Party Politics* 18, 6: 865–884.

Art, D. (2011) *Inside the Radical Right: The Development of Anti-Immigrant Parties in Western Europe*, Cambridge: Cambridge University Press.

Bale, T. (2003) 'Cinderella and her ugly sisters: The mainstream and extreme right in Europe's bipolarising party systems', *West European Politics* 26, 3: 67–90.

Bale, T. (2007) 'Are bans on political parties bound to turn out badly? A comparative investigation of three "intolerant"democracies: Turkey, Spain, and Belgium', *Comparative European Politics* 5, 2: 141–157.

Bale, T. (2008) 'Turning round the telescope: Centre-right parties and immigration and integration policy in Europe', *Journal of European Public Policy* 15, 3: 315–330.

Bale, T., Green-Pedersen, C., Krouwel, A., Luther, K. R. and Sitter, N. (2010) 'If you can't beat them, join them? Explaining social democratic responses to the challenge from the populist radical right in Western Europe', *Political Studies* 58, 3: 410–426.

Berman, S. (2008) 'Taming extremist parties: Lessons from Europe', *Journal of Democracy* 19, 1: 5–18.

Betz, H.-G. (1994) *Radical Right-Wing Populism in Western Europe*, New York: St. Martin's.

Betz, H.-G. (2007) 'Against the "green totalitarianism": Anti-Islamic nativism in contemporary radical right-wing populism in Western Europe', in Liang, C. S. (ed.) *"Europe for the Europeans." The Foreign and Security Policy of the Populist Radical Right*, Aldershot: Ashgate, pp. 33–54.

Betz, H.-G. and Meret, S. (2009) 'Revisiting Lepanto: the political mobilization against Islam in contemporary Western Europe', *Patterns of Prejudice* 43, 3–4: 313–334.

Bischof, D. (forthcoming) 'Towards a renewal of the niche party concept: Parties, market shares and condensed offers', *Party Politics*.

Bolleyer, N. (2007) 'Small parties: From party pledges to government policy', *West European Politics* 30, 1: 121–147.

Bomberg, E. (2002) 'The Europeanisation of green parties: Exploring the EU's impact', *West European Politics* 25, 3: 29–50.

Brocker, M. and Künkler, M. (2013) 'Religious parties: Revisiting the inclusion-moderation hypothesis – introduction', *Party Politics* 19, 2: 171–185.

Buelens, J. and Hino, A. (2008) 'The electoral fate of new parties in government', in Deschouwer, K. (ed.) *New Parties in Government: In Power for the First Time*, London: Routledge, pp. 157–174.

Budge, I. and Laver, M. (1986) 'Office seeking and policy pursuit in coalition theory', *Legislative Studies Quarterly* 11, 4: 485–506.

Canovan, M. (2002) 'Taking politics to the people: Populism as the ideology of democracy', in Mény, Y. and Surel, Y. (eds) *Democracies and the Populist Challenge*, New York: Palgrave Macmillan, pp. 25–44.

Capoccia, G. (2002) 'Anti-system parties: A conceptual reassessment', *Journal of Theoretical Politics* 14, 1: 9–35.

Carter, E. (2005) *The Extreme Right in Western Europe: Success or Failure?* Manchester: Manchester University Press.

Curran, G. (2004) 'Mainstreaming populist discourse: the race-conscious legacy of neo-populist parties in Australia and Italy', *Patterns of Prejudice* 38, 1: 37–55.

Dalton, R. J. (2013) *Citizen Politics: Public Opinion and Political Parties in Advanced Industrial Democracies*, Washington, DC: CQ Press.

Damen, S. (2001) 'Strategien tegen extreem-rechts: Het cordon sanitaire onder de loep', *Tijdschrift voor Sociologie* 22, 1: 89–110.

De Lange, S. L. (2007) 'A new winning formula? The programmatic appeal of the radical right', *Party Politics* 13, 4: 411–435.

De Lange, S. L. (2012a) 'New alliances: Why mainstream parties govern with radical right-wing populist parties', *Political Studies* 60, 4: 899–918.

De Lange, S. L. (2012b) 'Radical right-wing populist parties in office: A cross-national comparison', in Backes, U. and Moreau, Ph. (eds) *The Extreme Right in Europe: Current Trends and Perspectives*, Gottingen: Vandenhoeck & Ruprecht, pp. 171–194.

De Lange, S. L. and Rooduijn, M. (forthcoming) 'Contemporary populism, the agrarian and the rural in Central Eastern and Western Europe', in Strijker, D., Voerman, G. and Terluin, I. J. (eds) *Right Wing Populist Parties and Rural Protest Groups*, Wageningen Academic Publisher.

De Swaan, A. (1973) *Coalition Theories and Government Formation*, Amsterdam: Elsevier.

Deschouwer, K. (ed.) (2008) *New Parties in Government: In Power for the First Time*, London: Routledge.

Downs, A. (1957) *An Economic Theory of Democracy*, New York: Harper and Row.

Downs, W. M. (2001) 'Pariahs in their midst: Belgian and Norwegian parties react to extremist threats', *West European Politics* 24, 3: 23–42.

Downs, W. M. (2002) 'How effective is the cordon sanitaire? Lessons from efforts to contain the far right in Belgium, France, Denmark and Norway', *Journal für Konflikt- und Gewaltforschung* 4, 1: 32–51.

Dumont, P. and Bäck, H. (2006) 'Why so few, and why so late? Green parties and the question of governmental participation', *European Journal of Political Research* 45, s1: S35–S67.

Elman, M. F. (2014) 'Does democracy tame the radicals? Lessons from the case of Israel's Shas', in Elman, M. F., Haklai, O. and Spruyt, H. (eds) *Democracy and Conflict Resolution: The Dilemmas of Israel's Peacemaking*, Syracuse, NY: Syracuse University Press, pp. 101–131.

Evans, J. and Ivaldi, G. (2010) 'Comparing forecast models of radical right voting in four European countries (1973–2008)', *International Journal of Forecasting* 26, 1: 82–97.

Ezrow, L. (2008) 'Research note: On the inverse relationship between votes and proximity for niche parties', *European Journal of Political Research* 47, 2: 206–220.

Ezrow, L., de Vries, C., Steenbergen, M. and Edwards, E. (2011) 'Mean voter representation and partisan constituency representation: Do parties respond to the mean voter position or to their supporters?', *Party Politics* 17: 3, 275–301.

Frölich-Steffen, S. and Rensmann, L. (2007) 'Conditions for failure and success of right-wing populist parties in public office in the new European Union', in Delwit, P. and Poirier, Ph. (eds) *Extrême Droite et Pouvoir en Europe*, Brussels: Editions de L'Université de Bruxelles, pp. 117–139.

Green-Pedersen, C. and Krogstrup, J. (2008) 'Immigration as a political issue in Denmark and Sweden', *European Journal of Political Research* 47, 5: 610–634.

Gurses, M. (2014) 'Islamists, democracy and Turkey: A test of the inclusion-moderation hypothesis', *Party Politics* 20, 4: 646–653.

Harmel, R. and Janda, K. (1994) 'An integrated theory of party goals and party change', *Journal of Theoretical Politics* 6, 3: 259–287.

Harmel, R., Heo, U., Tan, A. and Janda, K. (1995) 'Performance, leadership, factions and party change: An empirical analysis', *West European Politics* 18, 1: 1–33.

Harmel, R. and Svasand, L. (1993) 'Party leadership and party institutionalisation: Three phases of development', *West European Politics* 16, 2: 67–88.

Helboe Pedersen, H. (2012) 'What do parties want? Policy versus office', *West European Politics* 35, 4: 896–910.

Ignacio, S. (2004) 'Party moderation and politicians' ideological rigidity', *Party Politics* 10, 3: 325–342.

Ignazi, P. (2003) *Extreme Right Parties in Western Europe*, Oxford: Oxford University Press.

Ivarsflaten, E. (2006) 'Reputational shields: Why most anti–immigrant parties failed in Western Europe, 1980–2005', paper prepared for the 2006 Annual Meeting of the American Political Science Association in Philadelphia.

Jupskås, A. R. (2013) 'Mainstream parties in the Nordic countries have tried to deal with the rise of the far-right through a mix of isolation, tolerance and even collaboration', paper presented at European Politics and Policy at LSE.

Kalyvas, S. N. and van Kersbergen, K. (2010) 'Christian democracy', *Annual Review of Political Science* 13: 183–209.

Karakaya, S. and Yildirim, A. K. (2013) 'Islamist moderation in perspective: comparative analysis of the moderation of Islamist and Western communist parties', *Democratization* 20, 7: 1322–1349.

Kenney, C. D. (1998) 'Outsider and anti-party politicians in power: New conceptual strategies and empirical evidence from Peru', *Party Politics* 4, 1: 57–75.

Kitschelt, H. (1989) *The Logics of Party Formation: Ecological Politics in Belgium and West Germany*, Ithaca, NY: Cornell University Press.

Kitschelt, H. (1995) *The Radical Right in Western Europe: A Comparative Analysis*, Ann Harbor, MI: Michigan University Press.

Kitschelt, H. (2002) 'Popular dissatisfaction with democracy: populism and party systems', in Mény, Y. and Surel, Y. (eds) *Democracies and the Populist Challenge*, New York: Palgrave Macmillan, pp. 179–196.

Kriesi, H., Grande, E., Lachat, R., Dolezal, M. and Bornschier, S. (2008) *West European Politics in the Age of Globalization*, Cambridge: Cambridge University Press.

Krouwel, A. and Lucardie, P. (2008) 'Waiting in the wings: New parties in the Netherlands', *Acta Politica* 43, 2: 278–307.

Laver, M. (1989) 'Party competition and party system change: The interaction of coalition bargaining and electoral competition', *Journal of Theoretical Politics* 1, 3, 301–324.

Laver, M. and Schofield, N. (1998) *Multiparty Government: The Politics of Coalition in Europe*, Ann Arbor, MI: University of Michigan Press.

Lucardie, P. (2000) 'Prophets, purifiers and prolocutors towards a theory on the emergence of new parties', *Party Politics* 6, 2: 175–185.

Lupia, A. and Strøm, K. (2008) 'Coalition governance theory: Bargaining, electoral connections and the shadow of the future', in Strøm, K., Müller, W. C. and Bergman, T. (eds) *Coalition Governance in Western Europe*, Oxford: Oxford University Press, pp. 51–83.

Lynch, P., Whitaker, R. and Loomes, G. (2012) 'The UK Independence Party: Understanding a niche party's strategy, candidates and supporters', *Parliamentary Affairs* 65, 4: 733–757.

Mackie, T. T. and Rose, R. (1983) 'Incumbency in government: Asset or liability?', in Daalder, H. and Mair, P. (eds) *Western European Party Systems*, London: Sage, pp. 115–137.

MacMillan, S. (2006) 'How to civilize Hamas: Will Wednesday's winners be too busy fixing potholes to wage Jihad?', *Slate*, 27 January, www.slate.com/articles/news_and_politics/foreigners/2006/01/how_to_civilize_hamas.html.

Mair, P. (2001) 'The green challenge and political competition: How typical is the German experience?', *German Politics* 10, 2: 99–116.

Marks, G., Wilson, C. J. and Ray, L. (2002) 'National political parties and European integration', *American Journal of Political Science* 46, 3: 585–594.

May, J. D. (1973) 'Opinion structure of political parties: The special law of curvilinear disparity', *Political Studies* 21, 2: 135–151.

McDonnell, D. and Newell, J. L. (2011) 'Outsider parties in government in Western Europe', *Party Politics* 17, 4: 443–452.

Meguid, B. M. (2005) 'Competition between unequals: The role of mainstream party strategy in niche party success', *American Political Science Review* 99, 3: 347–359.

Meguid, B. M. (2008) *Party Competition Between Unequals: Strategies and Electoral Fortunes in Western Europe*, Cambridge: Cambridge University Press.

Meret, S. and Siim, B. (2012) 'Gender, populism and politics of belonging: Discourses of right-wing populist parties in Denmark, Norway and Austria', in Siim, B. and Mokre, M. (eds) *Negotiating Gender and Diversity in an Emergent European Public Sphere*, Basingstoke: Palgrave MacMillan, pp. 78–97.

Miller, B. and Meyer, T. (2010) 'To the core of the niche party: Conceptual clarity and valid measurement for a much employed concept', http://staatswissenschaft.univie. ac.at/uploads/media/Miller___Meyer_-_To_the_core_of_the_niche_party__Novem ber_2010_.pdf (accessed 16-07-2015).

Minkenberg, M. (2001) 'The radical right in public office: Agenda-setting and policy effects', *West European Politics* 24, 4: 1–21.

Minkenberg, M. (2006) ' Repression and reaction: Militant democracy and the radical right in Germany and France', *Patterns of Prejudice* 40, 1: 25–44.

Minkenberg, M. (2013) 'From pariah to policy-maker? The radical right in Europe, West and East: Between margin and mainstream', *Journal of Contemporary European Studies* 21, 1: 5–24.

Mudde, C. (2007) *Populist Radical Right Parties in Europe*, Cambridge: Cambridge University Press.

Mudde, C. (2013) 'Three decades of populist radical right parties in Western Europe: So what?', *European Journal of Political Research* 52, 1: 1–19.

Müller, W. C. and Strøm, K. (eds) (1999) *Policy, Office, or Votes? How Political Parties in Western Europe Make Hard Decisions*, Cambridge: Cambridge University Press.

Müller, W. C. and Strøm, K. (2000) *Coalition Governments in Western Europe*, Oxford: Oxford University Press.

Müller-Rommel, F. and Poguntke, T. (eds) (2002) *Green Parties in National Governments*, London: Frank Cass.

Narud, H. M. (1996) *Voters, Parties and Governments. Electoral Competition, Policy Distances and Government Formation in Multi-Party Systems*, Oslo: Institute for Social Research.

Norris, P. (2005) *Radical Right: Voters and Parties in the Electoral Market*, Cambridge: Cambridge University Press.

NRC (14-09-2013) 'Mensen zien ons als een serieus alternatief', www.nrc.nl/ha ndelsblad/van/2013/september/14/mensen-zien-ons-als-een-serieus-alternatief-1292 987 (accessed 16-06-2015).

Nu.nl (07-05-2014) 'CIDI hekelt samenwerken PVV met extreem rechts', www.nu. nl/politiek/3769162/cidi-hekelt-samenwerken-pvv-met-extreem-rechts.html (accessed 17-07-2015).

Otjes, S. P. (2012) "Imitating the newcomer. How, when and why established political parties imitate the policy positions and issue attention of new political parties in the electoral and parliamentary arena: the case of the Netherlands," Doctoral Thesis, Leiden University.

Pedersen, M. (1982) 'Towards a new typology of party lifespans and minor parties', *Scandinavian Political Studies* 5: 1–16.

Pharr, S. J. and Putnam, R. D. (eds) (2000) *Disaffected Democracies: What's Troubling the Trilateral Countries?* Princeton, NJ: Princeton University Press.

Przeworski, A. and Sprague, J. (1986) *Paper Stones: A History of Electoral Socialism*, Chicago, IL: University of Chicago Press.

Rooduijn, M. (2014) 'The nucleus of populism: In search of the lowest common denominator', *Government and Opposition* 49, 4: 573–599.

Rovny, J. (2013) 'Where do radical right parties stand? Position blurring in multidimensional competition', *European Political Science Review* 5, 1: 1–26.

Rydgren, J. and van Holsteyn, J. (2005) 'Holland and Pim Fortuyn: A deviant case or the beginning of something new?', in Rydgren, J. (ed.) *Movements of Exclusion: Radical Right-Wing Populism in the Western World*, New York: Nova Science Publishers, pp. 41–63.

Sartori, G. (1976) *Parties and Party Systems: A Framework for Analysis*, Cambridge: Cambridge University Press.

Scarrow, S. E. (1996) 'Politicians against parties: Anti-party arguments as weapons for change in Germany', *European Journal of Political Research* 29, 3: 297–317.

Schedler, A. (1996) 'Anti-political-establishment parties', *Party Politics* 2, 3: 291–312.

Schwedler, J. (2011) 'Can Islamists become moderates? Rethinking the inclusion-moderation hypothesis', *World Politics* 63, 2: 347–376.

Schwedler, J. (2013) 'Islamists in power? Inclusion, moderation, and the Arab uprisings', *Middle East Development Journal* 5, 1: 1–18.

Schofield, N. and Sened, I. (2006) *Multiparty Democracy: Parties, Elections and Legislative Politics*, Cambridge: Cambridge University Press.

Schumacher, G., de Vries, C. and Vis, B. (2013) 'Why political parties change their position: environmental incentives and party organization', *Journal of Politics* 75, 2: 464–477.

Sened, I. (1996) 'A model of coalition formation', *Journal of Politics* 58, 2: 350–372.

Sjöblom, G. (1968) *Party Strategies in Multiparty Systems*, Lund: Studentlitteratur Lund Sweden.

Smith, G. (1997) 'In search of small parties, problems of definition, classification, and significance', in Mueller-Rommel, F. and Pridham, G. (eds) *Small Parties in Western Europe. Comparative and National Perspectives*, London: Sage, pp. 23–40.

Somer, M. (2014) 'Moderation of religious and secular politics: A country's "centre" and democratization', *Democratization* 21, 2: 244–267.

Somer-Topcu, Z. (2009) 'Timely decisions: the effects of past national elections on party policy change', *The Journal of Politics* 71, 1: 238–248.

Strøm, K. (1990a) 'A behavioral theory of competitive political parties', *American Journal of Political Science* 34, 2: 565–598.

Strøm, K. (1990b) *Minority Government and Majority Rule*, Cambridge: Cambridge University Press.

Strøm, K., Budge, I. and Laver, M. J. (1994) 'Constraints on cabinet formation in parliamentary democracies', *American Journal of Political Science* 38: 303–335.

Strøm, K. and Muller, W. C. (eds) (1999) *Policy, Office, or Votes? How Political Parties in Western Europe Make Hard Decisions*, Cambridge: Cambridge University Press.

Tepe, S. (2012) 'Electoral constraints, ideological commitments, and the democratic capacities of religious parties in Israel and Turkey', *Political Research Quarterly* 65, 3: 467–485.

Valen, H. and Narud, H. (2007) 'The conditional party mandate: A model for the study of mass and elite opinion patterns', *European Journal of Political Research* 46, 3: 293–318.

Van der Brug, W. (2003) 'How the LPF fuelled discontent: Empirical tests of explanations of LPF support', *Acta Politica* 38, 1: 89–106.

Van der Brug, W., Fennema, M. and Tillie, J. (2000) 'Anti-immigrant parties in Europe: Ideological or protest vote?', *European Journal of Political Research* 37, 1: 77–102.

Van Heerden, S. C. (2014) "What did you just call me? A study on the demonization of political parties in the Netherlands between 1995 and 2011", Doctoral thesis, University of Amsterdam.

Van Kersbergen, K. and Krouwel, A. (2008) 'A double-edged sword! The Dutch centre-right and the "foreigners issue", *Journal of European Public Policy* 15, 3: 398–414.

Van Praag, P. (2003) 'The winners and losers in a turbulent political year', *Acta Politica* 38, 1: 5–22.

Van Spanje, J. (2010) 'Contagious parties: Anti–immigration parties and their impact on other parties' immigration stances in contemporary Western Europe', *Party Politics* 16, 5: 563–586.

Van Spanje, J. (2011a) 'Keeping the rascals in: Anti-political-establishment parties and their cost of governing in established democracies', *European Journal of Political Research* 50, 5: 609–635.

Van Spanje, J. (2011b) 'The wrong and the right: A comparative analysis of "anti–immigration" and "far right" parties', *Government and Opposition* 46, 3: 293–320.

Van Spanje, J. and van der Brug, W. (2007) 'The party as pariah: The exclusion of anti-immigration parties and its effect on their ideological positions', *West European Politics* 30, 5: 1022–1040.

Vrij Nederland (11-11-2013) 'De nieuwe extreme-rechtse vrienden van Wilders', www.vn.nl/Archief/Samenleving/Artikel-Samenleving/De-nieuwe-extreemrechtse-vrienden-van-Wilders-1.htm (accessed 17-07-2015).

Vrij Nederland (21-05-2014) 'Hoe Wilders over zijn eigen grens ging', www.vn.nl/Archief/Politiek/Artikel-Politiek/Hoe-Wilders-over-zijn-eigen-grens-ging.htm (accessed 16-06-2015).

Wagner, M. (2012) 'Defining and measuring niche parties', *Party Politics* 18, 6: 845–864.

Walgrave, S. and van Aelst, P. (2006) 'The contingency of the mass media's political agenda setting power: Toward a preliminary theory', *Journal of Communication* 56, 1: 88–109.

Zaslove, A. (2011) 'The populist radical right in government: The structure and agency of success and failure', *Comparative European Politics* 10, 4: 421–448.

Zúquete, J. P. (2008) 'The European extreme-right and Islam: New directions?', *Journal of Political Ideologies* 13, 3: 321–344.

Part I

Comparative analyses

2 Into the mainstream?

A comparative analysis of the programmatic profiles of radical right-wing populist parties in Western Europe over time

Tjitske Akkerman, Sarah L. de Lange and Matthijs Rooduijn

Introduction

Radical right-wing populist parties have developed into relevant parties in various countries in Western Europe. In many cases, they have gained coalition potential or office experience. These positions may have pressured them to mellow their programmatic positions, broaden their scope of issues or tone down their populist stances. This chapter addresses in a general and comparative way the question whether and in what ways radical right-wing populist parties have moved from the margins into the mainstream. The case studies in this volume will shed light on this question using in-depth, mostly qualitative data. However, in order to discern general patterns, it is important to begin with systematic analyses based on cross-country and cross-time data. In this chapter, we provide such analyses based on both existing and new quantitative data.

In the previous chapter, 'mainstreaming' has been defined as a process in which radical right-wing populist parties change to become more like mainstream parties, and this concept has been specified as having four dimensions. These dimensions include the extent to which radical right-wing populist parties can be qualified as radical, niche, or anti-establishment parties and the extent to which they have an extremist reputation. In this chapter, we will focus on the first three of these dimensions, which are all related to the programmatic profiles of this party family. The fourth dimension, which examines whether radical right-wing populist parties have toned down or abandoned their extremist reputation, is extremely difficult to assess quantitatively. It is therefore not included here. This aspect of mainstreaming will be studied extensively in the country chapters.

This chapter proceeds as follows. First, we operationalise the three dimensions of mainstreaming and describe the data that we will use to measure them (for a summary, see Table 2.1). Second, we analyse changes in party scores in order to discern whether we can find general patterns of mainstreaming. In other words, we study whether the programmatic profiles of radical right-wing populist parties have changed over time, and if so, whether these changes signal that these parties have become more like mainstream parties.

Measuring mainstreaming

The three dimensions of mainstreaming examined in this chapter differ fundamentally with respect to what should be measured: party positions or issue salience. Whether radical right-wing populist parties have changed their radicalness and anti-establishment character can best be measured by looking at party positions, whereas their 'nicheness' is primarily a matter of issue salience – that is, how strongly these parties emphasise certain issues.

Various practices to estimate party positions and their salience exist (for overviews and discussions, see Benoit and Laver 2006; Budge *et al.* 2001; Klingemann *et al.* 2006; Laver 2001; Volkens *et al.* 2013). The most commonly used methods for the estimation of party positions and their salience are (1) the analysis of election manifestos, sometimes referred to as the 'behavioural' or, more specifically, 'manifesto-based approach' and (2) the analysis of actors' (e.g., experts, party elites, party members, voters) *perceptions* of parties' positions and their salience, sometimes referred to as a 'second-hand approach' (Benoit and Laver 2006). Because they are highly standardised, both the manifesto-based and perception-based approaches share a high level of popularity in studies making cross-national and cross-temporal comparisons. They are widely used to study different aspects of party competition, such as electoral competition and the competition for government.[1]

Manifesto-based and perception-based estimates of parties' positions differ on many accounts. A comparison by Benoit and Laver (2006: 90–92) illustrates that the two approaches each have unique characteristics and have particular advantages and disadvantages (see also Laver 2001). While manifesto-based approaches produce more reliable estimates because they rely on an extensive,

Table 2.1 Dimensions of mainstreaming

Dimensions of non-mainstreamness	Evidenced by	Indicators for mainstreaming
Radical party	Positions on core issues, such as immigration and integration, European integration and law and order are radical	Core positions are moderated
Niche party	Issue agenda is limited to sociocultural issues	Issue agenda is expanded and socioeconomic issues are emphasised more strongly
Anti-establishment party	Populist positions	Populist positions moderated

predetermined coding scheme, perception-based approaches produce more valid estimates since they tap more easily into a general notion of left and right, and other party attitudes. In sum, 'systematic comparison clearly shows that none of the approaches can claim absolute truth in determining the relevant policy dimension and the "true" positions of parties on them' (Volkens 2007: 117).

Measuring radicalness

The first dimension of mainstreaming requires an assessment of radical right-wing populist parties' positions on the core issues of immigration and integration, and European integration and authoritarianism. To measure these positions over time, we can partly use expert surveys. They have been praised because they come with 'a certain weight and legitimacy', give a timely account of a party's position, are 'quick, easy, and comprehensive', and generate 'highly *comparable* and *standardized* data' (Mair 2001: 24). For our purposes, the most important expert surveys have been administered in the context of the Chapel Hill Expert Survey (CHES).[2] The CHES asks experts to estimate party positions on a variety of issues since 1999 (Bakker *et al.* forthcoming; Hooghe *et al.* 2010; Steenbergen and Marks 2007) and has been conducted in 1999, 2002, 2006 and 2010. In the CHES surveys, experts estimate party positions on a variety of policy dimensions – including immigration, multiculturalism and European integration – and on overarching dimensions, such as the left-right economic dimension and the Green-Alternative-Libertarian versus Traditional-Authoritarian-Nationalism (GALTAN) dimension.[3] The issues of immigration and multiculturalism are, however, relatively new additions to the dataset and have only been measured in 2006 and 2010. This time-span is too short to properly detect changes in programmatic profiles, and therefore, the CHES data on immigration and multiculturalism are not useful for our analysis. We use the CHES data only to assess radical right-wing populist parties' positions on European integration and on the GALTAN dimension, which provides an indication of these parties' positions on, amongst others, questions of authoritarianism (see Table 2.2).

Unfortunately, the CHES dataset does not include all the parties that are studied in this edited volume. It contains information about changes in the positions of seven radical right-wing populist parties in six countries: the Austrian FPÖ, the Belgian VB and FNb, the Danish DF, the French FN, the Italian LN, and UKIP from the United Kingdom.[4] The positions of these

Table 2.2 Measuring radicalness on the basis of the CHES data

Issue	Extreme 1	Extreme 2	Range
European integration	Strongly opposed	Strongly in favour	1–7
GALTAN	Libertarian/ postmaterialism	Traditional/ authoritarian	0–10

parties have been measured relative to the mean positions of the other parties in their respective countries.

Measuring immigration and integration positions

As explained above, the CHES dataset does not suit our aims of assessing party positions about immigration and integration over time. Since immigration and integration can be considered core issues of radical right-wing populist parties (Mudde 2007), it is necessary to assess positions on these issues accurately and over a longer time-span. An alternative dataset has therefore been used. This dataset is based on a Nativist Immigration and Integration Policy (NIIP) index that enables a fine-grained and differentiated analysis of concrete policy proposals in election manifestos (see Akkerman 2012, 2015). The NIIP index distinguishes at the highest level of analysis the broad policy domains 'immigration' and 'integration'. Each of these domains consists of several subcategories, which are presented in Table 2.3. The domain 'immigration' consists of five subcategories: worker immigration, access to citizenship (referring to those conditions that are not covered under integration, such as duration of residence, the acceptance of a dual nationality or the conditions for second or third generations), asylum, illegality (referring to the degrees of tolerance for the '*sans papiers*') and family reunification. The domain 'integration' consists of three subcategories: integration trajectories, social rights and religion/Islam. Integration trajectories consist primarily of language courses and tests, but may also include courses and tests focusing on civic orientation, culture and history. Because radical right-wing populist parties have increasingly defended the welfare state as a system exclusively meant for those belonging to the nation, the policy proposals regarding access of immigrants to housing, social security, and so on, have been included as important conditions for, or hurdles to, integration. Finally, as mentioned above, radical right-wing populist parties have increasingly identified cultural threats and problems of integration as being related to Islam. Hence, religious issues related to the integration of newcomers have become important issues for these parties. These subcategories are sufficiently comprehensive to cover all relevant pledges in party manifestos.

The range of positions the NIIP index covers is based on a cosmopolitan-nationalist dimension (see Akkerman 2012, 2015). All policy proposals that are restrictive with regard to immigration and assimilationist regarding integration are denoted as nationalist, whereas proposals favouring open borders and cultural pluralism are regarded as cosmopolitan. This dimension ranges from positive scores on the nationalist side to negative scores on the cosmopolitan side.

Table 2.3 Coding scheme

Immigration					Integration		
Worker immigration	Citizenship	Asylum	Illegality	Family reunification	Integration trajectories	Social rights	Religion/ Islam

To clarify how the coding of manifestos has been done, we will give examples regarding nationalist proposals. Restrictiveness with respect to immigration implies that radical nationalists are in favour of high hurdles for, or a wholesale stop to, worker immigration, asylum and family reunion alongside zero tolerance for, and expulsion of, '*sans papiers*'. Naturalisation is barricaded off from those not belonging to the nation, and permanent residency is highly conditional (Howard 2010). With regard to citizenship, radical right-wing populist parties will prefer a status exclusively based on *jus sanguinis*. Dual nationalities are highly distrusted, perceived as threats to loyalty and national identity. High barriers for residence permits or naturalisation are raised to protect the nation from disintegration (Bauböck *et al.* 2006; Howard 2010; Odmalm 2007; Vink 2010). With respect to integration, cultural assimilation and loyalty to the nation are highly valued. For instance, radical right-wing populist parties set relatively high standards for knowledge of language, extend integration requirements to civic orientation, history and culture, and tend to demand loyalty oaths and commitment to political and cultural values. At the same time, these tests are used as high hurdles for entry, residence or naturalisation (Bauböck and Joppke 2010; Goodman 2010; Jacobs and Rea 2007; Joppke and Morawska 2003). Radical right-wing populist parties are also welfare chauvinist, regarding social rights as exclusive entitlements for members of the nation. They are in favour of restrictive policies regarding social security, housing, education, the labour market and health care for immigrants (Betz 1994; Mudde 2007). Finally, these parties have increasingly focused on immigration from Muslim countries, identifying integration problems as being mostly related to Islam. They tend to regard Islam generally as a threat to national culture and liberal democracies. Christian culture – or a mixture of Christianity, Humanism and sometimes Judaism – is contrasted as being core to an authentic native culture (Betz and Meret 2009; Zúquete 2008). These parties therefore propagate a restrictive policy regarding Islamic attire (e.g. headscarves or burkas), the building of mosques, Islamic schools, and so on, while they tend to privilege Christian attire, buildings, schools, and the like. All these aspects of immigration and integration policies together are the core issues that need to be looked at systematically in order to assess whether radical right-wing populist parties have radicalised or moderated their positions.

Positions of mainstream and radical right-wing populist parties can vary substantially, especially on the nationalist side. Radical right-wing populist parties are more restrictive and assimilationist than mainstream right-wing parties. To do justice to the differences between radical and moderate positions, a 5-point scale has been developed. All pledges diverging from the status quo in a cosmopolitan direction score negatively, varying from −0.5 to −1, while all pledges diverging in a nationalist/nativist direction score positively, varying from 0.5 to 1. Pledges affirming the status quo score 0. For each subcategory, positions have been refined in order to enable this differentiation (see Appendix). The unit of analysis is the pledge. Compared to quasi-sentences, sentences or other text units, pledges provide the most substantive understanding of party positions and are therefore the best units to use when analysing positions. Pledges are defined as a stated commitment to carry out some action or produce some outcome.

Manifestos differ substantially in size and in character; they vary from a few pages to 50 pages or more. Some tend to devote a lot of space to rhetoric while others are relatively focused on pledges, and some present a detailed list of pledges, whereas others only mention essentials. This variation may heavily influence the position score because we have to consistently count all pledges. Following the solution provided by Laver and Garry (2000), we take account of the relative space devoted to pledges. The scores have been estimated in proportion to the total number of pledges in the policy field of immigration and integration. Finally, policy positions can be measured absolutely, or they can be measured relatively, by estimating the distances in relation to the positions of other parties. We have also measured the average positions of mainstream parties since this measurement has the advantage of capturing interaction patterns and reflecting wider shifts in policy courses. The parties included in this analysis are the DF, FN, FPÖ, PVV, SVP and VB.

Measuring 'nicheness'

The second mainstreaming dimension focuses on the changes in the niche character of radical right-wing populist parties. The aim is to assess whether the policy agenda of the parties has emphasised sociocultural issues above all or whether it has increasingly focused on socioeconomic issues as well. Our analysis of the salience of socioeconomic and sociocultural issues has been executed within the framework of the Manifesto Research Group, today named the Comparative Manifesto Project (CMP) (Budge *et al.* 2001; Klingemann *et al.* 2006; Volkens *et al.* 2013).[5] The CMP generates a 'solid basis and reliable estimates as a general standard for validating other methods' (Budge 2001: 210) that 'are quite good as compared to other accepted approaches' (Gabel and Huber 2000: 94). The approach relies on the sentence-by-sentence coding of manifestos presented by parties at election time. The CMP has chosen a saliency (or valence) approach, assuming that 'parties argue with each other by emphasizing different policy priorities rather than by directly confronting each other on the same issues' (Budge and Bara 2001: 6–7). In other words, the CMP believes that issues are salient in nature – that is, parties give attention to some issues and neglect others, regardless of their positions on these issues. Thus, the CMP measures *how often* parties mention certain issues in their manifestos rather than the *positions* they take on these issues. For this reason, the CMP is the best database for cross-country and cross-time analyses of the salience that parties attach to particular issues and policy dimensions, but it is less comprehensive when it comes to measuring positions (De Lange 2007; Pellikaan *et al.* 2003, 2007). In the CMP coding scheme, law and order, for instance, is considered to be a valence issue. Hence, parties' positions on this issue, which is important to radical right-wing populist parties, cannot be derived from the dataset. Another disadvantage is that the database was developed in the 1970s and that, consequently, the coding categories it employs are dated. The coding scheme does not include, for instance, the item of immigration, which has become a contested issue in more recent years (Akkerman 2012; Budge 2001; Petry and Landry 2001; Protsyk and Garaz 2013).[6] In sum, to assess how radical the positions of radical right-wing populist parties are on key issues such as immigration and integration, law and order, and European integration, the CMP data have too many shortcomings to be useful.

The dataset can, however, be successfully used to estimate how important traditional socioeconomic issues are to these parties and to help determine their 'nicheness'. Since it measures how many sentences are devoted to a particular topic, adding up these numbers provides an indication of the percentage of a party's manifesto devoted to groups of issues. For the purpose of this study, we distinguish between issues that belong to the traditional socioeconomic dimension and the newer sociocultural dimension. In the first category fall issues like free market economy, corporatism, protectionism, welfare state expansion, and the like (401 to 414 and 504 to 507 in the CMP coding scheme), while in the second category fall issues like national way of life, traditional morality, and law and order (601 to 608). Thus, emphasis on socioeconomic issues has been measured by adding up the scores on 401 through to 414 and 504 through to 507, while the emphasis on sociocultural issues has been calculated by adding up the scores on 601 through to 608. We have calculated the salience scores for the radical right-wing populist parties included in both the CMP dataset and this study. With the exception of UKIP, all radical right-wing populist parties studied in the country chapters are covered in the CMP dataset. In addition, we have also computed the average mainstream salience scores in every country in order to be able to contrast the salience profile of radical right-wing populist parties to that of mainstream parties.

Measuring anti-establishment positions

The third dimension of mainstreaming concerns the anti-establishment attitudes and behaviour of radical right-wing populist parties (Abedi 2004; Schedler 1996). In this chapter, we focus on attitudes only because comparing anti-establishment behaviour across cases and over time is complicated. The anti-establishment attitudes of radical right-wing populist parties stem from their populist ideas. Populism is defined here as 'a [thin] ideology that considers society to be ultimately separated into two homogeneous and antagonistic groups, "the pure people" versus "the corrupt elite", and which argues that politics should be an expression of the *volonté générale* (general will) of the people' (Mudde 2007: 23). This particular set of ideas makes populists fiercely criticise the political establishment for not listening to ordinary citizens.

The CMP and CHES datasets do not contain information about the extent to which parties and their platforms can be qualified as anti-establishment or populist. Several studies have attempted to assess to what extent political parties express a populist discourse (Deegan-Krause and Haughton 2009; Hawkins 2010; Pauwels 2011; Rooduijn *et al.* 2014; Rooduijn and Pauwels 2011). In this chapter, we employ the automated content analysis method that was developed by Rooduijn and Pauwels (2011). It has been shown that this measure of populism generates both valid and reliable results, and that it can be employed to assess large amounts of texts (in different languages) at the same time.

The measure relies on a dictionary approach, in which a computer programme (Yoshikoder) counts the words that are considered to be populist. An important advantage of such a computer-based content analysis over a classical content analysis (in which human coders conduct the analyses) is that it is much less time consuming and expensive. In our computerised content analysis, words instead of pledges or (quasi-)sentences are the units of measurement. Although words can have different meanings in different contexts, Laver and Garry (2000) have demonstrated that in most cases, it is possible to code words unambiguously. Initially, the method aimed at coding words that refer to either people-centrism or anti-elitism. However, it turned out that a measurement of people-centrism by means of individual words is almost impossible. For instance, 'the people' is often referred to by the words 'we' and 'our' (e.g., 'we [the people] need to raise our voice'). Yet not every mention of the words 'our' or 'we' is a reference to the people. These words could also refer to the political party instead of the people (e.g. 'we [the party] propose our plans in the next chapter'). It was therefore decided to focus only on words that refer to anti-elitism. Rooduijn and Pauwels (2011) have demonstrated that anti-elitism is a good indicator of populism because criticism towards elites is mostly motivated by the argument that elites betray the ordinary people. Moreover, and maybe even more importantly, this bias towards the anti-elitism component of populism is not problematic for our purposes here because we are mainly interested in the anti-establishment positions of parties, and not so much in their people-centrism.

The selection of dictionary words was based on both empirical and theoretical reasoning. Election manifestos of populist parties (that have not actually been analysed) were used as a source of inspiration. Words that populist parties used to express their negativity towards elites were put on a list. However, the final decision whether or not to include these words in the dictionary was based on theoretical considerations; only those words have been selected that were used to position the evil elites against the good people. Developing such a dictionary was not an easy task. Not every word that *could* refer to anti-elitism does always refer to it, while, at the same time, many occurrences of anti-elitism can easily be overlooked because it is impossible to include every single word beforehand that *might* refer to anti-elitism. The dictionary was translated into four languages as accurately as possible. Besides the translated 'core words', some 'context-specific words' were also added. These context-specific terms are words that are too context specific to be translated from one language to another. For instance, populists in the Netherlands sometimes refer to '*regenten*' (regents) to express anti-elitism. This word refers to the Dutch political rulers in the sixteenth, seventeenth and eighteenth centuries. The *regenten* formed a rather closed group that reserved government offices for themselves. This specific term is not used by populists in countries other than the Netherlands.

For a complete overview of the dictionary of populist terms used to measure anti-establishmentarianism, see Table 2.4. We have computed the proportion of these words vis-à-vis all words within the election manifestos of several political parties in six of the countries under analysis in this volume (Austria, Belgium, France, the Netherlands, Switzerland and the United Kingdom) during various elections between 1995 and 2012 (provided that election manifestos are available). These countries have been selected because various radical right-wing populist parties have been successful there. Moreover, the dictionary was developed in Dutch, English, French and German.

From radical party to mainstream party?

Our analyses show that there is no trend towards the mainstream when it comes to radical positions on the core issues immigration and integration, European integration and authoritarianism. The analysis of the CHES data (used to assess European integration and authoritarianism) makes clear that, in general, the parties have hardly or not at all moderated their positions on European integration (see Figure 2.1a) and on the GALTAN dimension since 1999 (see Figure 2.1b). Only on European integration is there a slight decrease in the gap between the average position of radical parties and the average position of all parties since 2006. On the GALTAN dimension, the gap with the mean position

Table 2.4 Dictionary (shortened words)

NL	UK	GE	FR
elit	elit	elit	élit
consensus	consensus	konsens	consensus
ondemocratisch	undemocratic	undemokratisch	antidémocratiq
corrupt	corrupt	korrupt	corromp
propagand	propagand	propagand	propagand
politici	politici	politiker	politicien
bedrog	deceit	täusch	tromp
bedreig	deceiv	betrüg	
verrad	betray	verrat	trahi
schaam	shame	scham	honte
schand	scandal	skandal	scandal
waarheid	truth	wahrheit	vérité
oneerlijk	dishonest	unehrlich	malhonnêt
establishm	establishm	establishm	établissement
heersend	ruling	herrsch	régnant
leugen		lüge	mensong
lieg	lying		ment

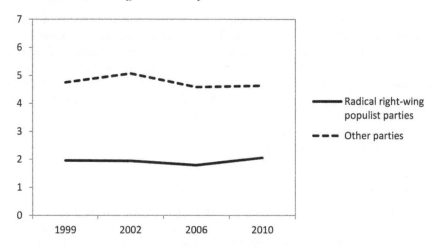

Figure 2.1a Average position on European integration

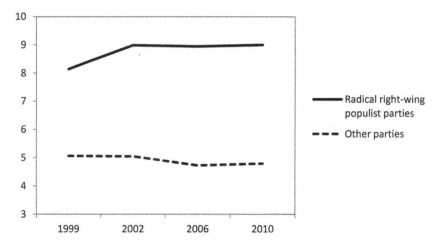

Figure 2.1b Average position on the GALTAN dimension

has even increased since 2002, with radical parties becoming more authoritarian and the mainstream parties, on average, slightly moderating their positions.

To see whether exceptions exist to the average trends in European integration and authoritarianism, we have added analyses of individual cases (see Appendix). With respect to European integration, the programmatic course of the DF appears to be exceptional. The party has consistently mainstreamed since 2002. Incidentally, there has been some moderation of other radical parties; the FPÖ slightly radicalised between 2002–06, but moderated again in 2010, the VB moderated slightly in 2002, the FNb slightly moderated over time, and the FN in 2010. UKIP is consistently Eurosceptical. With respect to authoritarianism, there is hardly any mainstreaming: the FPÖ radicalised in 2002; the VB incidentally moderated in 2002, FNb remained consistently authoritarian; the FN radicalised in 2002, moderated in 2006 and radicalised again in 2010; the DF radicalised in 2002, moderated in 2006 and radicalised again in 2010; UKIP radicalised slightly until 2006 and moderated again in 2010.

When we look at immigration and integration (see Figure 2.1c), it can be observed that, on average, the positions of the radical parties have become more radical over time, and the gap with mainstream parties has increased. If one looks at the parties individually (see Appendix1), it is noteworthy that some parties are not far from the mainstream. The gap with the mainstream parties (the average of the main left-wing and the main right-wing parties) is relatively small in the cases of the DF, FPÖ and FN. The DF has mainstreamed since 2005; the FPÖ radicalised in 2006, but moderated again in 2008; and the FN moderated in 2007 and 2012. The other parties that are central in the casestudies (the PVV, SVP and VB) are more radical. The PVV[7] narrowed the gap with mainstream parties somewhat in 2012, but the SVP and VB radicalised over time and increased the gap with the mainstream parties.

Overall, there is no indication that radical right-wing populist parties are becoming less radical. The thesis that parties with office opportunities tend to mainstream apparently needs to be qualified with regard to the radicalness of radical right-wing populist parties. Of the parties included in the datasets, the DF has been most continuously in national office since the turn of the millennium. The DF is also the party that has most clearly mainstreamed. It is the only example that fully confirms a correlation between experience in a coalition government and mainstreaming. In contrast, the SVP has also been continuously in office, but this party has become more radical over time.[8] The Swiss case seems to be most clearly contradicting the general theory, but it may be an exceptional case (see Chapter 9). The mixed evidence for the FN and

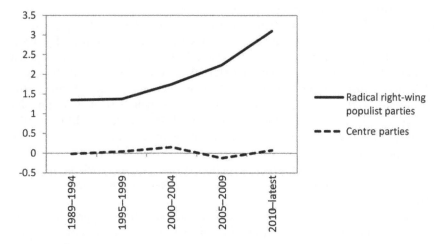

Figure 2.1c Average position on immigration and integration issues

UKIP makes clear that parties without any office opportunities may also have good reasons to mainstream, at least incidentally. The VB, on the other hand, is most consistently radical – with the exception of 2002 – and this is in line with its lack of office opportunities. The incidental moderation of the FPÖ and the PVV may be related to their one-time (and not very successful) experience in office (see Chapters 4 and 7). In the case of the FPÖ, a return to opposition (after 2005) went along with radicalisation until new perspectives of office may have incited the party to moderate again after 2008. For the PVV, the semi-office participation between 2010 and 2012 seems to have had a partly moderating effect, but the case study (Chapter 7) can throw more light on the long-term effects after 2012.

From niche party to mainstream party?

Existing research suggests that niche parties devote more attention to niche party issues (e.g. environmental issues, in the case of green parties; immigration and integration, and law and order issues, in the case of radical right-wing populist parties) than to traditional socioeconomic left-right issues (e.g., Meguid 2005, 2008; Meyer and Miller 2015; Wagner 2012). And indeed, radical right-wing populist parties devote, on average, more attention to sociocultural issues than to socioeconomic issues. In this respect their issue profile differs from that of mainstream parties, which place more emphasis on socioeconomic issues than on sociocultural issues (see Figure 2.2a and Figure 2.2b).

However, when studying the manifestos of radical right-wing populist parties, it can be observed that these parties differ greatly in their issue profiles. Some radical right-wing populist parties devote more attention to socioeconomic issues than others, and the same can be said about sociocultural issues (see Appendix). For the DF, FN, PVV and VB, for example, sociocultural issues make up a substantial part of their manifestos (e.g. more than 50 per cent for the DF in 2001, 40 per cent for the FN in 1997, 50 per cent for the PVV in 2006, and 40 per cent for the VB in 2010). For other parties, socioeconomic issues take priority. Examples are the FPÖ (around 50 per cent in 2002 and 2006), FrP (more than 60 per cent in 2001), LPF (almost 50 per cent in 2002), PS (almost 60 per cent in 1995), and SVP (more than 50 per cent in 1999). Moreover, the balance between the salience of the two types of issues differs between radical right-wing populist parties as well. Throughout the period analysed, the FPÖ, FrP, LPF and PS, always pay more attention to socioeconomic issues than to sociocultural issues. In this respect, they do not meet the criteria formulated for niche party status in the literature. Other radical right-wing populist parties put more emphasis on sociocultural issues than on socioeconomic issues and can therefore more easily be classified as niche parties.

Also when comparing the issue profiles of radical right-wing populist parties to the issue profiles of other parties in the system, the picture is more complex than the literature assumes. Few radical right-wing populist parties focus more systematically on sociocultural issues and less systematically on socioeconomic issues than the average party represented in parliament. In this sense, they do not conform to the image of the niche party that is presented in the literature. The DF, FN, FPÖ, PS and PVV mention sociocultural issues more often than other parties, whereas the FrP and LPF discuss socioeconomic issues more frequently. All in all, a difference in issue profiles is observable between so-called neo-liberal populist parties (e.g., FrP, LPF) and nationalist populist parties (e.g., DF, FN, PVV, VB) (e.g., Betz 1993, 1994; De Lange 2007; Mudde 2007). In the first group of parties, socioeconomic issues prevail by and large over sociocultural issues, whereas it is the other way around in the second group. However, not all radical right-wing populist parties neatly fall into either of these categories. The patterns observed in Austria and Switzerland, for example, are more complex and raise questions about the validity of the distinction between neo-liberal and national populist parties.

When it comes to the mainstreaming of radical right-wing populist parties – that is, the broadening of their issue profile by emphasising sociocultural issues less and socioeconomic issues more – the picture is also not particularly uniform. From the early 2000s onwards, radical right-wing populist parties have on average begun to devote more attention to socioeconomic issues, which could be taken as a sign of mainstreaming. However, in the late 1990s mainstream parties also experienced a period in which they emphasised these issues more than before (see Figure 2.2a), which makes the change in the agenda of radical right-wing populist parties less distinct. Moreover, radical right-wing populist parties have started to pay more attention to sociocultural issues in the same period, thereby reinforcing their niche party profile (see Figure 2.2b).

When studying individual cases, the pattern becomes even more complex (see Appendix). In some cases, increases (or decreases) in the salience of socioeconomic issues correspond to decreases (or increases) in the salience of sociocultural issues and the two appear like communicating vessels (e.g., in the case of the BZÖ, DF, FrP, LPF, PVV and VB). In those cases, processes of radicalisation or mainstreaming can clearly be distinguished. For instance, the radicalisation of the LPF and VB and the mainstreaming of the BZÖ and PVV can be clearly observed. The first two parties gradually devote more attention to sociocultural issues and less to socioeconomic issues, while the latter two move in the opposite direction. In the case of the Norwegian FrP, the party mainstreams between 1997 and 2001, only to radicalise again between 2001 and 2009. An inverse pattern can be observed in Denmark, where the DF radicalises sharply between 1998 and 2001 and slowly de-radicalises afterwards.

In the other cases (Austria, Finland, France and Switzerland), the two trends are not as clearly associated. Moreover, the radical right-wing populist parties in these cases appear to go through different phases. The FPÖ, for example, mainstreams between 1995 and 1999, prior to its entrance into government. Once in office, between 1999 and 2002, it radicalises again and reverts to its old issue profile. In subsequent years, however, developments are less clear-cut. The attention to socioeconomic issues goes up but initially does not go down for sociocultural issues. The FN experiences a similar trajectory. Between 1997

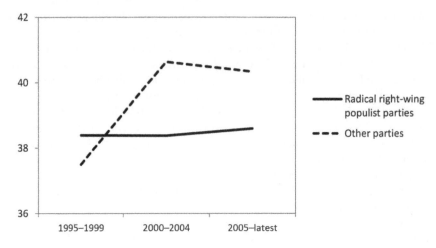

Figure 2.2a Average salience of socioeconomic issues

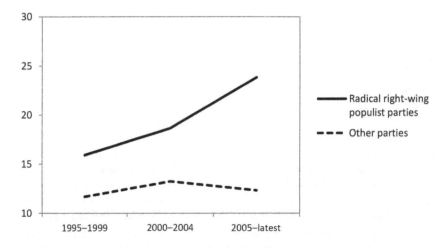

Figure 2.2b Average salience of sociocultural issues

and 2002, the party mainstreams, decreasing the salience of sociocultural issues and increasing the salience of socioeconomic issues. From 2002 onwards, the salience of sociocultural issues remains more or less constant. The attention devoted to sociocultural issues, however, decreases between 2002 and 2007, and increases between 2007 and 2012. For this period, it is therefore difficult to argue that the party either mainstreams or radicalises. The PS radicalises after 2007, when the former agrarian party joins the radical right-wing populist party family. However, the changes to the issue profile of the PS prior to this period are more difficult to understand. The SVP devotes far less attention to socio-economic issues in 2011 as compared to 1995, but this development does not coincide with increasing salience of socioeconomic issues. Hence, within the context of our framework, the party does not completely develop into a niche party.

Moreover, when evaluating and interpreting these patterns, it should be taken into consideration that in many countries, changes in the salience of sociocultural and socioeconomic issues in the manifestos of radical right-wing populist parties correspond to general shifts in salience in the party system. In other words, the scores for the radical right-wing populist parties tend to trend in the same way as the party system average. In these circumstances, it is difficult to speak of radicalisation or mainstreaming because although the radical right-wing populist parties change their issue profiles, they become neither less mainstream nor less radical than the other parties in the party system.

In other words, no clear and consistent mainstreaming of radical right-wing populist parties (i.e., decreased salience of sociocultural issues and increased salience of socioeconomic issues) can be observed over time, with the exceptions of the BZÖ and PVV. However, in a number of other cases, evidence of some temporary mainstreaming can be found. The DF, FN, FPÖ and FrP all mainstream at a specific point in time, and often for only one parliamentary period. Consequently, regarding issue profiles and niche party status, rather than studying which radical right-wing populist parties do or do not mainstream, it seems more fruitful to examine why radical right-wing populist parties mainstream at a certain point in time, focusing on factors that are related to the specific elections in which the mainstreaming takes place.

The comparative analysis also suggests that mainstreaming could indeed be related to questions of participation in government and therefore to shifts from vote- to office-seeking. The mainstreaming of the DF, FPÖ, FrP and PVV occurred prior to the elections in which these parties assumed office or in which they started to support a minority government. Inversely, the VB radicalised after a period of exclusion through the well-known *cordon sanitaire*. At the same time, several radical right-wing populist parties appear to re-radicalise during or after their government participation. This observation could indicate that being in office has a perhaps temporary mainstreaming effect.

From anti-establishment party to mainstream party?

Radical right-wing populist parties accuse the established political order of being out of touch with ordinary citizens. Yet, it could be expected that the longer these parties participate in the electoral arena, the more they will *themselves* become part of the establishment they criticise – especially in countries like Austria, Switzerland and the Netherlands, where they have participated in government coalitions. As a result, they will find it increasingly difficult to present themselves as political outsiders and to express a fierce anti-establishment critique. We therefore expect that radical right-wing populist parties have moderated their anti-establishment attitudes over the years.

Figure 2.3 displays the average populism scores (proportion of populist words compared to all words in a manifesto) of radical right-wing populist parties and the two mainstream left- and right-wing centre parties over time. The scores from all countries under analysis have been combined in this graph. The graph clearly shows that, contrary to the expectations, the degree of populism has not *decreased* but *increased* over the years. Apparently, radical right-wing populist parties have not moderated their critique towards the established political order. Instead, they have intensified their populist discourse. Between 1995 and 2004, mainstream parties and radical right-wing populist parties expressed almost equal amounts of populism. However, since 2005, radical right-wing populists have strongly intensified their populist discourse, whereas centre parties have slightly moderated their critique towards the elite. In the time period 2005–09, radical right-wing populist parties were almost four times as populist as centre parties, and between 2010 and the latest election under analysis, they were almost five times as populist.

When we look at the six countries separately (see Appendix), we can see that in four, radical right-wing populist parties have become more populist. Between 1997 and 2010, UKIP's populism score almost quadrupled. Mainstream parties in the United Kingdom have also become more populist – but only to a very limited extent. A more detailed assessment of UKIP's election manifestos shows that the party has supplemented its Eurosceptic position towards Brussels with a more unfavourable position towards the mainstream parties *within* the United Kingdom as well (see also Chapter 12). The SVP in Switzerland was not populist at all in 1995 (and also much less so than the centre parties). Yet, over the years, the party became increasingly negative about the political elite, and in 2011, the party was five times as populist as the average centre party. This shift towards more populism from the 1990s onwards coincides with the more nativist and

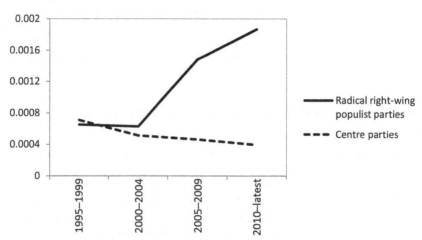

Figure 2.3 Average anti-establishment scores of radical right parties and centre parties over time

Eurosceptic agenda that the party adopted in these years. A similar trend can be observed in Austria. In 1995, the FPÖ was not populist at all. But in later years, the party increasingly incorporated the populist message. In 2008, the FPÖ was three times as populist as the centre parties. The FN was only very moderately populist in its manifestos in 2002 and 2007. However, the degree of populism more than doubled in the manifesto written for the 2012 elections. The critique was now focused on the UMPS (a combination of the acronyms of the two main centre parties, the UMP [Union for a Popular Movement] and PS [Socialist Party]). The centre parties in France were not populist at all in 2012. The degree of populism in the Netherlands increased as well. But contrary to the cases discussed so far, this increase was not due to an existing radical right-wing populist party increasingly employing populist discourse. Instead, the rise of populism in the Netherlands is caused by the appearance of the PVV on the political stage. The PVV has expressed a strongly populist message during all the elections in which it has participated (2006, 2010 and 2012). It has, however, become less populist over these years. This decrease is most likely due to the increasing length of the party's election manifestos. Its 2006 manifesto was very brief and contained only very few concrete and detailed policy proposals. It is likely that, as a result of this lack of attention to policy details, the populism score of the PVV's 2006 manifesto was slightly biased. The Dutch LPF became slightly more populist between 2002 and 2003. On average, the VB in Belgium became slightly less populist over the years. The degree of populism decreased between 1995 and 1999, but then increased between 1999 and 2003. It slightly decreased again between 2003 and 2010. However, the party is still much more populist than the centre parties in Belgium.

To sum up, five parties from five different countries (FPÖ, FN, LPF, UKIP and SVP) have become *more*, not less, anti-establishment over the years. Only the Dutch PVV moderated its populist discourse. The evidence in Belgium is mixed. Based on these findings, we can conclude that mainstreaming is not taking place in the anti-establishment dimension. To the contrary, parties have become more, not less, populist over the years.

Conclusion

Our analyses indicate that radical right-wing populist parties hardly move into the mainstream. Mainstreaming has been measured with respect to radical positions on European integration, authoritarianism and immigration/integration. Our conclusion is that the parties included in our datasets have, on average, become more radical. The distance to other parties with respect to positions on GALTAN and on immigration/integration has increased since the turn of the millennium. Only with respect to European integration has there been some mainstreaming. Radical positions on immigration/integration have most clearly moderated in the case of the DF and FN. The DF has also most consistently moderated regarding European integration. Office opportunities are clearly insufficient to explain mainstreaming in individual cases. While the

DF has mainstreamed in office, the SVP has not. During their exclusion from office, the VB has radicalised but the FN has not.

The evidence for the mainstreaming of the niche profile of radical right-wing populist parties is, at best, mixed. Although the parties pay on average more attention to socioeconomic issues in their manifestos, the salience of sociocultural issues has also increased over time. When disaggregating these findings, it becomes apparent that some radical right-wing populist parties mainstream (BZÖ, FN, PVV, and SVP), while others do not. Moreover, mainstreaming is often a temporary phenomenon, which appears to be related to participation in government coalitions. Office opportunities seem to play a role in the mainstreaming of the DF, FPÖ, FrP and PVV. Inversely, the VB radicalised after a period of exclusion through the well-known *cordon sanitaire*. At the same time, several radical right-wing populist parties appear to re-radicalise after their government participation, suggesting that the mainstreaming effect of government responsibility is usually short-lived. It should also be noted that not all radical right-wing populist parties included in this part of the study have a clear niche party profile. Some radical right-wing populist parties (FPÖ, FrP, LPF and PS) consistently pay more attention to socioeconomic issues than to sociocultural issues. This finding can be interpreted in various ways, for example as an indication that these parties are perhaps not fully-fledged members of the radical right-wing populist party, or as a sign that 'nicheness' is possibly not a distinctive feature of being not mainstream.

With regard to their populist positions, radical right-wing parties have clearly become more populist after the turn of the millennium. Since 2005, radical right-wing populists have strongly intensified their populist discourse, whereas centre parties have slightly moderated their critique towards the elite. Radical right-wing populist parties became eventually five times as populist as centre parties.

On all three dimensions – radical positions on core issues, salience of cultural issues, and anti-establishment positions – the average trends do not indicate that radical right-wing populist parties have mainstreamed. For several reasons we must be cautious about this general finding, however. First of all, quantitative analyses cannot provide the whole picture. Qualitative comparisons are required to get more complete and accurate assessments of mainstreaming. Apart from official documents such as election manifestos or secondary estimates by experts, we also need direct analyses of alternative sources, such as party websites, press releases, election debates, campaign material, interviews with politicians, parliamentary behaviour, voting patterns, and so on. Case studies are required to provide a more complete and accurate picture.

Second, individual cases indicate partial moderation, but these displays of mainstreaming seem to be rather volatile. Whether these incidental signs of moderation are the result of office seeking or of being in office is to be further investigated in the case studies.

Notes

1 Other approaches are available (e.g., media analysis, roll-call analysis, and the analysis of expenditure flows) but are less often used in comparative studies (but see Kriesi *et al.* 2006).
2 Other cross-national expert surveys include those by Castles and Mair (1984), Laver and Hunt (1992), Huber and Inglehart (1995), Lubbers (2000) and Benoit and Laver (2006).
3 The GALTAN dimension is first and foremost concerned with parties' views on democratic freedoms and rights. According to the CHES codebook 'Libertarian' or 'postmaterialist' parties favour expanded personal freedoms – for example, access to abortion, active euthanasia, same-sex marriage or greater democratic participation. 'Traditional' or 'authoritarian' parties often reject these ideas; they value order, tradition and stability, and believe that the government should be a firm moral authority on social and cultural issues.
4 Non-EU members Norway and Switzerland have only been included in 2010, so these two countries cannot be assessed over time. The countries and parties included are the following: Austria: FPÖ and BZÖ; Belgium: VB; Denmark: DF; Finland: PS; France: FN; Italy: LN; Netherlands: PVV; United Kingdom: UKIP.
5 In recent years, alternative techniques to code manifestos have been developed (e.g., De Lange 2007; Klemmensen *et al.* 2007; Laver and Garry 2000; Pellikaan *et al.* 2003, 2007; Pennings and Keman 2002).
6 With respect to integration, the items 607 and 608 (multiculturalism positive/ negative) of the CMP coding scheme would be useful in principle. However, the coding of this item is not always consistent. For example, the VB scores positive on this issue, although the party is quite negative when it comes to multicultural practices or rights of immigrants. The positive score is probably due to its regionalist promotion of Flemish culture. A clear definition of multiculturalism is lacking.
7 Only parties with data available for more than two points in time have been included in the general analyses of mainstreaming (Figures 2.1 to 2.3). Parties with data available for two or less points in time (PVV, LPF, PS, BZÖ) have only been included in the Appendix.
8 It should be noted, though, that we have only data about immigration/integration for the SVP. The CHES dataset includes only recent data for Switzerland.

References

Abedi, A. (2004) *Anti-Political Establishment Parties: A Comparative Analysis*, New York: Routledge.
Akkerman, T. (2012) 'Comparing radical right parties in government: Immigration and integration policies in nine countries (1996–2010)', *West European Politics* 35, 3: 511–529.
Akkerman, T. (2015) 'Immigration policy and electoral competition in Western Europe. A fine-grained analysis of party positions over the past two decades', *Party Politics* 21, 1: 54–67.
Bakker, R., De Vries, C., Edwards, E., Hooghe, L., Jolly S., Marks, M., Polk, J., Rovny, J., Steenbergen, M. and Vachudova, M. (forthcoming) 'Measuring party positions in Europe: The Chapel Hill Expert Survey trend file, 1999–2010', *Party Politics*.
Bauböck, R., Ersbøll, E., Groenendijk, K. and Waldrauch, H. (eds) (2006) *Acquisition and Loss of Nationality. Policies and Trends in 15 European States*, Amsterdam: Amsterdam University Press.

Bauböck, R. and Joppke, C. (eds) (2010) 'How liberal are citizenship tests?', *EUI Working Paper RSCAS 2010/*41. San Domenico di Fiesole: European University Institute.

Benoit, K. and Laver, M. (2006) *Party Policy in Modern Democracies*, London: Routledge.

Betz, H.-G. (1993) 'The two faces of radical right-wing populism in Western Europe', *The Review of Politics* 55, 4: 663–686.

Betz, H.-G. (1994) *Radical Right-Wing Populism in Western Europe*, Basingstoke: Palgrave Macmillan.

Betz, H.-G. and Meret, S. (2009) 'Revisiting Lepanto: the political mobilization against Islam in contemporary Western Europe', *Patterns of Prejudice* 43, 3–4: 313–343.

Budge, I. (2001) 'Validating party policy placements', *British Journal of Political Research* 31, 1: 179–223.

Budge, I. and Bara, J. (2001) 'Manifesto-based research: A critical review', in Budge, I. Klingemann, H.-D., Volkens, A., Bara, J. and Tanenbaum, E. (eds) *Mapping Policy Preferences: Estimates for Parties, Electors, and Governments 1945–1998*, Oxford: Oxford University Press, pp. 51–75.

Budge, I., Klingemann, H.-D., Volkens, A., Bara, J. and Tanenbaum, E. (2001) *Mapping Policy Preferences: Estimates for Parties, Electors, and Governments 1945–1998*, Oxford: Oxford University Press.

Castles, F. G. and Mair, P. (1984) 'Left-right political scales: Some "expert" judgements', *European Journal of Political Research* 12, 1: 73–88.

Deegan-Krause, K. and Haughton, T. (2009) 'Toward a more useful conceptualization of populism: Types and degrees of populist appeals in the case of Slovakia', *Politics & Policy* 37, 4: 821–841.

De Lange, S. L. (2007) 'A new winning formula? The programmatic appeal of the radical right', *Party Politics* 13, 4: 411–435.

Gabel, M. J. and Huber, J. (2000) 'Putting parties in their place: Inferring party left-right ideological positions from party manifestos data', *American Journal of Political Science* 44, 1: 94–103.

Goodman, S. W. (2010) 'Integration requirements for integration's sake? Identifying, categorising and comparing civic integration policies', *Journal of Ethnic and Migration Studies* 36, 5: 753–772.

Hawkins, K. A. (2010) *Venezuela's Chavismo and Populism in Comparative Perspective*, Cambridge: Cambridge University Press.

Hooghe, L., Bakker, R., Brigevich, A., de Vries, C., Edwards, E., Marks, G. and Vachudova, M. (2010) 'Reliability and validity of the 2002 and 2006 Chapel Hill expert surveys on party positioning', *European Journal of Political Research* 49, 5: 687–703.

Howard, M. M. (2010) 'The impact of the far right on citizenship policy in Europe: Explaining continuity and change', *Journal of Ethnic and Migration Studies* 36: 5.

Huber, J. and Inglehart, R. (1995) 'Expert interpretations of party space and party locations in 42 societies', *Party Politics* 1, 1: 73–111.

Jacobs, D. and Rea, A. (2007) 'The end of national models? Integration courses and citizenship trajectories in Europe', *International Journal on Multicultural Societies* 9, 2: 264–283.

Joppke, C. and Morawska, E. (eds) (2003) *Toward Assimilation and Citizenship: Immigrants in Liberal Nation-States*, Basingstoke: Palgrave Macmillan.

Klemmensen, R., Hobolt, S. B. and Hansen, M. E. (2007) 'Estimating policy positions using political texts: An evaluation of the Wordscores approach', *Electoral Studies* 26, 4: 746–755.

Klingemann, H.-D., Volkens, A., Bara, J., Budge, I. and Macdonald, M. (eds) (2006) *Mapping Policy Preferences II: Estimates for Parties, Electors, and Governments in Eastern Europe, European Union, and OECD 1990–2003*, Oxford: Oxford University Press.

Kriesi, H., Grande, E., Lachat, R., Dolezal, M., Bornschier, S. and Frey, T. (2006) 'Globalization and the transformation of the national political space: Six European countries compared', *European Journal of Political Research* 45, 6: 921–956.

Laver, M. (ed.) (2001) *Estimating the Policy Positions of Political Actors*, London: Routledge.

Laver, M. and Garry, J. (2000) 'Estimating policy positions from political texts', *American Journal of Political Science* 44, 3: 619–634.

Laver, M. and Hunt, W. B. (1992) *Policy and Party Competition*, New York: Routledge, Chapman and Hall.

Lubbers, M. (2000) *Expert Judgement Survey of West European Political Parties*, Amsterdam: Steinmetz Archive.

Mair, P. (2001) 'Searching for the positions of political actors: A review of approaches and a critical evaluation of expert surveys', in Laver, M. (ed.) *Estimating the Policy Position of Political Actors*, London: Routledge.

Meguid, B. (2005) 'Competition between unequals: The role of mainstream party strategy in niche party success', *American Political Science Review* 99, 3: 435–452

Meguid, B. (2008) *Party Competition Between Unequals: Strategies and Electoral Fortunes in Western Europe*, Cambridge: Cambridge University Press.

Meyer, T. M. and Miller, B. (2015). 'The niche party concept and its measurement', *Party Politics* 21, 2: 259–271.

Mudde, C. (2007) *Populist Radical Right Parties in Europe*, Cambridge: Cambridge University Press.

Odmalm, P. (2007) 'One size fits all? European citizenship, national citizenship policies and integration requirements', *Representation* 43, 1: 19–34.

Pauwels, T. (2011) 'Measuring populism: A quantitative text analysis of party literature in Belgium', *Journal of Elections, Public Opinion & Parties* 21, 1: 97–119.

Pellikaan, H., de Lange, S. L. and van der Meer, T. (2003) 'The road from a depoliticized to a centrifugal democracy', *Acta Politica* 38, 1: 23–49.

Pellikaan, H., de Lange, S. L. and van der Meer, T. (2007) 'Fortuyn's legacy: Party system change in the Netherlands', *Comparative European Politics* 5, 3: 282–302.

Pennings, P. and Keman, H. (2002) 'Towards a new methodology of estimating party policy positions', *Quality and Quantity* 36, 1: 55–79.

Petry, F. and Landry, R. (2001) 'Estimating interparty policy distances from election programmes in Quebec, 1970–1989', in Laver, M. (ed.) *Estimating the Policy Positions of Political Actors*, London: Routledge, pp. 133–146.

Protsyk, O. and Garaz, S. (2013) 'Politicization of ethnicity in party manifestos', *Party Politics* 19, 2: 296–318.

Rooduijn, M., de Lange, S. L. and van der Brug, W. (2014) 'A populist Zeitgeist? Programmatic contagion by populist parties in Western Europe', *Party Politics* 20, 4: 563–575.

Rooduijn, M. and Pauwels, T. (2011) 'Measuring populism: Comparing two methods of content analysis', *West European Politics* 34, 6: 1272–1283.

Schedler, A. (1996) 'Anti-political-establishment parties', *Party Politics* 2, 3: 291–312.

Steenbergen, M. and Marks, G. (2007) 'Evaluating expert judgments', *European Journal of Political Research* 46, 3: 347–366.

Vink, M. (2010) 'Citizenship attribution in Western Europe: International framework and domestic trends', *Journal of Ethnic and Migration Studies* 36, 5: 713–734.

Volkens, A. (2007) 'Strengths and weaknesses of approaches to measuring policy positions of parties', *Electoral Studies* 26, 1: 108–120.

Volkens, A., Bara, J., Budge, I., McDonald, M. D. and Klingemann, H.-D. (2013) *Mapping Policy Preferences from Texts: Statistical Solutions for Manifesto Analysis*, Oxford: Oxford University Press.

Wagner, M. (2012) 'Defining and measuring niche parties', *Party Politics* 18, 6: 845–864.

Zúquete, J. P. (2008) 'The European extreme-right and Islam: New directions?', *Journal of Political Ideologies* 13, 3: 321–344.

3 Closing the gap?

A comparison of voters for radical right-wing populist parties and mainstream parties over time

Matthijs Rooduijn

Introduction

Various scholars have investigated whether mainstream parties and radical right-wing populist parties have become increasingly alike (e.g., Bale *et al.* 2010; Bale 2003; Immerzeel *et al.* 2015; Van Spanje 2010). So far, however, researchers have not investigated whether a similar development has been taking place at the level of *voters*. Have the electorates of radical right-wing populist parties and those of mainstream parties become more and more similar? Convergence of these two electorates could be the result of two processes: radical right-wing populist voters becoming more like mainstream voters (I call this process 'mainstreaming') or mainstream voters becoming more like radical right-wing populist voters (I call this second process 'radicalisation').

Various scholars have argued that those who vote for radical right-wing populist parties differ from mainstream voters in three main respects. First, radical right-wing populist voters have been claimed to be 'losers of globalisation' (Kriesi *et al.* 2006, 2008); they are on average lower educated and have lower class positions than those who vote for mainstream parties. Second, it has been shown that most radical right-wing populist voters support these parties because they agree with them on issues such as immigration (e.g., Ivarsflaten 2008; Van der Brug *et al.* 2000) and European integration (Arzheimer 2009; Werts *et al.* 2013). Third, it has been demonstrated that those who are politically dissatisfied are overrepresented among the electorates of radical right-wing populist parties (e.g., Bergh 2004; Swyngedouw 2001).

These three differences between mainstream and radical right-wing populist electorates have been studied extensively. But so far only little attention has been paid to the question as to how these differences have developed over time. Have the differences in socioeconomic status between these two groups of voters diminished over the years? Have the attitudes of those who vote for radical right-wing populist parties become increasingly like the attitudes of those who vote for mainstream parties? The main aim of this chapter is to assess whether these changes have occurred. Based on an analysis of voting behaviour and public opinion data from four Western European countries (Belgium, Denmark, France and Switzerland), I assess whether radical right-wing populist voters and mainstream voters have become increasingly alike.

The chapter proceeds as follows. In the next section, I describe in which respects radical right-wing populist voters have been shown to differ from mainstream voters, and I present the main research hypotheses of this study. Next, I discuss various processes that could lead to convergence of the two groups of voters. In the following section, I discuss case selection, measurement and method. After an elaborate discussion of the main findings, I conclude the chapter by positioning the findings within a broader theoretical perspective and by discussing possible avenues for future research.

Closing the gap?

Various scholars have shown that – especially when it comes to issues such as immigration and integration – mainstream parties are influenced by radical right-wing populist parties (e.g., Akkerman 2012; Bale 2003; Bale et al. 2010; Curran 2004; Immerzeel et al. 2015; Norris 2005; Van Spanje 2010). At the same time, it has been claimed that radical right-wing populist parties have increasingly come to resemble mainstream parties over the years (Rydgren 2005). This alleged convergence of radical right-wing populist parties and mainstream parties suggests that the electorates of these two groups of parties have also become increasingly alike.

In order to test this 'convergence hypothesis', it is of essential importance to first assess on which dimensions the two electorates have traditionally differed. In general, the existing literature distinguishes three main dimensions.[1]

Three Dimensions of Convergence

Many studies of radical right-wing populist voting have indicated that those who vote for radical right-wing populists tend to have a lower socioeconomic status in terms of their education, income and class. Betz (1994) refers to these voters as the 'losers of modernity' because they have to compete with immigrants for low-skilled jobs. In later studies, Kriesi et al. (2006, 2008) similarly argue that a new political cleavage distinguishes the winners from the losers of globalisation. The winners are those who profit from international competition (e.g., highly educated entrepreneurs), and the losers are those who feel threatened by the opening of borders (e.g., lower educated employees in traditionally protected sectors). Kriesi et al. (2008: 19) argue that the losers of globalisation are likely to vote for radical right-wing populist parties: 'In most countries, it is [the] parties of the populist right who have been able to formulate a highly attractive ideological package for the "losers" of economic transformations and cultural diversity.' Various cross-national studies have confirmed this relationship between socioeconomic status and radical right-wing populist voting (Arzheimer 2009; Lubbers et al. 2002; Werts et al. 2013; Rydgren 2013).

If the convergence hypothesis holds, it might be expected that radical right-wing populist voters and mainstream voters have begun to resemble each other in terms of their socioeconomic status. I therefore hypothesise:

H1: The differences between voters for radical right-wing populist parties and voters for mainstream parties in terms of their socioeconomic status have diminished over the years.

Although it can be meaningful to look at the socioeconomic status of radical right-wing populist voters, assessing their socioeconomic characteristics tells us nothing about the *reasons* why citizens vote for these parties. In order to explain why individuals vote for radical right-wing populists, one has to look beyond these background characteristics and assess their actual policy positions (Ivarsflaten 2008; Van der Brug *et al.* 2000) – the second way in which populist radical right-wing voters differ from mainstream voters. Research has indicated that the two electorates mainly differ in their positions on immigration and European integration.

Those who vote for radical right-wing populist parties hold strongly nativist opinions; that is, they connect a strong emphasis on the nation-state with an aversion to 'dangerous others' (people who, according to them, do not belong to the nation and therefore pose a threat to the nation's identity and culture) (Dunn forthcoming). More specifically, radical right-wing populist voters hold negative attitudes towards immigrants (e.g., Ivarsflaten 2008; Rydgren 2007; Van der Brug *et al.* 2000). Attitudes towards European integration are related to radical right-wing populist voting as well (e.g., Arzheimer 2009; Lubbers and Scheepers 2007; Werts *et al.* 2013). Increasing European integration has led to political indignation among voters who believe that integration has violated the popular sovereignty of the European Union (EU) member states and that the process of integration should therefore be slowed down, stopped or even turned around. Because radical right-wing populist parties hold strong Eurosceptic positions, Eurosceptic voters are likely to vote for these parties.

If voters for radical right-wing populist parties and voters for mainstream parties are increasingly alike, it might be expected that these two groups of voters have also become increasingly similar when it comes to these attitudes.

H2: The differences between voters for radical right-wing populist parties and voters for mainstream parties in terms of their positions on immigration (H2a) and European integration (H2b) have diminished over the years.

Radical right-wing populist voters can be distinguished from voters for mainstream parties in another respect. Various studies have indicated that those who vote for radical right-wing populists are significantly less satisfied with politics (Arzheimer 2009; Bélanger and Aarts 2006; Betz 1994; Knigge 1998;

Mayer and Perrineau 1992; Norris 2005; Swyngedouw 2001; Zhirkov 2014). The main explanation for this difference is that radical right-wing populist parties present themselves as political outsiders (Barr 2009). They claim that established political parties have messed things up and no longer listen to ordinary citizens. Individuals who vote for radical right-wing populist parties usually agree with this attitude about politics (Bergh 2004). For them, political dissatisfaction is an important motive to vote for the radical right-wing populist alternative.[2]

If convergence is taking place, it might well be that the differences between radical right-wing populist voters and mainstream voters have become less clear-cut over the years (Mair 2002; Mudde 2004). I therefore expect that:

> H3: The differences between voters for radical right-wing populist parties and voters for mainstream parties in terms of their political (dis)satisfaction have diminished over the years.

Mainstreaming and Radicalisation

Convergence of the radical right-wing populist and mainstream electorates could be caused either by mainstreaming or by radicalisation.[3]

The process of mainstreaming could be the result of two possible mechanisms. First, the radical right-wing populist electorate could become increasingly similar to the mainstream electorate because the *composition* of the radical right-wing electorate changes. This might for instance be the case when radical right-wing populist parties become more mainstream – for example, by moderating their core positions, anti-establishment attitudes and/or reputations (see Rydgren 2005 and the introduction to this volume). Voters who previously felt attracted to these parties' ideas but found them still too radical might now consider voting for these parties. It could also be the case that some core voters decide not to support these parties any longer because they now conceive of them as being too moderate. In both cases, the outcome regarding the electorate's composition is the same; the proportion of the core voters decreases compared to the proportion of the new, more mainstream voters. As a result, the radical right-wing populist electorate increasingly resembles the mainstream electorate.

This type of mainstreaming most likely takes place when radical right-wing populist parties are office seeking or have had office experience, and want to signal their *Salonfähigkeit* – that is, social acceptability – to mainstream parties and voters (Berman 2008). After all, it is less likely that they would moderate their core positions if they were policy seeking or if they were competing for votes in niche segments, thus needing to keep up strong ideological profiles (see Müller and Strøm 1999).

Yet mainstreaming need not be the result of a changing proportion of core radical voters compared to new moderate voters. A second reason why mainstreaming could occur is a change among the core radical right-wing populist voters themselves. This change could, for instance, be a result of radical right-wing populist parties convincing their core constituencies to become more moderate. Various studies have shown that citizens often look for elite cues and adjust their views based on the information that they are exposed to – especially if these cues are expressed by a party to which they are attracted (Lupia and McCubbins 1998; Singh and Roy 2014; Sniderman *et al.* 1993; Zaller 1992). In other words, 'citizens take cues from political elites, including party leaders, and adjust their views to be more in line with those elites' (Steenbergen *et al.* 2007). When it comes to attitudes towards the EU, various studies have demonstrated that party elite cues affect public opinion (Anderson 1998; Ray 2003). Core voters might also moderate because of other reasons. They might, for instance, be affected by the media. Various studies have shown that media messages have a direct effect on public opinion (Brandenburg and Van Egmond 2011; Dalton *et al.* 1998; De Vreese and Boomgaarden 2006; Zaller 1996). And, of course, it could also be the case that mainstream voters moderate for other reasons, such as changing external socioeconomic circumstances.

Just like mainstreaming, the process of radicalisation could be the result of two possible mechanisms. First, the composition of the electorate of mainstream parties could change, and the proportion of more radical voters (who previously voted for radical right-wing populist parties) could increase compared to the proportion of the more moderate voters – for example, when mainstream parties become more radical in their positions on immigration (Bale *et al.* 2010; Bale 2003; Curran 2004; Van Spanje 2010) and when they use populist discourse (Mudde 2004). By radicalising their message, these parties might convince voters who previously supported radical right-wing populist parties to vote for them. But radicalisation of mainstream parties could also result in the more moderate voters leaving the party. These voters could now decide to switch to, for instance, green or radical left-wing parties. In both cases, the outcome is the same; the composition of the mainstream electorate changes because the proportion of radical voters increases compared to the proportion of the more moderate voters.

The party strategy of radicalisation is not necessarily an electorally successful one. Findings regarding the electoral outcomes of this strategy are mixed (Mudde 2007). Some studies have found this approach to be successful (e.g., Kitschelt and McGann 1995), whereas others have shown that it legitimises the radical right-wing populist parties, thereby decreasing the success of mainstream parties (e.g. Arzheimer and Carter 2006). Yet whether the strategy is electorally successful or not is not of importance for the mechanism described here. A mainstream party may well lose some of its moderate voters subsequent to its radicalisation. The party's voter base, however, may still become more radical if former radical right-wing populist voters decide to vote for it because of its radicalisation.

A second development leading to radicalisation could be when the existing pool of mainstream voters is cued to become more radical. In other words, those who in the past have voted for mainstream parties and now do so again might become more like those who vote for radical right-wing populists. Such a transformation may come about either because mainstream voters are influenced by 'their' radicalised party leaders or because of certain factors such as changing media coverage and socioeconomic conditions.

In practice, it will be difficult to assess which mechanisms underlie the processes of mainstreaming or radicalisation. In the remainder of the chapter, I will therefore only assess whether the gap between radical right-wing populist voters and mainstream voters is narrowing and, if so, whether this decrease is the result of mainstreaming or radicalisation.

Research design

Case Selection

To assess the attitudes and sociodemographic characteristics of those who vote for radical right-wing populist parties, I have employed the European Social Survey (ESS). I focus on four Western European countries where a radical right-wing populist party has been electorally successful for an extended period of time: Belgium, Denmark, France and Switzerland. In many other Western European countries, radical right-wing populist parties have only recently become electorally successful (e.g., the United Kingdom Independence Party [UKIP] in Britain, the Party for Freedom [Partij voor de Vrijheid, PVV] in the Netherlands, the Sweden Democrats [Sverigedemokraterna, SD] in Sweden or the Finns Party [Perussuomalaiset, PS] in Finland) or have so far not been electorally successful at all (e.g., Germany and Spain). The ESS dataset does not cover enough elections in all countries of potential interest (e.g., Austria and Italy). Indeed, France, Belgium, Denmark and Switzerland are the only cases for which the ESS has enough data to allow over-time comparisons of radical right-wing populist voters and mainstream voters. I included all six waves of the ESS (2002–12) in order to be able to assess whether any changes have occurred over the years. Those who voted for the Flemish Interest (Vlaams Belang, VB), the Danish People's Party (Dansk Folkeparti, DF), the National Front (Front National, FN) and the Swiss People's Party (Schweizerische Volkspartei, SVP) are classified as radical right-wing populist party voters.

Measurements

The dependent variable is based on which party a respondent voted for during the last national election. I recoded this variable so that a respondent scores a '1' if he or she voted for a radical right-wing populist party and a '0' if he or she voted for one of the mainstream parties. Parties have been categorised as mainstream when they are liberal, social democratic, Christian democratic or conservative. If a respondent voted for another party the variable has been set to missing.

The main socioeconomic independent variables are education and class.[4] Education is measured by means of a 5-point ordinal scale: 1 = less than lower secondary education (International Standard Classification of Education [ISCED], level 1); 2 = lower secondary education completed (ISCED 2); 3 = upper secondary education completed (ISCED 3); 4 = post-secondary non-tertiary education completed (ISCED 4); and 5 = tertiary education completed (ISCED 5–6).[5] Class was measured with the Erikson-Goldthorpe-Portocarero (EGP) classification scheme (Erikson *et al.* 1979). This class scheme was recoded into a variable with 6 categories: (1) semi- and unskilled manual workers and agricultural labourers; (2) manual supervisors and skilled manual workers; (3) small self-employed and farmers; (4) routine non-manual workers; (5) lower level professionals and managers; and (6) higher level professionals, managers and entrepreneurs.

Attitudes towards immigration are measured by adding up three variables, which all sit on a scale from 0 to 10.[6] The resulting variable has a scale from 0 (very negative about immigration) to 30 (very positive about immigration). Citizens' attitudes towards the EU were measured by means of the following question: 'Some say European integration should go further. Others say it has already gone too far. What best describes your position?' Answers ranged from 0 (integration has already gone too far) to 10 (integration should go further). Political satisfaction was measured by means of the question 'On the whole, how satisfied are you with the way democracy works?' The answers ranged from 0 (extremely dissatisfied) to 10 (extremely satisfied).

I controlled for several attitudes and sociodemographic variables that have been shown to correlate with radical right-wing populist voting. I measured attitudes towards homosexuality with the statement 'gay men and lesbians should be free to live their own life as they wish' (see Spierings and Zaslove 2015 for more information about the effect of this variable on voting for radical right-wing populist parties), and attitudes on income redistribution (see Zhirkov 2014) with the claim that 'the government should take measures to reduce differences in income levels'. The answers range from 1 (agree strongly) to 5 (disagree strongly). I further included age, gender (0 = male, 1 = female), unemployment (0 = employed, 1 = unemployed), religiosity (ranging from 'not at all religious' [0] to 'very religious' [10]) and a variable measuring whether a respondent comes from a rural (1) or an urban area (2) (see Arzheimer 2009; Lubbers *et al.* 2002).

For an overview of all the variables, see Table 3.1.[7]

Method

As the analysis is based on a binary dependent variable (voting for either a radical right-wing populist party or a mainstream party), I estimated logistic regression models. Because respondents are nested within both countries and years, I included country- and year-fixed effects. The observations are weighted using the population size weights and the design weights as provided by the ESS. The main purpose of the analysis is to assess to what extent voters for radical right-wing populist parties resemble those who vote for mainstream parties. I estimated separate regression models for all the different waves of the ESS. For every

Table 3.1 Descriptive statistics

	Observations	Mean	Std. Dev.	Min	Max
Vote	48992	0.10	0.31	0	1
Education	48802	3.25	1.27	1	5
Class	41407	3.57	1.73	1	6
Immigration	45712	15.55	6.03	0	30
EU	28037	5.14	2.55	0	10
Political satisfaction	48123	5.65	2.44	0	10
Homosexuality	47575	2.09	1.14	1	5
Income redistribution	48452	2.28	1.13	1	5
Age	48909	51.87	16.89	18	102
Gender	48963	0.52	0.50	0	1
Unemployed	48725	0.03	0.18	0	1
Religiosity	48722	4.92	2.90	0	10
Rural area	48899	1.58	0.49	1	2

variable of interest, I have displayed how the regression coefficients (and their 95 per cent confidence intervals) have changed over time. My main expectation is that the effects are increasingly close to 0 (which means that radical right-wing populist voters do not differ from mainstream voters). In order to show whether differences between mainstream voters and radical right-wing populist voters are due to radicalisation of mainstream voters or to mainstreaming of radical right-wing populist voters, I also show how the mean scores for both groups have developed over the years.

Results

Figure 3.1 displays the regression coefficients for every separate wave of the ESS.[8] Panel 1a shows that the effect of education is consistently negative and did not change over the years.[9] Panel 2b confirms this finding and indicates that there is a considerable gap between mainstream voters and radical right-wing populist voters, which also did not change over the years. Panel 2a displays the effects of class over time. The effect is consistently negative. Only in 2008 did the regression coefficient fail to reach statistical significance. The graph in Panel 2b shows that the class level for both groups has increased in 2012 – slightly more for the radical right-wing populist voters. In general, we can conclude that from a socioeconomic perspective, radical right-wing populist voters have not become increasingly like mainstream voters. On average, radical right-wing populist voters have a lower education and come from lower classes. This status has not changed in the last decade. Hypothesis 1 should therefore be rejected.

Regarding attitudes towards immigration, the difference between voters for radical right-wing populist parties and voters for mainstream parties has remained fairly stable over the years (Panel 3a). It is slightly larger only in 2010 (the regression coefficient in 2010 is significantly different from the coefficient in 2002), and did not endure; in 2012, the regression coefficient decreased again to a level comparable to the previous years. Looking at the development of the mean (Panel 3b), we see stability but no other trend. The graph indicates that both

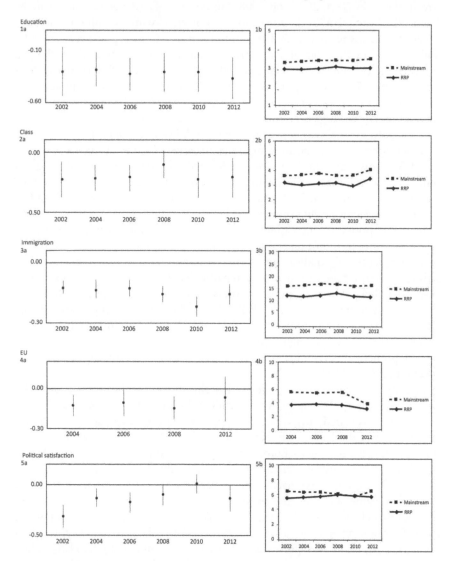

Figure 3.1 Regression coefficients for different variables explaining vote for radical right-wing populist (RRP) party (1) or mainstream party (0) over the years and average scores on these variables per electoral group

groups were slightly more negative about immigrants in 2010 compared to 2008. The radical right-wing populist voter became even more negative in 2012, whereas the mainstream voter once again became more positive in that year. Yet the changes over the years are very small, which indicates that Hypothesis 2a should be rejected.

When it comes to attitudes towards European integration, we can observe that radical right-wing populist voters are significantly different from mainstream voters in 2004, 2006 and 2008, but not in 2012 (Panel 4a). Interestingly, Panel 4b shows that both voters for radical right-wing populist parties and voters for mainstream parties have become more Eurosceptic between 2008 and 2012 – but the latter much more so than the former. As a result, the gap between the two groups decreased considerably. Hypothesis 2b is therefore confirmed: voters for radical right-wing populist parties increasingly resemble voters for mainstream parties in their attitudes towards the EU. My analysis shows that this attitudinal convergence results from the radicalisation of the mainstream voter and not from the mainstreaming of the radical right-wing populist voter.

When it comes to political satisfaction, we also see some changes over time. Panel 5a shows that in 2002, voters for radical right-wing populist parties differed from voters for mainstream parties. The negative effect of political satisfaction endured in 2004, 2006 and 2008. However, in 2010 and 2012, the effect was no longer statistically significant. This result indicates that voters for radical right-wing populists increasingly resemble voters for mainstream parties when it comes to their political satisfaction. Panel 5b shows that between 2002 and 2008, voters for radical right-wing populists have become slightly more satisfied, whereas voters for mainstream parties have become slightly less satisfied. In 2010, radical right-wing populist voters were even slightly *more* satisfied than voters for mainstream parties. In 2012, the 'traditional' difference between the two groups was apparent again; the mainstream electorate was more satisfied with politics than the radical right-wing populist electorate. The findings indicate that Hypothesis 3 is confirmed for 2002–10. However, the trend seems to be reversed again in 2012.

In general, these findings indicate that the differences between those who vote for radical right-wing populist parties and those who vote for mainstream parties have decreased only when it comes to European integration and political satisfaction (for the latter, only between 2002 and 2010). To better understand these developments vis-à-vis European integration and political satisfaction, Figure 3.2 displays the means for each country separately. Panel 1a displays the results for Belgium. This graph shows that the net difference between the attitudes of voters for mainstream parties and the attitudes of voters for radical right-wing populist parties did not really change over the years. When mainstream voters became more positive about European integration, a similar development took place among the radical right-wing populist voters (for instance between 2006 and 2008). Similarly, when voters for mainstream parties became less enthusiastic about European integration, voters for radical right-wing populist parties became more Eurosceptic as well (for instance between 2008 and 2012). Panel 1b displays the results for Switzerland. In both groups, attitudes towards Europe became steadily more negative over the years. However, between 2008 and 2012, Euroscepticism among voters for mainstream parties increased more strongly than among voters for radical right-wing populist parties, resulting in a much smaller difference between the two groups in 2012. Panel 1c shows that a similar development took place in Denmark; a strong increase in Euroscepticism among mainstream voters coincided with a much less pronounced growth among radical right-wing populist voters. In France, the attitude towards the EU did not really change in the group of radical right-wing populist voters (Panel 1d). However, just as in the previous cases, Euroscepticism increased sharply among mainstream voters, and as a result, we can observe a declining gap between the two groups of voters. Convergence can thus be observed in three out of the four countries under investigation.

Regarding political satisfaction, the pattern is much less clear-cut. We see that in Belgium, the gap between radical right-wing voters and mainstream voters narrowed between 2006 and 2010, but then increased again between 2010 and 2012 (Panel 2a). In Switzerland, however, the gap seems to have increased a little over the years (Panel 2b). Both groups of voters have become more satisfied, but this growth in satisfaction has been more pronounced among voters for mainstream parties. In Denmark, just like in Switzerland, both groups of voters are rather satisfied with politics (Panel 2c); mainstream voters are only slightly more satisfied. In 2012, however, this difference is more pronounced. Panel 2d shows that the developments in France are different. Between 2002 and 2008, the gap between the two groups dwindled (with the mainstream voters becoming less satisfied and the radical right-wing populist voters becoming more satisfied). Yet, in 2010, both groups became less satisfied, and in 2012, more satisfied again. In sum, when it comes to political satisfaction, the patterns over time are very different across countries. We cannot therefore conclude that the gap between the two groups of voters has diminished over the years. Even the observed convergence between 2002 and 2010 took place in only two of the four countries under analysis.

Conclusion

Have voters for radical right-wing populist parties and voters for mainstream parties become increasingly alike? In this chapter, I have argued that such convergence could be the result of two possible processes: (1) radical right-wing populist voters becoming increasingly similar to mainstream voters (mainstreaming) and (2) mainstream voters becoming increasingly similar to radical right-wing populist voters (radicalisation). I have argued that convergence could have occurred with respect to the dimensions on which the radical right-wing populist electorate traditionally differs from the mainstream electorate: (1) socioeconomic status, (2) positions on immigration and EU integration and (3) political (dis)satisfaction. Based on an analysis of public opinion data, information about socioeconomic status and voting behaviour in four different countries (Belgium, Denmark, France and Switzerland), I have assessed whether the gap

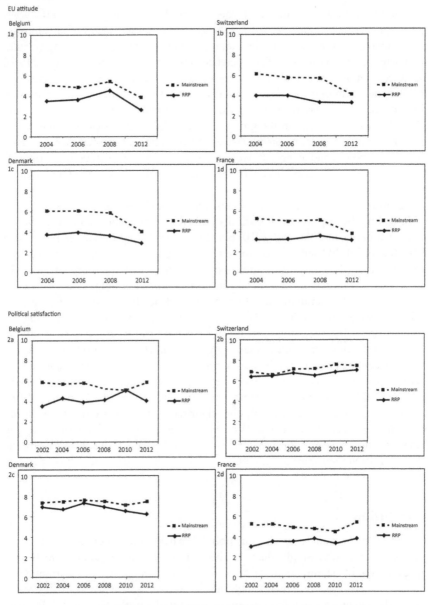

Figure 3.2 Average EU attitude and political satisfaction per electoral group per country over the years

between the populist radical right-wing electorate and the mainstream electorate has indeed narrowed over the years.

The findings show that regarding socioeconomic status, the gap is not narrowing; the differences in education and class between the mainstream electorate and the radical right-wing populist electorate did not decrease over the years. A similar conclusion can be drawn vis-à-vis positions on the issue of immigration; there is a strong difference between the two groups of voters, and this difference has not become less clear-cut over the years. When it comes to citizens' positions on European integration, however, a process of convergence seems to be at work. Both voters for radical right-wing populist parties and voters for mainstream parties have become increasingly sceptical about European integration. Yet, because Euroscepticism increased more among mainstream voters, the two groups of voters have become increasingly alike. This process of convergence is thus not due to the mainstreaming of the radical right-wing populist electorate but to the radicalisation of the mainstream electorate. In some countries, convergence can also be observed when it comes to political satisfaction; mainstream voters have become less satisfied (radicalisation) whereas radical right-wing populist voters have become more satisfied (mainstreaming). However, this process of mainstreaming can be observed only in France and Belgium, and only between 2002 and 2010. After 2010, the two groups of voters have once again grown apart.

These conclusions suggest that *if* convergence takes place, it is most likely caused by the radicalisation of mainstream voters and not by the mainstreaming of radical right-wing populist voters. Radicalisation might be due to three reasons. First, by radicalising their attitudes, mainstream parties may have convinced voters who used to vote for radical right-wing populist parties to switch to mainstream parties. If so, average attitudes within mainstream electorates will have become more radical because more radical voters have been added to the mainstream voting base. Second, moderate mainstream voters may have moved away to green parties or radical left-wing parties, for example, resulting in a mainstream electorate whose composition has changed and become more radical overall. Third, radicalisation of mainstream voters might also be the result of changing attitudes among the core constituencies of mainstream parties. For example, attitudes might have been affected by the economic crisis, increasingly radical media messages or radicalising mainstream parties.

Unfortunately, because I do not have panel data which allow me to detect vote-switching behaviour, I am unable to assess which of these mechanisms has most likely been taking place. Future studies should focus more specifically on the mechanisms of mainstreaming and radicalisation that have been discussed in this chapter. Such research could be undertaken by using panel data with information about which parties individuals (intend to) vote for over several years. By following individuals over time, one gathers much more information about the changing electorates of mainstream parties and radical right-wing populist parties.[10]

In this study, no attention has been paid to mainstreaming in respect to the salience of certain issues. The discussed mechanisms of mainstreaming and radicalisation as well as the dimensions on which they were expected to take place allow for the expectation that mainstream voters increasingly believe that niche issues are important (e.g., immigration and European integration), whereas radical right-wing populist voters increasingly emphasise typical mainstream issues (e.g., socioeconomic redistribution). Future studies might well assess this matter.

In addition, it would be interesting to assess the electoral potential of a party – that is, the pool of voters that is likely to vote for a particular party (Van der Brug *et al.* 2013). This information would help us to better understand with which parties radical right-wing populists compete.

Finally, we can only speculate about why mainstreaming has only taken place regarding European integration. The timing of radicalisation suggests that it has to do with the financial crisis between 2008 and 2012. Future studies should assess whether and to what extent this is indeed the case.

Notes

1 The three dimensions on which radical right-wing populist voters differ from mainstream voters discussed in this chapter are not exhaustive. Various scholars have argued, for instance, that these two groups of voters also differ from each other regarding their personalities (see Adorno 1982) and their attitudes towards crime (see Dunn forthcoming). Yet, the findings are still mixed. The three dimensions discussed in this chapter are the most salient ones in the literature on the radical right.

2 Although voting for a radical right-wing populist party is seen by some as irrational behaviour, I follow Van der Brug *et al.* (2000) by arguing that, in many cases, voting for such a party should be conceived of as a rational act. After all, voting for a party that is ideologically close to one's own way of thinking is not irrational. Even when the only motivation to vote for such a party is political dissatisfaction, radical right-wing populist voting behaviour should be conceived of as rational. After all, political (dis)satisfaction is just like policy positions on for instance immigration or European integration an attitude that might legitimately guide citizens' voting behaviour.

3 Of course, in practice, both processes could be taking place at the same time.

4 Income has not been included because of a large number of missing observations in some country-years. Unemployment has been left out of the analysis because of the low absolute numbers of radical right-wing populist voters that are unemployed.

5 I did not employ the newer ES-ISCED measure because these data were not available for France in 2002 and 2004.

6 The first variable asks: 'Would you say it is generally bad or good for [country]'s economy that people come to live here from other countries?' Values range from 0 = bad for the economy to 10 = good for the economy. The second one is: 'Would you say that [country]'s cultural life is generally undermined or enriched by people coming to live here from other countries?' Values range from 0 = cultural life undermined to 10 = cultural life enriched. And the final one is: 'Is [country] made a worse or a better place to live by people coming to live here from other countries?' Values range from 0 = worse place to live to 10 = better place to live.

7 In this chapter, I focus only on sociodemographic variables and positions of voters. It could also be expected that the gap between mainstream voters and radical right-wing populist voters has decreased because (1) radical right-wing populist voters increasingly believe that non-niche issues (e.g. socioeconomic matters) are important or (2) mainstream voters believe that typical niche issues (e.g., immigration and European integration) have become more important over the years. However,

because of a lack of data on issue salience among voters, this chapter does not look at this type of mainstreaming.

8 The full regression tables are available upon request.

9 Although the variables education and class have not been measured on a continuous scale, I have displayed the means here for reasons of clarity. Reporting proportions leads to substantively similar results.

10 Note that based on the theory discussed in this chapter, one might expect that the smaller the voter base of a radical right-wing populist party (compared to previous years), the more radical the average attitude towards issues such as immigration and European integration. After all, a small voter base suggests that only 'core' voters support the party. The results show, however, that this is not necessarily the case. In France, for instance, the FN was more strongly anti-immigration and Eurosceptic when its voter base was larger (the results are available upon request). The reason may be that even a small voter base could contain a large segment of noncore voters. We need panel data to assess which supporters are actual core voters and which are vote switchers.

References

Adorno, T. W. (1982) *The Authoritarian Personality*, New York: W.W. Norton.

Akkerman, T. (2012) 'Comparing radical right parties in government: Immigration and integration policies in nine countries (1996–2010)', *West European Politics* 35, 3: 511–529.

Anderson, C. J. (1998) 'When in doubt, use proxies attitudes toward domestic politics and support for European integration', *Comparative Political Studies* 31, 5: 569–601.

Arzheimer, K. (2009) 'Contextual factors and the extreme right vote in Western Europe, 1980–2002', *American Journal of Political Science* 53, 2: 259–275.

Arzheimer, K. and Carter, E. (2006) 'Political opportunity structures and right-wing extremist party success', *European Journal of Political Research* 45, 3: 419–443.

Bale, T. (2003) 'Cinderella and her ugly sisters: The mainstream and extreme right in Europe's bipolarising party systems', *West European Politics* 26, 3: 67–90.

Bale, T., Green-Pedersen, C., Krouwel, A., Luther, K. R. and Sitter, N. (2010) 'If you can't beat them, join them? Explaining social democratic responses to the challenge from the populist radical right in Western Europe', *Political Studies* 58, 3: 410–426.

Barr, R. R. (2009) 'Populists, outsiders and anti-establishment politics', *Party Politics* 15, 1: 29–48.

Bélanger, E. and Aarts, K. (2006) 'Explaining the rise of the LPF: Issues, discontent, and the 2002 Dutch election', *Acta Politica* 41, 1: 4–20.

Bergh, J. (2004) 'Protest voting in Austria, Denmark, and Norway', *Scandinavian Political Studies* 27, 4: 367–389.

Berman, S. (2008) 'Taming extremist parties: Lessons from Europe', *Journal of Democracy* 19, 1: 5–18.

Betz, H.-G. (1994) *Radical Right-Wing Populism in Western Europe*, Basingstoke: Macmillan Palgrave.

Brandenburg, H. and van Egmond, M. (2011) 'Pressed into party support? Media influence on partisan attitudes during the 2005 UK general election campaign', *British Journal of Political Science* 42, 2: 441–463.

Curran, G. (2004) 'Mainstreaming populist discourse: The race-conscious legacy of neo-populist parties in Australia and Italy', *Patterns of Prejudice* 38, 1: 37–55.

Dalton, R. J., Beck, P. A. and Huckfeldt, R. (1998) 'Partisan cues and the media: Information flows in the 1992 presidential elections', *The American Political Science Review* 92, 1: 111–126.

De Vreese, C. H. and Boomgaarden, H. G. (2006) 'Media message flows and interpersonal communication: The conditional nature of effects on public opinion', *Communication Research* 33, 1: 19–37.

Dunn, K. (forthcoming) 'Preference for radical right-wing populist parties among exclusive-nationalists and authoritarians', *Party Politics*, doi: 10.1177/1354068812472587.

Immerzeel, T., Lubbers, M. and Coffe, H. (2015) 'Competing with the radical right: Distances between the European radical right and other parties on typical radical right issues', *Party Politics*, doi: 10.1177/1354068814567975.

Ivarsflaten, E. (2008) 'What unites right-wing populists in Western Europe?' *Comparative Political Studies* 41, 1: 3–23.

Kitschelt, H. P. and McGann, A. (1995) *The Radical Right in Western Europe: A Comparative Analysis*, Ann Arbor, MI: University of Michigan Press.

Knigge, P. (1998) 'The ecological correlates of right-wing extremism in Western Europe', *European Journal of Political Research* 34, 2: 249–279.

Kriesi, H., Grande, E., Lachat, R., Dolezal, M., Bornschier, S. and Frey, T. (2006) 'Globalization and the transformation of the national political space: Six European countries compared', *European Journal of Political Research* 45, 6: 921–956.

Kriesi, H., Grande, E., Lachat, R., Dolezal, M. and Bornschier, S. (2008) *West European Politics in the Age of Globalization*, Cambridge: Cambridge University Press.

Lubbers, M., Gijsberts, M. and Scheepers, P. (2002) 'Extreme right-wing voting in Western Europe', *European Journal of Political Research* 41, 3: 345–378.

Lubbers, M. and Scheepers, P. (2007) 'Euro-scepticism and extreme voting patterns in Europe: Social cleavages and socio-political attitudes determining voting for the far left, the far right, and non-voting', in Loosveldt, G., Swyngedouw, M. and Cambré, B. (eds) *Measuring Meaningful Data in Social Research*, Leuven: Acco, pp. 71–92.

Lupia, A. and McCubbins, M. D. (1998) *The Democratic Dilemma. Can Citizens Learn What They Need to Know?* Cambridge: Cambridge University Press.

Mair, P. (2002) 'Populist democracy vs party democracy', in Mény, Y. and Surel, Y. (eds) *Democracies and the Populist Challenge*, New York: Palgrave Macmillan, pp. 81–98.

Mayer, N. and Perrineau, P. (1992) 'Why do they vote for Le Pen?', *European Journal of Political Research* 22, 1: 123–141.

Mudde, C. (2004) 'The populist zeitgeist', *Government and Opposition* 39, 3: 541–563.

Mudde, C. (2007) *Populist Radical Right Parties in Europe*, Cambridge: Cambridge University Press.

Müller, W. C. and Strøm, K. (1999) *Policy, Office, or Votes? How Political Parties in Western Europe Make Hard Decisions*, Cambridge: Cambridge University Press.

Norris, P. (2005) *Radical Right: Voters and Parties in the Electoral Market*, New York: Cambridge University Press.

Ray, L. (2003) 'When parties matter: The conditional influence of party positions on voter opinion about European integration', *Journal of Politics* 56, 4: 978–994.

Rydgren, J. (2005) 'Is extreme right-wing populism contagious? Explaining the emergence of a new party family', *European Journal of Political Research* 44, 3: 413–437.

Rydgren, J. (2007) 'The sociology of the radical right', *Annual Review of Sociology* 33, 1: 241–262.

Rydgren, J. (2013) *Class Politics and the Radical Right*, New York: Routledge.

Singh, S. P. and Roy, J. (2014) 'Political knowledge, the decision calculus, and proximity voting', *Electoral Studies* 34: 89–99.

Sniderman, P. M., Brody, R. A. and Tetlock, P. E. (1993) *Reasoning and Choice: Explorations in Political Psychology*, Cambridge: Cambridge University Press.

Spierings, N. and Zaslove, A. (2015) 'Conclusion: Dividing the populist radical right between "liberal nativism" and traditional conceptions of gender', *Patterns of Prejudice* 49, 1–2: 163–173.

Steenbergen, M. R., Edwards, E. E. and de Vries, C. E. (2007) 'Who's cueing whom? Mass-elite linkages and the future of European integration', *European Union Politics* 8, 1: 13–35.

Swyngedouw, M. (2001) 'The subjective cognitive and affective map of extreme right voters: Using open-ended questions in exit polls', *Electoral Studies* 20, 2: 217–241.

Van der Brug, W., Fennema, M. and Tillie, J. (2000) 'Anti–immigrant parties in Europe: Ideological or protest vote?', *European Journal of Political Research* 37, 1: 77–102.

Van der Brug, W., Fennema, M., De Lange, S. L. and Baller, I. (2013) 'Radical right parties: Their voters and their electoral competitors', in Rydgren, J. (ed.) *Class Politics and the Radical Right*, New York: Routledge, pp. 52–74.

Van Spanje, J. (2010) 'Contagious parties: Anti-immigration parties and their impact on other parties' immigration stances in contemporary Western Europe', *Party Politics* 16, 5: 563–586.

Werts, H., Scheepers, P. and Lubbers, M. (2013) 'Euro-scepticism and radical right-wing voting in Europe, 2002–2008: Social cleavages, socio-political attitudes and contextual characteristics determining voting for the radical right', *European Union Politics* 14, 2: 183–205.

Zaller, J. (1992) *The Nature and Origin of Mass Opinion*, Cambridge: Cambridge University Press.

Zaller, J. (1996) 'The myth of massive media impact revived: New support for a discredited idea', in Mutz, D., Brody, R. and Sniderman, P. (eds) *Political Persuasion and Attitude Change*, Ann Arbor, MI: University of Michigan Press, pp. 17–79.

Zhirkov, K. (2014) 'Nativist but not alienated: A comparative perspective on the radical right vote in Western Europe', *Party Politics* 20, 2: 286–296.

Part II
Case studies

4 The mainstreaming of the Austrian Freedom Party

The more things change…

Reinhard Heinisch and Kristina Hauser

Introduction

In this chapter we examine the Austrian Freedom Party's[1] (Freiheitliche Partei Österreichs, FPÖ) approach to mainstreaming as well as its goals and strategies by distinguishing four periods: before office, in office, immediately after office, and the long run. Specifically, we look for evidence that moderation has occurred in any of the dimensions of non-mainstreamness outlined in the theoretical framework underlying this volume. Since its transformation into a radical right-wing populist party in the 1980s under the leadership of Jörg Haider, the FPÖ has exhibited the characteristics of a radical party, a niche party, and an anti-establishment party with extreme right reputation. However, these traits neither manifested themselves to an equal measure nor were they constant over time or across all nine regional party branches. In our analysis, we rely on case analyses of FPÖ policy positions from 2000 to 2013, the various election programmes, as well as data from the Chapel Hill Expert Survey (CHES).[2] The challenge of this assessment lies in pinpointing the FPÖ's positions at different times because the party repeatedly shifted its orientations and ignored its party programmes when it was politically inconvenient.[3] Instead, it relied on shorter-term 'action programmes' and public statements by party leader Haider (Horner 1997).

Founded in large part by former Nazi-sympathisers and war veterans in 1956, the FPÖ initially represented a German-nationalist but also libertarian and anti-clerical tradition dating back to the nineteenth century. It opposed Austria's post-war *partitocrazia* established by the two major parties, the Christian-Democratic Austrian People's Party (Österreichische Volkspartei, ÖVP) and the Austrian Social Democratic Party (Sozialdemokratische Partei Österreichs, SPÖ). However, the FPÖ's radical right character locked the party into a political ghetto (Luther 1995: 138), preventing it from forming effective organisational linkages to mainstream institutions such as labour unions and employer organisations. Polling around 5 per cent in national elections, the FPÖ slowly gained political acceptance in the 1960s and 1970s, but remained a marginal force overall. In 1970 it supported a Social Democratic minority government in exchange for a favourable electoral reform and in 1983 it formed a coalition with the SPÖ. However, government participation exposed irreconcilable differences between nationalists and liberals, allowing the young and charismatic Haider, leader of the regional Carinthian party branch, to take over the chairmanship in 1986. Subsequently, he transformed the FPÖ into a radical right-wing populist party by adopting a relentless voter-seeking strategy (Zöchling 1999: 156; Luther 2008: 107). The breakthrough elections had already come in 1986 when the FPÖ nearly doubled its vote share with 9.7 per cent (see Table 4.1). After initially mobilizing against excessive regulation and public corruption, the FPÖ focused increasingly on immigration and Euroscepticism in the 1990s. It continued to increase its electorate in every subsequent election except for 1995 until peaking in 1999 with 26.9 per cent and even surpassing the Christian-Democrats. By then, it emerged as the second largest party in five of Austria's nine provinces and was also driving public policy in areas such as immigration and law-and-order (Fassmann 2013: 695–712).

Mainstreaming

In this section, we analyse the development of the FPÖ based on the selected indicators for mainstreaming in four distinct periods.

Table 4.1 Percentage of votes in national elections

	Political Parties[1]						
Year of election[2]	Greens	Social Demo-crats (SPÖ)	People's Party (ÖVP)	Freedom Party (FPÖ)	Alliance (BZÖ)	Team Stronach	Liberals Neos
1983		47.7	43.2	5.0			
1986	4.8	43.1	41.3	9.7			
1990	4.8	42.8	32.1	16.1			
1994	7.3	34.9	27.7	22.5			6.0
1995	4.8	38.1	28.3	21.9			5.5
1999	7.4	33.2	26.9	26.9			
2002	9.5	36.5	42.3	10.0[3]			
2006	11.1	35.3	34.3	11.0	4.1		
2008	10.4	29.3	26.0	17.5	10.7		
2013	12.4	26.8	24.0	20.5	–	5.7	5.0

Notes: 1 The parties are ordered along the left–right dimension. Grey cells indicate the parties forming the government after the respective elections.
2 Legislative sessions and government periods do not always correspond exactly. General elections often take place at the end of the calendar year and new governments take office much later, often at the beginning of the following year (this was, e.g. the case in 1987, 1996, 2000, 2003, and 2007).
3 The second ÖVP-FPÖ cabinet lasted only until April 2005, when the BZÖ formally replaced the FPÖ as the ÖVP's coalition partner, without new elections being called.
Source: data from Federal Ministry of the Interior.

We suggest that prior to the elections of 1999 past experiences, expediency, and the initial political outlook made it difficult for Haider to commit fully to office-seeking. Thus, the party pursued a mixed approach of noisy radicalism stressing its positions on European integration, public safety, and immigration as well as substantive policy proposals. Nevertheless, the FPÖ became an acceptable coalition partner for the ÖVP but was not adequately prepared for incumbency. Unable to manage internal conflicts, the FPÖ collapsed in the polls, losing two out of every three voters (see Table 4.1). Pre-empting a full-scale revolt by the FPÖ's base, Haider and many moderates broke away in 2005 to form a new party called Alliance (for the) Future of Austria (Bündnis Zukunft Österreich, BZÖ). The latter continued on in government until 2007, whereas the (rump) FPÖ reverted to an aggressive vote-seeking strategy. In doing so, it rebuilt its electoral support to levels similar to the 1990s while the vote shares of SPÖ and ÖVP had significantly declined.

Before public office

Following a temporary electoral setback in 1995 (see Table 4.1) in the sense that the party did not grow by large margins as in the past but actually lost votes, the FPÖ internally reorganised and adopted a new programme in line with its Austro-patriotic election manifesto of 1994 (FPÖ 1994). It began embracing more fully Austrian cultural traditionalism and Catholic conservatism – remarkable for a previously German-national, libertarian, and anti-clerical party. Its 1997 party programme invoked the idea of Europe as a Christian project, stressed European subsidiarity and social solidarity, and launched a family agenda (see FPÖ 1997). As such, the FPÖ called for infant money for mothers, increases in subsidies for farmers, and stricter approaches to policing and prosecutions. These changes in FPÖ positions have to be seen in the context of conditions set out in the mid-1990s by Andreas Khol, leader of the ÖVP's parliamentary caucus that the FPÖ would have to meet to be a viable coalition partner. He had demanded that the FPÖ give up radical designs of creating a plebiscitary democracy, support neo-corporatist economic governance, accept Austrian European (Union) integration, and distance itself unambiguously from Nazism (Khol 1996: 209–10).

At the time, the FPÖ also revived aspects of its market-liberal heritage by demanding a flat tax, cuts in the state bureaucracy and public expenses while calling for a better targeting of welfare-state spending (‘*Treffsicherheit*’). This appealed to groups in the ÖVP whose policy ideas had been stymied for years by their Social Democratic coalition partner. Simultaneously, however, the FPÖ also engaged xenophobic mobilisation, talking about Austria's ‘over-foreignisation’ and categorically opposing the EU's East European enlargement to maintain its radical populist profile (Heinisch 2002: 125–26, 217–21) – conflicting with the ÖVP's clearly Europhile position. In the run-up to the 1999 national elections, Haider campaigned with populist xenophobic messages and benefited from the fact that the campaign itself and its political implications of change were becoming the centre of attention (Pallaver *et al.* 2000: 180). The FPÖ bested the ÖVP by 415 votes, coming in second behind the SPÖ. Drawing support largely from former voters of the mainstream parties, the FPÖ had gained an additional 160,000 votes and was thus in an ideal position to influence government formation in 2000.

In this period we see evidence of mainstreaming in all four dimensions: The FPÖ moderated core positions (i.e., dropping the demand for systemic reform in favour of a plebiscitary democracy), expanded its issue-oriented agenda to include specific socioeconomic policy goals and signalled respect for the rules of the game (i.e., Haider honouring his commitment in 1999 to serve out his term as governor of Carinthia). It also launched a new party programme in 1997, designed to move the FPÖ away from German nationalism. Moreover, in an effort to distance his party from anti-Semitism, Haider promoted the Austrian-Jewish intellectual Peter Sichrovsky as candidate for the European parliamentary elections in 1996 and later as party secretary (Heinisch 2002: 97). We may attribute these processes of mainstreaming to office-seeking given that the FPÖ was reaching out to the Christian-Democrats (Luther 2006b: 22). However, Haider's populist discourse overshadowed the more substantive shifts in the party's agenda and sharpened its profile as a radical populist party.

In public office 2000–2005

In 2000 the FPÖ met all the conditions presented by the Christian-Democratic Party negotiating team so that ÖVP leader Schüssel and Haider quickly came to an agreement. Facing national and international pressure, hostile national media and a sceptical Austrian Federal President Thomas Klestil, Schüssel and Haider signed a preamble to their government programme, reconfirming their commitment to EU membership and vowing to protect tolerance in Austria (Müller 2006: 195). Haider also acquiesced when President Klestil rejected two designated FPÖ ministers.[4] To avoid further controversy and focus on his position of state governor, Haider resigned the FPÖ chairmanship in 2000 in favour of his confidante Susanne Riess-Passer, who also became vice-chancellor.

The FPÖ obtained important ministries such as Finance, Justice, Defence, Social Affairs, and Transportation and Infrastructure (Luther 2006a: 382), but the shortage of personnel with policy expertise hampered the ability to translate the FPÖ's agenda into public policy (Fallend 2001: 245). Still, the new government changed the patterns of party competition in Austria, aiming for substantial and swift reforms (Müller and Fallend 2004: 809–17). Raising the retirement age, introducing university student fees, and the introduction of hospital fees were only some of the more controversial policy decisions by the centre-right government (Heinisch 2003: 104). Although uncharacteristic for Austria, these measures were substantively mainstream policies and in line with neo-liberal programmes elsewhere. By themselves, they are not evidence of mainstreaming because the FPÖ had long since attacked what it considered excessive state and corporatist meddling in the economy. While this fit with the culturally conservative and market-liberal agenda designed to attract (former ÖVP) middle-class voters, it contradicted the party's other strategy of styling itself as 'advocate of the little man' by promoting for example an increase in the financial support for families (see FPÖ 1999). Whereas the tension between these goals could be papered over in opposition, this mix of positions proved to be a problem in public office (Heinisch 2003: 104–09).

Other FPÖ calls for expanding plebiscitary mechanisms, a new procedure for appointing high court judges, and tougher libel laws to muzzle journalists corresponded more to the party's extremist and populist course but were prevented by the ÖVP or not pursued vigorously by the party leadership (Heinisch 2003: 108). The FPÖ also engaged in a campaign against the constitutional court. This and Governor Haider's refusal to implement the court's decision were seen by the opposition and constitutional lawyers as a threat to the rule of law (Heinisch 2003: 106; Fallend 2012), and constituted an area where the party strayed furthest from the mainstream.

In terms of immigration policy, the FPÖ insisted on a very restrictive regime regarding immigrant quotas and family reunions. It prevailed despite massive objections by industry because the agenda was supported also by hard-line conservatives in the ÖVP and represented little more than an extension of the measures introduced by previous governments (Minkenberg 2001; Fassmann 2013). In this issue domain, the mainstream parties had been moving steadily toward positions staked out by the FPÖ as can be gleaned from the data about FPÖ positions on immigration in the Appendix which indicate a convergence on more restrictive policies (see the Appendix, Austria).

The policy dimension that most stands out as representing evidence of mainstreaming in government is the FPÖ's position on European integration. The 1997 party programme talked about Europe in vague terms referring to its Christian (anti-Islamic) character and calling it a community of destiny. While it supported European Security and Defence Policy, it rejected Brussels' 'omni-competence' and a 'federal' Europe (FPÖ 1997: 10–12). Some of the FPÖ's later moderation was designed to reach out to the ÖVP while other aspects were the result of socialisation due to the sanctions. Not only was the FPÖ pressured into signing an explicit commitment to Austria's EU membership but Austria wanted to remain a trusted EU partner and showed sensitivity concerning its past. Thus, though the bilateral sanctions should have constituted a tempting target for a radical right-wing populist party for all-out mobilisation (Heinisch 2002: 242–59; Luif 2006: 876–77), the FPÖ reacted with relative restraint knowing that the staunchly pro-European ÖVP would otherwise break off the coalition. The ÖVP-FPÖ government even concluded an €420 million restitution settlement with some 149,000 surviving forced labourers of the Nazi regime. These measures have to been seen also in light of the FPÖ's attempts to move away from its extreme right reputation. Nevertheless, the FPÖ continued to criticise specific EU office holders, policy decisions, and developments deemed unfavourable such as EU enlargement (Heinisch 2003: 106–09).[5] FPÖ officials also threatened to block Czech and Slovenian accession to the EU if the grievances of the ethnic Germans expelled after the war were not addressed and the construction of a nuclear power plant near the Austrian border not stopped. In all these instances, the ÖVP ensured that the FPÖ could not determine the final policy outcome while the FPÖ refrained from breaking up the government and unanimously supported all cabinet decisions (Heinisch 2002: 264–65).

Still, the FPÖ's overall position on Europe is hard to pinpoint because the party had a tendency to ignore its own programmes when it was politically convenient. Moreover, programmes were generally phrased broadly, thus allowing for different interpretations. Under Haider, statements of the party leader and slogans on campaign posters provided a more definitive indication of the precise direction and salience of an issue. It is clear, however, that the FPÖ had started out as a pro-European party that became steadily more Eurosceptical in the 1990s, even opposing Austria's EU accession.

In government, FPÖ representatives generally adopted a public tone that reflected moderation. Eschewing controversy, they criticised Haider's efforts to boost the party's political fortunes in the Vienna regional election in 2001 by injecting anti-Semitism into the campaign. Moreover, when he hosted a meeting of European radical right party leaders in 2002, FPÖ chairwoman Riess-Passer publicly and unmistakably rebuked him (Heinisch 2003: 111). In terms of style, the political relationship between the government teams of ÖVP and FPÖ was exceptionally good and stood in marked contrast to that of ÖVP and SPÖ in earlier coalitions and to the tensions within the FPÖ itself (Müller and Fallend 2004). In fact, the FPÖ Finance Minister Karl-Heinz Grasser subsequently switched to the ÖVP, staying on through 2007. Thus, the FPÖ was no longer demonised but increasingly a welcome partner against the Social Democrats and Greens. Yet, the FPÖ's rank-and-file was dissatisfied with the party's moderation on key positions and its neo-liberal policies. These aspects were perceived by many as concessions to the ÖVP for which the FPÖ was paying the political price (Heinisch 2003: 109). FPÖ members outside the government referred, for example, to the restitution settlement as "'protection money" to safeguard "Austrian trade relations with the US'" (Heinisch 2003: 107).

Referring to the indicators of mainstreaming employed in this volume we may qualify the above policy measures as representing both an expanded issue agenda and a stronger emphasis on socioeconomic issues. In this sense, they were a departure from the previous populist rhetoric of 'Advocacy on behalf of little people' (*Eintreten für kleine Leute*) (Plasser and Ulram 2000: 227). This reorientation is evidenced also by growing internal disagreements over political direction within the party and by increasing voter defections. The party lost three state elections in a row during its first two years in office (Dachs 2006: 1014–15) when especially working-class voters returned to the Social Democrats. In voter terms, mainstreaming appeared to cost the FPÖ 2 per cent in the state elections in Styria (2000), 4.8 per cent in Burgenland (2000), and (with a tendency to rise as incumbency went on) 7.7 per cent in Vienna (2001).

The reactions by the rank-and-file and voters have to be seen as a mutually reinforcing dynamic. The FPÖ's base had also previously experienced changes in direction initiated by the leadership but always acquiesced because of

Haider's successes at the polls. However, the electoral defeats after 1999, persistently low opinion poll numbers, and the negative media coverage (Schausberger 2013: 83–121) encouraged those groups in the party dissatisfied with the new course to criticise the leadership, which lacked Haider's standing in the party. When the conflict escalated, the base brought down its own leadership and thus the government (Luther 2003: 139–41). In the impromptu elections that followed, the FPÖ lost nearly two-thirds of its electorate, achieving barely 10 per cent whereas the ÖVP gained 15.4 per cent, taking 42.3 per cent of the votes overall (see Table 4.1).

In the subsequent cabinet Schüssel II (2003–2007), the FPÖ was much diminished, controlling only three ministries (Luther 2006a: 382). As a result, it played the role of spoiler by seeking to block certain neo-liberal policies while partially returning to protest party rhetoric (i.e,. calling for a tax on the 'super-rich'). Attempting to reconnect with its former voter base, the FPÖ was moving away from the ÖVP, drifting to the left on economic and social policy. This development in economic policy is also reflected by the CHES data (Bakker *et al.* 2013) (see Figure 4.1). Although the time period covered is too large for pin-pointing this shift, we notice that the FPÖ shifted to the left on socioeconomic issues after 2002 but discontinued its direction as it focused again more strongly on sociocultural issues.[6]

The FPÖ's diminished weight in the government precluded effective action short of breaking up the government. The conflict in the FPÖ over the political direction continued, eventually culminating in a split of the FPÖ in April 2005 along vote-seeking and office-seeking (see Luther 2008). In response, Haider founded the BZÖ, taking with him most of the FPÖ government team. Orchestrated with Schüssel's approval (Luther 2011: 465), this move resulted in a reconfigured coalition, now involving the ÖVP and BZÖ, which served out the legislative term until 2007. As a consequence, the (rump) FPÖ elected, as their new party leader, the radical head of the Vienna party branch, Heinz-Christian Strache, a vocal critic of FPÖ's government team.

After public office 2005–2008

Facing a 2006 national election turning on the issue that the government 'cared more about deficits than people' (Fallend 2007: 879), Strache refocused his party on immigration, crime, and Turkey's EU accession (SORA/Institut für Strategieanalysen 2006: 15). Although the FPÖ formally kept the 1997 party programme[7] (until 2011), it played little role in campaigning. Strache resembled Haider from the 1990s by being 'loud, offensive, uncooperative, and expressive of extreme positions', and 'frame[d] [the FPÖ's] policy priorities through a cultural conservative lens using the language of heritage and homeland [*Heimat*]' (Williams 2013: 82). In response, the BZÖ also campaigned partly on chauvinistic and anti-Islamic themes but achieved only 4.1 per cent of the vote (SORA/ Institut für Strategieanalysen 2006: 15). Nonetheless, the BZÖ tried to style itself as a more acceptable alternative to voters with protest sentiments for whom the

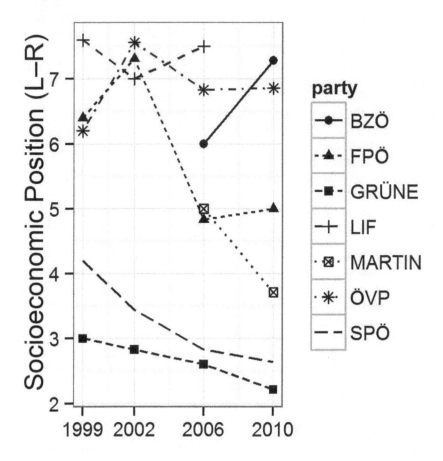

Figure 4.1 Socioeconomic position (left/right); Austrian parties

FPÖ was too extreme. The growing emphasis of sociocultural issues in the FPÖ under Strache in 2006 and beyond is also reflected in the CHES data (see Appendix, Austria).

The strategy of vote maximisation had some success as the FPÖ won 11 per cent of the votes, thus one percentage point more than in 2002, whereas the Social Democrats narrowly defeated the Christian-Democrats. The BZÖ succeeded only in Carinthia where Haider's party had the organisational advantage over the FPÖ. The ensuing SPÖ-ÖVP coalition lasted only from January 2007 to October 2008. It gave way to a campaign pandering to issues popular with the tabloid media (e.g. the SPÖ promised to make future EU treaty revisions subject to referenda and the ÖVP promised a tougher stance on crime).[8] In this context, BZÖ and FPÖ campaigned especially on the issues of immigration and Europe. The FPÖ's 2008 election programme demanded curbing social rights for foreign labourers (i.e., lesser social insurance coverage) and warning against African organised-crime rings. For the most part (on senior citizens, the military, healthcare, etc.), the election programme was not especially radical but rather vague, mixing leftist and conservative positions (FPÖ 2008): Taxes were to be lowered, government services (eldercare) expanded, individual tax exemptions increased, revenues procured from slashing the bureaucracy, and Europe was to be a union of sovereign nation-states. Still, the overall tone had moderated compared to 2006 (see FPÖ 2006, 2008; Fallend 2009: 890). By comparison, the BZÖ's positions were more compatible with those of the mainstream parties, indicating a continued interest in public office. The election programme of 2006 emphasised the party's performance in government, while in 2008, Haider's 'Carinthian model' was heavily promoted (BZÖ 2006, 2008). In the end the FPÖ made sizeable gains, especially at the expense of the ÖVP as voters were concerned about immigration (SORA/Institut für Strategieanalysen 2008: 25). Nonetheless, Strache excluded his party from being considered as a potential coalition partner by making excessive political demands such as an immediate referendum on the Lisbon Treaty and Turkish EU accession.

The FPÖ after 2008 – the long run

In the 2009 campaign for the European Parliament, the FPÖ maintained its distance from the mainstream, calling the EU corrupted by power struggles and engaged in 'asylum madness' (Fallend 2010: 885). The party's policy proposals such as on social issues were filtered through a xenophobic lens and far from what would be tolerable for mainstream parties (Fallend 2010: 886). However, from 2010 onward, the FPÖ began showing signs of a selective re-engagement with the mainstream by moderating its discourse and distancing itself from extreme positions. For example, after the FPÖ's candidate for the federal presidency, Barbara Rosenkranz, became embroiled in controversy when downplaying the Holocaust, Strache signalled distance and, uncharacteristically, called for her resignation following her unsuccessful bid.

In order to indicate a break with the old Haider FPÖ, Strache unveiled a new programme in 2011. Reflecting some resurgence of right-wing German-nationalist party factions, it emphasised again more explicitly Austria's German cultural character (Horaczek and Reiterer 2009: 86). The new programme promised to introduce direct democracy, and is remarkable for its brevity and vagueness, being half the length of the 1997 programme (see FPÖ 2011). It was rather Eurosceptical (calling for an 'association of free peoples and autonomous fatherlands') (FPÖ 2011: 3, 17), rejected the fiscal union and similar steps toward further integration, and revived demands in favour of ethnic Germans expelled from the Czech Republic and Slovenia (FPÖ 2011). However, in the subsequent electoral campaigns for the national parliament in 2013 and the European Parliament in 2014, the FPÖ did not call for Austria to exit the EU[9] or even the Eurozone.[10]

In the elections to the European Parliament in 2014, the FPÖ was relatively measured in tone even though the circumstances were rather favourable for

Euroscepticism. When the FPÖ's only MEP, Andreas Mölzer, made racist comments about an Austrian soccer star of African descent, Strache distanced the party from Nazism and racism, forcing Mölzer to withdraw his candidacy (*Der Standard* 2014b). Nonetheless, we may qualify the FPÖ's approach to mainstreaming as selective because it pertained mainly to its style and tone but less to the substance of its policies (Fallend 2002).

Overall, the FPÖ fared quite well in the elections in 2013 and 2014 mainly because the BZÖ was in disarray after Haider's death in 2008 and could not regain its political footing. Despite a political environment favourable to protest politics – given the widespread unhappiness with the governing grand coalition, the Euro-crisis, and bank bailouts – the FPÖ's more moderate tone compared to the campaigns in 2006 and 2008 hinted at Strache's willingness to cooperate with other parties (see our assessment in Table 4.2). However, this push toward moderation was episodic and limited to the national level. Regionally, the FPÖ varied its style and approach depending on the political circumstances and personalities involved.

If we analyse the mainstreaming process of the FPÖ over the four periods covered, we may argue that the FPÖ paid a political price for mainstreaming in the pursuit of office. The shift toward office-seeking in the later 1990s as well as its period in office led to some mainstreaming in all four dimensions of analysis. But when the party elites showed greater respect for the rules of the game, distanced themselves from the FPÖ's extreme right reputation, de-emphasised its anti-establishment legacy (by no longer calling for a plebiscitary democracy), and moderated several core positions (European integration, restitution settlement, commitment to tolerance), the party became embroiled in conflict during incumbency. Following a string of electoral defeats after 2000, plummeting poll numbers, and extremely negative media coverage about the FPÖ in office, the base rebelled. At the time, the party did not have, as will be discussed subsequently, a strategy for compensating for the cost of moderation expressed mainly by the massive decline in voter support and loss in legislative and executive power (Luther 2006a: 382). To extricate itself from this situation, the FPÖ reverted to a radical vote-seeking strategy by 2005, facilitated by the departure of the party moderates. Since 2010 the FPÖ has indicated some renewed interest in pursuing public office and will have undoubtedly learned from its past mistakes.

The FPÖ's goals and strategies

In this segment we examine the goals and strategies underlying the FPÖ's positions and its reaction to political challenges encountered as a result of its experience in public office.

Before public office, 1990–2000

FPÖ leader Haider was clearly motivated by attaining public office. He made this intention unmistakably clear in a speech in 1995 (Piringer 2001: 409) and in

Table 4.2 Dimensions of mainstreaming – Austrian Freedom Party

Dimensions of non-mainstreamness	Evidenced by	Pre-Incumbency (1995–99)	Incumbency (2000–2005)	Post-incumbency (2005–2014)
			Indicators for mainstreaming (in bold)	
Radical Party	Rejection of EU membership/radical opposition to further integration	Position mostly maintained	**Accepts EU/no sustained action on enlargement**	**Qualified acceptance-EU**/wants powers devolved to national level
Niche Party	Sociocultural issues emphasised: immigration, 'over-foreignisation'	**Also emphasis on socioeconomic agenda**	**Main focus on socio-economic issues**	Focused on sociocultural issues/immigration
Anti-establishment	Call for plebiscitary democracy/radical change of economic governance model	**De-emphasised**	**Plebiscitary democracy dropped**/supports weakening unions	Plebiscitary democracy revived/**change of government model not salient**
Extreme Right Reputation	German nationalism, ambivalent statements/Nazi period, Holocaust/extreme rhetoric	New Austro-patriotic agenda/some extreme rhetoric	**Distancing from anti-Semitism, Holocaust/supports settlement/moderate rhetoric**	German nationalism revived but low salience/**inconsistent distancing & rhetoric**

similar pronouncements in the media subsequently (e.g., Seiler 2006). Despite this, the FPÖ had not come any closer to national public office. Haider's brief stint as state governor (1989–1991) had ended abruptly following his favourable comments about the Nazi employment policy after which the local ÖVP pulled its support (Czernin 2000: 31). Yet, the Christian-Democrats remained Haider's preferred partner and the FPÖ supported the ÖVP in parliament in 1996 in a vote against the latter's coalition partner SPÖ (Piringer 2001: 418). It was also Haider who offered the chancellorship to ÖVP leader Schüssel (Heinisch 2002: 229). His acceptance of this offer represented a clear shift on the part of the Christian-Democrats from an exclusionary to an inclusionary strategy and was met with resistance in his party. The FPÖ's own strategic choices and main party reactions are summarised in Table 4.3 below.

Throughout the 1990s the internal dynamics of the FPÖ were characterised by frequent reshuffles of personnel and significant internal conflict resulting in the exodus of the liberal wing in 1993, the expulsions of previous FPÖ leaders, entire regional groupings, and even exponents of the party's German-nationalist segment. All this drained the available talent pool for public office and created an air of permanent revolution, which interfered with political mainstreaming (Luther 1997: 290; Heinisch 2002: 94–103). Following the FPÖ's setback in the 1995 parliamentary elections, Haider experimented with reorganising the party, imposing in 1998 more discipline from the top after even threatening to leave the FPÖ to form his own party (Heinisch 2002: 94–102).[11]

The FPÖ embraced an overall strategy to assemble a broad coalition of voters discontented with the status quo. Whereas the FPÖ's radical right-wing populist messages (i.e. on immigration) were intended to appeal to disaffected Social Democratic voters in urban areas, especially Vienna where the FPÖ saw its largest potential for growth, the more substantive policy agenda was aimed at Christian-Conservatives and neo-liberal groups within the ÖVP. Haider could do so as public office did not seem a realistic option until late in the 1999 campaign when ÖVP leader Wolfgang Schüssel vowed to take his party into opposition if it fell behind the FPÖ. As a result, committing the FPÖ to a seemingly unrealistic office-seeking strategy which might have ultimately backfired and cost votes would have been hard to justify.

Table 4.3 Strategic party behaviour (national level); Austrian Freedom Party and main parties

	Pre-incumbency	Incumbency	Post-incumbency
FPÖ's strategy	inconsistent office-seeking	office-seeking; partly policy-seeking	initially vote-seeking; recently office-seeking
Main parties' strategies	exclusionary	ÖVP inclusionary	rather exclusionary

In public office, 2000–2005

For a party long cut out from formal political influence, a key goal of office-seeking was the power and privilege of government itself. As such, the FPÖ did not hesitate to fill all available posts in public institutions, enterprises, and the bureaucracy with loyal partisans (Fallend 2002: 907–09), although this practice explicitly deviated from professed principles.[12] In this context, the long-term success of Haider's governorship in the economically troubled state of Carinthia depended also on powerful political allies in the national government.[13]

In terms of policies, it was clear that the FPÖ and ÖVP would prioritise those issues where the convergence was greatest while wanting to avoid areas of potential conflict: This elevated the policy issues of balancing the budget, social insurance reform, and welfare state restructuring to a priority (Heinisch 2002: 90). Both ÖVP and FPÖ saw this also as an opportunity to decisively weaken the Social Democrats institutionally. Nevertheless, a problem for the FPÖ was that this issue cut both ways politically. Whereas many voters of the FPÖ were critical of the 'apparatchiks' in corporatist institutions and thus supported reform when the issue was framed in certain ways, the social partnership still enjoyed considerable popularity, which was demonstrated once the unions began mobilising against the Schüssel government. This is also the reason why the FPÖ pivoted toward social policy after losing several regional elections and the national elections in 2002. Egged on by the party base, the FPÖ veered increasingly to the left on social policy, as it tried to block or water down further social cuts, even collaborating clandestinely with the leftist Chamber of Labour to acquire relevant policy expertise (Hinterseer 2014). Yet, as a much weaker coalition partner after 2002, the FPÖ found few realistic opportunities to undercut the ÖVP's drive to reform what Schüssel considered wasteful spending.

The issue of European integration constituted the most important area of moderation. The FPÖ never fully pushed anti-EU policy issues and, despite its stated opposition, did not seek to block the EU's Eastern enlargement from going forward. Even on Turkish accession, Austria's strong opposition owed as much to sentiments among Christian-Democrats as it did to the Freedom Party. Other aspects of policy convergence such as on crime and security as well as immigration were the result of culturally conservative trends in both FPÖ and ÖVP. More-over, especially on immigration, official policy had already moved so far in the direction of the FPÖ that the government's course no longer looked especially radical. In most cases, voters who approved of these reforms credited the chancellor and the more competent ÖVP.

Although the split within the FPÖ was largely over policy and ideology, there were also structural factors that played a role (see Luther 2006a: 383–84): importantly, the party apparatus was overstrained, failing to maintain the party organisation and support the government team properly. Whereas the ÖVP had deep roots in the ministerial bureaucracy and corporatist associations for the purpose of policy development and drafting legislation, the FPÖ had no such equivalent. Also, the FPÖ's personnel were generally not up to the task, adding to the image of political amateurism. Unlike Haider himself, who could credibly pivot toward the political mainstream and back away again when the circumstances dictated (Heinisch 2002: 50–4, 86–90), the post-Haider FPÖ leadership was frequently outmanoeuvred by Schüssel and the ÖVP (Heinisch 2003: 116).

The mainstreaming processes the FPÖ underwent were influenced by four important factors. First, there was the composition of the government group, which consisted generally of moderates with some experience in regional governments and in business. Second, Haider himself transitioned into public office by becoming governor in Carinthia. This required him to change his posture to secure support locally from either ÖVP or SPÖ. Third, Haider's departure from the FPÖ leadership in favour of a less controversial person, Riess-Passer, also mattered. Fourth, there was a genuine overlap in agendas between conservative groups in the ÖVP and the FPÖ which served as a mutual anchor.

Yet, it is remarkable that the FPÖ completely failed to anticipate the cost of mainstreaming and never developed a consistent and unified response. For example, the FPÖ did not settle on a log-rolling strategy (see Akkerman and de Lange 2012) or extract a major concession from the ÖVP on an issue dear to FPÖ voters that could have compensated for the FPÖ's acquiescence on European integration and enlargement.

After public office, 2005–2008

Arguing that the FPÖ was damaged beyond repair, Haider founded the BZÖ in an attempt to allow 'his' government team to remain in office. Haider was committed to incumbency through 2007 and even beyond if Schüssel's memoir is to be believed (Schüssel 2009: 271). Returning to populist opposition politics with the small BZÖ, a situation he had encountered more than 20 years earlier, must have held little appeal for an ambitious national figure of advancing age after years as a popular state governor.

The 2006 parliamentary elections were the first in which Haider's BZÖ and the 'new' FPÖ led by Strache competed directly against each other. They also had to contend with a new Eurosceptical protest group founded by former Social Democratic MEP Hans-Peter Martin (*Liste Hans-Peter Martin*, HPM), who was supported by Austria's largest tabloid newspaper *Neue Kronenzeitung*. Therefore, FPÖ and the BZÖ were trying hard to appeal to voters concerned about immigration and European integration. When the SPÖ focused on social policy issues, the FPÖ was in the best position to take ownership of the immigration issue and, by extension, the opposition to Turkish EU accession. The FPÖ had far more credibility with voters on these issues than HPM and was also more unequivocally anti-EU than the BZÖ, which pursued a strategy of qualified Euroscepticism (Taggart and Szczerbiak 2004: 4).

When the strategy of the BZÖ met with success only in Carinthia, Haider sought to underscore his party's distinctiveness by positioning it as a market-liberal party that competed nonetheless for right-wing voters (Heinisch 2002: 59). This meant that whereas the FPÖ focused nearly exclusively on patriotism, immigration, security and welfare (i.e., immigrants should be denied social benefits), the BZÖ sought to appeal to voters with market liberal orientations (i.e., cutting the bureaucracy, privatisation, reducing inflation). The BZÖ had nonetheless reservations about European integration (i.e., a referendum on Turkey and the Lisbon Treaty). Only in Carinthia, where Haider was governor, did he engage in ethnic mobilisation by playing on resentments against the local Slovene minority to ensure as large a victory as possible to compensate for expected losses elsewhere. Otherwise, the BZÖ presented itself as a more acceptable alternative to the FPÖ. Haider, who was still governor and ran as the BZÖ top candidate only in 2008, tried to recast himself, compared with Strache, as the more statesmanlike and rules-oriented politician (*Der Spiegel* 2008). His was a more qualified criticism of the EU (BZÖ 2008) than the blanket indictment presented by the FPÖ (FPÖ 2008). Nonetheless, the latter's more uncompromising position propelled the FPÖ to a clear victory, validating Strache's vote-seeking strategy.

The FPÖ after 2008 – the long run

With the death of Haider in 2008 the BZÖ was increasingly in disarray over its political direction and no longer represented an existential threat to the FPÖ. Also the disappearance of HPM from the domestic political scene eliminated another rival for the Freedom Party. Yet, the FPÖ continued its radical sociocultural messaging to boost its support in two state elections. In the state of Styria, the party demanded a ban on the construction of mosques and minarets. In Vienna, the FPÖ ran on an anti-immigration and anti-Muslim platform, reminding voters of the Ottoman siege of Vienna, and more than doubled its share from 10.9 to 25.8 per cent (Jenny 2011: 907–08).

The 2013 national elections saw the new protest parties Team Stronach (TS) and New Austria (Das Neue Österreich und Liberales Forum, NEOS) compete. This was unwelcome news for the 'traditional' protest parties FPÖ and BZÖ. Especially TS proved initially a formidable challenge to the FPÖ because of the former's anti-EU position, criticism of public corruption and gridlock, and its charismatic leader. However, the political inexperience of the Austro-Canadian tycoon Frank Stronach, who headed the party, caused so many missteps that in the end TS garnered only 5.7 per cent, followed by NEOS with 5 per cent (SORA/Institut für Strategieanalysen 2013: 1). Whereas the BZÖ dropped out of parliament entirely, the FPÖ achieved 20.5 per cent but could have done even better in both the national elections in 2013 and the European Parliament elections in 2014. Many Austrians were reeling from fallout from the financial crisis and had little love left for the coalition government. The appeal and initial success of Stronach showed that a significant share of the electorate was willing to vote for protest party alternatives provided the latter were not especially radical or had ties with extremists. TS stayed away from xenophobia and extremist positions on sociocultural issues. It was noticeable that Strache adopted a more moderate tone in his public appearances (*Die Presse* 2013). He even proclaimed that 'there is room for Muslims in the FPÖ' (*Salzburger Nachrichten* 2015).

Austrian politics and the FPÖ seem to have come full circle. After winning three national elections in a row since 2005 and facing an unpopular main-party coalition, the FPÖ is once again contemplating public office. Strache has even hinted at wanting to collaborate with the SPÖ (*Der Standard* 2012; *Kleine Zeitung* 2013). A coalition with the SPÖ would reduce the cost of mainstreaming because both parties are likely to pursue popular social policies. The FPÖ could make its mark by holding the line on immigration and possibly Europe – an issue not as central to the SPÖ as to the ÖVP. The interest in pursuing office-seeking may be motivated by the fact that the FPÖ's monopoly on protest politics is no longer assured. Recent developments show that even the ultra-stable Austrian political system can produce new protest formations seemingly from nowhere. At the same time, the FPÖ does not wish to relive its near-death experience of 2005 and would be cautious to commit itself to a strategy and positions that alienate its voters and fuel internal divisions. This makes Strache's approach of selective re-engagement a strategically plausible course of action: Regionally, radical populist messages continue to be part of the FPÖ's discourse,[14] whereas in areas of great visibility there have been efforts to distance the party from political radicalism. The 2011 party programme supports this direction in that it is sufficiently vague on key policy matters to allow for a range of political avenues to be pursued. However, none of this has deterred the FPÖ from trying to form a common faction in the European Parliament with the French National Front, the Italian Northern League, the Flemish Interest and the Dutch Freedom Party (*Kurier* 2014; EurActiv 2014).

Conclusion

This chapter examined processes of mainstreaming in the Austrian Freedom Party (FPÖ) by tracing its development before, in, and after incumbency. In the run-up to the 1999 elections, the FPÖ embraced culturally conservative and market-liberal positions, which appealed to the ÖVP and middle-class voters. Haider also pursued a strategy stressing radical positions on European integration, public safety and immigration to court the blue-collar electorate in the East where the FPÖ saw its largest potential for growth. Crucially, the radical positions on foreign immigration and EU enlargement overshadowed its substantive socio-economic proposals. Moreover, as the FPÖ could not anticipate being in a situation to enter government in 1999, it did not fully commit to office-seeking and failed to develop a strategy for compensating for the cost of moderation. Following internal shakeups, the party was also poorly prepared for public office in terms of organisation and personnel. In order to enter into a coalition with the ÖVP in 2000, the FPÖ had to meet a series of conditions set out by the Christian-Democrats, including a commitment to European integration and an unambiguous rejection of Nazism. Thus, we conclude that mainstreaming took place as a result of an office-seeking strategy with regard to de-emphasising anti-establishment positions and greater emphasis on socioeconomic issues. When faced with incumbency, the socioeconomic focus was enhanced, positions on the European Union moderated, and the party distanced itself clearly from anti-Semitism as well as its demands for plebiscitary democracy. This clearly shows the moderating effect on the FPÖ by the inclusionary approach pursued by the ÖVP.

After a short period in government, the FPÖ was confronted with a backlash of voters alienated by the party's new course. The consecutive losses in elections exacerbated internal divisions and eventually led to the breakup of the government and split of the party along office-seeking moderates and vote-seekers. The reasons for why the FPÖ failed to deliver in the voters' eyes are complex: (a) in some areas, existing policies were already rather restrictive (immigration) and could hardly be tightened much further; (b) the unfamiliar softer rhetoric conflicted with expectations about the party's typically unambiguous messaging; (c) the amateurish performance of FPÖ members stood in marked contrast to their pre-election claims; (d) a large share of the electorate was surprised by the neoliberal dimension of the FPÖ's programme; and (e) the party had genuinely moderated in all four dimensions of non-mainstreamness. Furthermore, moderation occurred especially with regard to European integration. In addition, it presented also a substantive socioeconomic agenda (compared to its track record). Lastly, FPÖ officials also showed respect for the rules of the game and distanced themselves from extremism. At the same time, the party's position on immigration remained rather unchanged during the (pre-)incumbency phase due to the approximation of the other parties to the FPÖ's position. Only after the split in 2005 did the party take a more extreme position.

In the final phase of incumbency the FPÖ tried to regain the voters' trust, by moving to the left on socioeconomic issues and assuming the role of defender of the 'man in the street'. In the two subsequent elections after leaving office, the FPÖ concentrated on xenophobic and anti-European mobilisation. Overall, the FPÖ's position on Europe has become more sceptical compared to its term in office but nonetheless its criticism appears more guarded than that of other European radical right-wing populist parties.

Following repeated successes in national elections, the FPÖ is signalling once again an interest in public office. Widespread dissatisfaction with the current SPÖ-ÖVP government may in due course present the FPÖ with the opportunity of securing an outright majority. This would force the issue of government participation sooner rather than later (*Der Standard* 2014a). There is no doubt that this would be a desirable development for FPÖ; but one where the party will try to have learned from past mistakes. From this perspective, moderation in tone and less in core positions is preferable.

Notes

1 On FPÖ's history and development, see Luther 1997; Höbelt 1999; Zöchling 1999; Heinisch 2002.

2 See Bakker *et al.* 2013. We also considered data from the Manifesto Project but found the coding wholly inconsistent with other empirical evidence about FPÖ positioning.
3 Despite increasing radicalisation, it formally retained its social-liberal and pro-European Salzburg Program of 1985 until 1997, which it then maintained until 2011 although undergoing profound changes in leadership and direction and even a split in 2005.
4 The ministers to be, Thomas Prinzhorn and Hilmar Kabas, were rejected on account of unacceptable statements made during the campaign (Fallend 2001: 242).
5 This was evident in criticisms ranging from the EU's handling of BSE and foot and mouth disease to ECJ rulings against Austria on transit traffic and bank secrecy laws.
6 When looking at these graphs one has to bear in mind that lines create the illusion of a trajectory even when positions change abruptly. The 'turning points' indicated in the graphs are not necessarily the moments when the direction changed but when a new survey captured this change.
7 The FPÖ reconfirmed the 1997 party programme with some minor changes on 24 April 2005 at the 27th party congress.
8 While the SPÖ's new strongman and later chairman Werner Faymann courted the support of the influential tabloid *Neue Kronenzeitung*, the Christian-Democrats propagated xenophobic slogans pandering to potential FPÖ voters (Fallend 2009: 886, 889).
9 This was suggested by Strache in an interview in 2005 (News 2005).
10 In an interview in 2011 Strache presented ideas for a specific currency zone for the economically stronger member states such as Germany, Belgium, the Netherlands, and Austria (Kurier 2011).
11 Haider created an electoral platform that abandoned the name FPÖ in favour of 'F-movement' (Die Freiheitlichen) and aimed at creating a Freedomite-led 'citizen movement' (Bürgerbewegung) called 'Alliance 98' (Bündnis 98).
12 This included especially the public broadcasting company (ORF), the central social insurance administration (Hauptverband der Sozialversicherungsträger), and the holding corporation of the state-owned enterprises (ÖIAG).
13 Haider's local 'baby check' initiative was rolled into the national infant money programme and the national government also committed itself to building a €6 billion high speed rail and tunnel project while looking away when evidence of political corruption and mismanagement in Haider's administration began surfacing.
14 The head of the parliamentary caucus, Johann Gudenus, talked about the 'Islamisation' of Vienna (FPÖ party homepage) whereas the chairman of the Lower Austrian party branch, Christian Höbart, referred to asylum seekers as 'cavemen' (Der Standard 2014c).

References

Akkerman, T. and de Lange, S. L. (2012) 'Radical right parties in office: Incumbency records and the electoral cost of governing', *Government and Opposition* 47, 4: 574–596.
Bakker, R., Jolly, S. and Polk, J. (2013) 'Measuring party positions in Europe: The Chapel Hill expert survey trend file, 1999–2010', *Party Politics* 23, 1: 43–152.
BZÖ (2006) 'Wahlprogramm', https://manifestoproject.wzb.eu/uploads/attach/file/5237/42710_2006.pdf (accessed 15-12-2015).
BZÖ (2008) 'Deinetwegen. Österreich. Das Wahlprogramm des BZÖ', https://manifestoproject.wzb.eu/uploads/attach/file/5242/42710_2008.pdf (accessed 15-12-2015).
Czernin, H. (2000) *Wofür ich mich meinetwegen entschuldige: Haider, beim Wort genommen*, Wien: Czernin Verlag.

Dachs, H. (2006) 'Parteiensysteme in den Bundesländern', in Dachs, H., Gerlich, P., Gottweis, H., Kramer, H., Lauber, V., Müller, W. C. and Tálos, E. (eds) *Politik in Österreich: Das Handbuch*, Wien: Manz, pp. 1008–1023.

Der Spiegel (2008) 'Der Wilde und der Milde', www.spiegel.de/spiegel/print/d-60403592. html (accessed 15-12-2015).

Der Standard (2012) 'Strache: "Bei Abwahl von Faymann wäre Zusammenarbeit mit SPÖ möglich"', http://derstandard.at/1326503588552/Chat-Nachlese-Strache-Bei-Abwa hl-von-Faymann-waere-Zusammenarbeit-mit-SPOe-moeglich (accessed 15-12-2015).

Der Standard (2014a) 'FPÖ würde bei Neuwahlen weit vorn liegen', http://derstandard.at/ 2000002013315/FPOe-wuerde-bei-Neuwahlen-weit-vorn-liegen (accessed 15-12-2015).

Der Standard (2014b) 'FPÖ-Spitze zwingt Mölzer zu völligem Rückzug', http://d erstandard.at/1395364560922/Moelzer-zieht-sich-als-FPOe-Spitzenkandidat-zurueck (accessed 16-10-2014).

Die Presse (2013) 'Straches Wahlkampf mit Schalldämpfer', http://diepresse.com/ home/politik/nrwahl2013/1452680/Straches-Wahlkampf-mit-Schalldaempfer (accessed 12-15-2015).

EurActiv (2014) 'Front National will europäische Rechtspartei gründen', www.euractiv. de/sections/europawahlen-2014/front-national-will-europaeische-rechtspartei-gruen den-309071 (accessed 03-12-2015).

Fallend, F. (2001) 'Austria', *European Journal of Political Research Political Data Yearbook* 40, 238–253.

Fallend, F. (2002) 'Austria', *European Journal of Political Research Political Data Yearbook* 41, 906–914.

Fallend, F. (2007) 'Austria', *European Journal of Political Research Political Data Yearbook* 46, 876–890.

Fallend, F. (2009) 'Austria', *European Journal of Political Research Political Data Yearbook* 48, 884–902.

Fallend, F. (2010) 'Austria', *European Journal of Political Research Political Data Yearbook* 49, 880–898.

Fallend, F. (2012) 'Populism in government: The case of Austria', in Mudde, C. and Kaltwasser, C. R. (eds) *Populism in Europe and the Americas: Threat or Corrective for Democracy?* Cambridge: Cambridge University Press, pp.113–135.

Fassmann, F. (2013) 'Migrations- und integrationspolitik', in Kriechbaumer, R. and Schausberger, F. (eds) *Die Umstrittene Wende 2000–2006*, Wien: Böhlau Verlag, pp. 695–712.

FPÖ (1994) 'Österreich-Erklärung', https://manifestoproject.wzb.eu/uploads/attach/ file/4158/42420_1994.txt (accessed 15-12-2015).

FPÖ (1997) 'Program of the Austrian Freedom Party', www.fpoe.at/fileadmin/Contentp ool/Portal/PDFs/Parteiprogramme/Parteiprogram_eng.pdf (accessed 15-12-2015).

FPÖ (1999) 'Wahlprogamm', https://manifestoproject.wzb.eu/uploads/attach/file/5244/ 42420_1999.pdf (accessed 03-12-2015).

FPÖ (2006) 'Wahlprogramm der Freiheitlichen Partei Österreichs FPÖ: Nationalratswahl 2006', https://manifestoproject.wzb.eu/uploads/attach/file/2214/42420_2006.pdf (accessed 15-12-2015).

FPÖ (2008) 'Österreich im Wort: Auswahl und Zusammenfassung inhaltlicher Ziele der freiheitlichen Partei Österreichs für die neue Legislaturperiode', *WIR für EUCH Deshalb FPÖ – HC Strache*, https://manifestoproject.wzb.eu/uploads/attach/file/ 5243/42420_2008.pdf (accessed 15-12-2015).

FPÖ (2011) 'Parteiprogramm der Freiheitlichen Partei Österreichs (FPÖ): Österreich zuerst', www.fpoe.at/fileadmin/Content/portal/PDFs/_dokumente/2011_graz_partei programm_web.pdf (accessed 13-12-2014).

Heinisch, R. (2002) *Populism, Proporz, Pariah: Austria Turns Right: Austrian Political Change, its Causes and Repercussions*, New York: Nova Science.

Heinisch, R. (2003) 'Success in opposition – failure in government: Explaining the performance of right-wing populist parties in public office', *West European Politics* 26, 3: 91–130.

Hinterseer, T. (2014) 'Sozialpartnerschaft m(M)acht Arbeitspolitik: wie institutionell bestimmtes Akteursverhalten am Beispiel der Sozialdemokratischen Partei Österreichs sowie des Gewerkschaftsbundes und der Arbeiterkammer den Einfluss der Sozial-partnerschaft auf arbeitspolitische Gesetzwerdungsprozesse (im Sinne der Guten Arbeit) bestimmt', unpublished PhD thesis at the University of Salzburg.

Höbelt, L. (1999) *Von der vierten Partei zur dritten Kraft: Die Geschichte des VdU*, Graz: Leopold Stocker Verlag.

Horaczek, N. and Reiterer, C. (2009) *HC Strache: Sein Aufstieg, seine Hintermänner, seine Feinde*, Wien: Wirtschaftsverlag Ueberreuter.

Horner, F. (1997) 'Programme–ideologien: Dissens oder konsens', in Dachs, H., Gerlich, P. and Gottweis, H. (eds) *Handbuch des Politischen Systems Österreichs: Die Zweite Republik*, 3rd edn, Wien: Manz, 235–247.

Jenny, M. (2011) 'Austria', *European Journal of Political Research Political Data Yearbook* 50, 901–912.

Khol, A. (1996) 'Die FPÖ im Spannungsfeld von Ausgrenzung, Selbstausgrenzung, Verfassungsbogen und Regierungsfähigkeit', in Khol, A., Ofner, G. and Stirnemann, A. (eds) *Österreichisches Jahrbuch für Politik 1995*, Wien and München: Böhlau Verlag, 193–221.

Kleine Zeitung (2013) 'Strache hält nur Zusammenarbeit mit SPÖ für umsetzbar', www. kleinezeitung.at/k/politik/4092109/Koaltion_Strache-haelt-nur-Zusammenarbeit-m it-SPO-fur-umsetzbar (accessed 15-12-2015).

Kurier (2011) 'FPÖ: Austritt statt Rausschmiss', http://kurier.at/thema/eurokrise/fpoe-a ustritt-statt-rausschmiss/731.074, accessed 13-15-2015.

Kurier (2014) 'FPÖ, FN und CO: Ringen um eine neue Rechtsfraktion', http://kurier. at/politik/eu/fpoe-fn-und-co-ringen-um-neue-rechtsfraktion/67.585.880   (accessed 03-12-2015).

Luif, P. (2006) 'Österreich und die Europäische Union', in Dachs, H., Gerlich, P., Gottweis, H., Kramer, H., Lauber, V., Müller, W. C. and Tálos, E. (eds) *Politik in Österreich: Das Handbuch*, Wien: Manz, 862–883.

Luther, K. R. (1995) 'Zwischen unkritischer Selbstdarstellung und bedingungsloser externer Verurteilung: Nazivergangenheit, Anti-Semitismus und Holocaust im Schrifttum der Freiheitlichen Partei Österreichs', in Bergmann, W., Erb, R. and Lichtblau, A. (eds) *Schwieriges Erbe. Der Umgang mit Nationalsozialismus und Antisemitismus in Österreich, der DDR und der Bundesrepublik Deutschland*, Frankfurt: Campus Verlag, pp. 138–167.

Luther, K. R. (1997) 'Die Freiheitlichen', in Dachs, H., Gerlich, P. and Gottweis, H. (eds) *Handbuch des politischen Systems Österreichs: Die zweite Republik*, 3rd edn, Wien: Manz, pp. 286–303.

Luther, K. R. (2003) 'The self-destruction of a right-wing populist party? The Austrian parliamentary election of 2002', *West European Politics* 26, 2: 136–152.

Luther, K. R. (2006a) 'Die Freiheitliche Partei Österreichs und das Bündnis Zukunft Österreich', in Dachs, H., Gerlich, P., Gottweis, H., Kramer, H., Lauber, V., Müller, W. C. and Tálos, E. (eds) *Politik in Österreich: Das Handbuch*, Wien: Manz, 364–388.

Luther, K. R. (2006b) 'Strategien und (Fehl-)Verhalten: Die Freiheitlichen und die Regierungen Schussel I und II', in Tálos, E. (ed.) *Schwarz-blau: Eine Bilanz des "Neu-Regierens"*, Wien: Lit, pp. 19–37.

Luther, K. R. (2008) 'Electoral strategies and performance of Austrian right-wing populism, 1986–2006', in Bischof, G. and Plasser, F. (eds) *The Changing Austrian Voter: Contemporary Austrian Studies*, New Brunswick, NJ: Transaction, pp. 101–122.

Luther, K. R. (2011) 'Of goals and own goals: A case study of right-wing populist party strategy for and during incumbency', *Party Politics* 17, 4: 453–470.

Minkenberg, M. (2001) 'The radical right in public office: Agenda-setting and policy effects', *West European Politics* 24, 4: 1–21.

Müller, W. and Fallend, F. (2004) 'Changing patterns of party competition in Austria: From multipolar to bipolar system', *West European Politics* 27, 5: 801–835.

Müller, W. C. (2006) 'Der Bundespräsident', in Dachs, H., Gerlich, P., Gottweis, H., Kramer, H., Lauber, V., Müller, W. C. and Tálos, E. (eds) *Politik in Österreich: Das Handbuch*, Wien: Manz, pp. 188–200.

News (2005) 'Strache verlangt EU-Austritt Österreichs: FPÖ-Obmann läuft Sturm gegen die Union', www.news.at/a/strache-eu-austritt-oesterreichs-fpoe-obmann-stu rm-union-114141 (accessed 15-12-2015).

ÖVP (1999) 'Wahlprogramm', https://manifestoproject.wzb.eu/uploads/attach/file/ 4150/42520_1999.txt (accessed 3-12-2015).

Pallaver, G., Pig, C., Gruber, G. W. and Fliri, T. (2000) 'Wahlkampf in den Fernseh-nachrichten. Eine Inhaltsanalyse der tagesaktuellen Berichterstattung', in Plasser, F., Ulram, P. A. and Sommer, F. F. (eds) *Das Österreichische Wahlverhalten*, Wien: Signum Verlag, pp. 175–206.

Piringer, K. (2001) 'Chronologie der FPÖ-Entwicklung 1986 bis Jahresmitte 2000', in Höbelt, L. (ed.) *Republik im Wandel. Die große Koalition und der Aufstieg der Haider-FPÖ*, Munich: Universitas Munich, 356–459.

Plasser, F. and Ulram, P. A. (2000) 'Rechtspopulistische Resonanzen: Die Wählerschaft der FPÖ', in Plasser, F., Ulram, P. A. and Sommer, F. F. (eds) *Das österreichische Wahlverhalten*, Wien: Signum, 225–241.

Salzburger Nachrichten (2015) 'Strache möchte die FPÖ für Muslime öffnen', 12-12-2015, 2.

Schausberger, F. (2013) 'Barometer, Denkzettel und Hausgemachtes', in Kriechbaumer, R. and Schausberger, F. (eds) *Die umstrittene Wende 2000–2006*, Wien: Böhlau Verlag.

Schüssel, W. (2009) *Offengelegt*, Salzburg: Ecowin-Verlag.

Seiler, C. (2006) 'Jörg Haider: Im Gegenteil', *Die Weltwoche*, www.weltwoche.ch/ausga ben/2006-02/artikel-2006-02-im-gegenteil.html.

SORA/InstitutfürStrategieanalysen (2006) 'Wahlanalyse Nationalratswahl 2006', www. sora.at/themen/wahlverhalten/wahlanalysen/nrw06.html (accessed 02-12-2015).

SORA/InstitutfürStrategieanalysen (2008) 'Wahlanalyse Nationalratswahl 2008', www.sora. at/fileadmin/downloads/wahlen/2008_nrw_wahlanalyse.pdf (accessed 07-07-2014).

SORA/InstitutfürStrategieanalysen (2013) 'Wahlanalyse Nationalratswahl 2013', www. sora.at/themen/wahlverhalten/wahlanalysen/nrw13.html (accessed 06-07-2014).

Taggart, P. and Szczerbiak, A. (2004) 'Contemporary Euroscepticism in the party systems of the European Union Candidate States of Central and Eastern Europe', *European Journal of Political Research* 43, 1: 1–27.

Williams, M. H. (2013) 'Tipping the balance scale? Rightward momentum, party agency and Austrian party politics', *Journal of Contemporary European Studies* 21, 1: 68–86.

Zöchling, C. (1999) *Haider: Licht und Schatten einer Karriere*, Wien: Molden.

5 The Danish People's Party

Combining cooperation and radical positions

Flemming Juul Christiansen

Introduction

The Danish People's Party (Dansk Folkeparti, DF) has found a permanent place in the Danish party system. In 2001 it became the third largest party in the *Folketing*, and at the general election in June 2015, it became second largest with 21 per cent and 37 seats out of 179. At the European Parliamentary Election in May 2014 it managed to become the largest party with 27 per cent of the votes and four seats out of 13 Danish MEPs. The success of the party has raised public debate about whether the party should join a cabinet. It has not been in office yet and in the government formation negotiations after the 2015 election it stayed outside and instead supported a minority government headed by the Liberal Party (Venstre, V) that only received 34 seats. This was in accordance with the line announced up to the election by the party leader since 2012, Kristian Thulesen Dahl who has advocated that a support party position is more advantageous, just like it happened between 2001 and 2011. From that position his party could seek policy influence through bargaining, perhaps from a strengthened position in number of seats and on more policy issues. These ten years of cooperation must be considered a crucial step towards the DF becoming a 'normal party'.

The DF was founded in 1995 by four members of the parliamentary group of the Progress Party (Fremskridtspartiet, FrP), itself founded in 1972 by a charismatic tax lawyer, Mogens Glistrup, on an anti-tax and anti-bureaucracy platform that from the mid-1980s came to include resistance towards immigration and Muslim immigration in particular. According to Bille (1989: 49), the FrP did possess anti-system characteristics in a broad sense of the term because it did not play by the parliamentary rules of the other parties, and because it was in opposition to a welfare system basically agreed to by the old parties represented before 1973. The party founder himself was expelled from the party in 1990. Before the 1995 split, two factions called 'tighteners' and 'looseners' rivalled for power, the latter headed by Pia Kjærsgaard, who also demonstrated persuasive communication skills in the media (Ringsmose 2003). Her faction wanted the party to interact more closely with other parties. After a party congress with public scenes of turmoil, Kjærsgaard took the initiative to found the DF.

Table 5.1 shows that the party has enjoyed considerable electoral success in the five general elections it has taken part in. Only in 2011 did the party have its first minor setback.

The party founder, Kjærsgaard, resigned voluntarily in 2012 and was succeeded by the parliamentary party group chairman, and co-founder of the party, Thulesen Dahl. Unlike the charismatic and passionate but also publicly divisive Kjærsgaard,[1] Thulesen Dahl has a calmer image and according to opinion polls he is perceived as a highly competent figure (*Politiken* 11-06-2014). For quite some time after his take-over, DF achieved support from 18 to 20 per cent of the population in opinion polls and performed even slightly better at the election in 2015.

The rise of the DF and its cooperation with parties of the mainstream right, including membership of the European Conservatives and Reformists (ECR) group in the European Parliament with the British Conservatives, raises the question whether the party itself is in a process of mainstreaming or has already has gone through such a process. The purpose of this chapter is to assess whether that is the case and also to evaluate the goals and strategies of the DF since it was founded.[2] In the next section mainstreaming of the DF will be measured. The following section discusses the strategy and goals of the party. The chapter concludes that the party has partly gone through a mainstreaming process with the radical policies towards immigration and the EU as the major exception. The party remains reluctant to take the whole step into government and prefers to seek policy influence as a parliamentary support party in order to avoid loss of votes.

Up the mainstream

To measure whether DF has become a mainstream party we will use the four dimensions outlined in the introductory chapter: the less the DF is still a radical, niche, and anti-establishment party with an extreme reputation, the more it can be said to have become mainstream.

Table 5.1 Electoral support for the DPP in general elections, 1998–2015

	Percentage	Number of parliamentary seats (N = 179. It includes four North Atlantic seats)
1998	7.4	13
2001	12.0	22
2005	13.3	24
2007	13.9	25
2011	12.3	22
2015	21.1	37

Maintaining radical positions on core issues

Political radicalism should in this context be understood as non-centrist political positions, primarily with regard to the sociocultural dimension central to radical right-wing populist parties in general, like opposition towards immigration and European integration as well as stricter policies concerning law and order. The political manifestos of the DF provide important data to assess these policy items and their development. The first 'principle programme' of the party from 1997 was 36 pages long and strikingly similar to that of the FrP both with regard to priorities and positions. The next, and current, principle program of the DF, is from 2002, and rather short (only 6 pages). The party has also passed much longer 'working programmes' written by the parliamentary group in 2001 (106 pages) and in 2009 (170 pages).

When the DF was formed, its first message to the public was a wish to continue the policies of the FrP with a marked resistance against immigration policies and against the European Union (Bille 1998: 212). The policies of the centre-left government on these issues were either supported or only vaguely challenged by the centre-right opposition (Green-Pedersen and Krogstrup 2008). The FrP was strongly against liberal immigration policies passed in 1983 in the *Folketing* against the votes of the party. When Glistrup was released from prison in 1986, after serving 3.5 years convicted for tax fraud, he declared that his new top priority would be the expulsion of Muslims (*Politiken* 18-09-1994).

On the European issue the FrP had switched position from campaigning for a 'yes' vote in the 1986 referendum over the Single European Act to a 'no' vote in the referendums in 1992 and 1993 over the Maastricht Treaty. The party supported a free market, but not the political aspects of European cooperation. All of the mainstream parties had then supported a 'yes' vote, and after the rejection in 1992, they had made 'a national compromise' on EU policies. So, also on this issue, the FrP stood out with a radical position in contrast to the mainstream parties.

The DF pledged to continue these radical positions of the FrP on immigration and the EU. The 1997 manifesto had many references to these issues. It stated that 'Denmark is not and should not become a country of immigration', 'refugees should not become permanent immigrants' and that 'the current mass integration is a serious threat against the existence of Denmark as peaceful welfare state' (Dansk Folkeparti 1997). Thus, from its very beginning, the party made an explicit link between immigration and the welfare state. Schumacher and Van Kersbergen (forthcoming) refer to the DF as pioneering 'welfare chauvinism', meaning that access to welfare should be restricted to the 'deserving' natives.

Concerning the European Union, the party stressed the independence of Denmark and sovereignty of the *Folketing*, and not the European Parliament, and it wanted to retain the veto power of individual nations. The 1997 programme advocated more police, anonymous witnesses, and stricter punishments. With these elements in place, the DF from its outset held 'radical' sociocultural positions, and it qualifies as a radical right-wing populist party. Its focus was 'nativist' seeing Denmark as an independent state under threat from immigration and European unification. Its promotion of stricter policies concerning law and order is towards the authoritarian end of a dimension with libertarian in the opposite.

Outside sociocultural policies, the party advocated a significant reduction of 'the tax burden' as well as public expenditure. This economic right-wing position was in accordance with the policies of the FrP. Nevertheless, both parties were also supportive of spending on health and education.

The current 2002 programme repeats the sociocultural positions on not becoming an immigrant country and a multi-ethnic society as well as resistance towards the EU. Furthermore, it advocates 'rapid convictions and punishment' for criminals (Dansk Folkeparti 2002). So, the party maintains its 'radical' policy positions on these issues. Remarks on tax reductions are no longer included, but replaced by very broad remarks that Denmark prospers because of the quality of work and ability to work together (Dansk Folkeparti 2002). The economic position is best labelled as 'centrist'.

The 2001 working programme in its introduction identified a number of threats against democracy and freedom in Denmark including immigration of people 'remote from Danish and European culture, and way of life', 'who cannot become integrated into Danish society'. The manifesto stated that due to high fertility, family reunions and organised illegal immigration, 'Danes will become a minority in Denmark during the 21th Century'. Ghettos, violence against women, illiteracy, crime and disorder were also mentioned as threats, together with the European Union, about to replace the national states with multiculturalism without identity (Dansk Folkeparti 2001).

The 2009 working programme repeats these threats with the same wording, although the remarks on fertility and Danes becoming a minority are no longer present – a slight moderation. The current party manifesto states that continued immigration will have 'far-reaching and destroying impact on the demographics of Denmark, societal structure and cohesion power' (Dansk Folkeparti 2009). It is combined with a number of specific proposals to tighten immigration policies. Concerning law and order, the 2009 programme prides itself with some of the achievements of the party as a support party after 2001, and it does appear more satisfied with present conditions than the previous manifestos. It is also more open to preventive measures but still demands swifter and stricter punishments. The party is against the European Union and its course towards becoming a federal state and prefers to maintain national and cultural differences. That still indicates an important element of 'nativism'. The party wants to uphold the four Danish 'opt-outs' negotiated after the no vote in 1992, including retaining a Danish currency. On economic policies, the party now promotes balanced finance politics with an efficient public sector. It further states that high income taxes are 'conditioned by the need for costs in the public sector as well as general economic policies' (Dansk Folkeparti 2009), i.e. necessary. It wants a gradual decrease of the tax level, especially for lower incomes. The socioeconomic position of the working programme can therefore still be considered 'centrist'. In April 2015, the party proposed further tightening of immigrant policies, in particular concerning family reunions (*dr.dk* 05-04-2015). The new party leader, Thulesen Dahl, states, though, that he believes 'reforms of Islam are possible', a more moderate stance than expressed by his predecessor, Kjærsgaard (*Weekendavisen* 08-05-2015).

As of 2015 the party prefers more growth in the public sector than the centre-left government. The party leader recently declared on national TV that his party views itself as to the left of the government on these matters (*dr.dk* 02-05-2015). In another remark, he criticised the former partners of the party:

> V has shifted to zero growth. We recommend them to go back to 0.8 per cent.
> (*Politiken* 31-05-2015)[3]

It wants a more generous unemployment benefit system than both the government and the centre-right opposition. These two topics appeared to be the most debated generally by the parties and public in the 2015 election campaign, and the V government formed after the election promises 'more than zero growth' with a direct reference to the electoral result.

In general, the DF has maintained radical sociocultural core positions not that different from those it inherited from the FrP. This observation is largely in accordance with the quantitative analysis presented in Chapter 2 (see Appendix). However, on socioeconomic policies the party has shifted from the right to centre or centre-left in its public statements and programs in accordance with the 'new winning formula' (De Lange 2007).

Main emphasis on immigration but broadened its profile to socioeconomic issues

The major issue emphasised in public by the DF during its first years was immigration, followed by crime and the conditions for the elderly citizens (see Bille 2006). Its economic policies were less emphasised in its communications and became even less prominent during the first years of the party, whereas taxation and a minimal state had been important for the FRP. Intellectually, the party got inspiration from among others the Danish Association – an issue-based political association established in 1987, known for anti-immigration stances and an 'ethno-nationalist outlook' (Rydgren 2004).[4] During the years as support party for the government of V and Conservatives (Konservative Folkeparti, K) between 2001 and 2011, its main concern according to the CMP data remained what the party and electoral researchers label 'value politics', what would be issues on a libertarian/authoritarian dimension (cf. Andersen 2007: 29). Over time the party has developed thematic issues such as animal welfare, the elderly, national culture as well as pro-US and pro-Israel positions in foreign affairs. The DF largely accepted the economic policies of the government leaving little room for a clear and independent profile. This was most likely a weakness for the party when the economic crisis caused the 2011 election to be dominated by economic themes (Stubager *et al.* 2013).

In opposition after 2011 and in particular since the change of party leader in 2012 – it selected the finance spokesperson for the party – the DF emphasises general economic issues such as public sector growth or the unemployment benefit system much more. When other parties now challenge the economic policies of the DF – blaming the party for 'economic populism' – it is a sign that the party now has a profile on economic policy that is clear enough to be electorally competitive, so that other parties feel the need to relate to it.

The CMP data from 1995 to 2010 confirm that the DF has been more concerned with sociocultural issues than Danish parties in general and less concerned with economic policies, but also that these issues have taken up more space after 2001 (see Appendix). During the 2015 election campaign the party very much emphasised its economic and welfare positions as well. With a broader issue agenda, the party has become much less of a niche party although immigration remains a prominent topic.

Parliamentary cooperation but anti-elite statements

To assess the development of an anti-establishment profile, two aspects will be analysed. First, we will look at the anti-elitism of the party. Second, it will be assessed whether the party respects or challenges the rules of the game in the parliamentary system.

The 1997 programme and the later ones are sparse on populist references representing the people against the elite. It does criticise the lack of democracy in the EU though, and it fears that EU policies will promote 'a politically correct idea' of more immigration to Europe and Denmark (Dansk Folkeparti 2009). In public debates such remarks are much more common. An example by the former party leader, Kjærsgaard illustrates this style when she states that 'the core of the problem' is 'a self-serving political and cultural elite' 'living in the right places' 'without the least sense of passion for the conditions of others and the people'. And also 'The people chose another immigration policy after 2001 against the wishes of this elite' (Kjærsgaard 2005). Other terms that often appear in public discourse are 'naive', 'betrayal', 'ordinary Danes' or just 'Danes', and 'political correctness'.[5] These terms are now to a certain extent used beyond the ranks of DF, and the party may in this manner impact on the agenda and framing of the public debate in Denmark, not least among Internet commentators. Thulesen Dahl, however, appears much more hesitant to use such phrases. This could be conceived of as a sign of mainstreaming.

From its outset the DF had the ambition to function as a 'normal' party (Ringsmose 2003). The 1997 principle programme stressed the need to play an active role in Danish parliamentary life and to become a party that could be counted on when entering political agreements (Dansk Folkeparti 1997). A party has to stick to legislative settlements (*forlig*) – described in more detail in the next section – in order to be considered 'responsible' by the established mainstream

Danish parties. The FrP did not follow these norms and reneged from agreements they had made several times, partly caused by internal turmoil. With minority governments as a permanent feature, this made it difficult 'to do business' with the party.

When the VK-government was formed in November 2001 it remained an open question whether the DF would after all be able to provide the needed support for the new government in a disciplined manner (Bille 2006: 23). The cooperation over policies started out with the bargaining over the state budget in early 2002. From then onwards DF became the primary partner of the minority government and took part in a high number of legislative settlements. There is not a single reported occasion in which the party did not behave according to the parliamentary norms of the huge number of legislative settlements it took part in.

Another feature of being considered a 'responsible' party in the *Folketing* is to vote yes to pass the annual state budget (Christiansen 2012).[6] However, unlike the mainstream centre-right parties, the DF voted against it during the years of centre-left governments up until 2001. When the party cooperated with the centre-right between 2001 and 2011, it voted yes to the state budget. Because the party was also part of a political settlement it was unclear whether it actually followed the norm to do so or acted as a result of the policy compromise. Yet, in opposition after 2011, the DF has continued to vote 'yes' presenting the same pro-system arguments used by other parties without being part of the state budget agreement.[7] So, the party has now clearly accepted this norm of being a 'responsible' party.

When a support party, the DF consistently voted in favour of 19 out of 20 pieces of legislation passed during the period between 2001 and 2011, also a sign of pro-system behaviour. The major exception to this cooperative pattern concerned European Union matters where the party did not and does not take part in the major settlement regulating EU policies (Christiansen and Pedersen 2012). Nevertheless, the party has supported 87 per cent of laws implementing EU regulation.[8] Matters concerning the European Union have remained an area in which the DF argues against the established parties. It also represents a problem to be dealt with if the party should someday achieve cabinet office. On the left the Socialist People's Party (Socialistisk Folkeparti, SF) was not considered ready for office before it had shifted position to become EU positive (Christiansen *et al.* 2014).

Put together, the DF manifestos have not been strongly anti-elitist, but its politicians do utter such statements occasionally. The party now clearly performs according to the parliamentary norms on legislative settlements and state budgets necessary for Danish minority governments to function. EU matters, however, remain an important exception. Thus, the party can only partially be characterised as an anti-establishment party.

Zero-tolerance of extremism with prominent exceptions

The DF was formed with the deliberate aim of breaking with the extreme style of the FrP. The DF did not want what it labelled as 'village loonies' with extreme utterances destroying the image of the party. When lower-ranking members of the DF present extreme or racist statements about immigrants, the party leadership most often reacts swiftly to such remarks by excluding the party members (*Fyens Stiftstidende* 24-06-2014). An example among several others was when the vice chairman of the local organisation in Sorø was excluded in 2012 after condoning violence against immigrants in Greece on her Facebook profile. Unlike the FrP, and most other parties, party rules allow for such exclusions without real possibilities for appeal (see Kosiara-Pedersen 2006). However, from more prominent party members the DF has tolerated extreme remarks. Several examples come from former MEP and current local councillor, Mogens Camre, who has stated that the 'German occupation forces 1940–45 behaved better in the streets than Muslim boys do today' (*Politiko* 28-10-2014). The now deceased MP Jesper Langballe confessed to and was convicted in court to pay a fine for a statement considered racist about 'Muslim uncles raping their nieces' without being excluded from the party (*Politiko* 03-12-2010). The party leader has stated that there is more leeway in these cases due to long service for the party (*Weekendavisen* 08-05-2015). However, in general the party cannot be said to promote or condone extreme or overtly racist utterances. Extremist utterances result in swift expulsion from the party unless they come from experienced and high-ranking party members. Tight leadership control over the party organisation is the key to understand how the party has managed to keep extremists out.

Partial mainstreaming

The DF is still a radical party when it comes to immigrant policies and socio-cultural issues more generally. It has, however, moderated its socioeconomic policies and moved towards the centre or even the centre-left of the socio-economic dimension. Its emphasis on economy and welfare has increased making it less of a niche party. It has retained a few elements of an anti-establishment outlook while sticking to the norms in parliament when it comes to legislative settlements and state budget. The party attempts to avoid extreme utterances from its members by maintaining a tight discipline within a highly centralised party organisation with limited party member democracy. So, there are elements of mainstreaming, but radical elements are upheld concerning core sociocultural policies.

The development of the goals and strategies of the DF

Basic party goals such as office, votes, policy purity and policy influence may often be in a trade-off against each other (see Chapter 1). To assess the dilemmas for a party like the DF for the two first decades of its 'lifecycle', it makes sense to divide its history into three phases where different conditions affect which choices and priorities the party has had to face: the founding phase (until 2001); the support party phase (2001–2011); and the current phase (since 2011). These phases correspond with shifts from a centre-left to a centre-right government and back.

The founding phase 1995–2001

In the first phase, between 1995 and 2001, the party had to get elected into parliament in its own right and remain there. Hence, votes were important. Emphasising its core sociocultural policies in a pure form turned out to be an effective means to achieve that goal. During the early years of the DF, the party very much promoted its agenda of stricter immigration policies, and until after the 1998 election it was quite alone with that issue prominent for many radical right-wing populist parties (Akkerman 2012; Green-Pedersen 2001). Electoral surveys show that the group of voters strongly critical towards immigration consistently constituted 35 to 40 per cent of the electorate between 1994 and 2001 (Nielsen 2003: 340). However, only 11 per cent of the group voted FrP in 1994. Yet DF got this number up to 20 per cent in 1998 and 27 per cent in 2001 (ibid.: 343). Within the strongly critical group there are many workers and voters with low levels of education (ibid.) The DF still polls strongly in these groups as of 2011 (Stubager and Hansen 2013). At this point in history it appears to have been difficult for the DF leadership to 'come across' to the public on other topics than immigration – such as welfare – even when it tried (*Berlingske Tidende* 04-10-1999).

During the 1990s, and in particular after the defeat in the 1998 election, the new chairman of V, Anders Fogh Rasmussen, was more ready than his predecessor to criticise the immigration policies of the centre-left government. According to Green-Pedersen and Krogstrup (2008: 622–623), the promotion of the immigration issue benefited the DF, very much at the expense of the Social Democrats (Socialdemokraterne, SD), thereby increasing the likelihood of a right-wing victory. It could also be said to legitimise the DF in the eyes of the voters.

The DF was founded with the declared aim of seeking influence like a 'normal party'. Challenging the parliamentary norms of the system had kept the FrP away from direct policy influence and reduced the manoeuvrability of the entre-right governments that had look across the centre to reach out for a majority (Green-Pedersen 2001). Contrary to this the DF declared that it was ready to negotiate with the other parties, including the centre-left government, in a realistic manner, also over important topics like the state budget (*Jyllandsposten* 03-10-1999). Despite this intention the party was not included in any important legislative bargaining and settlement until 2001 (Bille 2006: 29). This may partly be explained by policy distance between the centre-left government and the DF, but partly it was also a result of a deliberate decision by the centre-left government at the time not to legitimise the party. In his address to the 1999 opening of the *Folketing*, the Social Democratic Prime Minister, Poul Nyrup Rasmussen made a widely cited remark towards the DF: 'you will never become Salonfähig' (Statsministeriet 1999).[9] Afterwards, the DF was deliberately kept out of negotiations by the government (Bille 2001: 71).

Cooperation with the centre-right government 2001–2011

With V pushing immigration policies on the political agenda, this topic became the single most important issue mentioned in the media during the 2001 election, occupying 42 per cent of the space compared to 14 per cent in 1998 (Van der Brugge and Voss 2003). The share of voters sceptical towards immigration did not change but it may have benefited the electoral fortunes of the DF when more voters decided how to vote with outset in the topic of immigration (Andersen 2003: 148)

In the phase from 2001 until 2011 the DF wanted to prove its parliamentary credibility as a permanent support party for the VK minority coalition government. In the 2001 electoral campaign, the V party leader, Fogh Rasmussen, had not made his intentions clear regarding the DF whereas he was ready to include two smaller centrist parties in government. The electoral result provided the VK-government a majority together with the DF and no need to include any minor centrist party. During its first months in office the support of the DF was still considered somewhat of an experiment, including its first major agreement, which was over the state budget for 2002 (Bille 2006: 23–29). Soon after an efficient working formula became the order of the day. It included support from the DF for the policies included in the coalition agreement of the government in return for policy influence on other topics such as immigration achieved through legislative settlements, state budget settlements, and by including the party at the early stages of preparation of legislation to be presented by the government (Christiansen and Pedersen 2014). In this manner the party was included in almost all legislation, except EU policies that the government agreed upon with other parties.

Now the DF did become part of the legislative settlements (*forlig*), making true its declared dedication. Thereby, the party agreed to informal yet important parliamentary norms in the *Folketing*. The parties involved hold veto powers on changing the agreement, and the parties got privileged access to information from the minister (Christiansen and Pedersen 2014). Hence, taking part in legislative settlement meant both policy influence and legitimisation as a pro-system actor.

The annual negotiations over the state budget became another means in which the DF achieved policy influence. Since the 1980s the passing of the annual state budget has become a forum for political bargaining and exchange of political support between the almost permanent minority governments in Denmark and opposition parties. The resulting agreements have covered many political topics and not only ones properly related to the state budget. Until 2001 they included different parties each year, but between 2001 and 2011 each and every year the VK-government made a major agreement with the DF and only minor supplementary agreements with other parties – still including the DF (Christiansen 2012). The financial spokesperson, Thulesen Dahl, was known for having a close political partnership with the three finance ministers during the period. In addition he was chairman of the Finance Committee of the *Folketing*. This position only holds limited formal powers – the chairman is more of a meeting leader than an actual agenda setter or veto player like in the United States – but to the public the tandem of the finance minister and chairman of the Finance Committee provided a strong image of the inclusion of the DF in the decision-making process. Thulesen Dahl was often filmed carrying around the state budget bill with a huge number of yellow post-its attached to it, likely to be questions and topics for negotiation with the government. Thulesen Dahl has in a newspaper interview described the state budget agreements as one of the most important pathways to policy influence for the DF (*Berlingske Tidende* 02-08-2003). Basically, the DF supported the general economic policies and goals set up by the government in its state budget proposal. In return, the party received concessions, very often of a strong symbolic character, when they bargained over the state budget. Examples include a paycheck for low-income pension receivers or specified amounts for the preservation of national historical and cultural heritage – such as a new roof for Roskilde Cathedral. Furthermore, the parties could also get concessions on non-economic policies such as harsher punishments or stricter immigrant policies. Thus, the state budget negotiations provided a setting for logrolling by the government and the DF (Christiansen and Pedersen 2014).

Since 1993 all of the Danish governments have issued public coalition agreements of increasing length (Christiansen and Pedersen 2014; Damgaard 2000). When Fogh Rasmussen was prime minister from 2001 to 2009, these documents were cornerstones in what he had coined 'contract politics' (Kurrild-Klitgaard 2011). Such promises could be risky in a multiparty system characterised by minority government. Nevertheless, the close cooperation with the DF enabled him to succeed and gave the government a command of policies in parliament unusual in a Danish setting. The government managed to pass major reforms with narrow majorities on local government and the labour market, reducing the role of the trade union movement and thereby corporatism more generally (Klitgaard and Nørgaard 2014). Originally, the DF had demanded influence on the policies of the government in order to support it, but when the VK-government was formed in 2001, it did not include the DF directly in the negotiations. Only a vague understanding seemed to have been reached that the DF would accept the coalition agreement in return for tightening of immigration policies. Neither did the DF take part in negotiating the coalition agreements after the elections in 2005 and 2007 although it did nod to the result. One foot in and one foot out gave the party some freedom to promote its points of view, i.e. retain some policy purity when making statements, albeit limited by the duties as support party. Meanwhile, the government enjoyed high degrees of freedom to pursue its core policies.

Christiansen and Pedersen (2014) compare one electoral period of the VK minority government permanently supported by the DF with periods of minority government without permanent support or with the rare occurrence of majority government.[10] They find that the permanent support party arrangement involved the government getting its policies passed with the support of the DF but also that a higher number of laws were included in legislative settlements – but *not* mentioned in the coalition agreement – than was the case for majority government and, more interestingly, for the minority government without such support. The implication of this is that the DF got compensated through concessions included in legislative settlements. A closer scrutiny of the bills passed points out that for areas such as immigration policies and law and order this pattern is much stronger than previously, and for other policy areas. So, apparently, it got influence on its core topics, and it was all part of major and quite institutionalised logrolls.

DF had influence or power when the centre-right parties did do something they would not otherwise have done by themselves. Whereas the mainstream parties have *not* been ready to openly defy human rights conventions, they have gone further than they probably would have done on their own. The border control mentioned below provides such an example since V had stated it was not their idea, and the party did not want to reinstate them. Non-policy could also be part of it. V did not promote a double citizenship bill while cooperating with DF but has supported such an initiative afterwards. So, to a certain extent, the support party did hold negative agenda-setting power on topics not mentioned in the coalition agreement. This comes close to a veto power.

Especially in the later years of support party status up to 2011, the idea of the party participating in government was also occasionally aired either by members of V or the party itself, including Kjærsgaard. She often stated in the press that the long-term purpose of her close cooperation with the government was not only to gain policy influence, but also to get the party recognised as a normal party, and that government participation would be the culmination of that process (*Politiken* 04-09-2010). Opinion polls suggested however that such a coalition would be a vote loser for the mainstream centre-right parties, and the Prime Minister, Lars Løkke Rasmussen, made it clear once more that the party would not be included in government after an election victory (*Berlingske Tidende* 06-09-2010). So, before 2011 there was still a marked public resistance against the DF joining the government and nothing came of it. Also the topic of the EU was considered an obstacle (Christiansen and Pedersen 2012).

One particular event before the 2011 election deserves further attention because it highlights the ultimate limitation of the cooperation. For some time the DF was hesitant to reduce the coverage of the unemployment scheme from four to two years, and the party also wanted to retain the early retirement scheme, popular among elderly voters with physically hard work. However, in 2011 the party agreed to a bargain shortly before the general election was about to take place. In return the party got permanent border control stations.[11] The 2011 bargain was different in the sense that the prime minister made a public dissolution threat if a bargain was not found over the scheme (Becher and Christiansen forth-coming). So, acceptance from the DF was needed to avoid a break-up of the coalition before the election. A bargain was found. In this situation the DF put loyalty towards its cooperation partners higher than the government did since the latter was ready to distance itself from the DF during an election campaign whereas the DF seemed to have seen an interest in avoiding that. This was the only time during the ten years of cooperation that bargaining with DF took place under an explicit dissolution threat (ibid.). The example also showed the difficulty of the DF main-taining its economic and welfare policies even after almost ten years as a support party. It had become a 'captive' of the government (cf. Bale and Bergman 2006).

To conclude on the phase between 2001 and 2011: the DF did not achieve cabinet seats proper but a semi-governmental position that provided inclusion in most legislation, including economic and welfare policies where it largely followed the line of the government. It got parliamentary recognition by other parties, and also some policy influence vis-à-vis its core sociocultural policy interests. This required compromise, meaning that the party could not pursue policy purity, neither on immigration nor on economic policies. Even though the DF upheld it votes during the general elections, its support role restrained the party from pursuing even more votes.

Preparing for the future? DF in opposition from 2011

In opposition 2011–2015 the DF was much less tied to the other parties of the right wing, and, as mentioned above, the new party leader emphasises economic and welfare policies, taking a centre-left position on these issues. Thereby, he reaches out to many voters with a leftist welfare position and a rightist position on immigrants and crime. Yet the DF has remained firm in its support for the party leader of V as their preferred Prime Minister, and is not yet ready to claim full government participation. It may seem like a paradox but the argument is that V is the party most likely to grant DF policy influence. The party leader of DF has repeatedly pointed at the bad experiences of SF, which was largely considered to have abandoned its policies in order to join the government in 2011 (cf. Christiansen *et al.* 2014) and afterwards lost most of its support in opinion polls before leaving government in 2014, as a reason to stay out of office.

In other words, the party leader does not seem ready to sacrifice policy purity, influence and votes for cabinet office. With increased support in the opinion polls prior to the 2015 election, the possibility of full government participation was debated in the media. In public statements, Thulesen Dahl has been less eager than his predecessor to become a minister himself. In August 2014 the party leader put forward four 'non-negotiable' points on the size of the public sector, immigration, crime, and the EU, as preconditions for government participation. He also stated that he did not expect the other parties to accept these points (dr.dk 06-08-2014). During the election campaign Thulesen Dahl speaks about his party being a 'free bird' 'not as a goal by itself' but 'as a method to achieve greater influence'.

We would like political influence. Then the others can be allowed to achieve a prestigious position.

(Politiken 31-05-2015)

If the DF gets more seats, this should be converted into policy influence:

We have a greater appetite for influence compared to the first 2000 decade. Then we tested the role of support party for the first time. We carry that in our storage now. It is obvious that if we get greater support at the election, then we want more influence.

(Politiken 31-05-2015)

The policy influence should extend to further areas than previously if the DF is once more to permanently support the policies of a prime minister from V.[12]

[Back then] … we accepted to a large degree that EU policies were done with the Social Democrats but now we have greater interest in affecting this.

(Politiken 31-05-2015)

Opinion polls before the 2015 election showed that 55 per cent of the electorate thought the party should join the government in the case of a right-wing victory, and that number includes 69 per cent of the DF electorate (*Politiken* 31-05-2015). On the first day of the election campaign the party leader of V, former PM Løkke Rasmussen, opened the possibility for government participation of all parties that could find agreements on policies, and he wanted compromise on important issues of public growth and unemployment benefits. However, on the next day, his deputy leader specified that any party joining a government should actively support a 'yes' vote in the referendum planned on revising one of the Danish opt-outs on judicial cooperation within the EU. The pro-EU parties have agreed to a referendum, and emphasised that this agreement is valid also after the election in 2015. This agreement excludes the EU-sceptical parties such as the DF and leaves much less leeway in policy negotiation on this topic for government formation after the election. In the government negotiations after the 2015 election DF largely stuck to the demands stated above that it had presented prior to the election. The party was blamed in public and by leaders of other parties for its reluctance to take office despite its strong result. Negotiations appeared to break apart on whether to challenge the Schengen Agreement, i.e. over the EU issue.

The centre-left government from 2011 to 2015 negotiated with the DF just like with any other party but the DF did not compromise with the government on welfare without V also taking part. At the invitation of the leader of the SF the two parties have developed a cooperation on welfare topics, and most prominently an agreement in May 2015 on one of the main topics of the electoral campaign to support easier access to the unemployment benefit system (*Politiko* 24-05-2014; *Jyllandsposten* 30-05-2015). This goes against the wishes of V and also puts the DF to the left of the government on this important issue during the electoral campaign. When the DF is no longer anathema to a leftist party such as SF, it has indeed become 'Salonfähig' in the eyes of the other parties despite policy agreements on a number of topics.

Put together, all of this indicates that the party remains reluctant to pursue cabinet office even with support from more than 20 per cent of the voters, but also that the party is ready to seek policy influence on a broader range of topics, primarily economy, welfare, and the European Union, than was previously the case. This reluctance to pursue full cabinet office must be understood as a fear of losing votes as happened to the SF in Denmark or the Norwegian Progress Party (Fremskrittspartiet, FrP). The result of the 2015 election is that the DF has been content with a semi-office position, supporting a minority government of V.

Conclusion

At its outset the stated goal of the DF was basically to keep the policies of the FrP that it broke away from, but to change the strategy to seek policy influence and become a normal party accepted by the other political parties. Thus, it wanted to mainstream its style while maintaining its radical policies. Two decades later the party has largely succeeded in reaching these goals and at the same time obtained consistent support from more than 10 per cent of the electorate; not least during the years as a support party for the VK minority government between 2001 and 2011 when the party participated in a huge number of political settlements and state budgets. The party remained loyal towards its partners, it got recognised as a 'normal party'. The party does have elements of anti-elitism in its public discourse though, and while it swiftly expels ordinary members for extreme or racist utterings, there are exceptions for higher-ranking and experienced members. In its first year, the DF strongly emphasised sociocultural issues like immigration, crime and the European Union, and was thereby somewhat of a niche party. This is much less the case now with the party addressing economic policies and welfare policies much more often. The DF has largely kept its positions of scepticism towards immigrants and the EU, and advocates stricter punishments for crime. However, the party has moved its economic and welfare policies from the right – as inherited from the FrP – to the centre, and lately also, centre-left. So, on the three indicators of mainstreaming – radicalism, niche and anti-establishment – the party has moved on all of them, albeit the least so concerning sociocultural policies and the EU.

Vote maximisation and policy influence appear to be major concerns for this long-term strategy and also for its reluctance to get cabinet seats. The party did find a group of voters unhappy with what they considered to be too liberal immigrant policies. In particular, there is a major group of voters – around 30 per cent – with a low level of education as one of its characteristics – with right-wing views on value politics and left-wing views on economy and welfare (Borre 2003). This is the position the DF has now found and with a more equal emphasis on both topics than previously.

Especially from 2001 onwards the DF managed to move voters from the left wing over to the right wing. This was an important reason for ten years of permanent majority in the Danish parliament – the longest period ever in Danish history. It had a major impact on public policies being passed. At the same time the DF was until 2011 still proving to the government that it was able to remain a loyal party. Some might even claim that it was not too influential on actual legislation. It makes sense to state that the VK minority government largely managed to get its economic policies through, and also that they did not go much further in their compromises with the DF than they would otherwise have been ready to accept. On the other hand, the DF did get concessions through legislative and state budget settlements on issues of interest for it. The party has also affected the topics of public discourse making it more focused and polarised, not least around issues of immigration and the EU. More research is needed on this type of impact of the DF but mainstream parties in Denmark are now reported massively to have adapted to 'welfare chauvinism' (Schumacher and Van Kersbergen forthcoming).

The DF itself explains its reluctance to join a government by the likelihood of getting more policy influence from outside. Experiences from other radical right-wing populist parties as well as from the SF in Denmark in 2011, also point to the risk of losing votes as a result of office-seeking. The party had success between 2001 and 2011 with one foot in and one foot out, and now wants to extend its areas of influence if possible after the election in June 2015.

The rise and mainstreaming of the DF may have had an impact on democracy broadly conceived. The party attracts a group of voters who might otherwise be dissatisfied with politics and the system more generally, but they have now found a voice inside the system able to seek actual policy influence. This could be one explanation why electoral turnout remains high in Denmark. Thereby, the DF could be said to integrate voters into the democratic system. Nevertheless, the organisation of the DF is highly centralised and party members enjoy fewer rights than those of other party organisations. They cannot prevent coalition building or mainstreaming, and they hardly affect party policy (Kosiara-Pedersen 2006). Kjærsgaard has often defended top leadership by referring to the FrP stating 'that the alternative is too frightening' (*Berlingske Tidende* 27-05-2000). An organisation with limited party democracy would have been unlikely to have success during the age of mass parties when member support was essential but as of 2014 the DF has about 14,500 members according to its own numbers (Dansk Folkeparti 2014). The party does find it important to have member support at local level (Kosiara-Pedersen 2006). The absence of members making racist or other errant remarks and strict discipline of the parliamentary group has most likely been a necessary condition for the mainstreaming of the DF to succeed and to be trustworthy in negotiations with other parties in order to gain policy influence. However, by the very limited internal party democracy, the DF differentiates itself from traditional democratic mainstream parties.

The DF represents an example of an electorally successful radical right-wing populist party that has managed to become a mainstream pro-system party achieving actual policy influence on its core sociocultural policies which remain radical. The DF has succeeded in becoming mainstream in style while maintaining to some extent the radical core of some of its most important policies just like it intended.

Notes

1 Ms Kjærsgaard was elected Speaker of Parliament after the 2015 election.
2 The study builds on existing literature as well as party manifestos and newspaper interviews and stories.
3 The DF wants an annual growth rate of 0.8 per cent in the public sector, which is more than the centre-left government. The centre-right parties V and K advocate zero growth. However, at the 2011 election, the present government parties argued for 1.4 per cent and V, K and DF 0.8 per cent (*Jyllandsposten* 07-10-2014). Like in the citation, the party has often pointed out in public debate that it is the other parties that have moved to the right while the DF has remained steady.
4 Furthermore, the party has recruited intellectual supporters and candidates from a Lutheran protestant network around a journal named Tidehverv (meaning 'turn of times') which represents a minor but theologically influential wing within the Danish National Church. Tidehverv dates back to the 1920s and was originally against 'sentimental' religious appeals but had turned political during the 1970s and 1980s adopting a mixture of nationalist and conservative positions.
5 References searched on the newspaper database Infomedia.
6 The logic is that state expenditures are primarily set by law and therefore the result of settled battles that should not be taken up again. This also secures the smooth operation of the state.
7 From readings in parliament found on www.ft.dk.
8 Such laws constituted about 14 per cent of the laws throughout 1998–2012.
9 The term is *stueren*, which also means 'house-trained'. It was a response to a proposal from Kjærsgaard at its previous annual party congress that parents and grandparents of non-Danish criminals should be expelled from Denmark and not just the criminal him- or herself.
10 The most recent one was from 1993 to 1994 and the previous one from 1968 to 1971.
11 These were removed again shortly after the election by the new government. They may have been against the Schengen Agreement.
12 In Denmark minority government means that the parties sustaining a government in office do not necessarily supports its policy initiatives.

References

Akkerman, T. (2012) 'Comparing radical right parties in government: Immigration and integration policies in nine countries (1996–2010)', *West European Politics* 35, 3: 511–529.
Andersen, J. G. (2003) 'Vælgernes nye politiske dagsorden', in Andersen, J. G. and Borre, O. (eds) *Politisk Forandring. Værdipolitik og Nye Skillelinjer ved Folketingsvalget 2001*, Århus: Systime, pp. 135–149.

Andersen, J. G. (2007) 'Samfundskonflikter, partier i bevægelse og vælgere med omtanke: Rids af en teoretisk ramme', in Andersen, J. G., Andersen, J., Borre, O., Møller Hansen, K. and Nielsen, H. J. (eds) *Det Nye Politiske Landskab. Folketingsvalget 2005 i Perspektiv*, Århus: Academica, pp. 11–55.

Bale, T. and Bergman, T. (2006) 'Captives no longer, but servants still? Contract parliamentarism and the new minority governance in Sweden and New Zealand', *Government and Opposition* 41, 3: 422–449.

Becher, M. and Christiansen, F. J. (forthcoming) 'Early elections and legislative bargaining in a parliamentary democracy', *American Journal of Political Science*.

Berlingske Tidende (04-10-1999) 'Ro i den rød-hvide lejr'.

Berlingske Tidende (27-05-2000) 'Medlemsflugt fra Pia'.

Berlingske Tidende (02-08-2003) 'Sommergruppemøde: DF: Vi har maksimal indflydelse'.

Berlingske Tidende (06-09-2010) 'Løkke holder døren for DF lukket'.

Bille, L. (1989) 'Denmark: The oscillating party system', *West European Politics* 12, 4: 42–58.

Bille, L. (1998) *Dansk Partipolitik 1987–1998*, København: Jurist- og Økonomforbundets Forlag.

Bille, L. (2001) *Fra Valgkamp til Valgkamp: Dansk Partipolitik 1998–2001*, København: Jurist- og Økonomforbundets Forlag.

Bille, L. (2006) *Det Nye Flertal: Dansk Partipolitik 2001–2005*, København: Jurist- og Økonomforbundets Forlag.

Borre, O. (2003) 'To konfliktdimensioner', in Andersen, J. G. and Borre, O. (eds) *Politisk Forandring: Værdipolitik og Nye Skillelinjer ved Folketingsvalget 2001*, Århus: Systime, pp. 171–186.

Christiansen, F. J. (2012) 'Raising the stakes: Passing state budgets in Scandinavia', *World Political Science Review* 8, 1: 184–200.

Christiansen, F. J. and Pedersen, H. H. (2014) 'Minority coalition governance in Denmark', *Party Politics*, 20, 6: 940–949.

Christiansen, F. J. and Pedersen, R. B. (2012) 'The impact of EU in a minority system: The case of Denmark', *Scandinavian Political Studies* 35, 3: 179–197.

Christiansen, F. J., Nielsen, R. L. and Pedersen, R. B. (2014) 'Friendship, courtesy and engagement: Pre-electoral coalition dynamics in action', *Journal of Legislative Studies* 20, 4: 413–429.

Damgaard, E. (2000) 'Denmark: The life and death of government coalitions', in Müller, W. C. and Strøm, K. (eds) *Coalition Governments in Western Europe*, Oxford: Oxford University Press, pp. 231–264.

Dansk Folkeparti (1997) 'Principprogram', København: Dansk Folkeparti.

Dansk Folkeparti (2001) 'Fælles værdier – fælles ansvar. Arbejdsprogram for Dansk Folkeparti', København: Dansk Folkeparti.

Dansk Folkeparty (2002) 'Principprogram', København: Dansk Folkeparti.

Dansk Folkeparti (2009) 'Dansk Folkepartis arbejdsprogram', København: Dansk Folkeparti.

Dansk Folkeparti (2014) 'Årsmødeberetning 2014. Dansk Folkepartis 19. Årsmøde', www.danskfolkeparti.dk/pictures_org/Beretning_%C3%A5rsm%C3%B8de.pdf.

De Lange, S. L. (2007) 'A new winning formula? The programmatic appeal of the radical right', *Party Politics* 13, 4: 411–435.

Dr.dk (06-08-2014) 'Dansk Folkeparti har fire krav for at gå i regering', www.dr.dk/Nyheder/Politik/2014/08/06/090043.htm.

Dr.dk (05-04-2015) 'DF foreslår markant stramning af regler for familiesammenføring', www.dr.dk/Nyheder/Politik/2015/04/04/04222147.htm.

Dr.dk (02-05-2015) 'Thulesen Dahl: Jeg ligger til venstre for Helle Thorning', www.dr.dk/nyheder/politik/2015/05/01/211314.htm.

Fyens Stiftstidende (24-06-2014) 'Klap i eller skrup af'.

Green-Pedersen, Ch. (2001) 'Minority government and party politics: The political and institutional background to the "Danish miracle", *Journal of Public Policy* 21, 1: 53–70.

Green-Pedersen, Ch. and Krogstrup, J. (2008) 'Immigration as a political issue in Denmark and Sweden', *European Journal of Political Research* 47, 5: 610–634.

Jyllandsposten (03-10-1999) 'Dansk Folkeparti vil med i finanslovsforliget'.

Jyllandsposten (07-10-2014) 'Politisk overblik. Sådan forholder partierne sig til de temaer, som vil præge de kommende måders valgkamp'.

Jyllandsposten (30-05-2015) 'SF og DF indgår alliance om dagpenge'.

Kjærsgaard, P. (2005) *De har deres på det tørre*, http://danskfolkeparti.dk/Pia_Kj%C3%A6rsgaard_De_har_deres_p%C3%A5_det_t%C3%B8rre%E2%80%A6_3821_171.

Klitgaard, M. B. and Nørgaard, A. S. (2014) 'Structural stress or deliberate decision? Government partisanship and the disempowerment of unions in Denmark', *European Journal of Political Research* 53, 2: 404–421.

Kosiara-Pedersen, K. (2006) *Driving a Populist Party: The Danish People's Party*, København: Institut for Statskundskab.

Kurrild-Klitgaard, P. (2011) 'Kontraktpolitik, kulturkamp og ideologi 2001–2011', *Økonomi og Politik* 84, 3: 47–62.

Nielsen, H. J. (2003) 'Indvandrere og indvandringspolitik', in Andersen, J. G. and Borre, O. (eds) *Politisk Forandring: Værdipolitik og Nye Skillelinjer ved Folketingsvalget 2001*, Århus: Systime, pp. 324–345.

Politiken (18-09-1994) 'Partiet, der kom ind i varmen – næsten'.

Politiken (04-09-2010) 'Pia K.: Løkke skal sige ja til DF i regering'.

Politiken (11-06-2014) 'Måling: Thorning og Løkke halter bagefter på troværdigheden'.

Politiken (31-05-2015) 'Hvis Løkke står fast på velfærd og EU, vil Thulesen være en fri fugl'.

Politiko (03-12-2010) 'Langballe dømt for racisme'.

Politiko (24-05-2014) 'SF-formand klar til samarbejde med Dansk Folkeparti'.

Politiko (28-10-2014) 'Her er 30 af Camres mest ekstreme udtalelser'.

Ringsmose, J. (2003) *Kedeligt Har det i Hvert Fald ikke Været: Fremskridtspartiet 1989–1995*, Odense: Syddansk Universitetsforlag.

Rydgren, J. (2004) 'Explaining the emergence of radical right wing populist parties. The case of Denmark', *West European Politics* 27, 3: 474–502.

Schumacher, G. and van Kersbergen, K. (forthcoming) 'Do mainstream parties adapt to the welfare chauvinism of populist parties', *Party Politics*.

Statsministeriet (1999) 'Statsminister Poul Nyrup Rasmussens replik ved åbningsdebatten i Folketinget 7. oktober 1999', www.stm.dk/_p_7628.html.

Stubager, R. and Møller Hansen, K. (2013) 'Social baggrund og partivalg', in Stubager, R., Møller Hansen, K. and Andersen, J. G. (eds) *Krisevalg: Økonomien og Folketingsvalget 2011*, København: Jurist- og Økonomforbundets Forlag, pp. 61–88.

Stubager, R., Møller Hansen, K. and Andersen, J. G. (2013) 'It's the economy, stupid!', in Stubager, R., Møller Hansen, K. and Andersen, J. G. (eds) *Krisevalg: Økonomien og Folketingsvalget 2011*, København: Jurist- og Økonomforbundets Forlag, pp. 15–44.

Van der Brugge, J. and Voss, H. (2003) 'Mediernes dagsorden', in Andersen, J. O. and Borre, O. (eds) *Politisk Forandring: Værdipolitik og Nye Skillelinjer ved Folketingsvalget 2001*, Århus: Systime, pp. 119–134.

Weekendavisen (08-05-2015) 'En håndsrækning til muslimerne'.

6 From the mainstream to the margin?

The radicalisation of the True Finns

Ann-Cathrine Jungar

Introduction

The True Finns (Perussuomalaiset, PS) made Finnish political history by five-folding the electoral support to 19 per cent in the parliamentary election of 2011. Never before has a political party witnessed such a vote increase between two consecutive elections. The PS were formed in 1995 as a successor party to the first postwar populist political party in Finland, the Finnish Rural Party (Suomen maaseudun puolue, FrP) (Arter 2012).[1] The PS was both organisationally and personally built upon the structures of the FrP. Whereas the FrP was defined as an agrarian populist party, the PS has been claimed to be 'populist par excellence' (Wiberg 2011), to represent the 'new radical right' (Pekonen 1999) and to be a member of the radical right populist party family (Jungar and Jupskås 2014). The radicalisation and transformation of PS has not impeded access to government. The transformation of PS to a radical right-wing populist party did not come about immediately with its formation in 1995, but the party has radicalised during the last decade. PS still cultivates some elements of its origin in agrarian populism speaking for the deprived ordinary people, and particularly the rural population, but has increasingly targeted groups – pensioners, unemployed and the sick – who have been under pressure with the weakening of the Finnish welfare state after the economic crises in the 1990s and post-2008 (Arter 2010). Moreover, PS is contrary to the predecessor party opposed to the European Union: its EU-scepticism gained further momentum with the euro-crisis and the post-2008 European economic recession. The party has strengthened its anti-immigration and anti-multiculturalism appeals, and increasingly criticised the rights of the Swedish-speaking minority in Finland.

The electoral results were modest until 2007, when the PS received 4.1 per cent of the vote in the parliamentary election (see Table 6.1). The vote started growing in the European Parliamentary elections of 2009 when the PS support doubled to 9.8 per cent compared to the national outcome in 2007. In the 2011 parliamentary election the party almost quintupled its vote share to 19.1 per cent. The PS took part in the preliminary governmental negotiations after these breakthrough elections, but abstained from joining government as that would have meant accepting the EU bailouts to Greece and Portugal, which

Table 6.1 Election results for the True Finns in national, local and EP elections 1999–2015

National elections		Local elections		European parliamentary elections	
1999	0.99% (1 mandate)	2000	0.66% (109 mandates)	1996	0.67% (0 mandates)
2003	1.57% (3 mandates)	2004	0.90% (106 mandates)	1999	0.79% (0 mandates)
2007	4.05% (5 mandates)	2008	5.39% (443 mandates)	2004	0.54% (0 mandates)
2011	19.05% (39 mandates)	2012	12.34% (1,195 mandates)	2009	9.79% (1 mandate)
2015	17.7% (38 mandates)			2014	12.9% (2 mandates)

the party had vociferously campaigned against. Even though the vote of PS diminished to 17.7 per cent in the 2015 parliamentary election the party leader Timo Soini did not hesitate to claim the result as a second '*jytky*' (great victory) following that of 2011, and as a sign of continued consolidation.

The PS support has grown in the municipal assemblies and has expanded organisationally as well. In 2012 there were 300 local branches, which are divided into 16 districts (Interview Marja-Leena Leppänen). The PS have contrary to the predecessor party FRP a national presence with representation in all electoral districts, the urban areas included. That is, the party has an organisation with national coverage. The PS membership has fourfolded since 1995: the party had 2,000 members in 1995, 2,700 in 2000, 5,000 in 2011 and 8,000 members in 2013 (Suomen vaalitutkimusportaali 2011; *Turun Sanomat* 15-04-2013). The PS received their first seat in the European parliament in 2009, and in the 2014 elections the party obtained two seats with 12.9 per cent of the vote. The PS were a member of the Europe of Freedom and Democracy (EFD) group between 2009 and 2014, and joined together with the Danish People's Party (Dansk Folkeparti, DF) the Europe of Conservatives and Reformists (ECR) group in 2014. The PS have established international contacts both within the European Parliament and bilaterally with the DF and the United Kingdom Independence Party (UKIP). During the electoral campaign of the parliamentary election of 2015 the first public meeting between the Sweden Democrats (Sverigedemokraterna, SD) and the PS took place (*Suomen Uutiset* 17-04-2015).

In this chapter the transformation of a populist party with agrarian roots to a radical right populist party is analysed. The radicalisation has gone hand in hand with the achievement of fundamental party goals like vote-seeking and office-seeking: PS has experienced electoral success due to its radicalisation, and despite this maintained governmental credibility among the other political parties. After the parliamentary elections of 2015 the PS became a member of government. The trade-offs between various party goals have so far been marginal, but with the recent entrance in government the party leadership has made preparations for possible costs in terms of policy compromises and above all, party cohesion. The chapter follows the template for analysing mainstreaming that has been formulated in Chapter 1. In the second and third parts the party strategies of the PS and the conditions that have influenced the behaviour of the party are accounted for. The contextual factors, in particular the political opportunity structures that have rendered it possible for a radicalising party to grow electorally and obtain office are identified. The chapter is based on various sources: official party documentation (party programmes, electoral manifestos, party journals), blogs, statements from party representatives, news information and personal interviews.

Populist legacies in Finland

Populism has an almost uninterrupted presence in the Finnish political system since Finland became an independent state in 1917 (Jungar 2015). Already in the 1920s anti-establishment appeals resonated in radical agrarian movements and political parties. Finnish populism manifests continuity as to its core ideas: the anti-establishment position, the rhetorical construction of a united, virtuous and threatened 'people' and promises of the restoration of popular sovereignty (Canovan 1999; Mudde 2007; Stanley 2008). These ideas have at irregular intervals been skilfully contextualised for political mobilisation and paved the way for electoral successes. In 1959 the Finnish Rural Smallholders' party (Suomen pientalouspoikien puolue, FrP) was formed as a splinter party from the Agrarian Union (Maaseudun Liitto, ML). The FrP was unsuccessful in its first parliamentary election in 1962, but in 1966 the party took its first parliamentary seat. The charismatic party leader and founder Veikko Vennamo presented himself as the spokesperson for the disaffected small farmers and the party has therefore been characterised as an 'agrarian populist party' (Sänkiaho 1971; Fryklund and Peterson 1981). The FrP defended the interests and the values of small rural holders, entrepreneurs and the rural population in the on-going process of rapid urbanisation and modernisation and spoke in favour of traditional (Christian) values that were perceived to be under threat. It was fiercely anti-communist, and critical of the 'subservient' Finnish foreign policy towards the Soviet Union, which in addition to its strong anti-establishment appeals, rendered it a party with no governmental potential. Commitment to the official foreign policy of 'friendship, cooperation and mutual cooperation' with the Soviet Union was a precondition for government participation (Jungar 2002).

The electoral breakthrough of the FRP came in the parliamentary elections of 1970. The party received 10.5 per cent of the vote (see Figure 6.1). Transformations in the opportunity structures paved the way for its electoral success. In 1966 a broad surplus majority government was formed that included – for the first time since 1948 – the Finnish Communist Party (Suomen Kansan Demokraattinen Liitto, SKDL). This party had a substantial following in the countryside in northern Finland, but as a party of government, it was no longer perceived as a credible protest party and a substantial number of its voters defected to FrP (Sänkiaho 1971: 35). After the general election of 1970, the party stabilised as a '5–10 per cent party' until it collapsed in the 1995 election leaving it with a public support of 1.3 per cent and only one MP (see Figure 6.1). The FrP was the first Nordic populist party to participate in government. When the longstanding president Kekkonen resigned in 1981 and the Soviet Union no longer accused the FrP of being extreme right or fascist, the party was invited to take part in government between 1983 and 1990. As a matter of fact, fascist parties were forbidden in Finland in the Peace Treaty that was signed with the Soviet Union after the Second World War. Assuming governmental responsibility was thus the beginning of the decline of the party. The decreasing electoral support in the 1990s was also due to internal conflicts. After the devastating electoral result in 1995 the deteriorating financial situation forced the party leadership to declare the party bankrupt.

Mainstreaming

In line with the general framework of this volume radical right populist parties are identified as simultaneously radical, niche and anti-establishment political parties (see Introduction). When the development of the PS is analysed along these dimensions a picture emerges of a mainstream political party that has become more radical. In other words, the party has moved further away from the mainstream by assuming more extreme policy positions on both immigration and European integration. The PS can from this point of view be compared with the Swiss People's Party (Schweizerische Volkspartei, SVP) which started radicalising in the late 1990s and from 2003 can be classified as a radical right-wing populist party. The SVP was also originally an agrarian party that gained

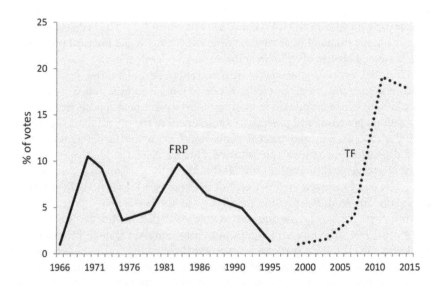

Figure 6.1 Electoral support in the parliamentary elections for the Finnish Rural Party
(FrP) and the True Finns (PS) 1966–2015

electoral success after radicalisation (Albertazzi 2008: 304–305; Art 2011). The PS are more radical than the predecessor party FrP: whereas anti-immigration and anti-EU positions were absent in the FrP they are salient and radical in the PS. The PS have constantly held a centre-left socioeconomic placement in the Finnish political system, but have expanded their appeal on the sociocultural dimension. The anti-establishment appeals are intact, and the party leadership has not distanced itself from extreme representatives and groups that have made racist statements or committed hate-speech. In the following the PS are analysed in greater detail along these four dimensions. The time period is from 1995 until present.

The radicalisation of a populist agrarian party

The PS have maintained quite a stable socioeconomic centrist location in the Finnish political system, but after 2003 gradually radicalised on the liberal-authoritarian dimension (see Figure 6.2, and the following section). The historic origin in agrarian populism with a social profile was largely imprinted on the programmatic profile of the PS during the first years:

> Inspired by a Christian-social base, the aim of the party is to bring together groups whose interests and social and economic equality have not been fairly taken care of. These are the families with children, pensioners, small- and family entrepreneurs, as well independent labourers, low wage-earners, civil servants, students and rural and forestal entrepreneurs.
>
> (Perussuomalaiset 1995)

The first party platform of the reformed party echoed both the socioeconomic concerns and value-conservatism of the FrP. From this follows that the PS *cannot* be characterised as a radical right-wing populist party from the outset (see Figure 6.3). The transformation has unfolded gradually and gained momentum particularly after 2003. The two issue areas where the greatest changes have taken place are immigration and European integration.

Compared to the other Nordic countries, immigration to Finland has been low. In 1995, 2 per cent of the population was foreign born, 3.5 per cent in 2005 and 5.8 per cent in 2015. Immigration has increased since 2005 and by now the Russians, Estonians and Somalis are the largest immigrant groups (*Tilastokeskus* 2014: 115–116). The Somalis are particularly discriminated against in Finland (European Union Agency for Fundamental Rights 2009: 35, 265–66). The radicalisation of the PS's anti-immigration rhetoric goes hand in hand with this development. The PS want to restrict immigration that has negative economic and cultural consequences (Perussuomalaiset 2011). In the 2015 electoral manifesto it was explicitly spelled out that immigration that is a burden on the public economy and the welfare state, or is related to religious extremism should be prevented. In a report published by the PS think tank Suomen Perusta in 2015

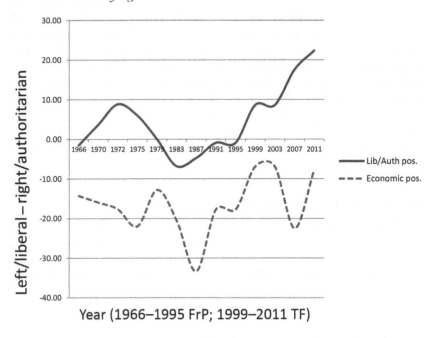

Figure 6.2 FrP and PS policy change on the socioeconomic left-right and liberal-authoritarian dimensions between 1966–2011

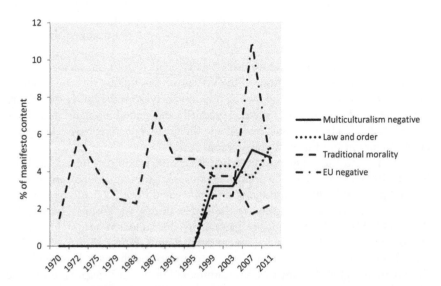

Figure 6.3 FP and PS manifesto content on four policy categories: multiculturalism, law and order, traditional morality, and the EU, 1970–2011

the costs and contributions of different immigrant groups were calculated. It was concluded that immigration that benefits Finland, that is primarily labour immigration, should be supported (Salminen 2015). The number of asylum seekers should be reduced to the figures of the 1990s, and the PS demand stricter immigration policies for family reunification in particular, and immigration in general. The demographic challenge should according to the PS not be solved by immigration, but by family policies supporting Finnish young people to form families and have more babies.

With regard to integration the PS initially voiced reciprocity and multicultural respect. These have now been replaced with one-sided assimilation and nativist appeals. In PS's first party programme of 1995 it was stated that:

> We welcome foreigners to build their lives here, but not to destroy our nation. They have to accept our society and legal system like we in our turn accept their culture and life-styles and give them the right to live with us as equal citizens.
>
> (Perussuomalaiset 1995)

That is, assimilation was conceived of as a reciprocal process and formulated as 'respect for the Finnish society and culture ... *like we respect their culture*' (Perussuomalaiset 1995, *italics added by the author*). However, the PS's integration policies radicalised gradually from 2003 onwards: in the 2003 electoral manifesto it is claimed that the peripheral location of Finland has been profitable in a world characterised by overpopulation and racial problems. This experience does not imply that Finland should close the borders entirely, but Finland should be sovereign to decide how many and which immigrants and refugees are welcomed. Therefore, international commitments should be resisted. Cultural practices that are alien to Finland – circumcision, child marriage and honorary culture – should be banned, and stricter demands on assimilation should be required from the immigrants (Perussuomalaiset 2003). This transformation coincides not accidentally with the recruitment of the former professional show-boxer and television celebrity Tony Halme as a parliamentary candidate to the PS for the 2003 parliamentary election. He personalised the radicalisation of both the anti-immigration and anti-EU position of the PS. In the 2003 parliamentary elections he received almost 17,000 personal votes and was nationally the fifth most popular parliamentary candidate. He profiled himself with anti-establishment and general provocative appeals, as well as with xenophobic and welfare-chauvinist statements. He said, for example, that Finnish citizens should be prioritised before immigrants, who were portrayed as receiving more social benefits than the titular population, and that foreign criminals and Islamic terrorists should be expelled (Hannula 2011: 37). However, Halme was with his street-level rhetorics, and as an alcohol- and drug-addict not the appropriate person to pursue the PS's transformation in a radical direction, but he paved the way for a more fully fledged transformation by revealing the existing electoral opportunity structure of anti-immigration mobilisation (Hänninen and Hänninen 2010: 59). During this period the PS increasingly attracted sympathisers and activists from national organisations and anti-immigration web-communities that considered the PS as a platform for influencing policies. Fenno-nationalism and nativism, including anti-Islam positions, have become more prevalent in the party's public documents. In addition to the sociocultural arguments against immigration, economic ones reflecting welfare-chauvinist positions became more frequent. In the 2007 electoral manifesto, for instance, the 'problem of *multiculturalism*' is formulated for the first time, and the message 'When in Rome do as the Romans' ('*maassa maan tavalla*') becomes a key expression. Public support for 'foreign' cultures and language-education were perceived as threats to Finnish culture and language. As formulated in the manifesto:

> It is not reasonable to have a system as the present one: you come to Finland to spend some time here, you look for your fortune and simultaneously the public administration by force tries to preserve the culture of the immigrants. To preserve the culture is the business of the immigrants, and state funding should not be used for that … Multiculturalism should not be cherished by neglecting our own culture.
>
> (Perussuomalaiset 2007)

According to the PS the Swedish approach that allows immigrant communities to constitute their own cultures within the titular culture, which subsequently is threatened, is a warning. In the 2011 electoral manifesto the section on immigration was further expanded and dressed in an even more outright nativist rhetoric as immigration was portrayed as a threat to the Finnish culture:

> Love for the fatherland and Finnishness unite people over social classes, income, education, party-political disagreement and other convictions … . The basis for our immigration policy is that the Finns themselves always have the right to decide on what condition foreigners can come and reside in our country.
>
> (Perussuomalaiset 2011)

In 2010 a group of nationalist minded activists, among which the publicly well-known anti-immigration and anti-Islam personality Jussi Halla-aho and several parliamentarians of the PS came together and wrote an immigration-critical manifest, the so-called *Nuiva Manifesti* – which was included in the PS electoral manifesto of 2010 (Nuiva Manifesti Maahanmuuttokriittinen manifesti 2010). The nationalist ethos is echoed in the call to protect Finnish culture and people, and the idea that the nation and the state should coincide. A common national identity is believed to strengthen the spirit of community, which is the basis of the societal contract, and the PS presents itself as a party of the Fennoman movement by stating that:

We want to protect Finnishness and develop it further. We want an unique culture, that not only enriches the proper people but the whole world, to thrive in our country.

(Perussuomalaiset 2011)

Nationalism also includes the protection of popular sovereignty, which means that 'only the people who constitute a separate unity have an eternal and unrestricted right to freely decide their own matters' (Perussuomalaiset 2011).

EU-scepticism

The PS were from the outset sceptical towards the EU. After a popular referendum in 1994 Finland became a full member state in the EU. The same year PS was formed out of the ashes of the FrP. Contrary to the FrP's favourable view of European integration, the PS have been ambivalent about it (Perussuomalaiset 1995). In concrete terms the PS proclaimed that Finland should not contribute to a federal development of the EU, but that intergovernmental cooperation should be the backbone of the European organisation. However, with the subsequent Amsterdam, Nice and Lisbon treaty reforms, and the enlargements of 2004 and 2007, EU-scepticism turned into a more salient issue. The European Union was a divisive political issue in Finland between 1994 and 2000, that is from the referendum on membership of the EU until joining the European Monetary Union in 1999. The division between EU-sceptical and EU-positive voters that had become manifest at the referendum remained but between the established political parties a consensus was developed after 2000: Finland should pursue pragmatic EU politics aimed at maximising influence (Raunio 2008). Moreover, the EU-sceptical parties the Greens (Vihreä Liitto, VIHR) and the Left Wing Alliance (Vasemmistoliitto, VAS) took part in the government that brought Finland into the EMU (Jungar 2002). However, with the European economic recession making itself more present in 2008, the gap between the EU-sceptical voters and a political elite more favourable to the European integration project became more evident. The PS successfully mobilised voters disappointed with the introduction of the euro since the 2000 parliamentary election, and in the 2011 elections the EU bailouts were timely targets in the PS parliamentary campaign (Borg 2012; Pernaa and Railo 2012). The PS can be characterised as a soft EU-sceptical party as it has not advocated the immediate withdrawal of Finland from the EU, but has made appeals for moderate reforms of the European integration process (Szczerbiak and Taggart 2008). The PS have advocated that Finland should withdraw from the EMU, and renegotiate its terms of membership, and that a referendum should be held thereafter. However, the PS backed away from a Finnish withdrawal at the party congress of 2013. The EU-criticism has become more salient in both anti-establishment rhetorics and nationalist ideas. The EU is conceived of as an elite project; and Soini frequently applies anti-establishment appeals in relation to the European economic crisis:

At the risk of being accused of populism, we'll begin with the obvious: It is not the little guy who benefits. He is being milked and lied to in order to keep the insolvent system running. He is paid less and taxed more to provide the money needed to keep this Ponzi scheme going. Meanwhile, a symbiosis has developed between politicians and banks: Our political leaders borrow ever more money to pay off the banks, which return the favor by lending ever more money back to our governments.

(Wall Street Journal 09-05-2011)

The PS oppose both further vertical and horizontal European integration. The party compares a federal EU to the undemocratic Soviet Union:

We protest against the development of the EU to a federal state, and if this development speeds up, we will demand that Finland leaves the EU, because the EU is as an idea as well as in practice an equally undemocratic project as the Soviet Union.

(Perussuomalaiset 2007)

The PS oppose in particular measures aimed at developing common EU taxes, economic redistribution between the EU member states and the further development of an EU social dimension. The EU should be a loose cooperation between independent member states. The EU is blamed for increasing economic inequality, the deprivation of the countryside and the welfare state. According to the PS the enlargement of the EU has reduced Finlands's relative influence in the EU, as well as increased the membership fee (Perussuomalaiset 2007). The PS have consequently politicised the EU in the previously quite consensual EU-policy-making. The PS's loud opposition to the bailouts is part of the explanation why the Finnish government required special guarantees, and has taken quite a reluctant position in the EU on economic support to Greece and other member states in crisis. The PS's decision not to take part in the governmental negotiations after the 2011 parliamentary election was due to the unwillingness of the party to compromise its EU-policies, on which the electoral gains in these elections largely depended. However, the PS have moderated their position on the euro and no longer demand a Finnish withdrawal. The party now formulates its EU stance alongside the UK and Dutch governments of a 'lighter and looser union' (Perussuomalaiset 2014). This transformation is related to the attainment of governmental office after the parliamentary election of 2015.

The radicalisation of the PS has come about by the inclusion of nationalist-minded anti-immigration and Islamophobic groups that previously have resided in civil society organisations or web communities (Koivulaakso *et al.* 2012; Lydén 2012). Persons and groups with roots in various Finnish nationalist organisations such as Suomen Sisu and online communities, such as the Hommafoorum (roughly 'the job forum'), have joined the party. In the midst of the 2000s individuals from these networks wanted to influence political decision-making and had to decide whether to form their own party or affiliate with an existing party (Hannula 2011). Many chose the latter option. The PS and Soini, whose success to that point had been modest, welcomed them with open arms. The strongly anti-immigration and in some cases outright Islamophobic factions gained legitimacy by joining the PS, which would probably not have been the case had they formed a party of their own. Obviously their acceptance was part of a vote-seeking strategy from the old party leadership. That strategy turned out to be very successful in 2011 when the PS fivefolded the vote and made inroads in the urban centres where the party historically had been weak. Soini has so far skilfully balanced the old agrarian factions with roots in the FrP and the nationalist faction against one another. After the election of 2011 representatives from the nationalist-minded group have received influential positions within the party organisation, such as the position of party secretary, chief editor of the party newspaper *Perussuomalainen/Suomen Uutiset* and director of the PS think tank Suomen Perusta. One third of the 40 parliamentarians of the PS who were elected to parliament in 2011 and 2015 have a background in Homma-foorum and Suomen Sisu (Lydén 2012: 132–33). The anti-immigration and anti-Islam personality Jussi Halla-Aho has been a key figure in this integration process in his capacity of an informal leader of these heterogenous and over-lapping nationalist-minded groups. He was elected as representative of the Helsinki City Council for the PS in 2008, became a party member in 2010, MP in the Finnish parliament in 2011, and an MEP in 2014.

The mobilisation of a new niche

The PS have moved towards the far right end of the sociocultural dimension. By taking more radical positions on immigration, the preservation of Finnish culture and identity and the EU after 1995, the PS have consistently politicised issues, which until the early 2000s had been fairly unimportant for political mobili-sation and competition (Grönlund and Westinen 2012). The other political parties have reacted by increasingly formulating policies on these two issues (see Figures 6.4 and 6.5).

However, it was only in 2011 that the sociocultural dimension became more salient than the socioeconomic dimension for the PS (see Figure 6.6). That is, the PS have strategically developed and increasingly competed on this niche in the Finnish political system by supplying unique policy programmes on the EU and immigration.

PS has throughout its existence maintained a centre-left position on the socio-economic dimension. It has never been a representative case of what Kitschelt (1995, 2007) considered to be a 'winning formula' for successful radical right populist parties in the 1990s, i.e. the combination of economic liberalism with authoritarianism (cf. De Lange 2007). On the socioeconomic dimension the PS support moderate state regulation of the market, a tax-based redistributive (Nordic) welfare state, and small and medium-sized entrepreneurship. The PS hold welfare-chauvinist opinions as

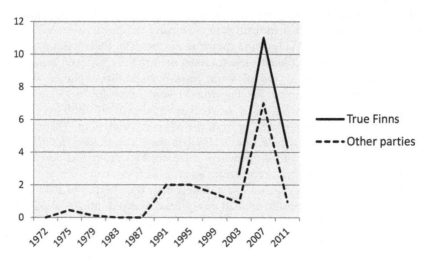

Figure 6.4 Saliency for the EU issue in Finland (% of manifesto content)

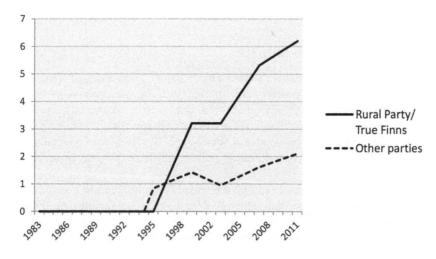

Figure 6.5 Saliency for the immigration issue in Finland (% of manifesto content)

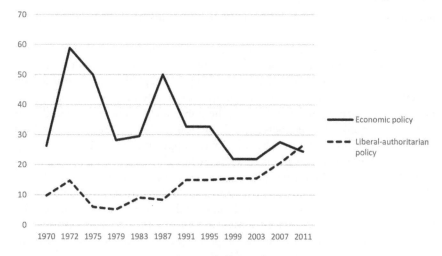

Figure 6.6 Saliency of economic versus liberal-authoritarian policy, as percentage of SMP/PS election manifesto content

they claim that the 'proper', or the particularly 'deserving' people (pensioners, war veterans and disabled) should be prioritised.

The salience of the sociocultural has thus increased, with a more pronounced resistance to immigration, multiculturalism, the rights of (the Swedish-speaking) minority, and strong support for the Finnish language, culture and traditions. Policy issues relating to the sociocultural dimension are thus presently more salient than socioeconomic issues for the PS (Bakker *et al.* 2015).

An anti-establishment party with governmental credibility

A central element in the populist ideology is the contra-positioning of a corrupt, unresponsive elite and a united, virtuous people. Anti-elitism and anti-establishment appeals constitute the historical core of Finnish populism. It is characterised both by protest against and criticism of the established political parties, the government and the bureaucracy, but also of the economic, cultural and academic elites that have distanced themselves from the values and lives of ordinary people. Soini has cultivated the populist rhetorical heritage of Veikko Vennamo by recycling many of the party founder's cogent expressions which are part of the Finnish common political vocabulary like 'Rotten Gentlemen' ('*Rötösherrat*') – corrupt, wheeling and dealing politicians – and the 'Theoretical Gentlemen' ('*Teoria-herrat*'), isolated in their academic ivory towers with no sense of what is happening on the ground. In contrast, 'yes, the people know' (*kyllä kansa tietää*) captures the idealised 'common sense' of the ordinary man (less often women). The anti-establishment appeals recur in the PS's criticism of power cliques, political nepotism, corruption, the tyranny of experts and the all-powerful EU bureaucrats who have turned a deaf ear to the opinions and values of ordinary citizens.

A recurrent theme in both old and contemporary populism is political corruption. The FrP and in particular Veikko Vennamo as a lawyer conducted many investigations of illicit contacts between political parties and enterprises, and criticised how politicians used public money for private purposes (Jungar 2015). He said that moral decay had infiltrated the political elite. The mission of the FrP was to make public the mischiefs of public persons and institutions. Soini walks in the footsteps of his predecessor by using every opportunity to talk about corrupt practices of Finnish politicians, of which there have been quite a lot during the last years. For instance, the former prime minister Matti Vanhanen was involved in illegal party financing, gifts from companies, dubious love affairs, and former minister Ilkka Kanerva had affairs with night club dancers, and there were other party financing scandals. However, the criticism of PS has been toned down after 2011, since several of their own representatives attracted substantial media attention when they became involved in scandals.

From 2003 the anti-establishment appeals are more frequent in the PS party programmes and electoral manifestos. The 'old' parties that have distanced themselves from the voters are contrasted with the PS that presents itself as:

> The only real political force with the capability, the will and the possibility to make the people take part in the decision making in a modern way. To challenge the power of the old parties and the monopoly of opinion is the main task for our party.
>
> (Perussuomalaiset 2003)

There has been a favourable opportunity structure for populist criticism of the established political parties with both home-made high-level political corruption, and the European political and economic leadership assuming more powers for the management of the euro-crisis. For instance, the political leadership are accused of having lied about the the benefits of the EU, and accused of devaluing the citizens when considering their negative opinions of the EU as lack of knowledge and irrationality (Perussuomalaiset 2007). The prevalence of surplus majority governments with limited alternation in power has been a breeding ground for the PS's anti-establishment appeals. The anti-establishment position has not been reflected in improper parliamentary behaviour except for extremist statements and behaviour, which are described in the section below.

Reputation: extremism and legitimacy

The entry of activists and representatives from nationalist organisations and anti-immigration web-communities has impacted on the party communication: racist and extremist statements have been common, even among some of the parliamentary representatives. The PS party leadership has been tolerant of misbehaving party representatives who break 'codes of conduct': it has been quite reluctant to discipline party activists making outright racist comments. In September 2011, Halla-aho was forced to take two weeks of leave from the parliamentary party group as he had stated that there was a need for strong military invention to calm down the demonstrations against the EU requirements on Greece. In April 2011, the new PS parliamentarian and sawmill owner Teuvo Hakkarainen in an interview with daily newspaper *Helsingin Sanomat* called for faster expulsion of rejected refugees, used expressions considered offensive racial slurs and made mocking imitation of a praying Muslim. When criticised he excused himself by referring to his rural background and outspokenness. He was called to a talk with Soini, who urged him to exercise more discretion (Yleisradio 28-04-2011).[2] In September 2013, the PS parliamentarian James Hirvisaari was forced to leave the party as he had invited a person with national-socialist sympathies to the parliament and had taken a photo of the person doing the Nazi-salute in the parliamentary chamber. 'It's completely clear that the inhumanity that Nazism represents is really unacceptable and will not be tolerated' (Yleisradio 04-10-2013).[3] A limit had been reached according to Soini:

> He's been warned, he has been regularly on the outside of the Parliamentary group. We've been trying to raise him like a difficult child in a family. We've tried to understand, to guide. Now comes the punishment.
> (Yleisradio 04-10-2013)

After the PS joined the government a new scandal broke out as member of parliament Olli Immonen, who also is the chairman of the nationalist organisation Suomen Sisu, had organised an event in which the national-socialist and anti-democratic organisation Finnish Defense League participated. Olli Immonen posted a photograph of himself with the participants on his Facebook account. The leader of the PS parliamentary group Sampo Terho reacted by stating that this was related to his private activities, and not to the PS, and Soini was of the same opinion. That is, even if the PS are in government the party apparently feels no need to distance itself clearly from extremist environments.

Even when party representatives were convicted in court, as a rule the leadership has reacted mildly. Two parliamentarians of the PS have been convicted by a Finnish court for hate-speech with no or modest reactions from the party. Party leader Soini stated in 2009 that he hoped that racists would leave the party rank and file, when Jussi Halla-aho was prosecuted for hate-speech (*Hufvudstadsbladet* 17-02-2009). At that point in time he was not a party member, but had been elected as representative in the Helsinki city assembly on the PS list. However, when Halla-aho was convicted, the member of parliament for the PS and the informal leader of the nationalist faction of the PS, was sentenced to pay 60-day fines by the highest court of justice for breaking religious peace and hate-speech, Soini did not demand his resignation despite the conviction (*Hufvudstadsbladet* 08-06-2012). The verdict related to a blog statement of 2008 when he compared

Islam to paedophilia. Jussi Halla-aho is an internationally well known anti-Islamist blogger, and his *Scripta* with the subtitle (translated from Finnish) *Writings from the sinking West* is connected to international anti-Islamist environments and published in translation on, for instance, the website Gates of Vienna. After the verdict he stated that the Highest Court of Justice expressed 'individual views of some persons', which aroused criticism within the party (*Iltasanomat* 11-06-2012). He had to resign from his chairmanship of the parliamentary committee in charge of administration and immigration issues, but could continue his parliamentary work. In December 2011 the parliamentarian James Hirvisaari was sentenced by a Finnish court (medium instance) to 25-day fines for hate-speech for having written disrespectfully on Muslims. Hirvisaari was temporarily excluded from the parliamentary group for improper statements and for not obeying a party recommendation.

Soini has thus responded vaguely to the scandals and transgressions of the party representatives, as well as to cases of racist and extremist talk among local representatives. He has instead pleaded for forgiveness, saying that the persons concerned are inexperienced or by stating that anyone can make a mistake and should be forgiven. Even if there was some pressure from the other factions within the PS to take firmer action against the extremists within the party, few statements in this direction have been made from the party leadership. For instance, the PS has not issued a general ban on membership of extremist organisations, but Soini has once stated that membership of the Finnish Defence League is not accepted. There have been candidates for the PS who are members of Blood and Honour, and above all the Suomen Sisu, an organisation that attracts hardcore nationalist–minded persons. The organisation is embedded in Finnish and European neo-fascist milieux, such as the Finnish journal *Sarastus*.

Goals and strategies

In the previous section the exploitation of the sociocultural dimension and the radicalisation of PS during the last decade have been analysed. This radicalisation has not hampered the party's accomplishment of fundamental party goals, i.e., vote-, policy- and office-seeking.

Vote-seeking

On the contrary, radicalisation is the key to the electoral growth of the party and has not been an impediment to the attainment of governmental office in 2015. The backdrop against the PS electoral breakthrough in 2011 was the European economic recession and the crisis of the Eurozone combined with cases of domestic high-level political corruption that fuelled political distrust among the Finnish voters against the established political parties. The four most impor-tant reasons mentioned by the voters for voting for PS were: to transform the ossified party system (80 per cent), restrictive immigration policies (65 per cent), to slow down Finland's integration in the EU (68 per cent) and Timo Soini's leadership qualities (70 per cent) (Borg 2012: 201). The anti-establishment position, the charisma of the party leader and anti-EU and immigration appeals paved the way for the electoral breakthrough. From this perspective the PS are in line with Ivarsflaten's (2006) finding that radical right-wing populist parties with a so-called reputational shield are more likely to successfully mobilise the anti-immigration, (and in this case also an anti-EU) vote. The PS, due to their historic ideological origin and experience of government, were conceived of as legitimate party with governmental credibility.

It is a surprising achievement that the PS successfully consolidated its support in the 2015 election as none of the three key issues that explained the PS success in 2011 – anti-EU and immigration, anti-establishment appeals – concerned the voters most in these elections (Jungar 2002). Against the background of the deteriorating Finnish economy the electoral campaign revolved largely around traditional socioeconomic issues, such as employment, the public debt and economic growth. The success of the PS in 2011 had not only originated in being the party successful in the mobilisation of non-voters, but also in the party managing to recruit voters who had previously voted for the Centre (Keskusta KESK), the Social- Democrats (Suomen Sosialidemokraattinen puolue, SDP) and the Conservatives (Kansallinen Kokoomus, KOK). Moreover, being in opposition allowed the PS to voice strong criticism of the highly unpopular government. Finally, the PS have (thanks to the increase in public party funding since 2011) been able to build up a party organisation with national presence, efficient channels of communication, and even a proper think tank, the Suomen Perusta, which was established in 2013. This has been helpful for the consolidation of an electorate and a presence in the public debate.

Office

Already after the electoral breakthrough in 2011 the PS was invited to take part in the governmental negotiations. According to informal parliamentary practice a party witnessing a substantial vote increase should be included in government to reflect responsiveness to the electoral result (Jungar 2002). The voters expected the party to assume governmental responsibility: 80 per cent of the PS voters wanted the party to transform and vitalise the 'ossified' Finnish party system (Borg 2012: 201). Party activists and the newly elected parliamentary representatives supported government participation as well, but Soini was far more reluctant. He feared that the compromises, in particular in relation to the EU, that had to be made in government would have a devastating effect on the recently gained electoral support. He said:

> If we would have joined the Katainen government we would have received six ministerial portfolios. ... Many among us believed that we should have joined government. We concluded that the crisis will

continue for several years. If we join government, and change our view of the EU, we (the party) will fall on that.

(Soini 2014: 118)

Hence, government participation would imply breaking promises made to the electorate on the EU, and risking electoral loss. Soini talked as a policy purifier to those who had an appetite for the spoils of office and wanted the PS to pursue the governmental negotiations:

You get trapped ... and the dreams of becoming a or pretending to be a minister is awakened, and suddenly Portugal is not that important anymore.

(Soini 2014: 115)

However, other costs connected with office probably bothered Soini more than policy purity. A common assumption is that populist parties because of their anti-establishment profile and democratic ethos of responsiveness to voter demands, rather than responsibility, are harder punished in government than other political parties (Canovan 1999: 12; Heinisch 2003; Mény and Surel 2002: 18). The experience of government by the FrP between 1983 and 1990 has been an important lesson for Soini in how to navigate the party between government participation, party cohesion and electoral consolidation. In his Master Thesis in political science of 1988 the student Soini, and at that point of time chairman of the FrP youth organisation (1984–1992) reflects on the transformation of the FrP from a party of opposition to a party in government (Soini 1988). The fatal dissolution of the FrP in 1995 was still some years ahead when the thesis was presented. Soini described the negative consequences of the decision of the FrP to join government. The period in government increased conflict within the party, not so much over policy, but over power and resources. Moreover, the incumbency costs were high for FrP. All in all, Soini was well aware of the trade-offs between policy, votes, office, and of the pressure that incumbency would put on the party organisation (Sjöblom 1968).

Moreover, what was not mentioned, but was obvious, was that the PS as a fast-growing party did not have many representatives with the necessary experience to assume governmental responsibility in 2011. The parliamentary group, which could be divided into two subgroups – the traditional populists representing the ideological roots of the FrP and the nationalist-minded faction – consisted predominantly of newcomers to parliament (Lydén 2012: 140–141). The party leadership had little information on how the parliamentary group would behave, particularly as the Finnish open list system where the voters vote for individual candidates provides the political parties with less influence over those ultimately elected as parliamentarians. As the PS do not have the means at their disposal to control which candidates get elected into parliament, the party has required of every candidate to sign a written agreement not to leave the PS parliamentary group during the legislative period (*Suomen Kuvalehti* 08-04-2011). 'We wanted to ensure a commitment of loyalty to the party from the candidates as the possible split of the party has been a recurrent theme in the media', Soini explained the juridically non-binding agreement (ibid.). Members of parliament are in principle free to act according to their own will. However, there was fear among the older PS parliamentarians that the new nationalist-minded PS parliamentarians connected to the Hommafoorum and Suomen Sisu could form a parliamentary group of their own (*Suomen Kuvalehti* 24-11-2011). As a matter of fact, there have been open confrontations within the PS parliamentary group. Soini nominated one of the former parliamentarians Päivi Ruohonen Lerner, a loyal trustee of himself, as the leader of the parliamentary group. Quite soon she had to take measures against misbehaving parliamentarians (see the section on extremism above), and she was increasingly criticised internally. In 2014 the parliamentary group voted her out as the leader, and she was replaced by Jari Lindström, who had better relations with the nationalist faction.

In addition to misbehaving parliamentarians, the distribution of economic resources has been another cause of conflicts between grassroots activists and the party leadership. With the increase of public party support from €900,000 to €7,000,000 in 2011 there were expectations that the regional and municipal party-units, which so far had operated predominantly on a voluntary basis, would be financially strengthened. It was decided that out of the party funding 12 per cent would go to the women's section, and 12 per cent to the local organisation, which was a disappointment for the grassroots activists (Yleisradio 19-04-2011). The dissatisfaction was also reflected in a grassroots protest against the party foundation, which is ruled by a selected few of the older party leadership and not elected, to which party funding was transferred (Yleisradio 24-04-2011).

In 2015, PS decided that the time for national office had come. The party became a member of a centre-right government including three of the four large political parties after the parliamentary election in April 2015. Life-span metaphors flourished when Matti Putkonen representing the party leadership announced that the PS would take part in the three-party government formed after the parliamentary election of 2015. As Matt Putkonen described:

> In 1995 this party was given birth to in a sauna by the lakes of Saarijärvi (by the four leading men of the bankrupt FRP Timo Soini, Raimo Wistbacka, Kari Bärlund and Urpo Leppänen). It took off electorally in its teens and now when reaching adulthood the time has become ripe to assume responsibility.
>
> (*Suomen Uutiset* 15-06-2015)

After three weeks of negotiations the central party organs – the party board, party assembly and the parliamentary group – had accepted the governmental programme and decided to join government. The long-time office aspiration of the PS was realised. Long-term office-seeking aspirations had been formulated

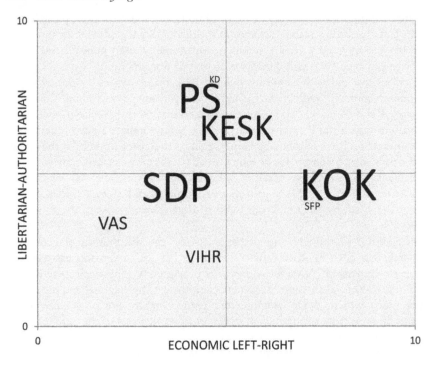

Figure 6.7 The Finnish party space (parties sized by vote share in the 2011 elections)

already in 2011, but now the time was ripe. The PS joined a centre-right cabinet with the KESK and the KOK, and received four ministerial portfolios in a government with a total of 14 portfolios: Minister of Foreign Affairs (Timo Soini), Defense (Jussi Niinistö), Social Affairs and Health (Hanna Mäntylä), and Justice and Employment (Jari Lindström). Soini had during the legislative period stated that the preferred government would be with the SDP and the KESK (*Suomen Kuvalehti* 28-06-2013) as this composition would imply less compromising on the socioeconomic dimension (see Figure 6.7).

The responsible party organs took the decision to join government unanimously, but the MP Veli-Matti Saarakkala, a former chairman of the PS's youth organisation and a representative of the PS's national faction, voiced his concerns that the party had to compromise its EU-policies. Soini demanded loyalty from the party representatives and the PS has so far demonstrated high party discipline. The leader of the more extreme nationalist group Jussi Halla-Aho had also warned about rushing into government unless the party had a blackmailing position and would get its prioritised policies through (*Turun Sanomat* 04-10-2014). However, only a week later he took his statement back, and said that the PS should aspire to office in order to be able to influence policy. The nationalist-minded group exhibits a greater concern for policy purity and is reluctant to compromise away the key concerns of the party, whereas the more moderate groups together with

Soini pursued long-term office-seeking by preparing for government after the 2011 election by institutionalising the party.

Pursuing a policy-influencing strategy in the three-party centre-right government will imply compromises for the PS, in particular on the socioeconomic dimension. A government including the SDP, which was the preferred composition of the party leader Timo Soini, would have been less costly for the PS. The government has set out to make substantial cuts in public expenditure without raising taxes. Welfare state entitlements to families with children, pensioners, unemployed and others dependent on public support will be reduced, which are groups that the PS have targeted (Valtioneuvoston kanslia 2015). Moreover, the cutting of car taxation, which was one of PS's core electoral promises in 2015, was not realised in the government programme. The reforms that need to be addressed with regard to pensions, labour market legislation and welfare entitlements require that the party can convince the voters that they benefit from PS being in office and also deserves credibility by assuming governmental responsibility in times of economic hardship. One possibility is to stress the party's influence on immigration and integration policies in the governmental programme, which differs from the previous government. In the 2015 governmental programme 'useful' labour market immigration is welcomed:

> The Government will promote work-related migration that enhances employment in Finland, boosts public finances, improves the dependency ratio and contributes to the internationalisation of the economy. The whole of Europe is ageing and will have to deal with the resulting problem of public deficits. Immigrants enhance our innovation capacity and increase our know-how by bringing their cultural strengths to Finnish society.
>
> (Valtioneuvoston kanslia 2015)

However, a more restrictive approach is taken to other types of immigration:

> The Government will encourage open debate about migration policy but will not tolerate racism. We will promote a tolerant and humane national discussion culture. An independent study of the costs of migration and its impact on Finnish society will be conducted to enable facts-based discussion, better integration policies and better decision-making.
>
> (Valtioneuvoston kanslia 2015)

Since Finland already implements restrictive immigration policies the possibilities of making major restrictions are limited: the refugee quota is annually 1,050 persons and 3,000 asylum seekers were accepted in 2014. Nevertheless, the governmental representatives talk about controlled immigration, and the PS have proposed lowering the refugee quota to 750 (*Hufvudstadsbladet* 13-05-2015; *Vasabladet* 22-05-2015). An independent inquiry will be set up to analyse the costs of immigration and its effect on society. The governmental aspiration of 'an open debate' on immigration should be a debate based on facts, and not on so-called 'world-bettering' or 'humanitarian values'. These statements resonate somewhat differently than those of the previous government for which immigration was conceived of in positive terms, and prevention of discrimination was a priority.

> Immigrants are a permanent and welcome part of Finnish society. The Government considers the integration of immigrants and the prevention of discrimination as essential activities during this Government's term of office. The Government aims for an immigration policy that supports the building of an unprejudiced, safe and pluralistic Finland, and enhances Finland's international competitiveness
>
> (Valtioneuvoston kanslia 2011)

The governmental policies on the EU are formulated in more restrictive terms. The EU must focus on the most essential issues; it is not necessary to deepen integration in all policy areas. The government will assess all EU regulation from the perspective of economic growth, competitiveness and jobs, and will also require a corresponding approach by EU institutions. Finland seeks 'less, but better and lighter, regulation than at present' (Valtioneuvoston kanslia 2015). However, the government's support for the maintenance of the present euro-policy will be a hard bite to swallow for the PS as the party until 2013 wanted Finland to leave the euro. In the 2011 electoral manifesto the PS stated that it was in the interest of Finland to leave the EMU immediately if the member states that break the rules of the stability pact are not forced to leave the EMU (Perussuomalaiset 2011: 33). The PS modified its policy in 2013 ahead of the EU parliamentary elections in order to secure that the Euroscepticism would not impede access to office:

> The PS accept the Finnish participation in the euro-zone as an existing fact, which can be modified. In contrast to the other political parties we are not politically dedicated to the euro, but exclusively to Finland's national interest.
>
> (Perussuomalaiset 2014)

This transformation was the entrance ticket for the PS to government, rather than a modification of the anti-immigration stance. For instance, during the electoral campaign of 2011, the incumbent Prime Minister Mari Kiviniemi said that the PS cannot be a member of government if it is not prepared to moderate its EU-criticism (*Dagens Nyheter* 09-04-2011).

Representatives of the nationalist faction in the PS have since 2011 replaced more traditional PS representatives on key positions within the party – as the party secretary, the vice chairman of the party, the editor in chief of the party journal *Perussuomalainen,* and as the director of the PS think tank Suomen Perusta. That is, advocates for more radical policies have assumed several important position within the party organisation. An explanation for this is that these representatives are well educated and hold academic degrees, even Ph.Ds, and possess the necessary skills and competences. They are in various ways engaged in the public debates and well represented in the media, and have thereby contributed to the public presence of the PS. Soini has so far balanced the various groups within the party by the means of his own undisputed status as the front figure of the party.

However, the experience of the FrP break-ups have been lessons for the PS. Not only has Soini demanded a declaration of loyalty from members of the parliamentary group, but the party has also managed to include a revision of the legislation on party funding in the governmental programme. This revision will be a disincentive for defection for members of the parliamentary group. In 1972, a clause was added in the legislation on public party funding that if a section of a parliamentary group leaves the party they have the right to a proportional share of the funding that goes to the parliamentary group. This decision was made in 1972 by the other political parties against the FrP and Vennamo and brought about a split in the FrP. In the governmental programme of 2015 this paragraph is to be removed. According to Soini, this had nothing to do with the anticipation of possible splits within the PS, but the making right of a historic wrongdoing (*Helsingin Sanomat* 27-05-2015).

The political opportunity structures

The PS have established themselves as the most credible alternative for the anti-immigration and EU-critical voters. The puzzle is why this radicalisation has not constituted an obstacle for the PS to be considered a legitimate party of government by the mainstream parties. However, the PS moderated their EU-position before entering government in 2015, and it is not unlikely that more moderation may be ahead. In this final section three aspects that have facilitated both the electoral growth and the attainment of office are presented. First, the (lack of) a reputation as an extreme and racist party will be discussed. Second, mainstream political parties have by playing the nationalist card and competing on the social-cultural dimension presented the PS with opportunities to enter the electoral market and thereby also constrained their ability to formulate credible criticism of the PS for being nationalist (Ellinas 2010). Third, the electoral strength and the centrist location on the socioeconomic dimension renders the PS an attractive member of government.

Reputational shield

An extremist reputation has been claimed to be an obstacle for the attainment of office and therefore radical right-wing populist parties need to distance themselves from extremist activists and racism. This has not been a serious problem for the PS. First, the PS has a reputational shield that helps to fend off allegations of extremism (Ivarsflaten 2006). Not only the PS itself, but also the mainstream parties and the media have fended off allegations of extremism by pulling forward the party's respectable origins in agrarian populism. The party secretary of the PS, Riikka Poutsalo-Slunga, reacted sharply when Sir Graham Watson, chairman of the Alliance of Liberals and Democrats in Europe (ALDE) group in the European Parliament, stated that the election of Soini as a Minister of Foreign and EU-Affairs is like making 'Dracula the CEO of a Blood Bank' (Asiakattaus 20-06-2015; Yleisradio 07-06-2015). The former Prime Minister and present Minister of Finance Alexander Stubb sided with the PS' party secretary by saying:

> I defend him in the sense that I think he and his party sometimes get put and lumped into the wrong corner with the likes of European far-right parties. ... Soini is very pragmatic and I think Europe should give the guy a chance.
>
> (*Financial Times* 17-06-2015)

Another example of the rejection of extremist allegations was made by the Finnish president Sauli Niinistö when he visited Stockholm a couple of days after the 2015 parliamentary elections. He explained for the Swedish media that:

> The Swedish debate on the governmental credibility of the PS is based on the false assumption that the PS are a similar type of anti-immigration party as the SD. I have acquainted myself with the ideas of the SD and I have seen a long time ago that we do not have Finland democrats. The PS are a different type of party.
>
> (Sveriges Television 28-04-2011)

The Finnish mainstream political parties have not condemned the party's policies and acceptance of racist and intolerant statements. During both the parliamentary campaigns of 2011 and 2015 no mainstream political party ruled out governmental cooperation with the PS. The mainstream parties have referred to parliamentary procedural rules, for instance, when the PS parliamentarians made transgressions.

Mainstream adaptation

According to Ellinas (2010), the response of the mainstream parties is vital for the development of radical right-wing populist parties. Ellinas suggests that when mainstream political parties first play the nationalist card by formulating anti-immigration policies, but then are compelled to retract, for instance in government, they enhance the opportunities of radical right-wing populist parties (Ellinas 2010: 29–30). A dynamic process incorporating the behaviour of mainstream political parties can facilitate both the entrance, the electoral growth as well as the attainment of office.

Compared to the other Nordic countries, Finland has always pursued restrictive immigration policies. The issue was not politicised until the early 1990s. With the implosion of the Soviet Union in 1991 and the economic downturn that followed in its aftermath more attention was given to immigration in the political debates (Förbom 2010; Lydén 2012). Issues of national identity had been put on the political agenda before the PS were formed in 1995 (Jungar and Jupskås 2014). However, in parallel with the PS's stronger mobilisation on immigration from 2003 (see above), the incumbent coalition government at that point of time (the KESK, the SDP and the SPP) played the nationalist card with the social-democratic Minister of Interior Kari Rajamäki at the forefront. He prepared a reformulation of the Immigration Act with restrictive immigration policies and preventive measures to curb illegal immigration, and he also coined expressions like 'asylum tourism' and 'asylum shopping'. Rajamäki opposed the fact that Finland could not choose the nationality quota refugees, and that Finland therefore was forced to welcome Muslim refugees (Lydén 2012: 36). The immigration debate sparked off in this period made the issue more salient (see Figure 6.4), as not only representatives from the PS voiced anti-immigration opinions, but representatives of some mainstream parties as well (see Lydén 2012: 21–23). Consequently, the mainstream parties started competing on national identity and thereby provided the PS with an opportunity to 'enter the media debate, gain media attention and publicise their views' (Ellinas 2010: 28). The mainstreaming of the anti-immigration debate continued after the 2008 municipal elections when the PS mobilised on immigration and increased its vote. (Raittila 2009). This coincided with the outbreak of the European financial crisis and a Eurosceptic opinion. The restrictive turn in immigration policies was reflected in how the Minister of Interior, Astrid Thors from the SPP, was criticised, even within government, when she proposed legislation that would increase the number of asylum seekers and facilitate family reunification and the reception of a permanent permit of residence (Lydén 2012: 85–89). The PS's mobilisation of anti-immigration policies developed within a dynamic process in which other political parties occasionally played the nationalist card, and then backed down, parallel to when the PS mobilised on immigration. The mainstream parties have by competing on the sociocultural dimension paved the way for the PS to establish itself as a more credible alternative. Moreover, the adaptation of PS's policies on immigration by mainstream parties made their criticism less credible.

Size and location: median party

The size and the strategic centrist position on the socioeconomic dimension renders the PS a potentially attractive governmental coalition partner. The socioeconomic dimension has been the most salient political cleavage in the Nordic countries, including Finland (Arter 2006: 48–49; Grönlund and Westinen 2012: 183). The Finnish party system has been characterised by a strong centre party (KESK), fuelled by the enduring cleavage between urban and rural interests. Its strongest competitors, however, have been the social-democratic SDP and the conservative KOK. An ethnoregionalist cleavage has been present since independence with the Swedish People's party SFP representing large segments of the Swedish-speaking minority (Arter 2006: 48). With the PS's electoral success of 2011 the Finnish party system contains four equally sized parties which together account for 80 per cent of the popular vote. Apart from the four main contenders, the Finnish party system also contains the VAS, the VIHR, the Christian Democrats (KD), and the Swedish People's Party (SFP). The positions of all current Finnish parliamentary parties are illustrated by a two-dimensional ideological space consisting of economic policy (left-right) and sociocultural values (libertarian-authoritarian), based on data from the 2010 Chapel Hill Expert Survey (Bakker *et al.* 2015).

Three main clusters of parties can be discerned: a left-libertarian party group consisting of SDP, VAS and VIHR; the economically right-wing and value-centrist KOK/SFP duo; and a centrist authoritarian cluster containing the KESK, the KD and the PS. Polarisation along the vertical axis is relatively low, but the saliency of the value dimension has increased (Nurmi and Nurmi 2012).

According to this snapshot PS is not alone in the centre-authoritarian corner, but is accompanied by both the KESK and the KD. PS assumes more extreme positions on immigration and law and order, whereas the Christian parties are more concerned about religion and family values. Hence, the position of the KESK and the KD on the libertarian-authoritarian dimension is the result of a different combination of issues. Moreover, the saliency of multiculturalism, nationalism and law and order is higher for the PS than for the two other parties. PS is far more radical on immigration than the KESK and KD.

PS has since the 2011 electoral breakthrough occupied the position of the median legislator party, which renders the party an attractive partner for both centre-right and centre-left government striving for policy-connected governments (Laver and Schofield 1991). On the socioeconomic dimension PS is most proximate both to the SDP and the KESK. The PS and the KESK are also close to one another on the liberal-authoritarian dimension. As a matter of fact, PS was the prioritised partner in government for the KESK party leader during the governmental negotiations in 2015: the KESK both anchored the first sketches of the 2015 governmental programme with the PS party leadership as well as providing generous time for bilateral governmental negotiations with the PS (*Helsingin Sanomat* 18-06-2015). In addition, the future Prime Minister Juha Sipilä gave in to the PS demands of a government consisting of three larger parties without the participation of any of the minor political forces, which has been the practice in Finnish parliamentarism. Thereby each and every party in three-partite government can blackmail the majority government, which is advantageous for the PS.

Conclusions

The PS represent a case of an anti-establishment party that gradually has radicalised from 2003 up to now. The radicalisation has taken place policy-wise with regard to issues like immigration and the EU, but also in terms of its populist appeals and anti-establishment behaviour. Thereby the PS established itself as a niche-party. The radicalisation has until recently gone hand in hand with the achievement of fundamental party goals. Vote-seeking was initially the primary goal, but long-term office-seeking was formulated already at the refusal of government participation after the electoral breakthrough election in 2011. After the parliamentary election of 2015 the PS became a member of government for which PS's stance on Finland's membership in the EMU was moderated. The trade-offs between the realisation of various party goals have so far been marginal, but with the recent entrance in government the party leadership has been prepared for possible costs in terms of policy compromises and party cohesion. For instance, representatives of the nationalist faction of the party voiced criticism about the concessions on the EU that the PS had to accept when joining government.

The opportunities on the electoral market and for office seeking have been favourable in several respects. Mainstream parties and the media have not demonised the party, but rather contributed to fending off allegations of extremism. Mainstream political parties also have by playing the nationalist card and competing on the social-cultural dimension presented the PS with opportunities to enter the electoral market and thereby constrained their ability to formulate credible criticism of the PS for hosting hardcore nationalists within its rank and file. The location on the socioeconomic dimension renders the PS an attractive member of government. The PS has been the median legislator party since 2011, which according to spatial coalition theory makes it an attractive partner both for the centre-right and centre-left. The context has so far been favourable for the PS fulfilment of vote- and office-seeking aspirations, but participation in government will constitute a first test of whether the electoral support and the internal cohesion can be maintained.

Notes

1 The Finnish party name Perussuomalaiset literally means ordinary, regular and basic Finns, translated into 'True Finns' as official English name. After the party's electoral success in 2011 the board of the party decided to adopt 'The Finns' as the official English name. According to the party leader Timo Soini the former name brought up wrong associations with extreme nationalism, and referred to an essentialist rather than a cultural 'common' Finnishness (*Helsingin Sanomat* 2011). The Finnish abbreviation PS is used throughout the text.

2 The interview can be seen here with English subtitles (Teuvo Hakkarainen, First day in parliament, 27-04-2011, www.youtube.com/watch?v=LMMakFNTbB4, accessed 20-06-2012).

3   Hirvisaari became a member and the only parliamentary representative of Muutos 2011, an extreme nationalist, anti-immigration and pro-direct democracy party during the remaining legislature, but he was not re-elected in 2015.

References

Albertazzi, D. (2008) 'Switzerland: Yet another populist paradise', in Albertazzi, D. and McDonnell, D. (eds) *Twenty-First Century Populism: The Spectre of Western European Democracy*, Basingstoke: Palgrave Macmillan, pp. 100–119.

Art, D. (2011) *Inside the Radical Right The Development of Anti-Immigration Parties in Western Europe*, Cambridge: Cambridge University Press.

Arter, D. (2006) *Democracy in Scandinavia: Consensual, Majoritarian or Mixed?* Manchester: Manchester University Press.

Arter, D. (2010) 'The breakthrough of another West European populist radical right party? The case of the True Finns', *Government and Opposition* 45, 4: 484–504.

Arter, D. (2012) 'Analysing "successor parties": The case of the True Finns', *West European Politics* 35, 4: 803–825.

Asiakattaus (20-06-2015) 'Europolitikko vertasi Soinia Draculaan – näin vastaa perussuomalaiset', http://asiakattaus.vuodatus.net/lue/2015/06/europoliitikko-vertasi-soinia -draculaan-nain-vastaa-perussuomalaiset (accessed 21-06-2015).

Bakker, R., de Vries, C., Edwards, E., Hooghe, L., Jolly, S., Marks, G., Polk, J., Rovny, J., Steenbergen, M. and Vachudova, M. (2015) 'Measuring party positions in Europe: The Chapel Hill expert survey trend file, 1999–2010', *Party Politics* 21, 143–152.

Borg, Sami (ed.) (2012) *Muutosvaalit 2011*, Helsinki: Oikeusministeriö.

Borg, Sami (ed.) (2013) *Demokratiaindikaattorit 2013*, Helsinki: Oikeusministeriö.

Canovan, M. (1999) 'Trust the people! Populism and the two faces of democracy', *Political Studies* 47, 1: 2–16.

Dagens Nyheter (09-04-2011) 'EU kris gynnar finska högerpopulister', www.dn.se/nyheter/ varlden/eu-kris-gynnar-finska-hogerpopulister/gerpopulister (accessed 18-06-2015).

De Lange, S. L. (2007) 'A new winning formula?', *Party Politics* 13: 411–435.

European Union Agency for Fundamental Rights (2009) *European Union Minorities and Discrimination Survey – Main Results Report*, http://fra.europa.eu/sites/default/files/fra_ uploads/663-FRA-2011_EU_MIDIS_EN.pdf (accessed 20-06-2015).

Ellinas, A. A. (2010) *The Media and the Far Right in Western Europe: Playing the Nationalist Card*, Cambridge: Cambridge University Press.

Financial Times (17-06-2015) 'Sick Finland ready for austerity medicine, says Alexander Stubb', www.ft.com/intl/cms/s/0/fb55b4f2-14fc-11e5-9509-00144feabdc0.html#ax zz3dmlUxjqc (accessed 21-06-2015).

Förbom, J. (2010) *Hallan vaara – merkintöjä maahanmuuton puhetavoista*, Helsinki: Into Kustannus.

Fryklund, B. and Peterson, T. (1981) 'Populism och Missnöjespartier i Norden: Studier av Småborgerlig Klassaktivitet', Doctoral disseration, University Lund.

Gates of Vienna, http://gatesofvienna.blogspot.se/ (accessed 20-06-2015).

Grönlund, K. and Westinen, J. (2012) 'Puoluevalinta', in Borg, S. (ed.) *Muutosvaalit 2011*, Helsinki: Oikeusministeriö (Ministry of Justice), pp. 156–188.

Hänninen, J. and Hänninen, J. (2010) *Tuhansien Aatteiden Maa. Ääriajattelua Nyky-Suomessa*, Helsinki: WSOY.

Hannula, M. (2011) *Maassa Maan Tavalla Maahanmuuttokritiikin Lyhyt Historia*, Helsinki: Otava.

Heinisch, R. (2003) 'Success in opposition, failure in government: Explaining the performance of right-wing populist parties in public office'. *West European Politics* 26, 3: 91–130.

Helander, V. (ed.) (1971) *Vennamolaisuus PJjoukkoliikkeenä*, Hämeenlinna: Karisto Publishers.

Helander, V. (1971) 'Populismi ja populistiset liikkeet', in Helander, V. (ed.) *Vennamolaisuus Populistisena Joukkoliikkeenä*, Hämeenlinna: Karisto Publishers, pp. 12–22.

Helsingin Sanomat (21-08-2011) 'Perussuomalaiset otti käyttöön englanninkielisen nimi', Helsinki.

Helsingin Sanomat (27-05-2015) 'Hallitus hautaa Lex Vennamon – varautuuko Soini perussuomalaisten ryhmän hajoamiseen?', www.hs.fi/politiikka/a1432700856911 (accessed 03-06-2015).

Helsingin Sanomat (18-06-2015) 'HS-raportti: Näin syntyi Sipilän hallitus', www.hs.fi/kotimaa/a1434514982708 (accessed 18-06-2015).

Hufvudstadsbladet (17-02-2009) 'Soini: Rasistdömda sparkas ur partiet', http://hbl.fi/nyheter/2009-02-17/soini-rasistdomda-sparkas-ur-partiet.

Hufvudstadsbladet (08-06-2012) 'Soini: Sannfinländarna behandlar inte Halla-ahos dom', http://hbl.fi/nyheter/2012-06-08/soini-sannfinlandarna-behandlar-inte-halla-ahos -dom (accessed 22-06-2015).

Iltasanomat (11-06-2012) 'Jussi Halla-aho vähättelee KKO: n tuomiota', www.iltasanomat.fi/kotimaa/art-1288476028993.html (accessed 29-09-2013).

Interview with Marja-Leena Leppänen, Administrative secretary at the PS party office, 2013.

Ivarsflaten, E. (2006) 'Reputational shields: Why most anti–immigrant parties failed in Western Europe, 1980–2005', Paper presented at the 2006 Annual Meeting of the American Political Science Association, Philadelphia.

Jungar, A.-C. (2002) 'A case of surplus majority government: The Finnish rainbow coalition', *Scandinavian Political Studies* 25: 57–83.

Jungar, A.-C. (2015) 'Agrarian populism in Finland', in Strijker, D., Voerman, G. and Terlin, I. (eds) *Rural Protest Groups and Populist Parties*, Wageningen: Academic Publishers.

Jungar, A.-C. and Jupskås, A. (2014) 'Populist radical right parties in the Nordic region: A new and distinct party family?', *Scandinavian Political Studies* 37, 3: 215–238.

Kitschelt, H. (1995) *The Radical Right in Western Europe: A Comparative Analysis*, Ann Arbor, MI: University of Michigan Press.

Kitschelt, H. (2007) 'Growth and persistence of the radical right in postindustrial democracies: Advances and challenges in comparative research', *West European Politics* 30, 5: 1176–1206.

Koivulaakso, D., Brunila, M. and Andersson, L. (2012) *Äärioikeisto Suomessa*, Helsinki: Into.

Laver, M. and Schofield, N. (1991) *Multiparty Government: The Politics of Coalition in Europe*, Oxford: Oxford University Press.

Lydén, M. (2012) *Jag är inte Rasist: Jag vill bara ha Främlingsfientliga Röster*, Helsingfors: Schildt and Söderströms

Mény, Y. and Surel, Y. (eds) (2002) *Democracies and the Populist Challenge*, Basingstoke: Palgrave Macmillan.

Mudde, C. (2007) *Populist Radical Right Parties in Europe*, Cambridge: Cambridge University Press.

'Nuiva Manifesti Maahanmuuttokriittinen manifesti' (2010) www.vaalimanifesti.fi (accessed 18-06-2015).

Nurmi, H. and Nurmi, L. (2012) 'The parliamentary election in Finland, April 2011', in *Electoral Studies* 31, 1: 234–238.

Pekonen, K. (ed.) (1999) *The New Radical Right in Finland*, Helsinki: The Finnish Political Science Association.

Pernaa, V. and Railo, E. (2012) *Jytky Eduskuntavaalien 2011 mediajulkisuus*, Turku: Kirja Aurora Turun yliopisto.

Perussuomalainen (2010–2011) (party journal).

Perussuomalaiset (1995) 'Perussuomalaisen puolieen erityisohjelma: Olen perussuomalainen' (party programme).

Perussuomalaiset (2003) 'Perussuomalaisten eduskuntavaaliohjelma 2003: Uusi suunta Suomelle – korjauksia epäkohtiin' (electoral manifesto).

Perussuomalaiset (2007) 'Oikeudenmukaisuuden, hyvinvoinnin ja kansanvallan puolesta. Eduskuntavaaliohjelma 2007' (electoral manifesto).

Perussuomalaiset (2011) 'Suomalaiselle sopivin Perussuomalaiset r.p:n eduskuntavaaliohjelma'. www.perussuomalaiset.fi/getfile.php?file=1536 (electoral manifesto) (accessed 13-04-2015).

Perussuomalaiset (2014) 'Perussuomalaisten EU-vaaliohjelma' (EU electoral manifesto).

Raittila, P. (2009) *Journalismin maahanmuuttokeskustelu: hymistelyä, kriittisyyttä vai rasismin tukemista?* https://enolerasisti.wordpress.com/2009/12/30/pentti-raittila-journalismin -maahanmuuttokeskustelu-hymistelya-kriittisyytta-vai-rasismin-tukemista/ (accessed 02-06-2015).

Raunio, T. (2008) 'The difficult task of opposing Europe: The Finnish party politics of Euroscepticism', in Szczerbiak, A. and Taggart, P. (eds) *Opposing Europe? The Comparative Party Politics of Euroscepticism: Volume 1, Case Studies and Country Surveys*, Oxford: Oxford University Press, pp. 168–180.

Salminen, S. (2015) *Maahanmuutot ja Suomen Julkisen Talouden Tulot ja Menot*, Helsinki: Suomen Perusta.

Sänkiaho, R. (1971) 'Populismi ja populistiset liikkeet', in Helander, V. (ed.) *Vennamolaisuus populistisena joukkoliikkeenä*, Hämeenlinna: Karisto Publishers.

Sarastus (n.d.) http://sarastuslehti.com (accessed 20-06-2015).

Scripta (n.d.) *Kirjoituksia uppoavasta lännestä*, www.halla-aho.com/scripta/ (accessed 04-11-2011).

Sjöblom, G. (1968) 'Party strategies in a multiparty system', Doctoral Thesis: University Lund.

Soini, T. (1988) 'Populismi – politiikka ja poltinmerkki SMPn roolinmuutos', Master Thesis: Helsinki University.

Soini, T. (2014) *Peruspomo*, Helsinki: WSOY.

Stanley, B. (2008) 'The thin ideology of populism', *Journal of Political Ideologies* 13: 95–110.

Suomen Kuvalehti (08-04-2011) 'Timo Soini vaati kirjallisen sitoumuksen: Perussuomalaisten kansanedustajilla loikkauskielto', http://suomenkuvalehti.fi/jutut/kotimaa/timo-soini-vaati-kirjallisen-sitoumuksen-perussuomalaisten-kansanedustajilla-loikkauskielto/ (accessed 25-03-2012).

Suomen Kuvalehti (24-11-2011) 'Veltto Virtanen syyttää Jussi Halla-ahoa', http:// suomenkuvalehti.fi/blogit/polkomfi/veltto-virtanen-syyttaa-jussi-halla-ahoa (accessed 28-03-2013).

Suomen Kuvalehti (28-06-2013) 'Soini menisi hallitukseen keskustan ja Sdp:n kanssa', http://suomenkuvalehti.fi/jutut/kotimaa/soini-menisi-hallitukseen-keskustan-ja-sdpn-kanssa/ (accessed 23-06-2015).

Suomen Sisu (n.d.) http://suomensisu.fi/esittely/ (accessed 20-06-2015).

Suomen Uutiset (17-04-2015) 'Maahanmuuttoseminaarissa vedottiin: "Älkää tehkö Ruotsin virheitä, älkää kulkeko Ruotsin tietä"', www.suomenuutiset.fi/maahanm uuttoseminaarissa-vedottiin-alkaa-tehko-ruotsin-virheita-alkaa-kulkeko-ruotsin-tieta/ (accessed 29-04-2015).

Suomen Uutiset (27-05-2015) 'Hallitukseen vai ei – tiedotustilaisuus', www.suomenuutiset. fi/hallitukseen-vai-ei-tiedotustilaisuus-klo-2100-alkaen/ (Streamed press conference online) (accessed 27-05-2015).

Suomen Uutiset (15-06-2015) 'Silloin oli savusauna ja neljö miestä, Nyt on neljö minis- teriä', www.suomenuutiset.fi/silloin-oli-savusauna-ja-nelja-miesta-nyt-nelja-ministeria (accessed 15-06-2015).

Suomen vaalitutkimusportaali (2011) 'Puolueiden jasenmaarien kehitys (ilmoitetut jasenrekisteritiedot', www.vaalitutkimus.fi/fi/kiinnittyminen/puolueiden_jasenmaarie n_kehitys.pdf (accessed 06-06-2015).

SVT (28-04-2015) 'Sannfinländarna är inte samma som Sverigedemokraterna', www. svt.se/nyheter/uutiset/svenska/sannfinlandare-ar-inte-samma-som-sverigedemokrater na-1 (accessed 07-01-2016).

Szczerbiak, A. and Taggart, P. (eds) (2008) *Opposing Europe? The Comparative Party Politics of Euroscepticism*, Oxford: Oxford University Press.

Tilastokeskus (2014) *Statistical Yearbook of Finland*, Helsinki: Statistics Finland.

Turun Sanomat (15-04-2013) 'Eduskuntapuolueisiin kuuluu 300 000 suomalaista – vain pikkupuolueet kasvavat', www.ts.fi/uutiset/kotimaa/474016/Eduskuntapuolueisiin+ kuuluu+300+000+suomalaista++vain+pikkupuolueet+kasvavat (accessed 13-06-2015).

Turun Sanomat (04-10-2014) 'Halla-aho: Apupuolueen asema hallituksessa olisi kuoli- nisku puolueelle', www.ts.fi/uutiset/kotimaa/713672/Hallaaho+Apupuolueen+asem a+hallituksessa+olisi+kuolinisku+puolueelle (accessed 23-05-2015).

Valtioneuvoston kanslia (22-06-2011) 'Pääministeri Jyrki Kataisen hallitusohjelma'.

Valtioneuvoston kanslia (29-05-2015) 'Valtioneuvoston tiedonanto eduskunnalle 29.5.2015 nimitetyn pääministeri Juha Sipilän hallituksen ohjelmasta'.

Vasabladet (22-05-2015) 'Finland sänker flyktingkvoten', http://online.vasabladet.fi/Arti kel/Visa/67308 (accessed 30-06-2015).

Wall Street Journal (09-05-2011) 'Why I don't support Europe's bailouts', www.wsj.com/arti cles/SB10001424052748703864204576310851503980120 (accessed 23-26-2015).

Wiberg, M. (ed.) (2011) *Populismi Kriittinen Arvio*, Helsinki: Edita.

Yleisradio (19-04-2011) 'Perussuomalaisten puoluetuki pompsahti kattoon', http:// yle.fi/uutiset/perussuomalaisten_puoluetuki_pompsahti_kattoon/5346058 (accessed 15-06-2015).

Yleisradio (24-04-2011) 'Puolueväki ei tiennyt perussuomalaisten säätiökikkailusta Säätiö oli melko varaton ennen huoneistokauppaa varten otettua miljoonalainaa', http://yle.fi/uutiset/puoluevaki_ei_tiennyt_perussuomalaisten_saatiokikkailusta/6009 237 (accessed 12-06-2015).

Yleisradio (20-06-2011) 'Soini puuttui Hakkaraisen puheisiin', http://yle.fi/uutiset/ soini_puuttui_hakkaraisen_puheisiin/2549776 (accessed 20-06-2015).

Yleisradio (04-10-2013) 'Soini on Hirvisaari: We've been trying to raise him like an unruly child', http://yle.fi/uutiset/soini_on_hirvisaari_weve_been_trying_to_raise_ him_like_an_unruly_child/6864717 (accessed 07-11-2014).

Yleisradio (07-06-2015) 'Sannf sura över jämförelse mellan Soini och Dracula', http:// svenska.yle.fi/artikel/2015/06/07/sannf-sura-over-jamforelse-mellan-soini-och-dracula (accessed 25-10-2015).

7 The Party for Freedom

Balancing between mission, votes and office[1]

Tjitske Akkerman

Introduction

The Party for Freedom (Partij voor de Vrijheid, PVV) was founded on 22 February 2006 by Geert Wilders. Before he founded the PVV, Wilders had been a parliamentarian for the liberal-conservative People's Party for Freedom and Democracy (Volkspartij voor Vrijheid en Democratie, VVD). Disappointed with the VVD's moderate nationalist course – and especially its favourable position regarding Turkey's accession to the European Union (EU) – he broke with the party in September 2004. He became an independent member of parliament until he founded the PVV two years later. The PVV adopted the classic profile of a radical right-wing populist party, focusing on niche issues such as immigration, Islam, law and order and European integration (Lucardie 2009; Van Heerden *et al.* 2014: 126; Vossen 2011). Indeed, it developed into a populist party quickly, vehemently critiquing the cultural and political elites (Vossen 2013: 79; Rooduijn 2013: 87).

The PVV's exclusive nationalist positions with respect to immigration and Islam have affected the party's perceived legitimacy, among both politicians and the public. Statements such as Wilders' claim that a 'head rag tax' should be introduced or that there should be fewer Moroccans in the Netherlands have caused backlashes. Wilders was frequently required by members of parliament and journalists to account for, or to distance himself from, manifestations of extremism – which included a call for support for the PVV that was published on extremist websites, the presence of neo-Nazis at a PVV demonstration and international contacts with parties like the National Front (Front National, FN) and Flemish Interest (Vlaams Belang, VB) (*NRC* 13-11-2007; *NRC* 25-09-2013). Particularly in its building-up stage, the PVV suffered some negative electoral effects due to its extremist reputation (Van Heerden 2014: 20–34, 91). The PVV's fate, however, was not unique. Anti-immigration parties tend to be demonised more than other party families in the Dutch media; that is, they are portrayed more frequently as absolutely evil and are associated with Nazism/fascism (Van Heerden 2014). Such demonisation can have a negative electoral impact because voters are willing to support anti-immigration parties only if they are perceived as legitimate (Bos and Van der Brug 2010).

The demonisation of Dutch anti-immigration parties, however, appeared to decrease after the turn of the millennium. In the 1990s, Dutch radical right-wing populist parties like the Centre Democrats (Centrum Democraten, CD) were heavily decried as morally abject; if it got any attention at all, the CD was portrayed as dangerously extremist in the media. The party suffered an informal *cordon sanitaire* following its promising electoral gains in the local elections of 1990. Its leader, Hans Janmaat, was ignored by mainstream politicians when he spoke in the Dutch parliament, and the media, too, largely ignored the CD and its leader. Janmaat was prosecuted and sentenced for discrimination based on racism. Electorally, the CD suffered and gained only 2.4 per cent of the votes in the 1994 national election.

The PVV was demonised less than the CD, and the party was never seen as a political pariah (Van Heerden 2014: 33). The PVV's path to legitimacy had to some extent been paved by the List Pim Fortuyn (LPF), a radical right-wing populist party that had been founded in 2002. At that time, Islamic terrorism had become a highly significant topic due to the 9/11 terrorist attacks. Tensions due to terrorist attacks in the name of Islam were revived in the Netherlands when film director and producer Theo van Gogh was murdered by a Muslim fundamentalist in 2004. Shortly before this event, Wilders had left the VVD. Having received death threats, he was put under strict and permanent surveillance. The death threats against Wilders and Fortuyn's murder signified how dramatically tensions over immigration and Islam had escalated in the Netherlands. As a result, the LPF and PVV did not face a *cordon sanitaire* by the media and political parties.

In addition, the parties potentially had better 'reputational shields' than previous Dutch anti-immigration parties; they were better equipped to fend off accusations of racism and extremism because they could not easily be associated with (neo-) Nazism or fascism (Ivarsflaten 2006). As PVV leader Wilders used to say: 'We have two main advantages compared to parties abroad. ... We descend from the respectable VVD and not from an obscure neo-Nazi movement. We are also pro-Israel, so one cannot accuse us of anti-Semitism' (*Vrij Nederland* 21-05-2014).

Moreover, since Wilders had been a member of parliament in a respectable party, his personal reputation very much dominated the reputations of the party's parliamentarians, who did not necessarily come from the mainstream. Radical right-wing populist parties are usually strongly personalised and leader-centred, and Wilders' position is exceptionally dominant. The PVV, in fact, has only two official members: Geert Wilders and the foundation Groep Wilders (since 2008, Stichting Vrienden van de PVV).[2] At the same time, it should be noted that although the PVV's genesis has given the party relative credibility with respect to both legitimacy and competence, its legitimacy is not as strong as that of vested parties (Bos *et al.* 2011).

Partly as a result of its reputational shield, the PVV managed to gain an unexpected 5.9 per cent of the vote and nine seats in parliament in the 2006 elections to the Lower House (Tweede Kamer) (Van Holsteyn 2007). The PVV became the third largest party in the 2010 national elections when it won 15.5 per cent of the vote (see Table 7.1) – almost matching the exceptional and spectacular result of 17.3 per cent that had been garnered by the LPF in 2002. Whereas the CD had not been able to break through electorally in the 1980s and 1990s, the LPF and PVV became the most successful new parties in Dutch history since the introduction of universal suffrage in 1918.[3]

As with the LPF in 2002, electoral success brought the PVV the opportunity to enter national office in 2010. The 24 seats in parliament that the PVV had gained in the 2010 elections appeared to be crucial for the survival of the right-wing minority cabinet of the VVD and the Christian Democratic Appeal (Christen-Democratisch Appèl, CDA), a cabinet led by the VVD prime minister Rutte. Since this cabinet did not have a majority in parliament, it needed the PVV's support. The Rutte I cabinet prematurely came to its end in April 2012, when the PVV pulled the plug on the coalition (more about this below). For various reasons, the PVV fell back to 10.1 per cent of the vote in the following elections in September 2012. It joined the opposition when the Rutte II cabinet, a coalition government of the VVD and the Labour Party (Partij van de Arbeid, PvdA), a social-democratic party, assumed office after the 2012 election. In the 2014 elections for the European Parliament, the PVV lost one seat.

The following part begins with an assessment of the extent to which the PVV has mainstreamed since it was founded in 2006. An analysis follows of how the PVV has shifted its party goals over the years and how this shift relates to its mainstreaming. Lastly, I will offer several explanations for the changes that have occurred since 2006 – for example, the effects of entering national office and the pressures for change coming from within the party. The analyses and explanations are based on a large variety of primary sources.[4]

Table 7.1 Electoral support for the PVV

	European Parliament	National Parliament	Provincial Council
2006		5.9%	
2009	17.0%		
2010		15.5%	
2011			12.4%
2012		10.1%	
2014	13.3%		

Source: Nationale Kiesraad.

To the mainstream and back

Since the PVV's foundation in 2006, its programmatic profile and political behaviour have gone through various stages. They are best divided into three time periods: 'before office,' 'in office' and 'after office'. We will look at the party's programmatic profile and political role during each period to assess whether or not the party has been moving into the mainstream.

2006–2010: tougher on immigration, softer on care

In its building-up stage, between 2006 and 2010, the PVV went through several noteworthy changes. First, it moved away from neo-liberalism towards a more mixed socioeconomic programme (see Figure 7.1a). In its election manifesto of 2010, 'The agenda of hope and optimism,' the PVV maintained its neo-liberal preferences for lower taxes and less government but opposed raising the retirement age and corroding job security (Partij voor de Vrijheid 2006, 2010). Second, the party radicalised its stances on the issues of immigration and integration (see Figure 7.1b). Most significantly, it emphasised the importance of Islam as the central theme in the immigration and integration debate, and presented a series of radical statements on the topic. The 2010 manifesto proposed, for instance, a ban on the Koran; Wilders made clear that the PVV regarded the Koran as a 'fascist book'. The profile that the PVV developed in this period can be characterised as 'tough on immigration, soft on care' (*de Volkskrant* 15-04-2014). This profile was not only propagated rhetorically but also practised in parliament. Analyses of PVV parliamentary members' voting patterns between 2007 and 2010 make clear that the party was indeed tough on immigration; the PVV consistently defended the most restrictive positions on this issue. In this respect, the gap between the PVV and other parties was wide (Otjes 2012: 216). The 'soft on care' take was apparent, given that the PVV often voted together with the populist left-wing Socialist Party (Socialistische Partij, SP) on welfare issues (Otjes and Louwerse 2013: 10). In these respects, the PVV's programmatic profile and behaviour in parliament were far from the mainstream.

The PVV's distance from the mainstream parties was also underlined by its anti-establishment profile. In its manifesto of 2010, elites were vehemently attacked, an alarm was raised about the state of the Dutch democracy, and actions (e.g., a march of common citizens to The Hague) and remedies (e.g. more direct democracy) were proposed. The party also demonstrated its outsider position by following a strong opposition dynamic in parliament; the PVV faction was active when it came to asking questions or submitting motions but passive with respect to submitting amendments and drafting legislation (Otjes and Louwerse 2013). Moreover, in 2007–10, the party presented 8 motions of confidence to bring down the Balkenende IV government – an extremely high number by Dutch standards.[5] The PVV also highlighted its anti-establishment profile in the Dutch parliament by challenging the political mores; representatives aimed 'to test the limits' of parliamentary behaviour, as Geert Wilders said

148   Tjitske Akkerman

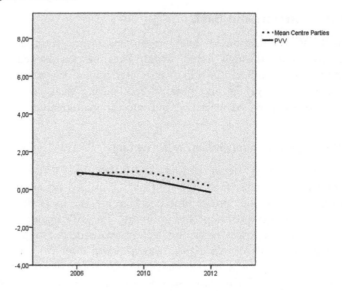

Figure 7.1a The position of the PVV on socioeconomic issues
Note: Analysis based on election manifestos. For details of measurement see De Lange 2007.

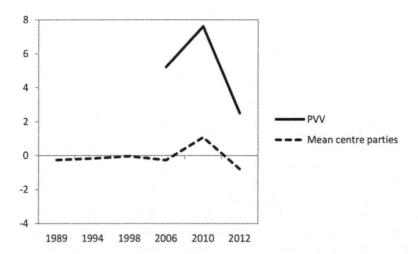

Figure 7.1b The position of the PVV on immigration and integration in election manifestos
Note: issues coded on 5 points-scale, with −0.5 or −1.0 attributed to pro-immigration and pro-multicultural pledges and +0.5 or +1.0 attributed to anti-immigration and assimilationist pledges. Mean represents average score of largest centre-left and largest centre-right party. For details of the codebook see Appendix.

(*NRC* 24-02-2007). The complete parliamentary group of the PVV ostenta-
tiously left parliament, for instance, when Wilders deemed a debate pointless
(*Trouw* 26-03-2009). Wilders cultivated a language that not only aimed to
communicate a clear, resolute and simple message but also to deliberately
challenge the (in)formal rules of political debates in parliament (Kuitenbrouwer
2012; Van Leeuwen 2009).

In one respect, however, the PVV began to resemble mainstream parties. It
developed a broader programmatic profile by shifting greater attention to socioeconomic issues. In the manifesto of 2010, socioeconomic issues had become as
salient as sociocultural issues (see Figures 7.2a and 7.2b). This broader programmatic profile came to the fore in the PVV's 2010 election campaign. An analysis
of televised election debates shows that the overall agenda of the election
campaign was heavily dominated by the financial crisis.[6] The themes of the
debates are predominantly set by the media, but in most debates, some room is
left for politicians to bring in their own issues.[7] This enables an assessment of how
much time Geert Wilders devoted to issues of his choice. Issues related to the
financial crisis appeared to dominate the agenda that Wilders was free to fill in.
The relatively high amount of time that Wilders chose to devote to welfare state
issues – in particular, to the care of the elderly – makes clear that he aimed to
highlight the PVV's socioeconomic profile (see Figure 7.3). To maintain the
spotlight on immigration and Islam, Wilders' strategy was to reframe welfare state
issues as immigration issues and vice versa. Welfare state issues were defended in
chauvinist terms in the election program – 'Henk and Ingrid pay for Ali and
Fatima' (Partij voor de Vrijheid 2010: 5) – and mass-immigration was opposed in
financial terms as costing the taxpayer dearly.[8] In sum, the PVV radicalised on the
core issues immigration and integration, and combined this radical position with a

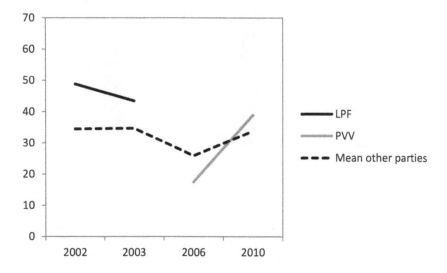

Figure 7.2a Salience of socioeconomic issues in the PVV manifestos

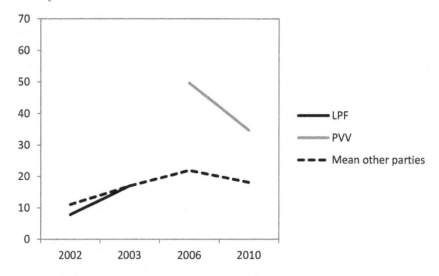

Figure 7.2b Salience of sociocultural issues in the PVV manifestos
Note: For details of measurement, see Chapter 2.
Source: Comparative Manifesto Project.

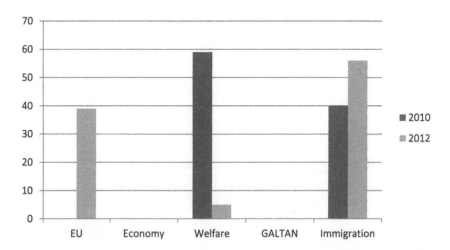

Figure 7.3 Attention devoted to socioeconomic and sociocultural issues by PVV in
election debates
Note: Based on coding of the following election debates: RTL4, Carré-debat,
26-05-2010; EenVandaag Lijsttrekkersdebat 07-06-2010; NOS Verkiezingsdebat
08-06-2010; NOS Nederland Kiest 11-09-2012; NOS Lijsttrekkersdebat 22-08-2012;
EenVandaag Lijsttrekkersdebat 06-09-2012; RTL4 Carré-debat 04-09-2012.

leftist profile on welfare issues. In the context of the financial crisis, the party began to broaden its profile by emphasising socioeconomic issues.

2010–2012: partial moderation

When the PVV became a support party of the minority cabinet Rutte I (14 October 2010 to 23 April 2012), the party was formally tied to the governing coalition parties VVD and CDA through a special policy agreement (*Gedoogakkoord*). The agreement implied that the PVV committed itself to voting in favour of cabinet proposals in four domains (immigration and integration, crime and security, elderly care, and finance) and to abstaining from supporting motions of no confidence proposed by the opposition parties (De Lange and Art 2011). In other words, the PVV had to change its behaviour in the parliamentary arena.

In comparison to the previous period, the PVV now presented itself as a reliable support party. The PVV parliamentarians voted in line with the *Gedoogakkoord* whenever the government coalition presented new legislation. In contrast to its radical opposition role in 2006–2010, the PVV presented no motions of confidence during this period.[9] The PVV also became more of a policy influencer. The party tended to cooperate more with other parties and appeared to be more willing to compromise in exchange for results. It fielded more amendments than in the former period and succeeded more often in getting amendments accepted by other parties (only 10 per cent in 2006–2010 versus approximately 50 per cent in 2010–2012). The party also cooperated more often with other parties when filing motions and parliamentary questions (Otjes and Louwerse 2013).

Yet, the PVV did not fully give up its radical, anti-establishment profile. Wilders optimally used the space that was left in the policy domains that were not part of the *Gedoogakkoord* – for example, foreign policy and Islam. Publicity was sought with radical statements and actions, such as Wilders' criticism of the Dutch queen for wearing a headscarf when visiting a mosque in the Middle East, his attendance at a controversial memorial service at Ground Zero, and the opening of a PVV website to report problems with Polish workers. The PVV was convinced that the coalition partners VVD and CDA would tolerate this opposition as long as the PVV was in line with the *Gedoogakkoord*.

From 2012 onwards: further radicalisation

After the government's collapse, the PVV steered a more radical programmatic course. The change can be clearly observed in the election campaign of 2012 (Partij voor de Vrijheid 2012). The PVV veered further left on socioeconomic issues (see Figure 7.1a). It highlighted the issue of European integration in its manifesto and in its campaign commercial, covering concerns about sovereignty, the financial crisis and immigration in one breath. In the election debates on television, immigration issues once again became the party's number one priority, even though the debates were dominated by the EU and economic issues (see Figure 7.3). The PVV adapted its agenda partly to this context by focusing more on the EU than in 2010 but emphasised its anti-immigration profile above all. In the television debates of 2012, Wilders emphasised economic issues and the party's leftist profile less than in 2010; welfare state issues now ranked third on the party's priority list.

After the fall of the Rutte I cabinet, the PVV changed tack in parliament. The party reverted to a strategy of radical opposition and once again became top scorer in motions of confidence.[10] Moreover, the party increasingly preferred solo actions. PVV members Fritsma and Van Klaveren initiated many policy motions in the domain of immigration and integration, but not one was accepted, and in most cases, only the PVV voted in favour.[11] Geert Wilders used to say in private conversations, 'the best motions are the ones that are exclusively supported by the PVV' (Interview 1, 02-06-2014). In 2013 and 2014, the percentage of PVV motions that were accepted reached rock bottom again, as in 2006–2010 (*Trouw* 12-01-2015).

Although in 2006–10 the PVV's influence in parliament had been low, the PVV became even more isolated in 2014 due to a controversial statement that Wilders made about Moroccan immigrants. On 19 March 2014, the day of the Dutch local elections, Wilders had rhetorically asked his audience whether they wanted fewer Moroccans, and the audience had chanted 'less, less, less' (*De Telegraaf* 05-06-2014). The reactions of other parties and the media were unanimously disapproving. Even the most popular right-wing newspaper, *De Telegraaf*, denounced Wilders' statement. Some months later, the PVV again highlighted its radical profile by fortifying its position that a temporary ban should be placed on the building of new mosques. In parliament, PVV member De Graaf stated that all mosques should be closed and that there should be no Islam in the Netherlands (*NOS* 26-11-2014).

The PVV returned to an anti-establishment course after 2012. It introduced a number of new obstruction methods in the Dutch parliament, such as filibustering. It engaged more in extra-parliamentary activities, such as a demonstration in The Hague and websites (e.g., MoskNee.nl) supporting complaints against the building of new mosques (Vossen 2013). Hence, the normalisation of the party's parliamentary behaviour ends abruptly after the fall of the minority coalition in 2012.

The PVV changed tack with regard to its international profile and relations. The Danish People's Party (Dansk Folkeparti, DF) had been a main source of inspiration for the PVV. While Wilders took care not to publicise the PVV's contact with parties like the Flemish Interest (Vlaams Belang, VB) or the National Front (Front National, FN) – to avoid putting the PVV's reputation at risk – the party advertised its contacts with the DF and United Kingdom Independence Party (UKIP). When the new FN leader Marine Le Pen sent Wilders a letter in 2010 to congratulate him on the electoral results, she got no reaction in return (*NRC* 14-09-2013). Likewise, representatives in the European parliament were keen to avoid seats next to FN representatives. As one of them, Van der Stoep, stated: 'We always tried to get seats as far away as possible from the FN ... If only because Bruno Gollnisch jumps up angrily every five minutes to make a point of order' (*Vrij Nederland* 21-05-2014).

However, negotiations about an alliance with DF and UKIP in the European Parliament broke off in 2011.[12] With the increasing importance of the EU issue and the approaching European elections in May 2014, the PVV needed new alliances in the European Parliament in order to get access to financial resources, amongst others. In 2013, Wilders began to formally ally with the Austrian Freedom Party (Freiheitliche Partei Österreichs, FPÖ), the FN, the Italian Northern League (Lega Nord, LN) and the VB, seeking their future cooperation in the European Parliament. The PVV's advances to parties that it used to shy away from signified that it was willing to risk increasing political isolation in The Hague.

Changing goals and priorities

The changes described above make clear that the PVV only temporarily mainstreamed its behaviour and programme while it supported the Rutte I cabinet. Before this experiment with participation in national office, the party had built up an increasingly radical profile as a niche party (although socioeconomic issues gained more salience for the PVV with the outbreak of the financial crisis in Europe). After its support role in office ended prematurely, the party not only returned to its old profile but also radicalised further by sharpening its anti-immigration positions and its anti-establishment profile through the initiation of additional extra-parliamentary actions. In the following part, the PVV's trajectory towards the mainstream and subsequent trajectory away from it will be assessed in terms of changing party goals.

2006–2010: maximising electoral support

In the build-up period, the party was mainly driven by vote-seeking. Immediately after its foundation, the PVV was doing poorly in the polls since it had to compete with both the successors to the LPF and the mainstream parties; thus, the primary goal became to gain support. As Vossen (2013: 60) argued, the most important reason for party change 'was without a doubt the continuously bad polls results and the lack of publicity with which the PVV struggled in the spring of 2006'. In the beginning, Geert Wilders was probing various themes to assess their electoral potential. During a study trip to the United States, for example, Wilders concluded, 'We don't have an anti-tax party in the Netherlands. That offers possibilities' (*NRC* 15-01-2005). Various actors involved with the PVV suggested that opinion polls and the comments section of *De Telegraaf*, a Dutch daily, informed the strategy of the party. According to Bart-Jan Spruyt, who initially collaborated with Geert Wilders, the PVV leader all of a sudden favoured closing the borders to Polish workers, even though that action went against his belief in the free market. Spruyt says: 'Wilders and Bosma waved *De Telegraaf* around, in which a Polish tsunami was discussed and they pointed at the polls of Maurice de Hond. The voters they were trying to reach were against, so they were against as well' (Vossen 2013: 55).

The programmatic course that was eventually developed aimed not only to attract radically right-wing voters but to broaden the appeal to left-wing voters who were also dissatisfied with immigration. Former PVV politicians unambiguously link the changes in the socioeconomic profile to the vote-seeking strategy of the party. Former MP for the PVV Joram van Klaveren, for example, claims that he frequently discussed the party strategy with Wilders. He states that:

> Geert said: 'It is correct that the course has become more left-wing on certain issues'. The consideration was that a purely right-wing party could never obtain more than 10 to 12 seats. That is too little to become a true people's party. So it was solely an electoral consideration: tough on safety and migration, soft on care.
>
> (*de Volkskrant* 15-04-2014)

In order to gain electoral support, the PVV had to rely mainly on free publicity by the media. The party had neither the organisation nor the money to allow for door-to-door campaigning, for cultivating contacts with social organisations, for building up reservoirs of activists for personal canvassing or for investing heavily in commercial campaigns. Although assessing the PVV's financial situation is difficult, most likely the party was and remains poor (Interview 3, 26-02-2015; see also Aalberts and De Keijser 2015). The PVV managed well relying mainly on free publicity through the media. In fact, Geert Wilders was exceptionally successful in drawing media attention. Beginning in October 2007, the media were preoccupied with Wilders' film Fitna (Scholten *et al.* 2008) for the next six months. A prominent news programme on television, *NOVA*, devoted 23 broadcasts to Fitna (Zwart 2009). After Fitna had been released on the Internet in March 2008, there was much media hype concerning Wilders' travels to London in 2009 (Bakker and Vasterman 2013). Wilders' media strategy was effective with regard to both the amount of exposure and agenda setting, and it contributed to increasing electoral support (Bos *et al.* 2011; Nienhuis 2010; Van Spanje and de Vreese 2015).

The search for an electorally attractive programme yielded profit. Between 2006 and 2010, the PVV managed to attract considerably more voters (from 5.9 per cent in 2006 to 15.5 per cent in 2010). With the highly promising results of both the 2009 European parliamentary elections and the local elections on 3 March 2010 – in which the PVV became the largest and the second largest party in Almere and Den Haag, respectively – the PVV could begin the campaign for the national election on 9 June 2010 with confidence.

During the election campaign in 2010, no programmatic changes indicated that the PVV was changing its vote-seeking course and that office-seeking was gaining priority. The PVV broadened its issue profile during the campaign for electoral reasons. When polls indicated that the party might not have sufficient credibility regarding socioeconomic issues, the PVV began to emphasise welfare issues more (Fennema 2011: 248; *de Volkskrant* 23-04-2010; Lucardie and Voerman 2012: 173). Strengthening the leftist socioeconomic profile made the PVV potentially less coalitionable, but vote-seeking apparently had priority. If the PVV were to seek office, a coalition with mainstream right-wing parties VVD and CDA would have been the only option because the PvdA had excluded the PVV as a potential coalition partner. Yet, the PVV never shifted back to the right on socioeconomic issues during the election campaign in order to signify its willingness to govern with VVD and CDA. While VVD and CDA promoted raising the retirement age to 67 in order to realise a large part of their proposed budget cuts, the PVV squarely opposed this measure. Although Wilders emphasised that the PVV was willing to enter government, his unwillingness to compromise on key socioeconomic issues hardly made this assertion credible. During the election campaign, Wilders repeated that the preservation of the retirement age of 65 would be a 'breaking point' in future negotiations about participation in a government coalition. A poll conducted in 2010 showed that 86 per cent of PVV voters were opposed to an increase of the retirement age to 67. For the PVV, vote-seeking was apparently more important than the opportunity to be in office (Afonso 2015: 12).

Although Wilders repeatedly emphasised his willingness to govern, promoting himself as 'the best vice-prime minister' (*NOS Verkiezingsdebat* 08-06-2010), this demonstration of being prepared for office should not be taken at face value. Interviews with former PVV parliamentarians indicate that the party was reluctant to assume office, or at the very least ambivalent about it, because of the risks involved. The PVV had to make complex choices. The financial crisis implied that budget cuts were necessary, and the party was not keen on taking responsibility for them. The PVV was also aware that some policy proposals, especially with regard to immigration, could not be realised (e.g., because of EU constraints). Finally, as a result of the national election on 9 June 2010, the PVV parliamentary group had almost tripled in size with its 24 seats, and it counted many new representatives. With so many newcomers, a coherent and disciplined group in parliament had yet to be formed. Hero Brinkman, a PVV member of parliament, had been unafraid to campaign for democracy within the party, and government participation would give him a strong position because of the bare majority in parliament (76 of the 150 seats). According to Brinkman: 'Those 24 seats in parliament imposed a huge problem for Geert, because some of these people were critical about the course of the party, like me, and others were new and enthusiastic about making a change and therefore willing to make compromises' (Van Heerden and Creusen 2014: 195).

Instead of acting as full coalition partner, the option of supporting a minority cabinet was an attractive alternative from the beginning of the election campaign (*NRC* 23-04-2010). The support role was less demanding in terms of internal organisation, and it might enable the PVV to keep some distance from the austere policies that were to be expected and to maintain a partly anti-establishment profile. This construction also avoided the difficulties of finding qualified candidates for office. Yet, after the elections on June 9, there was no internal consensus about the strategy the PVV should follow. According to one of our interviewees, Wilders and most of the old hands in the PVV were against entering office; it was in their view too early for a party that was organisationally still weak (Interview 1, 02-06-2014). However, now that the PVV had gained 24 seats, sufficient to make a majority in parliament with the VVD and the CDA, Wilders was afraid that a refusal to govern would cost him voters. Moreover, the majority of the PVV faction wanted to start negotiations with the VVD and the CDA (Interview 1, 02-06-2014; Van Heerden and Creusen 2014: 195). The VVD, winner of the elections, wanted to involve the PVV because it feared the PVV's electoral pressure. During the campaign, VVD leader Rutte had already confidentially stated his preference for a right-wing cabinet that included the PVV (Interview 1, 02-06-2014). But the PVV was not prepared for office, and Wilders was secretly relieved when the Christian Democrats appeared unwilling to join a minority cabinet supported by the PVV (Interview 1, 02-06-2014). When alternative options failed, however, a right-wing cabinet with the PVV came back in view. Wilders felt that he had no other option than to accept a support role in the new cabinet. With cold feet, the PVV began negotiations to enter national office.

2010–2012: mainstreaming as an effect of office

The result of the negotiations was that the PVV committed itself to severe budget cuts. In exchange, the PVV managed to include some proposals about family reunification and entrance conditions for asylum seekers in the *Gedoogakkoord*. These proposals were inspired by the programme of the Danish People's Party, which had been successfully implemented when this party supported a minority government between 2001 and 2011 (see Chapter 5). The strategy pursued by the DF had thus become an important source of inspiration for the PVV. During the *Gedoogakkoord* negotiations for the Rutte I cabinet, the PVV involved DF foreman Messerschmidt as adviser. He suggested including a paragraph in which the parties agreed to disagree about Islam (*Vrij Nederland* 21-05-2014). This move enabled the PVV to continue advertising its radical anti-Islam profile.

Of greater difficulty for the PVV was the socioeconomic part of the agreement. As Afonso (2015) has argued, vote-seeking strategies of radical right-wing populist parties that appeal to left-leaning blue collar workers will generally pose a trade-off dilemma with office-seeking; opportunities to hold office are restricted to coalitions with right-wing parties that are generally not supportive of welfare arrangements that protect the positions of this part of the electorate. The *Gedoogakkoord* between the PVV and the governing parties VVD and CDA implied that the PVV had to make important concessions on its socioeconomic positions; the breaking-point about retirement age had to be more or less swallowed, and severe budget cuts (18 billion euros) were accepted. Although the PVV managed to some extent to steer budget cuts away from vulnerable social sectors such as health and elderly care, the vote-seeking strategy appealing to left-leaning voters was clearly weakened due to entering office as a support party.

At the beginning of 2012, a combination of factors made the PVV decide to revoke its commitment to office. The coalition agreement was to be renegotiated to include further budget cuts. Wilders had threatened more than once that he would only accept new budget cuts in exchange for significant restrictions in immigration policy, including an opt-out of EU immigration policy if necessary (*De Telegraaf* 26-11-2011). These demands were unrealistic, and Wilders knew it. He entered negotiations with the second-best option of focusing budget cuts on development cooperation. An agreement was almost in sight late in April 2012, after seven weeks of negotiations, but unexpectedly Junior Minister of Development Cooperation Ben Knapen, a Christian Democrat, refused to accept severe cuts (*de Volkskrant* 22-02-2014). The negotiations now became very difficult for Wilders.

Wilders' position had already been weakened at the start of the negotiations due to dissent within his party. PVV member of parliament Brinkman left the faction on 2 March 2012. With the loss of one seat, the majority in parliament was jeopardised. Former PVV members Brinkman, Bontes and De Mos argue that Brinkman's defection and Wilders' fear of more dissidence were the main reasons why Wilders revoked his support of government and reshuffled the list of candidates. According to Bontes: 'Geert Wilders said that he could not go on with this faction and with 75 seats' (*NPO* 25-05-2014; *Nu.nl* 22-05-2014). When the last straw – the April agreement – eluded him, Wilders had no plan B left, and on the spur of the moment, he withdrew his support (Interview 1, 02-06-2014). Afraid that the majority of the parliamentary faction would prefer to continue the negotiations, he decided to inform the PVV faction of his decision only after the fact (Interview 3, 26-02-2015). On 21 April 2012, the government fell. This premature ending can only be partly ascribed to external conditions such as the difficult financial conditions in which the cabinet had to operate and the reluctance of coalition partner CDA to sacrifice development cooperation, which would have enabled the PVV to save face. Most important of all was that the PVV did not have a commitment and a well-considered strategy to seek and maintain office based on internal stability.

From 2012 onwards: a return to vote-seeking

After the collapse of the government, the PVV returned to a strategy that was first and foremost vote-seeking. The PVV suffered a considerable loss in the national election of 12 September 2012, going from 24 to 15 seats. After these elections, Geert Wilders' primary goal was not only to remit this loss but also to gain the electoral upper hand. He had earlier declared that the 'PVV wants to become the largest party' (*RTL4* Premiersdebat 26-08-2012). Soon after the elections, the polls indicated that the PVV had begun to reap profit of its vote-seeking course; in the second half of 2013, they pointed to the PVV as being the largest party, and at the end of 2014, it again reached this top score (see

Peilingwijzer 31-08-2013, 10-12-2014). Wilders chose an uncompromising course. His contentious speech, in which he asked his listeners whether they wanted fewer Moroccans, further isolated the PVV politically, but in terms of vote-seeking, no damage was done. Indeed, polls indicated that almost all PVV voters agreed with Wilders and that voters in general substantially supported the statement that 'there should be fewer Moroccans in the Netherlands' (*De Telegraaf* 22-04-2014). Wilders' statement was well prepared, and the audience had been instructed beforehand to chant 'fewer, fewer, fewer' (*De Telegraaf* 05-06-2014). The statement may have been intended to provoke a *cordon sanitaire* in the two cities (Almere and Den Haag) where the PVV had participated in elections and where it had come first and second, respectively. PVV defectors have argued that Wilders did not wish to enter local government because he feared internal conflicts and competition (NRC 06-05-2014). The effect of Wilders' speech was that the PVV was excluded from local government and became increasingly isolated in parliament. The VVD denounced Wilders' statement about Moroccans univocally, and some parties (PvdA, SP and the party for senior citizens, 50PLUS) decided to no longer initiate policy motions with the PVV (*Trouw* 12-01-2015).

Policy goals are highly important to Wilders and the members of the loyal group around him. The aim of Wilders' speech may have been to avoid local office, but the primary goal of the provocative statement about Moroccans was most likely to draw attention to the party's radical anti-immigration message. Another indication of this strategy was the party's intensification of its anti-Islam position by proposing a ban on all mosques. In other words, the PVV radicalised its positions regarding immigration and Islam primarily in order to highlight its programmatic profile and to gain electoral support. Seeking attention for its pro-grammatic profile on the part of the PVV should not be perceived as being purely instrumental to vote-seeking. Policy goals, especially the fight against Islam, are also important in their own right for Wilders. Wilders repeatedly emphasised that fighting Islam was the PVV's principal *raison d'être*: 'The reasons why I have founded my party: less immigration, less Islam' (*NOS*-lijsttrekkersdebat 22-08-2012). He also stated that 'I have entered politics for one reason and one reason only: to fight Islam. To defend freedom' (*Nu.nl* 09-03-2014). Martin Bosma, a confidant from the beginning and the PVV's foremost ideologist, emphasised that he and Wilders were missionaries rather than politicians. He stated that 'We are politicians, but also missionaries … . We not only want to arrange things here and now, but also feel it as our duty to change public opinion' (*NRC* 25-09-2010).

Wilders and Bosma demonstrated their missionary zeal not only rhetorically. Wilders risked his life and had to lead a nomadic life after receiving the first of many death threats in 2004. Bosma gave up a good job to work for Wilders, initially without a salary. Yet, in the end, it is hard to say whether Wilders' radical anti-Islam statements are merely a means to gain media attention and electoral support, or whether they are primarily driven by an ideological and sometimes prophetic mission to warn against the apocalypse of Islamisation. Former insiders tend to disagree whether Wilders is first and foremost a cool and calculating politician for whom strategic considerations regarding vote-seeking are most important or a politician still driven primarily by a mission (Interview 1, 02-06-2014; Interview 2, 02-06-2014). Until now, Wilders has not been faced with a hard trade-off between policy mission and electoral support. As long as the PVV's policy principles have not been put to this test, one can only speculate what comes first – policy purity or vote-seeking.

Although the PVV had lost credit as a coalition partner, Wilders argued that an electorally powerful PVV would not be ignored by the other parties:

> I can make the PVV the biggest party in the Netherlands. The strength of the party is also its size and when you become big, a lot becomes liquid. And the PVV will not only support a government, but it will govern … . Trust me, they are all power parties. They would sell their mother-in-law to assume office.
>
> (*Nu.nl* 09-03-2014)

The PVV, in contrast, was not willing to sell anything in exchange for assuming office. Wilders indicated that he was also content with indirectly influencing policy: 'I have learned a thing since I have been a politician. We have supported a government, we have been a member of the opposition. At the moment the PVV has 0.0 power, but a lot of influence. You do not need power to have a lot of influence' (*NOS* 11-05-2014).

With a diminished prospect of national office after 2012, Wilders apparently felt free to risk political isolation in return for media attention, indirect influence and electoral support. Any short-term prospect for office had become remote with the PVV's political isolation after the breakup of the Rutte I cabinet and the party's radicalisation. Wilders maintained, however, that a long-term prospect for office was still in the picture. He argued that other parties' unwillingness to govern with the PVV would disappear as soon has the PVV had achieved an electoral plurality. As far as one can go by the polls, gaining an electoral plurality is not an unrealistic goal for the PVV. But whether Wilders will pursue a realistic office strategy is doubtful. Hardly any party is willing to form a coalition with the PVV. Apart from this difficulty in finding coalition partners, the PVV faces obstacles that may pose an even greater problem (see below).

Explanations for the mainstreaming and subsequent radicalisation of the PVV

In this section, we will examine explanations for the changes in strategy described above. Whether these strategies are successful and can be upheld in the long run depends on external and internal conditions. As outlined in the introduction to this volume, the external environment comprises social and political conditions (see Chapter 1, Figure 1.1). Social conditions have generally been favourable for the PVV's vote-seeking strategy. Research has shown that particularly the anti-immigration and anti-Islam messages of radical right-wing populist parties are well received by the electoral market (Ivarsflaten 2008).

This finding holds true for the PVV. Polls repeatedly indicate that the PVV manages to gain electoral support for its anti-immigration statements even when other parties and media deplore these messages. What is questionable, however, is whether this anti-immigration profile is in such high demand when combined with a leftist, pro-welfare profile. Some scholars have argued that such a combination fills an important niche in the electoral market (Van der Brug and van Spanje 2009). However, the PVV has not obviously profited electorally from its leftward turn after 2006. Our analysis of the electoral gains made by the PVV in 2010 shows that new voters were not significantly more centrist or left wing in their socioeconomic orientation, despite the changes in the PVV programme and rhetoric (see Figure 7.4). This result indicates that the PVV's electoral gains should probably not be (exclusively) attributed to the change in course towards a more left-wing socioeconomic profile. Our analysis makes clear, however, that new voters in 2010 were more moderate on sociocultural issues and less Eurosceptic. In 2012, the PVV lost these relatively moderate voters again (see Figure 7.4). Mainstreaming between 2010 and 2012 not only occurred at the supply side but was also reflected in the electoral support for the PVV.

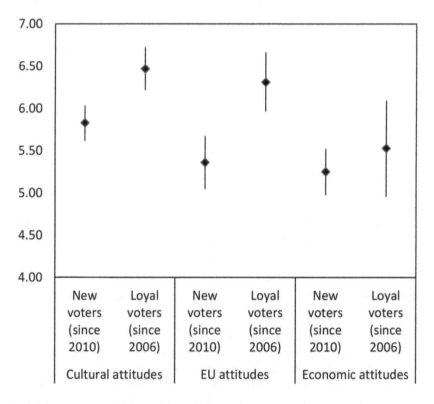

Figure 7.4 Attitudes of PVV supporters in 2010
Source: Dutch national parliamentary election study 2010.

With respect to the political conditions, they were initially relatively favourable for the PVV's vote-seeking strategy. The party suffered some problems with legitimacy in its building-up stage, but overall tendencies to demonise anti-immigration parties had decreased in the Netherlands after the turn of the century. Difficulties with legitimacy hampered the opportunity to enter national office – causing divisiveness within the Christian Democratic party about a coalition with the PVV – but these problems did not form an insurmountable obstacle. After 2012, when the PVV had pulled the plug on the Rutte I cabinet, the PVV became more isolated politically. Although the party maintained sufficient electoral strength to be a serious contender for office, conditions for joining a coalition had deteriorated, with few potential partners left. As the PVV radicalised its position on immigration and Islam, the media also became unanimously critical. The fact that Wilders will have to face a new trial for alleged discrimination indicates that legitimacy problems are far from resolved. Yet, in terms of vote-seeking, the legitimacy problems of the PVV have not damped down electoral success (Van Spanje and de Vreese 2015). Office-seeking, in contrast, has become more difficult as a result of political isolation.

Internal conditions are highly important for the success of new parties. In the case of the PVV, internal organisation is the principal problem that the party faces. Poor organisation is an obstacle to office-seeking, and in the long run, a party's institutionalisation is a condition for success in many other respects. For most political parties, institutionalisation takes years or even decades. The PVV had some years to build itself up, but the party had no members and no adequate mechanisms to create a reservoir of activists socialised through their participation in local and regional branches of the party. Rapid growth (such as in 2010, when the party gained 24 seats in parliament) posed a huge problem for the PVV, due to this lack of an internal reservoir of personnel. The PVV party elite partly consists of 'old hands' who are loyal, but new recruits still lack commitment to the party (De Lange and Art 2011). The negative example of the LPF – a party that dissolved quickly while in national office due to organisational weakness and internal conflicts – has induced Wilders to develop a strong and centralised control of the party. A successful office-seeking strategy is hampered by Wilders' autocratic leadership and by the difficulty of finding qualified candidates. Candidates not only have to be willing to join a party that suffers a social stigma, but they will also have little room to put their own stamp on the PVV programme or to pursue a political career. A high degree of loyalty to Wilders and to the party is required. Media contacts are supervised. Fleur Agema, a confidant of Wilders, controls both the media contacts and the parliamentary initiatives of all the members of parliament. Ex-PVV members complain that Wilders tends to demand exclusive media attention. For example, Wilders turned down a campaign film for the European elections that did not feature him prominently (Interview 4, 07-04-2015). PVV member Hero Brinkman openly advocated more freedom of media contacts and more say on the selection of candidates but lost his case and left the PVV. Members of a small and loyal group of confidants supervise the parliamentary committees and report to Wilders (Interview 1, 02-06-2014; Interview 3,

26-02-2015). Control of regional and local representatives is maintained by the mechanism of combining functions outside and inside The Hague (Interview 4, 07-04-2015; Lucardie and Voerman 2012: 180). Yet, central control from the top was sometimes difficult to extend beyond The Hague; interviews with ex-PVV members provide examples of some autonomy for representatives outside The Hague. For instance, members of the EU group contacted UKIP about future cooperation without informing Wilders, but this action did not have any repercussions (Interview 4, 07-04-2015). Although there appears to be some leeway for local and regional party groups, and for individual members with peripheral portfolios, dissidents complain about being whistled back by Wilders when they had demonstrated some initiative, such as making a policy report (Interview 1, 02-06-2014; Interview 4, 07-04-2015). Most important of all, according to PVV dissidents, there is little room for discussion. As one interviewee remembered, the election programme was drafted by a small group of loyalists, and he and other members of the parliamentary faction then 'got twenty minutes to read the draft' (Interview 3, 26-02-2015). Neither is there room for discussion within the parliamentary party about the assignment of portfolios (Aalberts and De Keijser 2015: 151–159). There are also various stories of critical PVV members being disciplined by being placed low on the candidate list, with no chance of being elected (Interview 1, 02-06-2014; Interview 4, 07-04-2015; see also Aalberts and De Keijser 2015; Hernandez 2012). In other words, internal support for party goals is mainly dependent on loyalty. With the option of giving voice being marginal, loyalty and exit have become the predominant features of interaction in the party's top ranks.

Wilders has difficulties in building consensus within the party on a strategy mainly aimed at vote-seeking. His explicit willingness to relinquish the spoils of office in order to maintain an uncompromising radical course is contested at the party's top level. PVV dissidents have been increasing in number in the parliamentary faction, European Parliament, Provincial Councils and local councils following the PVV's exit from national office in 2012. In particular, the exodus is notable in the Provincial Councils. The PVV had 69 members in the Provincial Councils following the 2011 elections; four years later, only 38 of these members were left. Eleven members had resigned, while 18 members had deserted the party but retained their seats in the councils (*NRC* 28-02-2015). Fourteen dissidents gave interviews complaining about the lack of openness in the party and Wilders' stubborn course (e.g., *Nu.nl* 24-04-2014). The dissidents were motivated to defect not only by Wilders' increasingly desecrating statements about immigrants but also his leftist course and the party's growing isolation. Two dissidents, Bontes and Van Klaveren, founded a new party, For the Netherlands (*Voor Nederland*, VNL), in May 2014. VNL positions itself as a respectable alternative to the PVV, at the far right of the political spectrum. Various other PVV dissidents have joined the new party, in particular former PVV members who were once elected to the Provincial Councils and the European Parliament (*Trouw* 08-01-2015).

The pressure of internal resistance, with dissidents voting with their feet, forced Wilders to modify his strategy somewhat. A few months before the

Provincial Council elections on 18 March 2015, Wilders decided to give provincial PVV representatives more leeway to pursue an office strategy.[13] Five of the 12 provincial PVV departments deleted the ban on civil servants wearing headscarves from their election programmes, and some of them explicitly did so in order to open up prospects for office (*Trouw* 29-01-2015). It is perhaps ironic that the party's organisational vulnerability puts pressure on Wilders to amend his undiluted vote-seeking course – the very vulnerability that was crucial in Wilders giving up national office in 2012 and setting all his cards on a vote-seeking course.

The PVV and mainstream politics

There is no sign that the PVV is going mainstream; on the contrary, the party is tending to radicalise. After the short-lived and failed experiment as a support party, the PVV stepped up its vote-seeking strategy and heightened its nativist and anti-establishment profile. The PVV's policy mission has become more pronounced, the party has become more isolated politically and the goal of office-seeking has been moved further from sight. Although the PVV moderated some policy goals between 2010 and 2012, the modifications were an effect of stumbling into office and of the commitment to a formal policy agreement, and not of a well-sustained office-seeking strategy.

Wilders has set the course of the PVV one-sidedly. He sought to enhance the anti-establishment profile and the nationalist profile of the party. He deliberately renounced his party's prospects of participating in local and regional office by intensifying the anti-immigrant and anti-Islam profile of the PVV. He appeared to have little ambition for office as long as this role demanded policy compromises and implied the risk of losing his strict grip on the party. An important reason for avoiding office has been the internal weakness of the PVV, but Wilders' efforts to maintain a strong hold on the party have been far from effective. His relinquishment of opportunities to enter office is one of the reasons that dissatisfaction within the party is increasing. As dissidents within the party have no voice, their only option is to exit. With various prominent PVV members voting with their feet against Wilders' vote-seeking course, he has been pressured to give some leeway to opponents in the party. Office-seeking, at least at the regional level, has made a wary and discreet comeback. As in 2010, the option of office is not sought by Wilders, but stumbled upon. The organisational obstacles that restrain Wilders from office-seeking are still fully in place. There is no sign that this situation will change anytime soon.

Notes

1 I would like to thank Sarah de Lange, Matthijs Rooduijn, Paul Lucardie and Cas Mudde for their valuable comments. Special thanks to Matthijs and Sarah for their contributions to the analyses of mainstreaming, again to Matthijs for his analysis of attitudes of PVV supporters and again to Sarah for her help with the interviews.
2 The foundation collects donations to support the PVV financially.

3 Except for new parties that resulted from mergers (see also Krouwel and Lucardie 2008).
4 For systematic analyses of the mainstreaming of PVV positions, I have made use of Chapel Hill Expert Surveys (CHES) (Bakker *et al.* forthcoming; Hooghe *et al.* 2010). To include recent elections and a broader analysis, the expert surveys have been complemented with content analyses of PVV election manifestos with respect to immigration/integration, socioeconomic positions and populism. For analyses of the salience of issues in the various PVV election campaigns, the Comparative Manifesto Project has been used (Volkens *et al.* 2013). I have added analyses of the main televised election debates of 2010 and 2012 to assess the salience of various issues in the PVV campaigns. The mainstreaming of the PVV's parliamentary behaviour has been systematically assessed by using the database www.tweedekamer.nl/kamerstukken. To track changes in voter profiles, the database Nationaal Kiezers Onderzoek has been used. A wide range of media sources, such as election debates and documentaries on television, newspapers and Internet sites have been used to assess the party's goals and strategies. In addition, interviews have been an important source for gaining insight into the goals of the PVV and for getting information about the internal organisation. I have interviewed four former PVV representatives – insiders who preferred to remain anonymous. Thanks to double functions and long-time experience in the PVV, these interviews covered a broad range of perspectives: the functioning of the PVV group in national parliament, in Provincial Councils and in the European Parliament. Besides experiences in representative fora, some of the interviewees had experience in back-stage positions as policy advisors or press managers. I have sent various requests for interviews to Wilders and other PVV members, as I am well aware that dissidents' perspectives may differ from those of loyal PVV members. To my regret, I received no response.
5 More than the six motions of confidence of other parties together.
6 According to public opinion, economic issues were highly important, but cultural issues such as tolerance and social cooperation were of even more concern (see SCP 2010).
7 Agendas for election debates on television are, to a large extent, set during nego-tiations between journalists and politicians about the issues to be addressed during the debates, but the outcomes are generally determined by journalists (see De Haan *et al.* 2014). However, although in 2006, the agendas of the very few election debates were completely preset, in 2010 and 2012, parts of the debates were left open.
8 In the election debates on television, this strategy was also apparent but was too incidental to assess quantitatively.
9 In the *Gedoogakkoord*, the PVV had explicitly committed itself not to present or support motions of confidence.
10 Six out of ten motions of confidence were initiated by the PVV (between 2012 and 2014).
11 Fritsma and Van Klaveren initiated 52 policy motions in 2010–2012; 35 were sup-ported only by the PVV, and 13 were also supported by the radical left-wing populist SP.
12 According to Wilders, the reason for breaking off the negotiations was that the PVV group in the European Parliament was divided about an alliance with UKIP. In one of our interviews, however, it was emphasised that Wilders did not like the prospect of working together with UKIP leader Farage and that negotiations were cancelled at his instigation (Interview 4, 07-04-2015).
13 'The provinces are completely free to make their own election programs. I have not interfered', Wilders said (*Trouw* 29-01-2015).

References

Aalberts, C. and de Keijser, D. (2015) *De Puinhopen van Rechts. De Partijen van Pim, Geert, Rita en Hero*, Delft: Eburon.

Afonso, A. (2015) 'Choosing whom to betray: Populist right-wing parties, welfare state reforms and the trade-off between office and votes', *European Political Science Review* 7, 2: 271–292.

Akkerman, T. (2012) 'Comparing radical right parties in government: Immigration and integration policies in nine countries (1996–2010)', *West European Politics* 35, 3: 511–529.

Bakker, P. and Vasterman, P. L. M. (2013) 'Wilders en de media', *Tijdschrift voor Communicatiewetenschappen* 41, 1: 82–98.

Bakker, R., de Vries, C., Edwards, E., Hooghe, L., Jolly, S., Marks, M., Polk, J., Rovny, J., Steenbergen, M. and Vachudova, M. (forthcoming) 'Measuring party positions in Europe: The Chapel Hill expert survey trend file, 1999–2010', *Party Politics*.

Bos, L. and van der Brug, W. (2010) 'Public images of leaders of anti–immigration parties: Perceptions of legitimacy and effectiveness', *Party Politics* 16, 6: 777–799.

Bos, L., van der Brug, W. and de Vreese, C. (2011) 'How the media shape perceptions of right-wing populist leaders', *Political Communication* 28, 2: 182–206

De Haan, Y., Groenhart, H., Hietbrink, N., Bakker, P. and van Liempt, A. (2014) 'Geven, nemen en keiharde voorwaarden. Onderhandelingen tussen politici en journalisten', in van Praag, Ph. and Brants, K. (eds) *Media, Macht & Politiek*, Diemen: AMB, pp. 45–65.

De Lange, S. L. (2007). 'A new winning formula? The programmatic appeal of the radical right', *Party Politics* 13, 4: 411–435.

De Lange, S. L. and Art, D. (2011) 'Fortuyn versus Wilders: An agency-based approach to radical right party building', *West European Politics* 34, 6: 1229–1249.

De Telegraaf (26-11-2011) 'Wilders: Nederland moet Denemarken achterna', www.tele graaf.nl/binnenland/20829115/__Geert_Wilders__Bagger__html (accessed 16-06-2015).

De Telegraaf (22-04-2014) 'PVV: 43% eens met minder Marokkanen', www.tele graaf.nl/binnenland/22535344/___43__eens_met_uitspraak_Wilders___.html (accessed 16-06-2015).

De Telegraaf (05-06-2014) 'Wilders vreest vervolging', www.telegraaf.nl/binnenland/ 22703992/__Wilders_vreest_vervolging__html (accessed 16-06-2015).

de Volkskrant (23-04-2010) 'Wilders: Niet voor Ali en Fatima', www.volkskrant.nl/dos sier-archief/wilders-niet-voor-ali-en-fatima~a987038/.

de Volkskrant (22-02-2014) 'Plots verzet in CDA velde Rutte I', www.volkskrant.nl/ dossier-archief/plots-verzet-in-cda-velde-rutte-i~a3601610/.

de Volkskrant (15-04-2014) 'Oud-PVV'ers in Kamer kiezen voor rechtse koers'. www.volkskrant.nl/dossier-archief/oud-pvvers-in-kamer-kiezen-voor-rechtse-koers~ a3635423/.

Fennema, M. (2011) *Geert Wilder Tovenaarsleerling*, Amsterdam: Prometheus.

Hernandez, M. (2012) *Geert Wilders Ontmaskerd. Van Messias tot Politieke Klaploper*, Soesterberg: Aspekt.

Hooghe, L., Bakker, R., Brigevich, A., de Vries, C., Edwards, E., Marks, G., Rovny, J. and Steenbergen, M. (2010) 'Reliability and validity of measuring party positions: The Chapel Hill expert surveys of 2002 and 2006', *European Journal of Political Research* 49: 684–703.

166   *Tjitske Akkerman*

Ivarsflaten, E. (2006) 'Reputational shields: Why most anti–immigrant parties failed in Western Europe, 1980–2005', Annual Meeting of the American Political Science Association, Philadelphia.

Ivarsflaten, E. (2008) 'What unites right-wing populists in Western Europe? Re-examining grievance mobilization models in seven successful cases', *Comparative Political Studies* 41, 1: 3–23.

Krouwel, A. and Lucardie, P. (2008) 'Waiting in the wings: New parties in the Netherlands', *Acta Politica* 43, 2: 278–307.

Kuitenbrouwer, J. (2012) *De Woorden van Wilders en Hoe Ze Werken*, Amsterdam: De Bezige Bij.

Lucardie, A. P. M. (2009) 'Rechts-extremisme, populisme of democratisch patriottisme? Opmerkingen over de politieke plaatsbepaling van de Partij voor de Vrijheid en Trots op Nederland', in Voerman, G. (ed.) *Jaarboek 2007 Documentatiecentrum Nederlandse Politieke Partijen*, Groningen: University of Groningen, pp. 176–190.

Lucardie, A. P. M. and Voerman, G. (2012) *Populisten in de Polder*, Amsterdam: Boom.

Nienhuis, A. (2010) 'Strafvervolging Wilders: Winst of Verlies? De Invloed van Strafvervolging Politicus voor zijn Uitspraken op Kiezers', Master Thesis, University of Amsterdam.

NOS Verkiezingsdebat (08-06-2010) 'Nederland kiest', www.npo.nl/nos-verkiezing sdebat/08-06-2010/10act0608natdeb (accessed 16-06-2015).

NOS-lijsttrekkersdebat (22-08-2012) http://nos.nl/video/409762-het-volledige-noslijst trekkersdebat.html (accessed 16-06-2015).

NOS (11-05-2014) 'Wilders', http://nos.nl/video/646673-volledig-europagesprek-met -wilders.html (accessed 16-06-2015).

NOS (26-11-2014) 'PVV: geen islam in Nederland', http://nos.nl/artikel/2005845-p vv-geen-islam-in-nederland.html (accessed 16-06-2015).

NPO (25-05-2014) 'Wilders Wereld', www.npo.nl/wilders-wereld/25-05-2014/AT_ 2013146 (accessed 16-06-2015).

NRC (15-01-2005) 'Wilders snuift in VS conservatieve thema's op', www.nrc.nl/ha ndelsblad/van/2005/januari/15/wilders-snuift-in-vs-conservatieve-themas-op-7717082 (accessed 16-06-2015).

NRC (13-11-2007) 'Extreem-rechts hielp partij Wilders', www.nrc.nl/handelsblad/van/ 2007/januari/13/extreem-rechts-hielp-wilders-11259075 (accessed 16-06-2015).

NRC (24-02-2007) 'Het koninkrijk van Allah zal er nooit komen', www.nrc.nl/hande lsblad/van/2007/februari/24/het-koninkrijk-van-allah-zal-er-nooit-komen-11281485 (accessed 16-06-2015).

NRC (23–04-2010) 'PVV wil rechts cabinet gedogen', www.nrc.nl/handelsblad/van/ 2010/april/23/pvv-wil-rechts-kabinet-gedogen-11880785 (accessed 16-06-2015).

NRC (25-09-2010) 'Ik denk, dus ik ben PVV', www.nrc.nl/handelsblad/van/2010/sep tember/25/ik-denk-dus-ik-ben-pvv-11947860 (accessed 16-06-2015).

NRC (14-09-2013) 'Mensen zien ons als een serieus alternatief', www.nrc.nl/handelsblad /van/2013/september/14/mensen-zien-ons-als-een-serieus-alternatief-1292987 (accessed 16-06-2015).

NRC (25-09-2013) 'Wilders: kabinet, ga naar huis – harde aanvaring met Pechtold', www.nrc.nl/nieuws/2013/09/25/wilders-opent-algemene-politieke-beschouwingen- ga-naar-huis/ (accessed 16-06-2015).

NRC (06-05-2014) 'Zuid-Hollands Statenlid is elfde PVV'er die uit de partij stapt', www.nrc.nl/handelsblad/van/2014/mei/06/zuid-hollands-statenlid-is-elfde-pvver-die- uit-d-1376010 (accessed 16-06-2015).

NRC (28-02-2015) 'PVV-politica Marjolein Faber huurde bedrijf van haar zoon in', www.nrc.nl/nieuws/2015/02/28/pvv-politica-marjolein-faber-huurde-bedrijf-van-haar-zoon-in/ (accessed 16-06-2015).

Nu.nl (09-03-2014) 'De mooiste tijden voor de PVV liggen nog voor ons', www.nu.nl/p olitiek/3721400/de-mooiste-tijden-pvv-liggen-nog-ons.html (accessed 16-06-2015).

Nu.nl (21-03-2014) 'Overzicht: vertrokken PVV'ers', www.nu.nl/geert-wilders/3732 850/overzicht-vertrokken-pvvers.html (accessed 16-06-2015).

Nu.nl (24-04-2014) 'Overzicht: vertrokken PVVérs', www.nu.nl/geert-wilders/373 2850/overzicht-vertrokken-pvvers.html (accessed 21-10-2015).

Nu.nl (22-05-2014) 'Wilders liet Rutte-I vallen om gedoe in PVV', www.nu.nl/poli tiek/3782877/wilders-liet-rutte-i-vallen-gedoe-in-pvv.html (accessed 16-06-2015).

Otjes, S. P. (2012) 'Imitating the newcomer. How, when and why established political parties imitate the policy positions and issue attention of new political parties in the electoral and parliamentary arena: The case of the Netherlands', Doctoral Thesis, Leiden University.

Otjes, S. and Louwerse, T. (2013) 'Een bijzonder meerderheidskabinet? Parlementair gedrag tijdens het kabinet Rutte-I', *Res Publica* 55, 4: 459–480.

Partij voor de Vrijheid (2006) 'Een Nederland om weer trots op te zijn', http://irs.ub. rug.nl/dbi/4c750f6f78d2c (accessed 16-06-2015).

Partij voor de Vrijheid (2010) 'De agenda van hoop en optimisme. Een tijd om te kiezen', http://irs.ub.rug.nl/dbi/4c333c0b343fc (accessed 16-06-2015).

Partij voor de Vrijheid (2012) 'Hún Brussel, ons Nederland', http://irs.ub.rug.nl/dbi/ 4ff53db3f079c (accessed 16-06-2015).

Peilingwijzer (31-08-2013) http://peilingwijzer.tomlouwerse.nl/search?updated-ma x=2013-11-01T10:57:00%2B01:00&max-results=3&start=24&by-date=false (accessed 16-06-2015).

Peilingwijzer (10-12-2014) http://peilingwijzer.tomlouwerse.nl/search?updated-max= 2015-02-23T17:13:00%2B01:00&max-results=3 (accessed 16-16-2015).

Rooduijn, M. (2013) 'A populist Zeitgeist? The impact of populism on parties, media and the public in Western Europe'. PhD thesis, University of Amsterdam.

RTL4 Premiersdebat (26-08-2012) 'Het Premiersdebat', www.youtube.com/watch?v= QrYC8GDc54M (accessed 16-06-2015).

Scholten, O., Ruigrok, N., Krijt, M., Schaper, J. and Paanakker, H. (2008) *Fitna en de Media. Een Onderzoek naar Aandacht en Rolpatronen*, Amsterdam: Nederlandse Nieuwsmonitor.

SCP (2010) *COB Kwartaalbericht 2010* (parts 1, 2 and 3), www.scp.nl/Publicaties/Alle_p ublicaties/Publicaties_2010/COB_Kwartaalbericht_2010_1; www.scp.nl/Publicaties/ Alle_publicaties/Publicaties_2010/COB_Kwartaalbericht_2010_2; www.scp.nl/Pub licaties/Alle_publicaties/Publicaties_2010/COB_Kwartaalbericht_2010_3 (accessed 16-06-2015).

Trouw (26-03-2009) 'PVV loopt woedend weg uit crisisdebat', www.trouw.nl/tr/nl/ 4324/nieuws/article/detail/1137456/2009/03/26/PVV-loopt-woedend-weg-uit-cri sisdebat.dhtml (accessed 16-06-2015).

Trouw (08-01-2015) 'Ontevreden PVV'ers nemen toevlucht tot VNL'. www.trouw.nl/ tr/nl/4492/Nederland/article/detail/3825396/2015/01/08/Ontevreden-PVV-ers-nem en-toevlucht-tot-VNL.dhtml (accessed 16-06-2015).

Trouw (12-01-2015) 'PVV geïsoleerd in Kamer sinds Wilders' Marokkanen-speech', www. trouw.nl/tr/nl/5009/Archief/article/detail/3827833/2015/01/12/PVV-geisoleerd-in-Ka mer-sinds-Wilders-Marokkanen-speech.dhtml (accessed 16-06-2015).

Trouw (29-01-2015) 'Hoofddoek mag soms toch van PVV', www.trouw.nl/tr/nl/5009/ Archief/article/detail/3839930/2015/01/29/Hoofddoek-mag-soms-toch-van-PVV.dh tml (accessed 16-06-2015).

Van der Brug, W. and van Spanje, J. (2009) 'Immigration, Europe and the "new" cultural dimension', *European Journal of Political Research* 48, 3: 309–334.

Van Heerden, S. (2014) 'What did you just call me? A study on the demonization of political parties in the Netherlands between 1995 and 2011', Dissertation, University of Amsterdam.

Van Heerden, S. and Creusen, B. (2014) 'Responding to the populist radical right: The Dutch case', in Sandelind, C. (ed.) *European Populism and Winning the Immigration Debate*, Falun: Scandbook, pp. 179–213.

Van Heerden, S., de Lange, S. L., van der Brug, W. and Fennema, M. (2014) 'The immigration and integration debate in the Netherlands: Discursive and programmatic reactions to the rise of anti-immigration parties', *Journal of Ethnic and Migration Studies* 40, 1: 119–136.

Van Holsteyn, J. J. (2007) 'The Dutch parliamentary elections of 2006', *West European Politics* 30, 5, 1139–1147.

Van Leeuwen, M. (2009) 'Het hoofdzinnenbeleid van Wilders: Over de stijl van Geert Wilders en Ella Vogelaar', *Tekst* 2, 6.

Van Spanje, J. and de Vreese, C. (2015) 'The good, the bad and the voter: The impact of hate speech prosecution of a politician on electoral support for his party', *Party Politics* 21, 1: 115–130.

Volkens, A., Bara, J., Budge, I., McDonald, M. D. and Klingemann, H.-D. (2013) *Mapping Policy Preferences from Texts: Statistical Solutions for Manifesto Analysis*, Oxford: Oxford University Press.

Vossen, K. (2011) 'Classifying Wilders: The ideological development of Geert Wilders and his Party for Freedom', *Politics* 31, 3: 179–189.

Vossen, K. (2013) *Rondom Wilders: Portret van de PVV*, Amsterdam: Boom.

Vrij Nederland (21-05-2014) 'Hoe Wilders over zijn eigen grens ging', www.vn.nl/ Archief/Politiek/Artikel-Politiek/Hoe-Wilders-over-zijn-eigen-grens-ging.htm (accessed 16-06-2015).

Zwart, J. (2009) '"Fitna Was een Splijtzwam". Onderzoek naar de Berichtgeving over Fitna door Nova', Master Thesis, University of Amsterdam.

8 The taming of the shrew

How the Progress Party (almost) became part of the mainstream

Anders Ravik Jupskås

Introduction[1]

Like most other radical right-wing populist parties in Western Europe, the Progress Party (Fremskrittspartiet, FrP) in Norway was initially dismissed as a short-lived vehicle of protest, and as a single-issue-oriented, ideologically extreme, and un-coalitionable party. However, since the mid-1990s, the party has become increasingly electorally successful, ideologically cohesive, organisationally institutionalised, and politically influential (Jupskås 2015). In 2013, the party even entered government at the national level for the first time as part of a right-wing minority coalition. Does this mean that the FrP has become part of the mainstream?

This chapter first sketches the general electoral and ideological evolution of the FrP, including its origin as an anti-tax revolt, gradual transformation to a more clear-cut radical right-wing populist party followed by a profound party crisis, and recent developments towards a junior partner in a right-wing governing coalition. The second section considers the degree to which the FrP has moved into the mainstream by assessing party change along four key dimensions: (1) programmatic scope, (2) ideological position on niche issues, (3) anti-establishment orientation and behaviour, and (4) linkages to right-wing extremism. The next section interprets the findings in light of changing goals and priorities by the party leadership. Finally, before summarising the main findings towards the end, the fourth section briefly discusses how these goals have been informed by internal and external constraints and opportunities.

Origin, ideology and electoral development

The FrP emerged in 1973 as an entrepreneurial issue party. Anders Lange's Party for a Strong Reduction in Taxes, Duties and Public Intervention (ALP) as the FrP was initially called, gained 5 per cent of the votes (and four seats in parliament) only a few months after the party had been founded (see Figure 8.1). Until the party picked up the anti-immigration issue in the late 1980s, it was primarily promoting a neo-liberal populist agenda (Goul Andersen and Bjørklund 2000). The electoral support was unstable and modest.

The ideological change from an anti-tax party towards a radical right-wing populist party mobilising on xenophobia had an immediate effect on the voters and the party organisation. In the electoral arena, support increased significantly and rapidly after the chairman played 'the immigration card' for the first time in the 1987 local elections (see Figure 8.1) (Bjørklund 1988). Two years later, in 1989, the FrP finished as the third largest party also at the national level. Internally, however, the shift towards xenophobic campaigning, in addition to a few other issues, contributed to growing factionalism. With the influx of new members and voters, the party was increasingly divided into three distinct factions: the libertarians (who dominated among the party elite), the Christian-conservatives and the national-populists (Iversen 1998). And while the libertarians won the first battle (i.e., the FrP downplayed the immigration issue in elections in the early 1990s), they lost the final battle over the party's soul (see below). After an agonising party convention in 1994, where the invaluable chairman since 1978, Carl I. Hagen, eventually sided with the two other factions against the libertarians, most of the libertarians left the party.

Since then, the party has clearly been a radical right-wing populist party, although it might be a milder version of (Kitschelt and McGann 1995: 121) or less nativist than (Mudde 2007: 47) similar parties elsewhere. First, the party is profoundly populist appealing to 'ordinary people', attacking the established parties and other elites, and promoting plebiscitarian democracy (Bjørklund 2004). Second, xenophobia and welfare chauvinism have been the most important issues for voters, members and candidates of the party since the late 1980s (Goul Andersen and Bjørklund 2000; Hagelund 2005; Jupskås 2015), even if other aspects of the party's policy are not particularly nationalist oriented (e.g., its rather libertarian cultural policies, and its ambivalence *vis-à-vis* Norwegian membership in the EU) (Hylland

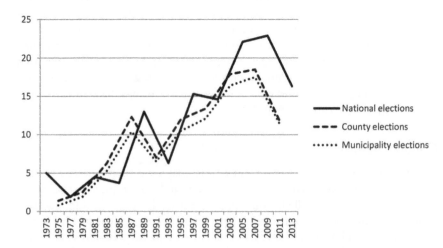

Figure 8.1 Electoral development of the FrP, national and subnational level 1973–2013 (in per cent)
Source: Statistics Norway.

2011; Skinner 2011). Third, the party has also been fairly authoritarian challenging for example the liberal approach to crime and punishment, often referred to as 'Nordic exceptionalism' (Pratt and Eriksson 2013).

In the most recent decades, the party has gained between 14.6 per cent (in 2001) and 22.9 per cent (in 2009) in national elections (Figure 8.1), to a large extent due to the immigration issue (Aardal 2003b; Aardal 2011a). Moreover, the support has become more equally distributed across the 19 electoral districts and the party has gradually penetrated the subnational level. In other words, the FrP has become more institutionalised, although voter loyalty and party identification continue to be at a fairly low level (Aardal 2011c: 24; Jupskås 2015: 118). In the 2011 local elections and 2013 national election, the FrP experienced a significant drop in electoral support. Despite (or perhaps due to) decreasing electoral support, the party was able to enter government for the first time as a junior partner in a minority right-wing coalition with the Conservatives (Høyre, H) in 2013. While the party has not been subjected to a *cordon sanitaire* to the same extent as a few other radical right-wing populist parties, it was not accepted as a governing party by the other parties until very recently. Two centrist parties – the Christian People's Party (Kristelig Folkeparti, KrF) and the Liberal Party (Venstre, V) – were also invited to take part in the coalition, but decided, for ideological reasons, to act only as formal parliamentary support parties (Allern and Karlsen 2014: 660). As a governing party, the support for the FrP has eroded even further, and current polls, in May 2015, suggest that at least one-fifth of the voters has left the party.[2]

Moving into the mainstream

Since the mid-1990s, the development of the party could be divided into four different phases regarding its relationship with the mainstream. Although such periodisation underestimates that party change tends to be characterised by gradual transition rather than fundamental rupture, these four phases differ to a greater or lesser extent with regard to the scope of the programmatic appeal, the degree of radicalism, the intensity of anti-establishment rhetoric and behaviour, and the existence of linkages to right-wing extremism. The first three of these phases concern how the party changed *before* it entered office, while the fourth and final phase is related to how the party has changed *after* it gained power in 2013.

1995–1999: radicalisation

After the party split in 1994, the FrP moved away from the mainstream. It quickly re-introduced and radicalised its position and rhetoric on the anti-immigration issue. Even if socioeconomic policies continued to occupy a central position in the party manifesto (see Appendix), the party became increasingly associated with the immigration issue in the public debate. In fact, the immigration issue came to dominate the party's agenda to the extent that commentators referred to the FrP as a 'single-issue party' (e.g., *Aftenposten* 22-04-1996). This perception was somewhat modified towards the end of the period when geriatric care emerged as another important issue (Aardal 1999: 24, see also Table 8.1). In 1997, the Labour party (Arbeiderpartiet, Ap) and the FrP tried to mobilise on almost identical slogans: 'elderly and health care first' (Ap) and 'health care and geriatric care – job number one' (FrP) (Bjørklund 2005: 450). However, the FrP was first and foremost known as an anti-immigration party. As noted by Hagelund (2003: 58), the campaign in 1999 started with politicians from the FrP 'appearing in what had come to be seen as their characteristic posture', namely 'open meetings on immigration politics'. At the opening of the campaign in Oslo in 1999, Hagen also turned immigration into a key issue by linking the influx of immigrants to rising housing prices (Ekeberg and Snoen 2001: 307).

The rhetoric and arguments were far more radical than they had been in the late 1980s. While the party initially criticised immigrants for being an economic burden and a problem for the welfare state, immigrants were increasingly seen as a source of increased criminality and/or a cultural threat (Hagelund 2003). Two controversial MPs – Vidar Kleppe and Øystein Hedstrøm – were particularly active in the public debate arguing that immigration leads to 'murder, drugs and other types of crime' and that the established parties were was about to 'ruin our nation with [immigrants]' (quoted in Hagelund 2003: 58).

The party did not only appear in public with a radicalised rhetoric, however; the manifesto was re-written too. Most importantly, in 1997, the official party manifesto included for the first time statements which could be interpreted as traditional biological racism. In short, it was argued that the current levels of immigration would lead to 'rapid changes of the general character associated with our population' (FrP 1997). Moreover, while the manifesto in 1993 explicitly stated that one had to fight racism and discrimination, this section had been deleted in the 1997 manifesto (Bjørklund and Goul Andersen 2002: 113). The party also radicalised with regard to law and order policies, and the new manifesto of 1997 argued in favour of re-introducing the death penalty (in cases related national emergency) (FrP 1997).

In this period of radicalisation, some factions in the FrP appeared to cultivate contacts and share policy ideas with extreme right groups and hardcore nationalist organisations (Jupskås 2015: 74–101). In 1995, for example, the above-mentioned MP, Hedstrøm, participated in a secret meeting with infamous extreme right activists in the eastern part of Oslo during the election campaign (Bjørklund 1999: 27), and it was later revealed that some of these activists had actually contributed to a controversial parliamentary motion demanding an 'immigration account' (Skarsbø Moen 2006: 254–55).

Anti-establishment behaviour and rhetoric once again emerged as core values. One commentator argued that Hagen seemed to re-create the protest movement he initially criticised in the late 1970s and 1980s (*Aftenposten* 31-03-1995). In parliament, the party was voting alone. While the parliamentary party disagreed with H in only one fifth of the votes in the first half of the 1990s, the level of disagreement increased to half of the votes in the late 1990s (see Figure 8.2). However, it should be noted that the party helped to pass the centrist government's state budget in 1997 and 1998 together with H (Narud and Valen 2007: 223). And while the party had issued several motions of non-confidence against the Ap-governments (1990–1997), no such motions were issued against the centrist government (1997–2000). These two observations certainly qualify the image of a profoundly anti-establishment-oriented party.

2000–2005: partial mainstreaming

At the beginning of the new millennium, the FrP changed its course, and the rhetoric regarding immigration policies was toned down. In 1999, the party selected two vice-chairmen who were seen as much more responsible and professional than previous vice-chairmen. Subsequently, in the year after, the most radical MPs were either excluded or forced to keep a low profile (Bjørklund 2003: 133). In the manifesto, the controversial concept *fjernkulturelle* (people who are culturally distant, 'alien') was replaced with the more neutral *utlendinger* (foreigners) and statements that could be interpreted as examples of biological racism were removed. Moreover, the manifesto included a completely new section on tolerance (Jupskås 2015: 87).

The programmatic appeal was further expanded and the party was no longer campaigning exclusively on anti-immigration. Prior to the national election in 2001, it was decided to focus less on the immigration issue. Instead, the party tried to mobilise on welfare, frequently in a welfare chauvinist manner (Bjørklund 2005: 447). And again, the party picked an almost identical slogan as the Ap.

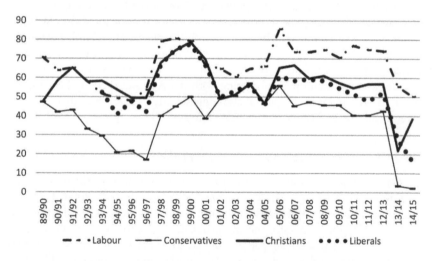

Figure 8.2 Disagreement index, parliamentary periods from 1989 to 2015
Note: The figure shows the level of disagreement in parliamentary votes between the FrP, the Conservatives (H), the Labour (the Ap), the Christians (KrF) and the Liberals (V). The index runs from 0 (no disagreement) to 100 (full disagreement on all votes). Source: NSD Voteringsarkiv.

When the latter said 'If welfare is most important, vote the Ap', the FrP responded 'Welfare *is* most important. Vote the FrP' (Bjørklund 2005: 450). The most important welfare issue was geriatric care (Bjørklund 2003: 139). While the increasing emphasis on welfare issues may seem paradoxical for a former anti-tax party, especially since the party continued to be sceptical of taxation, large public oil revenues allowed the party to promote *more* welfare and *less* taxation at the same time. The slogan from 2001 – 'We can afford!' (Hagen 2007: 395) – is a good illustration. Spending so-called 'oil-money' has been an important mobilising issue for the FrP since 2001 (Aardal 2003c; Narud and Aardal 2007). Also in 2005, the party was campaigning on a wide range of issues, including law and order, immigration, and the combination of right-wing (e.g., privatisation and anti-taxes) and left-wing economic policies (e.g., increased public spending on welfare) (Sitter 2006: 578).

In sum, these changes indicate that the party was trying to get rid of its reputation as being not respectable and single-issue oriented. However, the actual anti-immigration policies remained equally, if not more radical (see below). Indeed, even if governmental policies became much more restrictive toward the end of the 1990s, there were still very significant differences between the FrP and the mainstream parties (Bjørklund and Goul Andersen 2002: 114). Moreover, the campaign strategy continued to be highly controversial. In 2005, for example, the party published a poster of an immigrant juvenile with a shotgun stating 'the perpetrator is of foreign origin'.

In parliament, the relationship with other parties continued to be characterised by ambivalence and lack of mutual trust. Although the FrP acted as a support party of the centre-right government on several state budgets (Narud and Valen 2007: 223), the collaboration was never formalised to the same extent as it was in Denmark when the Danish People's Party (Dansk Folkeparti, DF) supported minority governments. On one occasion, the government threatened to resign in order to get the support from the FrP and on another, the government ended up collaborating with the Ap instead of the FrP. Voting patterns in parliament in this period also suggest fairly high levels of disagreement between the FrP and other parties (see Figure 8.2).[3]

2006–2012: less anti-establishment, yet still radical

The gradual transformation toward the mainstream was fortified after Siv Jensen replaced the longstanding chairman, Carl I. Hagen, in 2006. First, the party consolidated a comprehensive platform. Socioeconomic issues still accounted for about half of the manifesto, and the manifesto as a whole became increasingly similar to that of the mainstream parties (Jupskås 2015: 57). Campaign issues in 2009 were infrastructure, health- and geriatric care, anti-tax and education, in addition to typical niche issues (law and order and immigration) (FrP 2009b). Second, voting patterns in parliament suggest that the FrP was gradually moving in the direction of the other parties between 2006 and 2012 – H in particular (see Figure 8.2). And while the party previously issued motions of non-confidence alone, either all or at least some of the other non-socialist parties supported such motions during the red-green government between 2005 and 2013. This suggests a development towards a more constructive rather than confrontational oppositional behaviour.

However, even these signs of moderation should not be exaggerated. Although the FrP has never challenged the formal rules of the game (Goul Andersen and Bjørklund 2000: 202), the party has behaved differently than other more mainstream opposition parties with regard to several aspects of ordinary parliamentary activity. This is particularly striking if we look at the number of written questions to the ministers. In fact, until the party entered office, the activity has been so high that one could see it as a way of 'bullying the executive' (see Figure 8.3). For example, it has been documented that at least some of the questions were not particularly well prepared (*Dagens Naeringsliv* 04-12-2012).

The ideological position on niche issues did not change much either. To be sure, the anti-immigration and integration arguments were presented within a pseudo-liberal, and therefore more acceptable discourse (Akkerman and Hagelund 2007; Jupskås 2015), yet the actual policies were increasingly radical. In the manifestos, the party became *more* restrictive throughout the 2000s, and continued to be the only party linking immigration with emerging cultural conflicts (Simonnes 2013: 155–56). Ever since 1997, the party's manifestos have argued that immigration (of asylum-seekers) will lead to 'serious clashes between ethnic groups [folkegrupper] in Norway' (Simonnes 2013: 149). Key party representatives have also continued to use fairly radical rhetoric (see also Fangen and Vaage 2015). For example, party leader Siv Jensen introduced the concept of 'sneak Islamisation' in the Norwegian public debate in 2009 (Jupskås 2015: 68) and MP Christian Tybring-Gjedde published a high

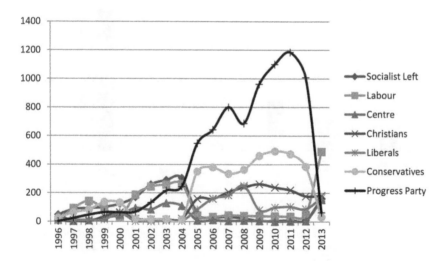

Figure 8.3 Number of written questions from members of parliament to the government 1996–2013

Source: Parliamentary registers for 1996–2008, see Rasch (2011). The author has collected figures for 2009–2013.

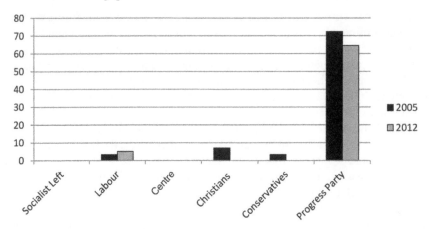

Figure 8.4 Support for the statement 'Immigration is a serious threat to our national
        culture' among members of parliament 2005–2012 (in per cent)
Note: The figure shows the percentage of MPs who agree completely or agree somewhat on a
Likert scale (1–5). The Liberal Party (V) is not included due to small number of respondents.
Source: Parliamentary surveys 2005 and 2012. Overall response rate was 69 per cent in
both surveys. The author has made the calculations.

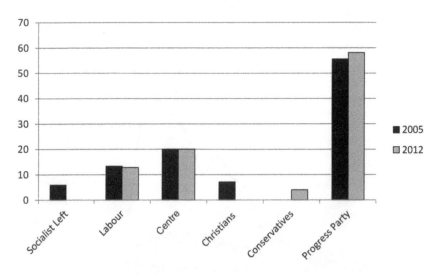

Figure 8.5 Support for the statement 'In bad times, we should first and foremost provide
        jobs for Norwegians' among members of parliament 2005–2012
Note: See previous figure.
Source: See previous figure.

profiled op-ed in 2010 in which he accused the Ap of 'cultural betrayal' (*Aften-posten* 26-08-2010). Generally speaking, although Islam and Muslims were hardly mentioned in the party manifestos, criticism of this particular religion and its followers played an important role in the public rhetoric of many prominent party representatives (Bangstad 2013).

Surveys among members of parliament in 2005 and 2012 corroborate these findings (see Figures 8.4 and 8.5). Asked whether or not 'immigration is a serious threat to our national culture', more than 70 per cent agreed completely or agreed somewhat in 2005. The figures were almost identical in 2012. Similarly, more than half of the MPs in 2005 and 2012 agreed completely or agreed somewhat that 'we should first and foremost provide jobs for Norwegian in bad times'. At both times, the uniqueness of the FrP is demonstrated. Neither the cultural threat perspective nor the economic chauvinist argument gained any support in other parties.

The authoritarian position has not changed much either, though recent manifestos put a stronger emphasis on preventive work and the bullet point on the death penalty has been deleted (FrP 2009a). Throughout the period, the party has argued in favour of much harsher punishments; the removal of 'quantity discount' when convicted for multiple violations of the law; introduction of medical treatment of repetitive serious sexual offenders; insuring that prisoners serve their time according to the actual length of sentences (FrP 1997, 2009a). In addition, the FrP has consistently criticised the system for being more concerned with perpetrators than victims (FrP 2005, 2009a). In 2011, a few months before the local elections, the party launched a controversial 10-point list on how to make the penal system significantly stricter, especially for foreigners (*Verdens Gang* 13-05-2011).

Again, surveys confirm this stability and clearly show the difference between the FrP and other parties. Asked whether or not preventive work is superior to tougher sentences as a way of curbing crime, more than 40 per cent of the congress delegates in the FrP in both 2001 and 2009 disagreed (see Figure 8.6). In all other parties, an overwhelming majority agreed that preventive work is the best strategy, with a very small authoritarian faction in H disagreeing.

Euroscepticism, an important niche issue of most radical right-wing populist parties, has been less important for the FrP. In Norway, which is highly integrated into but not formally a member of the EU, Euroscepticism has first and foremost been mobilised by centrist and socialist parties (e.g., Aardal 2003a: 63). The FrP has struggled with the issue, not least due to internal division as to whether or not Norway should join the EU (Saglie 2002), and the manifestos have therefore been neutral on this issue (i.e., arguing in favour of a new referendum) (FrP 1997, 2009a). Over time, however, the party has drifted towards a more revisionist Eurosceptic position, preferring the EU as it was pre-Maastricht (Skinner 2011). In short, there has been a growing aversion to the deepening of integration, the EU's social dimension, EU bureaucracy, EU regulation and foreign policy cooperation. Moreover, a growing share of congress delegates and members of parliament is against joining the EU (Jupskås and Gyárfášová 2012: 167–169).

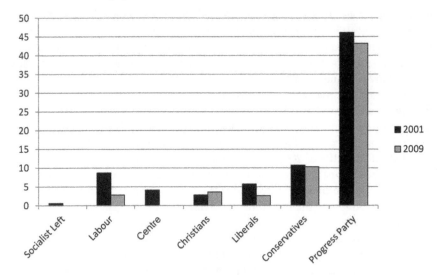

Figure 8.6 Disapproval of the statement 'To curb crime, preventive work is better than tough sentences' among congress delegates 2001–2009 (in per cent)

Note: The figure shows the percentage of MPs who disagree completely or disagree somewhat on a Likert scale (1–5). Don't knows are included. The author has made the calculations.

Source: Congress delegate survey 2009. Overall response rate was 49 per cent.

2013–2015: further mainstreaming with an emerging Janus face

The gradual transformation towards a mainstream party has been reinforced after the party entered office in 2013. The party has become less anti-establishment and less radical in its immigration rhetoric and policies, though there seems to be an emerging division between the party in government and the party in parliament.

The parliamentary party votes together with H on basically all issues and quite often with the parliamentary support parties (less than 20 per cent disagreement with V and between 20 per cent and 40 per cent disagreement with KrF) (see Figure 8.2). Also with regard to the number of written questions to the ministers, the FrP seems to behave according to its newly acquired role as a more responsible party. Very few written questions have been sent from the parliamentary group to the government (see Figure 8.3).

As regards the immigration issue, there were few signs of moderation before entering office. The most recent manifesto was quite similar to previous manifestos (FrP 2013) and the level of immigration was criticised for being 'culturally unsustainable' during the campaign (*NRK* 08-08-2013). However, not many of the party's ideas were included in the government platform. In fact, the narrative about immigration presented there was almost the complete opposite of xenophobia and welfare-chauvinism: 'Immigration has contributed to economic growth in Norway and made us a more diversified [mangfoldig] nation' (H/FrP 2013: 14).

Moreover, there seems to be a profound shift of rhetoric, especially among those representing the party in government (Fangen and Vaage 2015: 61–62). While the party in opposition argued that racism was caused by a liberal immigration policy, the party in government has focused more on poor integration. Consequently, the FrP representatives propose different policies in order to solve 'the problem' – either less *immigration* (party in opposition or those outside the government apparatus) or better *integration* (party in government). Furthermore, whereas the party in opposition was highly critical of the Ap, the party in government has emphasised cross-partisan agreement concerning the continuation of a strict immigration policy. And last but not least, while the party in opposition promoted (and still promotes) xeno-phobic narratives, the party in government has provided a qualified view and/or positive evaluation of immigration policies and immigrants. For example, Minister of Children, Equality and Social Inclusion, Solveig Horne (FrP), recently stated that 'immigration is good for society' (*Aftenposten* 16-03-2015).

However, the parliamentary party has challenged this mainstreaming of the party in government. As in the 1990s, there are signs of an emerging Janus face (Fangen and Vaage 2015: 57–61). Most notably, the parliamentary party has proposed refer-endums regarding immigration twice (i.e., about the level of immigration in general and Syrian refugees in particular), although this has not been official govern-mental policies (*Verdens Gang* 11-02-2014; *Aftenposten* 12-05-2015). A prominent member of parliament, Christian Tybring-Gjedde (2014), published a dystopic book with the Titanic-inspired title *While the orchestra continues to play* in which he strongly condemned the government's immigration policies. Vice-chairman, Per Sandberg (2013), also published an autobiography in 2013 in which he criticised the pro-fessionalisation of the party. And more recently, in early 2015, Sandberg gained extensive coverage in the press after publicly accusing KrF for having indirectly contributed to the recruitment of so-called 'foreign fighters' to the Islamic State (*Aftenposten* 22-02-2015).

Changing goals and priorities

The assessment of the FrP's development in recent decades suggests a gradual yet incomplete transformation into a mainstream party. On the one hand, the party has clearly done away with previous linkages to extreme right milieux, as well as de-radicalised its rhetoric regarding immigration policies, not least after the party entered government. The FrP has also become less anti-establishment oriented and further expanded its socioeconomic profile. On the other hand, a growing tension about immigration policies within the party became apparent. The next section will assess the partial changing course towards the mainstream with reference to changing party goals.

1994–1999: vote-maximisation and double communication

After the party split in 1994, the FrP was first and foremost driven by vote-seeking motives. As a consequence of the internal struggle between the libertarians and other factions in the party, the support had dropped below the electoral threshold (*Verdens Gang* 06-05-1994) and chairman Hagen believed that the only way to recover electorally was by pursuing a purely oppositional strategy (Ekeberg and Snoen 2001: 260). Votes were considered a necessary requisite for future positions and policy influence (FrP 1996). Hagen had previously experienced the mobilising capacity of the immigration issue and he was hoping it could bring the party above the threshold and back into Norwegian party politics (Hagen 2007: 251). Initially, however, the radicalising strategy only paid off partially. Yet, when it emerged as a salient issue towards the end of the 1995-campaign (due to Hedstrøm's participation in a secret meeting with other extreme right activists), Hagen (2007: 251) deliberately and successfully exploited the situation and criticised the establishment for being unwilling to discuss the problems of immigration. Almost all voters who were concerned with anti-immigration policies voted for the FrP (Bjørklund 1999: 183).

Although the radicalised position and linkages to more extreme groups provided the FrP with much needed publicity in the media and electoral growth, it alienated some voters, as well as prominent representatives and potential coalition partners at the subnational level (Ekeberg and Snoen 2001: 266, 274). The FrP was widely perceived as promoting racist immigration policies or exploiting racist tendencies among the public, even if elites (i.e., other parties, intellectuals and the media) usually argued that neither the leader nor the party as a whole could be considered racist – only as 'indecent' (Hagelund 2003; Jupskås 2015). In order to minimise the costs related to a radicalising position, it was widely argued that Hagen pursued a strategy of 'double communication' in this period (*Aftenposten* 09-09-1996; *Verdens Gang* 09-09-1997; *Aftenposten* 30-07-1999). On the one hand, Hagen never disassociated himself from radical statements from other MPs, and he supported the uncompromising strategy at the local level and put a lid on all kinds of internal criticism (Bjørklund and Saglie 2002: 12; Ekeberg and Snoen 2001: 266, 278). On the other hand, Hagen himself usually 'managed to keep [his] criticism of immigration and refugee policies within socially acceptable limits' (Goul Andersen and Bjørklund 2000: 205). And whenever the FrP was linked to other anti-immigration parties abroad, Hagen always claimed that the party was much more moderate and respectable (Jupskås 2015: 81–83).

2000–2005: preparing for office – but not without trade-offs

The change of course at the turn of the millennium towards a party with less radical immigration policies and rhetoric, and consolidation of its reputation as a non-extremist party suggest that office-seeking motives became increasingly important among the party's leadership. To some extent, the seeds (for such a strategy) had been sowed a few years earlier when the party finished as the largest non-socialist party in the 1997 national election. For the first time the chairman started day-dreaming about getting the party into office (Hagen 2007: 309–310) and Hagen (somewhat unsuccessfully) warned against turning the party into a single issue party (*Verdens Gang* 20-02-1999). Moreover, the party tried to improve its relationship with other non-socialist parties by functioning as a fairly reliable support party for the newly created centrist government. In fact, in budget negotiations between the centrist government and right-wing parties, the FrP was usually more pragmatic and yielding than H (Ekeberg and Snoen 2001: 299).

This office-strategy was further strengthened in 2000 when the national council agreed that the party would seek office after the next parliamentary election in 2001 (FrP 1999/2000: 27–28). Hagen had already been launched as a candidate for Prime Minister (Ekeberg and Snoen 2001: 329) and the leadership was referring to the party as a governing party in the media (e.g., *NTB* 20-02-2000). As head of the pro-gramme committee, the newly elected vice-chairman, Siv Jensen, was able to change the manifesto in the direction of being more socioeconomically centrist, rhetorically less radical, and more pragmatic (Ekeberg and Snoen 2001: 330; Skarsbø Moen 2006: 300). The party was no longer in favour of two waiting days before paying during sick leave. Controversial anti-immigration concepts and arguments were removed from the manifestos (FrP 2001). And most of the reforms were now supposed to be implemented gradually rather than immediately. A more centrist profile in economic policies was adopted primarily due to vote-seeking motives (i.e., to take more working-class voters from the Ap),[4] but it also brought the party closer to the centrist parties, which have never been particularly right-wing in their economic policies (Narud and Valen 2007: 140, 173).

Not surprisingly, this new office-seeking strategy was not without trade-offs. Internal democracy was further limited and electoral results were disappointing compared to the promising polls. While the dominant parliamentary faction wanted – in the words of Hagen (2007: 359) – to 'continue the development towards a more serious party', a minority of seven MPs wanted the party to remain anti-establishment oriented and radical in immigration policies. This situa-tion was not only problematic with regard to party cohesion, but it also constituted one of the main obstacles for future government participation (Ekeberg and Snoen 2001: 330ff; Skarsbø Moen 2006: 295). Hagen was fully aware of the problem:

> We are talking about straightening things up in the party; to take into account our political opponents in other parties who think that we are disorderly. If this is the reason for not wanting to have anything to do with us, we need to get rid of those bad things.
>
> (*Dagbladet* 21-07-2000)

After a brutal struggle for power in which a variety of different tactics were deployed (e.g. interference in nomination processes, op-eds in the party maga-zine, and public statements about alleged infiltration), an already centralised party organisation was further centralised and all except one of the oppositional MPs were forced to leave the party (Jupskås forthcoming; Skarsbø Moen 2006: 315).[5] In the media, Hagen was frequently portrayed as a 'party owner' (e.g., *Aftenposten* 14-11-2000), and former allies accused him of paranoia (*Aftenposten* 06-02-2001) or authoritarian leadership style (Hagen 2007: 379).

Another and more important challenge was related to the electoral arena. Hagen knew that many of the controversial MPs were popular in their own constituencies and that any party washing its dirty linen in public eventually will suffer in the polls. Indeed, this was exactly what happened. While the FrP had been the largest party with an astonishing 32 per cent in the polls in September 2000, the support decreased substantially after months of infighting.[6] The result at the national election in 2001 was that the party was no longer bigger than H.

Allegedly, the FrP wanted to be included in the government negotiations after the election (Hagen 2007: 399). However, the centre-right parties had ruled out any formal cooperation with the FrP already during the campaign due to policy distances, not least on immigration policies (Narud and Strøm 2011: 76, 80). And since Hagen (2007: 400) had repeatedly promised a change of government in the campaign, the party ended up as a *de facto* parliamentary support party for a new centre-right government consisting of H, KrF and V (see also Aardal 2007b: 17). In return, the centre-right government made several concessions to the FrP, on policies as well regarding the distribution of positions, even if such 'contract parliamentarism' was highly unusual in Norway (Narud and Strøm 2011: 74). For a while the FrP was quite satisfied. It was the largest party in the polls and it was influential in parliament. Hagen called it a 'dream position' (*Dagbladet* 05-07-2002). Internally, the party continued to prepare for government; both a government committee and a 'minister school' were created (Skarsbø Moen 2006: 327).

However, even if office-seeking and policy-seeking motives clearly emerged among party elites in this period, and more consistently than in the 1980s (Strøm 1994), vote-seeking motives continued to play an important role for the leadership. In fact, chairman Hagen's resistance towards too radical rhetoric on niche issues was also motivated by a vote-seeking strategy. After having been almost exclusively associated with the immigration issue in the 1999 local elections, the chairman seemed to realise that even if this issue was very important for some voters, the radical rhetoric and single-issue orientation pushed other voters away, partly due to the role of media. Hagen stated:

> The Progress Party has two groups of voters: those who vote for us due to our immigration policy, and those who vote for us in spite of it. We have scared the latter to vote for the Conservatives. I underestimated what a hostile media was capable of producing on the basis of these meetings [immigration meetings by Kleppe and Hedstrøm]. If I had realised that, I would have done more to stop them [Kleppe and Hedstrøm].
>
> (Ekeberg and Snoen 2001: 313–314)

Furthermore, the decision to support a centre-right coalition led by a centrist Prime Minister rather than a Conservative single-party government seems somewhat puzzling. According to Narud and Strøm (2011: 76–77), this behaviour must have been related to 'longer-term electoral and parliamentary strategies, in which [the party] saw itself benefiting from political responsibility (not allowing a weak govern-ment to take office) and from a clear separation between itself and future governing parties (so as to be able to benefit from any prospective popular disapproval)'. The latter strategy was also played out in parliament where the FrP voted rather frequently together with the left-wing opposition (see Figure 8.2), and in the media where Hagen came out with strong accusations of political opponents, especially the Prime Minister (Skarsbø Moen 2006: 328). According to Hagen (2007: 439–440), this was part of a deliberate strategy in which the party wanted to demonstrate the weakness of the government and to show that the FrP's support could not be taken for granted.

The inclusion of socioeconomic issues as part of a programmatic appeal in both national and local elections should also be interpreted primarily as a vote-seeking strategy. As demonstrated by election surveys and content analyses, welfare issues emerged as the most important political issues in the 1990s and early 2000s (e.g., Bjørklund 2005; Bjørklund and Saglie 2002). The FrP was constantly competing with the Ap regarding issue ownership of the immigration issue and geriatric care (see Table 8.1). It was certainly more successful on the first than the latter, but emerged as the owner of geriatric care in 2001. The initial tax-issue, to the contrary, was consistently owned by either the Ap or H.

At the end of the parliamentary period in 2005, the party changed its strategy again. Hagen seemed to realise that anti-establishment behaviour was damaging the relationship with possible coalition partners. In June 2004, an internal com-mittee headed by Siv Jensen presented a new strategy in which the party took partly criticism for the lack of cross-partisan collaboration (Skarsbø Moen 2006: 331). From now on, it would behave more responsibl and seek political compromises. Hagen publicly stated that he regretted many of his controversial statements about the policies of the other non-socialist parties (*Aftenposten* 25-06-2004). However, the FrP continued to be rejected by the other non-socialist parties. Consequently, a few months before the election, Hagen switched strategy and removed the centre-right government's parliamentary base by announcing that his party would no longer support a government led by Prime Minister Kjell Magne Bondevik (KrF). Although the decision obviously made a centre-right government less likely, it provided Hagen with maximum

Table 8.1 Issue ownership to immigration, geriatric care and taxation 1997–2013 (in per cent)

	Immigration			Geriatric care			Taxation		
	FrP	Ap	H	FrP	Ap	H	FrP	Ap	H
1997	28	27	8	18	19	5	–	–	–
2001	28	21	11	25	19	7	13	16	41
2005	32	22	14	21	38	6	18	33	25
2009	33	25	15	14	37	11	16	35	26
2013	23	20	16	12	25	15	8	29	30

Source: Norwegian election surveys 1997–2013. The author has made the calculations.

publicity and polls went up about three percentage points during the campaign (Sitter 2006: 578).

2006–2012: gaining office by maximising the votes and building alliances

The course of events was almost identical in 2009. Again, the FrP tried to convince the other non-socialist parties to accept it as a coalition partner (Allern 2010: 905). And again, the centrist parties consistently rejected the party on the basis of ideological distance. The Conservative activists were more positive, but the party elite seemed to prefer the centrist parties (*Verdens Gang* 04-09-2009). The FrP, for its part, had promised the voters that it would not under any circumstances support a government from which it was excluded and Jensen attacked both the incumbent red-green government and the former centre-right government (*NTB* 17-01-2009). The party even launched Jensen as its candidate for Prime Minister and argued that it could very well govern alone (Allern 2010: 905). This time, however, the strategy was unsuccessful and the support decreased in the polls before the election, partly because the non-socialist block was portrayed as a chaos by the media and opponents (Narud 2011). The red-green alliance was re-elected, and notwithstanding having received more votes than ever before, the FrP was very disappointed (FrP 2009/2010: 9).

Having been able to push both H and the Ap towards a more restrictive position on immigration policies (Notaker 2012: 286–303; Simonnes 2013), moderating the position on niche issues was considered electorally risky. Instead, the party adopted a strategy of anti-establishment moderation in parliament and anti-establishment radicalisation in public. While the party was publicly (re-)launched as a 'protest movement' founded upon the principle of being against the system (*Aftenposten* 24-04-2010), the leadership tried to improve non-socialist alliances in parliament. It was noted in internal documents that the FrP had to demonstrate its governing capacities and skills as a cooperative party (FrP 2011/2012: 1). Moreover, the leadership constantly reminded all representatives and activists about the importance of maintaining the image of being 'serious, responsible and thorough' (FrP 2009/2010: 2; 2011/2012: 1; 2012/2013: 1).

Eventually, this new strategy seemed to pay off. The party elites in KrF and V decided to open the door for the FrP in 2012. In public, the party leaders from the non-socialist block agreed that collaboration between the four parties had improved significantly. Among the factors mentioned by the non-socialist party leaders as being particularly important were the successful cross-partisan parlia-mentary negotiations regarding climate policies, and the leadership succession in the FrP from Hagen to Jensen, since the former was perceived as unpredictable (*Aftenposten* 10-11-2012).

2013–2015: one foot in, one foot out

Being a novel constellation in Norwegian postwar history, a pure right-wing minority coalition including the FrP with two centrist parties formally acting as parliamentary support parties was expected to be challenging, especially for FrP. Indeed, as predicted by Allern and Karlsen (2014: 661), the FrP faced the most significant challenges in terms of trade-offs between party goals. The government platform clearly showed that the FrP sacrificed many of its policies in order to gain office. Effective log-rolling between the four non-socialist parties was extremely difficult, if not impossible, due to opposing views on several issues considered important for at least two of the parties. Most importantly, the FrP gained only marginal results with respect to immigration policies (*Aftenposten* 01-03-2014). This was simply because both KrF and V were campaigning on the complete opposite of the FrP, namely a more liberal policy. Moreover, several other symbolic issues (e.g., abolition of road tolls and the level of 'oil-money' spending) were put away due to disagreement with both H and the centrist parties (*Verdens Gang* 25-06-2014). Many voters and representatives were disappointed.

The FrP's response has been two-fold thus far. First, according to interviews with key actors, the party was eager to demonstrate its ability to behave responsibly and simultaneously avoid 'The Socialist Left-trap' (*Verdens Gang* 02-05-2014).[7] In short, the FrP has organised a number of seminars or used information channels to make sure that the party organisation has been prepared for and informed about the inevitable consequences of political compromises. Some of the most anti-establishment-oriented representatives have been co-opted into the government apparatus as deputy secretaries. Lastly, Jensen has been less present in the media, opening up public space for other ministers.

Second, the party has also pursued the strategy of keeping 'one foot in, one foot out' (Albertazzi and McDonnell 2005). Already before entering office, Jensen argued that the FrP would 'be honest about defeats and preoccupied with victories' (*Verdens Gang* 02-05-2014). As noted by one commentator, the party actually promised to inform the voters about 'what the government means and what the FrP would have meant if it wasn't in government' (*Morgenbladet* 13-12-2013). It was repeatedly emphasised that the parliamentary group was elected on the basis of the party manifesto and not the government platform. In recent months, this strategy seems to have become increasingly important – not least because the first strategy of acting responsibly seemed unsuccessful. Just like the Socialist Left (Sosialistisk Venstreparti, SV), the FrP experienced decreasing support in the polls (from 16.6 per cent in the election to 10.3 per cent in March 2015) and membership figures have consistently decreased for the first time since the mid-1990s (−27 per cent since 2011 and −14 per cent since 2013) (FrP 2011/ 12, 2012/13, 2013/14, 2014/15). Moreover, surveys suggest that government policies were more in line with the preferences of H-voters than the FrP's constituencies (*Aftenposten* 15-11-2014). It remains to be seen whether this new strategy proves more successful than the first one.

Party strategies and the impact of external and internal conditions

This final section briefly presents some explanations for the changing party strategies as described above. After all, such strategies are not developed in a vacuum. Party leaders are facing internal and external constraints and opportunities when deciding on which party goals to emphasise. The social conditions in Norway since the 1990s have been favourable for the FrP's vote-seeking strategies. The salience of the immigration issue has increased (from 6 per cent in 1997 to 16 per cent in 2009) and a large share of the electorate holds fairly negative views on immigration, although different surveys show slightly different trends and levels (Aardal 2011b: 86–87; Karlsen and Aardal 2011: 134)

The salience of law and order issues has usually been somewhat lower, but several surveys have shown widespread authoritarian views on sentences and criminal foreigners; in 2005, for example, 89 per cent agreed that criminals should be punished more severely and 85 per cent agreed that criminal foreigners should be expelled from the country (Aardal 2007a: 43). As previously noted, the FrP has successfully exploited both these issues.

Notwithstanding its importance, the immigration issue has previously put – and continues to put – the party on a knife-edge. On the one hand, radical statements might threaten its 'reputational shield' (Ivarsflaten 2006) and damage its relationship to potential coalition partners (see below). A survey carried out in 1999 after a period of radicalisation suggested that 3 out of 5 voters agreed that the FrP's immigration policies could be considered racist (*Verdens Gang* 01-09-1999). Even among the FrP's own voters, 23 per cent agreed with the statement. After the terrorist attack by an Islamophobic right-wing extremist on 22 July 2011, the legitimacy of the party's anti-Islam position was challenged once again (Andersson 2012), also by some of the FrP's own representatives (*Adresseavisen* 15-08-2011).[8] On the other hand, the gradual mainstreaming on niche issues taking place after the party entered office might be a key factor explaining the decreasing support in the polls and defecting party members, though leaders of local branches also seem to be dissatisfied with the lack of impact on road tolls and level of 'oil money'-spending (*Dagens Naeringsliv* 20-10-2014).

The party system and institutional setting are also favourable for a vote-seeking strategy. The consensus-oriented and de-polarised party system with multiple minority governments of different political orientation has reinforced the party's image as the only alternative to the existing order, and the FrP has faced little competition from the established parties on its niche issues. Moreover, the absence of an investiture vote has allowed the party to constantly weigh policy influence against vote maximisation whenever centre-right has been in government.

In spite of being beneficial for the FrP's vote-seeking strategy, the ideological position of potential coalition partners and their preferred governing alternatives have made any office-seeking strategy more complicated that it would have been otherwise. In short, both KrF and V have been ideologically closer to the Ap than the FrP, and they have consistently preferred the former rather than the latter in government (Narud and Strøm 2011: 77–80). Hence, the reluctant acceptance by the centrist parties of the FrP as *salonfähig* prior to the 2013 election can hardly be explained without reference to the existence of a majority 'red-green government', i.e. the Ap, SV and agrarian Centre Party

(Senterpartiet, Sp), between 2005 and 2013. In this period, the centrist parties had very little policy influence and they were increasingly marginalised.

The office-seeking strategy of the FrP was also helped by internal factors. An increasingly centralised and institutionalised organisation has made the party more cohesive and prepared for government responsibility (Jupskås forthcoming). Furthermore, the well-planned leadership succession from Hagen to Jensen in 2006 was probably necessary in order to improve the relationship with other non-socialist parties. While the FrP became increasingly conventional under the leadership of Hagen (Goul Andersen and Bjørklund 2000: 200–201), especially with regard to its organisational structure, his confrontational style and to some extent unpredictable behaviour were damaging for the party's reputation. Jensen, by contrast, was widely perceived as a competent and trustworthy politician, not least due to having chaired the powerful finance committee in parliament between 2001 and 2005. As noted by Widfeldt (2015: 110), Jensen was 'more of a mainstream politician than Hagen who could not, or did not want to, quite shake off his populist style'.

However, we should not focus exclusively on the party leadership and end up overestimating the importance of a systematic integration of the party at the subnational level (Flo 2008: 145). The FrP penetrated municipalities and counties towards the end of the 1990 (see Figure 8.1) and the number of mayors increased significantly after the turn of the millennium: from one mayor only in 1999 to 13 in 2003 and 17 in 2007 (Bjørklund and Saglie 2005: 29). Since the *cordon sanitaire* has never been consistently implemented in subnational politics, the FrP has gained valuable experience as a governing party. Interestingly, one study finds that the difference between the FrP's representatives and the representatives of the other parties was smaller at the local level than at the national level (Fimreite 2003 cited in Flo 2008). In other words, experience from the local level may have contributed to an increasing acceptance of trade-offs between vote, policy and office-seeking goals within the FrP.

Part of 'the mainstream', but for how long?

The FrP has clearly moved into the mainstream since the mid-1990s. Two events appear to be particularly important: (1) the electoral success in 1997; and (2) government inclusion in 2013. The first event proved at least two things. First, the FrP was able to gain more votes than H and, second, the party could successfully mobilise voters on welfare issues previously owned by the Ap. An office-strategy was gradually adopted, though it never replaced vote-strategies completely. In fact, due to the political opportunity structure, vote-seeking was perceived as instrumental to office-seeking; by becoming the largest party, the other non-socialist parties would have no other option than accepting the FrP as a governing party. Hence, the party became less anti-establishment oriented, but kept its radical position on key niche issues.

The second event – government inclusion and participation – also proved at least two things. First, the FrP was eventually accepted as a governing party not because of mainstreaming, but because of an emerging two-bloc system after eight years of a majority centre-left government, though less anti-establishment behaviour played an important role too. Second, the party was willing to give up on many niche issues in the phase of government formation and subsequent participation. Office-seeking strategies obviously trumped vote-seeking and policy-seeking goals. The extent to which H has been able to 'tame the shrew' once and for all, however, remains to be seen. After all, the 'one foot in, one foot out' strategy might be further strengthened if the costs of governing turn out to be unacceptable.

Notes

1 Thanks to Tjitske Akkerman for many valuable comments on earlier drafts of this chapter.
2 The mean support in the polls is collected by Professor Bernt Aardal and presented at his website: www.aardal.info/partibarometre.html (accessed 06-07-2015). All references to polling results are from this website.
3 FrP also disagreed extensively with the Conservatives in this period, which was to be expected since the latter was in government with two centrist parties.
4 In the late 1990s, the party was increasingly popular among the working class. Surveys suggested that 20 per cent of unionised members were inclined to vote for the FrP (Skarsbø Moen 2006: 285).
5 Hagen was able to expel four of the most prominent figures of the internal opposition (three before the election and one after). Two others left more or less voluntarily. The only MP who remained in the party disappeared from the public debate and re-joined Hagen's faction.
6 The support also declined due to a large sex-scandal which involved one of the vice-chairmen (Skarsbø Moen 2006: 313).
7 'The Socialist Left trap' has recently emerged as an important narrative in Norwegian politics and it refers to how the Socialist Left party lacked cohesion; was overshadowed by the Labour party; and declined electorally and organisationally after entering office for the first time in 2005.
8 Both party leader Jensen and MP Tybring-Gjedde publicly apologised for some of their statements in the after-math of the terrorist attacks on 22 July 2011. However, they rapidly went back to 'business as usual'.

Bibliography

Aardal, B. (1999) 'Kapittel 1: Stortingsvalget 1997', in Aardal, B., Valen, H., Narud, H. M. and Berglund, F. (eds) *Velgere i 90-årene*, Oslo: NKS-forlaget, pp. 8–31.
Aardal, B. (2003a) 'Flyktige stemningsbølger eller politiske grunnverdier', in Aardal, B. (ed.) *Velgere i villrede … En analyse av stortingsvalget 2001*, Oslo: Damm & Søn, pp. 47–82.
Aardal, B. (2003b) 'Ideologi og stemmegivning', in Aardal, B. (ed.) *Velgere i villrede … En analyse av stortingsvalget 2001*, Oslo: Damm & Søn, pp. 83–106.
Aardal, B. (2003c) 'Kritiske velgere', in Aardal, B. (ed.) *Velgere i villrede … En analyse av stortingsvalget 2001*, Oslo: N. W. Damm & Søn, pp. 207–224.
Aardal, B. (2007a) 'Saker og standpunkter', in Aardal, B. (ed.) *Norske velgere. En studie av stortingsvalget 2005*, Oslo: N.W. Damm & Søn AS, pp. 41–58.
Aardal, B. (2007b) 'Velgere på evig vandring? Hva skjedde ved stortingsvalget i 2005?', in Aardal, B. (ed.) *Norske velgere. En studie av stortingsvalget 2005*, Oslo: N.W. Damm & Søn AS, pp. 13–40.

Aardal, B. (2011a) 'Det politiske landskap – stabile grunnholdninger og skiftende par-itpreferanser', in Aardal, B. (ed.) *Det politiske landskapet. En studie av stortingsvalget 2009*, Oslo: Cappelen Damm, pp. 97–130.

Aardal, B. (2011b) 'Folkeopinionen – demokratiets grunnvoll', in Aardal, B. (ed.) *Det politiske landskapet. En studie av stortingsvalget 2009*, Oslo: Cappelen Damm, pp. 65–96.

Aardal, B. (2011c) 'Mange blir valgt, men få blir gjenvalgt', in Aardal, B. (ed.) *Det poli-tiske landskapet. En studie av stortingsvalget 2009*, Oslo: Cappelen Damm Akademisk, pp. 13–39.

Adresseavisen (15-08-2011) 'Innvandring truer ikke norske verdier'.

Aftenposten (31-03-1995) 'Hagen I Anders Langes fotefar' (L. Hellberg).

Aftenposten (22-04-1996) 'Intet svar'.

Aftenposten (09-09-1996) 'Gjenvalgt, men fikk dagen ødelagt'.

Aftenposten (30-07-1999) 'Sentrum ofrer ikke Fr.p.-samarbeidet'.

Aftenposten (14-11-2000) 'Misbruk av tillit'.

Aftenposten (06-02-2001) 'Gundersen om Hagen: nærmer seg paranoia'.

Aftenposten (25-06-2004) 'Angrer skarpe utfall'.

Aftenposten (24-04-2010) 'Helsekøer minner om Sovjetunionen'.

Aftenposten (26-08-2010) 'Drøm fra Disneyland' (Andersen, K. and Tybring-Gjedde, C.).

Aftenposten (10-11-2012) 'Fire partiledere snakker varmt om samarbeid, men bare disse to vil være med på gruppebilde'.

Aftenposten (01-03-2014) 'Her er innvandringssakene Frp har droppet', www.aftenp osten.no/politikk/Her-er-innvandringssakene-Frp-har-droppet-7487289.html (accessed 03-06-2015).

Aftenposten (15-11-2014) 'FrP er nok misfornøyd med tempoet'.

Aftenposten (16-03-2015) 'Solveig Horne: Innvandring er bra for samfunnet'.

Aftenposten (12-05-2015) 'Kvalte opprør i egne rekker'.

Aftenposten (22-02-2015) 'Belastning for Regjeringen, men en befrielse for Frp-velgerne'.

Akkerman, T. and Hagelund, A. (2007) '"Women and children first!" Anti–immigration parties and gender in Norway and the Netherlands', *Patterns of Prejudice* 41, 2: 197–214.

Albertazzi, D. and McDonnell, D. (2005) 'The Lega Nord in the second Berlusconi government: In a league of its own', *West European Politics* 28, 5: 952–972.

Allern, E. H. (2010) 'Survival of a majority coalition: The Norwegian parliamentary election of 14 September 2009', *West European Politics* 33, 4: 904–912.

Allern, E. H. and Karlsen, R. (2014) 'A turn to the right: The Norwegian parliamentary election of September 2013', *West European Politics* 37, 3: 653–663.

Andersson, M. (2012) 'The debate about multicultural Norway before and after 22 July 2011', *Identities* 19, 4: 418–427.

Bangstad, S. (2013) 'Eurabia comes to Norway', *Islam and Christian–Muslim Relations* 24, 3: 1–23.

Bjørklund, T. (1988) 'The 1987 Norwegian local elections: A protest election with a swing to the right', *Scandinavian Political Studies* 11, 3: 211–234.

Bjørklund, T. (1999) *Et lokalvalg i perspektiv: valget i 1995 i lys av sosiale og politiske endringer*, Oslo: Tano Aschehoug.

Bjørklund, T. (2003) 'Fremskrittspartiet gjennom 30 år', *Nytt Norsk Tidsskrift* 20, 2: 129–145.

Bjørklund, T. (2004) 'Norsk populisme fra Ottar Brox til Carl I. Hagen', *Nytt Norsk Tidsskrift* 21, 3–4: 410–420.

Bjørklund, T. (2005) 'Stortingsvalget 2005: velgere som velferdsklienter', *Nytt Norsk Tidsskrift* 22, 4: 444–454.

190   *Anders Ravik Jupskås*

Bjørklund, T. and Goul Andersen, J. (2002) 'Anti-immigration parties in Denmark and Norway: The Progress Party and Danish People's Party', in Schain, M. A., Zolberg, A. and Hossay, P. (eds) *Shadows Over Europe: The Development and Impact of the Extreme Right in Western Europe*, New York: Palgrave Macmillan, pp. 107–137.

Bjørklund, T. and Saglie, J. (2002) 'Velferdsstat og valenspolitikk: lokalvalget i 1999', *Norsk statsvitenskapelig tidsskrift* 18, 1: 3–27.

Bjørklund, T. and Saglie, J. (2005) 'Valgresultatet i 2003. Bakgrunn og perspektiver', in Saglie, J. and Bjørklund, T. (eds) *Lokalvalg og lokalt folkestyre*, Oslo: Gyldendal Akademisk, pp. 22–41.

Dagbladet (21-07-2000) 'Må fjerne de dumme tingene'.

Dagbladet (05-07-2002) 'Jeg er i drømmeposisjon'.

Dagens Næringsliv (04-12-2012) 'Har 870 budsjettspørsmål'.

Dagens Næringsliv (20-10-2014) 'Frp-misnøye med oljepengebruk'.

Ekeberg, J. O. and Snoen, J. A. (2001) *Kong Carl: en uautorisert biografi om Carl I. Hagen*, Oslo: Kagge.

Fangen, K. and Vaage, M. N. (2015) 'FrP-politikeres innvandringsretorikk i posisjon og opposisjon', *Agora* 31, 3–4: 30–63.

Flo, Y. (2008) 'Partiet, kommunen og draumen om det nye samfunnet', in Helgøy, I. and Aars, J. (eds) *Flernivåstyring og demokrati*, Bergen: Fagbokforlaget, pp. 123–152.

Fremskrittspartiet (FrP) (1996) 'Fremskrittspartiets strategi'.

Fremskrittspartiet (FrP) (1997) Handlingsprogram.

Fremskrittspartiet (FrP) (1999/2000) Sentralstyrets årsberetning.

Fremskrittspartiet (FrP) (2001) Handlingsprogram.

Fremskrittspartiet (FrP) (2005) Handlingsprogram.

Fremskrittspartiet (FrP) (2009a) Handlingsprogram

Fremskrittspartiet (FrP) (2009b) 'Vi er klare til å fornye Norge'.

Fremskrittspartiet (FrP) (2009/2010) Sentralstyrets årsberetning.

Fremskrittspartiet (FrP) (2011/2012) Sentralstyrets årsberetning.

Fremskrittspartiet (FrP) (2012/2013) Sentralstyrets årsberetning.

Fremskrittspartiet (FrP) (2013) Handlingsprogram.

Fremskrittspartiet (FrP) (2013/2014) Sentralstyrets årsberetning.

Fremskrittspartiet (FrP) (2014/2015) Sentralstyrets årsberetning.

Goul Andersen, J. and Bjørklund, T. (2000) 'Radical right-wing populism in Scandinavia: From tax revolt to neo-liberalism and xenophobia', in Hainsworth, P. (ed.) *The Politics of the Extreme Right: From the Margins to the Mainstream*, London: Pinter, pp. 193–223.

Hagelund, A. (2003) 'A matter of decency? The Progress Party in Norwegian immigration politics', *Journal of Ethnic and Migration Studies* 29, 1: 47–65.

Hagelund, A. (2005) 'The Progress Party and the problem of culture immigration politics and right-wing populism in Norway', in Rydgren, J. (ed.) *Movements of Exclusion: Radical Right-Wing Populism in the West*, New York: Nova Science Publishers, pp. 147–164.

Hagen, C. I. (2007) *Ærlig talt: memoarer 1944–2007*, Oslo: Cappelen.

Hylland, O. M. (2011) 'Fremskrittspartiets kulturpolitikk-kulturpolitisk opposisjon i utvikling', *Nordisk kulturpolitisk tidsskrift* 14, 1–2: 51–70.

Høyre/Fremskrittspartiet (H/FrP) (07-10-2013) 'Politisk platform for en Regjering utgått av Høyre og Fremskrittspartiet'.

Ivarsflaten, E. (2006) 'Reputational shields: Why most anti-immigrant parties failed in Western Europe, 1980–2005', Annual Meeting of the American Political Science Association, Philadelphia.

Iversen, J. M. (1998) *Fra Anders Lange til Carl I. Hagen: 25 år med Fremskrittspartiet*, Oslo: Millennium.

Jupskås, A. R. (forthcoming) 'Persistence of populism. The Norwegian Progress Party, 1973–2009', PhD thesis, University of Oslo.

Jupskås, A. R. (forthcoming) 'Between a business firm and a mass party: The organization of the Norwegian Progress Party', in Heinisch, R. and Mazzoleni, O. (eds) *Understanding Populist Party Organization: A Comparative Analysis*, Basingstoke: Palgrave Macmillan.

Jupskås, A. R. and Gyárfášová, O. (2012) 'The appeal of populism', in Baldersheim, H. and Bátora, J. (eds) *The Governance of Small States in Turbulent Times: The Exemplary Cases of Norway and Slovakia*, Opladen: Barbara Budrich Verlag, pp. 157–185.

Karlsen, R. and Aardal, B. (2011) 'Kamp om dagsorden og sakseierskap', in Aardal, B. (ed.) *Det politiske landskap. En studie av stortingsvalget 2009*, Oslo: Cappelen Damm Akademisk, pp. 131–162.

Kitschelt, H. and McGann, A. J. (1995) *The Radical Right in Western Europe: A Comparative Analysis*, Ann Arbor, MI: University of Michigan Press.

Morgenbladet (13-12-2013) 'Høyre er sammen med tre partier som ønsker å være litt gravide. I politikken er det kanskje mulig' (Bonde, A.).

Mudde, C. (2007) *Populist Radical Right Parties in Europe*, Cambridge: Cambridge University Press.

Narud, H. M. (2011) 'Politiske avstander og regjeringsalternativ ved valget i 2009', in Aardal, B. (ed.) *Det politiske landskap. En studie av stortingsvalget 2009*, Oslo: Cappelen Damm Akademisk, pp. 195–224.

Narud, H. M. and Aardal, B. (2007) 'Økonomisk stemmegivning i oljefondets skygge', in Aardal, B. (ed.) *Norske velgere. En studie av stortingsvalget 2005*, Oslo: Damm & Søn, pp. 173–200.

Narud, H. M. and Strøm, K. (2011) 'Coalition bargaining in an unforgiven environment: The case of Bondervik II in Norway', in Andeweg, R. B., Winter, L. D. and Dumont, P. (eds) *Puzzles of Government Formation. Coalition Theory and Deviant Cases*, Abingdon: Routledge/ECPR Studies in European Political Science, pp. 65–87.

Narud, H. M. and Valen, H. (2007) *Demokrati og ansvar. Politisk representasjon i et flerpartisystem*, Oslo: N.W. Damm & Søn.

Notaker, H. (2012) *Høyres historie 1975–2005. Opprør og moderasjon*, Oslo: Cappelen Damm.

NRK (08-08-2013) 'De borgerlige steiler av Frp-utvalg', www.nrk.no/valg2013/de-borgerlige-steiler-av-frp-utvalg-1.11194790 (accessed 03-07-2015).

NTB (20-02-2000) 'FrP vil bli regjeringsparti'.

NTB (17-01-2009) 'Jensen: Frps strategi ligger fast'.

Pratt, J. and Eriksson, A. (2013) *Contrasts in Punishment: An Explanation of Anglophone Excess and Nordic Exceptionalism*, London: Routledge.

Rasch, B. E. (2011) 'Behavioural consequences of restrictions on plenary access: Parliamentary questions in the Norwegian Storting', *The Journal of Legislative Studies* 17, 3: 382–393.

Saglie, J. (2002) *Standpunkter og strategi. EU-saken i norsk partipolitikk, 1989–1994*, Oslo: ISF og Pax Forlag.

Sandberg, P. (2013) *Mot min vilje – oppklæring av et politisk liv*, Oslo: Juritzen forlag.

Simonnes, K. (2013) 'I stjålne klær? En analyse av endringer i Høyres, Arbeiderpartiets og Fremskrittspartiets innvandrings- og integreringspolitikk', *Norsk statsvitenskapelig tidsskrift* 29, 2: 144–158.

Sitter, N. (2006) 'Norway's Storting election of September 2005: Back to the Left?', *West European Politics* 29, 3: 573–580.

Skarsbø Moen, E. (2006) *Profet i eget land: historien om Carl I. Hagen*, Oslo: Gyldendal.

Skinner, M. S. (2011) 'From ambiguity to euroscepticism? A case study of the Norwegian Progress Party's position on the European Union', SEI Working Paper No 124. EPERN Working paper No 25, Sussex: Sussex European Institute.

Strøm, K. (1994) 'The Presthus debacle: Intraparty politics and bargaining failure in Norway', *American Political Science Review* 88, 1: 112–127.

Tybring-Gjedde, C. (2014) *Mens orkesteret fortsetter å spille*, Oslo: Cappelen Damm.

Verdens Gang (06-05-1994) 'Carl I. Bånn'.

Verdens Gang (09-09-1997) 'Motbydelig!'.

Verdens Gang (20-02-1999) 'Advarer mot hets'.

Verdens Gang (01-09-1999) 'FrP+Sp=sant'.

Verdens Gang (04-09-2009) 'Nå vil de begge ha Erna som statsminister'.

Verdens Gang (13-05-2011) 'Frps fengselsreform (mest for utledinger): hard og simpel soning'.

Verdens Gang (11-02-2014) 'Vil gjøre som Sveits'.

Verdens Gang (02-05-2014) 'Slik unngår Siv SV-fella'.

Verdens Gang (25-06-2014) 'Dette er Frps største seire og nederlag'.

Widfeldt, A. (2015) *Extreme Right Parties in Scandinavia*, Abingdon: Routledge.

9 Staying away from the mainstream

The case of the Swiss People's Party

Oscar Mazzoleni

Introduction

When radical right-wing populist parties acquire experience as part of a coalition government, it raises the question of whether they will begin to act more like mainstream parties. Of course, this could be a crucial point for parties that initially emerge as anti-establishment and/or niche parties and then go on to enter into a government coalition following a period of electoral success. This issue is also important for moderate parties in marginal positions within the party system that undergo a process of de-mainstreaming or conversion towards radical-right and anti-establishment stances (e.g., De Lange 2007; Mény and Surel 2000: 260–262). Another scenario, probably more rare, is that of parties that form part of a government coalition and simultaneously experience a process of radicalisation and thence develop anti-establishment positions. This chapter examines a case of this kind, namely that of the Swiss People's Party (the Schweizerische Volkspartei, SVP), which has risen to the fore as Switzerland's leading party since the 1990s. While it appears to resemble the many other radical right-wing populist parties that have gained experience in government coalitions around Western Europe, it is the only party considered to belong to this family that has been continuously present as part of the national government coalition, without interruption either before or during its period of de-mainstreaming, except for a very short period in 2008 (Mazzoleni 2013a).

So how has the SVP managed to be enduringly present in government, while to some extent remaining a radicalised, anti-establishment, and niche party? Has its participation in government lately changed in such a way that it has needed to become more moderate and more credible? To respond to these questions we must acknowledge that political parties are often faced with difficult choices and ambivalent situations, linked to both internal and external factors (Müller and Strøm 1999; Strøm 1990; Wolinetz 2002). In the case of the SVP it is important to underline that its strategy was based on a new leadership and a profound organisational change, and that it also had to take account of a specific institutional and political pattern: the country is governed by a long-term, stable coalition of parties without a common government programme, and allows for particularly extensive referendum rights that can be used by all parties, including those in the government coalition, to contest any law passed by parliament and to propose changes to the federal constitution (Burgos *et al.* 2011; Deschouwer 2001; Kerr 1987; Mazzoleni and Rayner 2009).

In this chapter, I will first show how the SVP has shifted from a conservative moderate wing towards a radical right-wing populist profile and how it has been able to consolidate a focus on certain specific issues and an anti-establishment stance. Second, I will analyse how the party managed to prioritise a vote-seeking strategy while it was part of a government coalition, focusing on how it fulfilled its role as a member of the federal government and its use of the referendum tools allowed by Swiss democracy. In the third and final part I will devote attention to the party's strategy dilemmas, examining a number of critical episodes from its split in the 2000s to the difficulties involved in implementing a consistent electoral strategy in the most recent federal elections.

Between mainstreaming and de-mainstreaming

The SVP has mainstream roots that reach back many decades: though officially constituted in 1971, the party's underlying foundations date to the 1910s (Skenderovic 2009a). Unlike other European radical right-wing populist parties, the SVP can claim a significant history as a rural conservative centre-right-wing party, traditionally a member of the national government. By 1929 a member of one of the two parties that would merge to form the SVP – the Bauern-, Gewerbe- und Bürgerpartei (BGB) – had joined the government federal coalition. In the decades that followed, the BGB became one of the pillars of the Swiss consociational government, and since 1959 in particular, a fully-fledged member of the 'magic formula', the grand coalition of all the main Swiss parties, namely the Freisinnig-Demokratische Partei (nowadays Die Liberalen, FDP), the Christlich-demokratische Volkspartei (CVP), and the Sozialdemokratische Partei der Schweiz (SP). In 1959, the smallest of the government parties, the BGB, was granted one seat on the Federal Council, while each of the other larger parties had two apiece.

In the second half of the 1980s and above all in the 1990s, the SVP under-went a profound ideological transformation (Mazzoleni 2008). Whilst in 1992, all the government parties, including the SVP, supported a change in foreign policy in favour of European integration, an emerging SVP faction headed by Christoph Blocher – a multi-billionaire entrepreneur and a national MP – conducted one of the most widely participated and most polarised referendum campaigns against Switzerland's entry into the European Economic Area (EEA): the turnout reached 78.7 per cent and 50.3 per cent said 'No' (Mazzoleni 2008). In its manifesto for the federal elections of 1991, the SVP supported Switzerland's integration into Europe, but in its 1995 manifesto, the party clearly rejected the project for Switzerland joining the EU (SVP 1991, 1995). More radically, the manifesto of 1999 denounced the 'bureaucratic' and 'centralistic' EU and the danger it was said to pose for Swiss welfare and popular rights (SVP 1999). Regarding immigration, the 1991 manifesto was in favour of immigration and the naturalisation of foreigners, but only one year later, in 1992, under pressure from Blocher, the SVP launched its first national popular initiative seeking to expel any asylum-seeker who illegally entered Switzerland. Over the course of the 1990s, the SVP became the Swiss party most intent on framing immigration issues in the public sphere, targeting immigrants and asylum-seekers as dangers for the country from both the cultural and the economic points of view (Giugni and Passy 2001: 54). Unsurprisingly, in its 1999 manifesto, the SVP denounced the increasingly 'dubious' claims for naturalisation and for a stabilisation of migrant flows, arguing that 'Switzerland is not a country of immigration' (SVP 1999: 7). The 1990s also produced a shift towards a clearly neo-liberal economic stance. In the 1991 manifesto, the party argued that any new state expenditures should be carefully evaluated, with particular attention to the less wealthy regions (SVP 1991: 6–7), but in 1995 it makes a clear claim for deregulation and privatisation, reducing state intervention (SVP 1995: 6–7). Moreover, a quantitative analysis of the federal manifestos shows an increase in right-wing socioeconomic stances from 41.4 per cent in 1995, to 56.5 per cent in 1999. At the same time, the degree to which socioeconomic issues accounted for the content of the federal election manifesto rose from 27.2 per cent to 37.2 per cent (Mazzoleni and Rossini 2014a: 6).[1] Alongside this, in public meetings and in the media, Blocher and his followers developed a critical discourse against the government and the 'political class', accusing them of betraying Swiss sovereignty, independence and neutrality, and against the mainstream bourgeois parties who were unable, they claimed, to disentangle themselves from statist and socialist policies (Niggli and Frischknecht 1998: 53 ff.). In sum, to an extent, the SVP became a neo-liberal and in part a niche party (Adams *et al.* 2006; Wagner 2012) focusing on immigration and EU issues, and developing an anti-establishment stance (Albertazzi 2007; Albertazzi and McDonnell 2015; Betz 2005; Mazzoleni 2008; Schedler 1996).

As the electoral success of the SVP in federal legislative elections went hand-in-hand with its persistent participation in government, the question arises as to whether the SVP is radicalising continuously, or whether it has been experiencing a process of re-mainstreaming in recent years – and, in particular, whether the party is in some way moderating its policy profile and its anti-establishment discourse. The answer is that the SVP has been able to maintain an organised ideological position, as well as an outsider posture. First of all, over the course of the 2000s and 2010s, the SVP's platform and behaviour has provided a persistent opposition against any openness towards supranational organisations, such as the UN and in particular the EU. The SVP launched several initiatives and referendums against the enlargement of the Swiss-EU agreements, in particular on free movement of persons. It also continues to be opposed to any 'excess' immigration, focusing on law and order dimensions (against foreign criminals), cultural components (the ability of immigrants to assimilate Swiss identity), and economic aspects (distinguishing between 'good' and 'bad' immigrants in relation to their capacity to undermine or to enhance Swiss well-being) – a blend very similar to that adopted by other radical right-wing populist parties in Europe (Kuisma 2013). At the same time, the party consolidated its neo-liberal stance, which is consistent with the hypothesis provided by Kitschelt (1995), according to which radical right-wing populist parties in Western Europe tend to combine restrictive discourse on immigration with a neo-liberal approach to the economy. On the one hand, the salience of socioeconomic issues falls slightly in the 2011 manifesto (to 32.4 per cent) whilst right-wing positions increase (to 72 per cent, with only 14.2 per cent centrist and 4.4 per cent left-wing positions).[2] The SVP's manifesto for the 2015 federal elections confirms this orientation, as the party 'rejects any increase in taxes and duties … for use in the restructuring of the social welfare system, as structural deficiencies must not be papered over with tax revenue', and claims that the health system should be reformed by increasing personal 'responsibility' (SVP 2015a: 57–58). Furthermore, the party has continued to criticise the 'political class', as well as the federal government as a whole, which has been accused of helplessness, incapacity, and even of 'betraying' the 'true concerns of the Swiss people'. For instance, when launching its most recent popular initiative, in March 2015, on the 'priority of Swiss laws against foreign judges', the party made claims against 'politicians, civil servants and professors unwilling for the people to have the last word, undermining popular sovereignty', and against 'the Federal Council, the other parties, the federal tribunal and the political class who give priority to international laws in respect to Swiss laws' (SVP 2015b: 1).

Prioritising a vote-seeking strategy

The process of de-mainstreaming in the 1990s coincided with a change towards a prevalent vote-seeking strategy, which aimed at maximising support in electoral arenas with the declared aim of becoming Switzerland's leading right-wing party. The vote-seeking goals of the 'new' SVP are consistent with the prioritisation of the electoral arena, alongside referendums and popular initiatives, and the radicalised ideological orientation and anti-establishment posture, permitting the development of an enduring strategy of demarcation vis-à-vis the other main parties. According to Downs (1957: 28), parties that pursue a vote-seeking strategy 'formulate policies in order to win elections, rather than winning elections in order to formulate policies'. According to the new strategy of the SVP, the objectives of the 'old' party, in particular its policy-seeking goals, have been partially pushed into second place.

The main consequence of the SVP's vote-seeking strategy is expressed by the most rapid and most enduring growth for a party in the last century of Swiss history. Between the 1990s and the second half of the 2000s, support for the SVP grew continuously, going from 15 per cent of the vote to 29 per cent in the period from 1995 to 2007. Since 1999, it has been the leading party in Switzerland in terms of votes at elections for the lower chamber of the Federal Assembly, attracting voters and political staff from extreme right-wing movements and parties (Altermatt and Kriesi 1994), but also from the centre-right-wing parties (Lutz 2012).

The vote-seeking strategy also has implications for the party's legislative behaviour. For a long time, the Swiss parliamentary decision-making processes were dominated by policy-seeking strategies, and a willingness to compromise in the name of the dominant rule of cooperation. Studies of electoral strategies in the 1970s and 1980s show two main types of coalition. In the first type, all of the parties in government contributed to the parliamentary decision-making process, while in the second, the main centre and right-wing parties were opposed to the Social Democrats and subsequently the Green Party. The marked autonomy between government and parliament and the opportunity for minority parties to resort to the use of referendums enabled parliamentary groups to arrive at solutions that were pragmatic, sometimes unexpected, and often characterised by a lack of party discipline, above all in the case of the two main centre-right-wing parties (see Lanfranchi and Lüthi 1999). In the 1990s, the strategy of the SVP's parliamentary group moved, first of all, towards some niche issues and protest stances, increasingly opposing the government and the mainstream parties on immigration, political asylum, the European Union, and fighting against the excessive costs of the welfare state, in the name of marked economic liberalism (Afonso 2013: 28–35; Mazzoleni and Skenderovic 2007). For instance, as can be seen through an in-depth analysis of 30 socioeconomic issues treated by the Swiss parliament in the 1999–2003 legislature, from the total of 6,350 votes, around 36 per cent set the SVP's MPs in opposition to the main parliamentary groups, including those of the centre-right-wing parties (Blanchard *et al.* 2009: 218–219).

In fact, the SVP's strategy includes the attempt to undermine the pivotal role of the centre-right-wing parties, the FDP and the CVP, which together have the majority in the upper chamber of the Federal Assembly (Schwarz and Linder 2006). This sometimes implies an original convergence in particular tactical alliances between the SVP and the Social Democrats, or with the Green Party, alliances that the centre-right-wing parties have lambasted as 'going against nature' (Mazzoleni 2013b). In other words, the role of the SVP contributes to challenging the coalitional legacy within parliament. The legislature that began in 1996 heralded a gradual decrease in traditional coalitions based on all government parties, and the increasingly autonomous legislative behaviour of the SVP parliamentary group. In this arena, too, the party highlighted its niche issues, opposing the government and the mainstream parties.

Under the new vote-seeking strategy, participation in government at any cost became less of a priority. As had also been the case during the 1990s, the Blocherian wing of the SVP often openly criticised the moderation of its own representative within the federal government. Since 1999, the party called for a change in the traditional government formula. In December 2003, the 'new' SVP succeeded in changing the government formula by obtaining a second seat at the expense of the Christian Democratic party. From 2003 to 2007, the Bernese representative Samuel Schmid sat alongside a new colleague on the Federal Council: Blocher, the national party leader from Zurich. Throughout the four-year period that he was in the executive, Blocher continued to act as the *enfant terrible* of Swiss politics, while his party, though temporarily down-playing its criticism of the government, continued to promote a populist agenda, particularly in the areas of foreign policy and immigration (Mazzoleni and Skenderovic 2007: 104 ss). However, this persistent radical strategy cost the SVP its seat in December 2007. Blocher was ousted from the executive, and replaced by Eveline Widmer-Schlumpf – a representative from the moderate wing of the SVP who was supported by the other parties. As the SVP had officially opposed the election of Widmer-Schlumpf, the party denounced her, declaring itself a party in parliamentary opposition for the first time since 1959. At the same time, the party expelled the moderate wing and its government representative, with whom Blocher had until then cohabited. In this sense, in 2008, there likely occurred a new apex in the radicalisation of the SVP, especially from the point of view of its anti-establishment discourse (see also Appendix). Since 2008, one of the main claims of the SVP has been the illegitimacy of the Swiss government and the Swiss 'political class', which constrains the main party of the country in the margin of power. Furthermore, although a party representative was once again elected to the government in December 2008, the SVP will persist with its vote-seeking strategy. Because of the split, in the federal elections in 2011, the SVP lost ground for the first time since 1995. However, it continues to remain the leading party, with 26.6 per cent of the votes in the elections for the lower chamber (based on a proportional system), as well as being the biggest group in the Federal Assembly under the persistent power of Blocher's leadership.

Strategic dilemmas

However, this doesn't exclude tensions or trade-offs between party goals. This ambivalence reflects the fact that the SVP has never been transformed into a pure anti-establishment and niche party, dealing with its mainstream legacy. Despite the rise and consolidation of Blocher's leadership within the party around the mid-1990s, the internal minority that was connected to the old SVP, and therefore more moderate and with less of a vote-seeking agenda, continued to play a role within the party for years. In the 1990s, the party's leaders often stated that they did not identify with their moderate representative in the executive (Mazzoleni and Skenderovic 2007). Between 2003 and 2007, the moderate representative of the SVP, Samuel Schmid, continued to show a cooperative attitude towards the government, despite the presence of Blocher in the same executive. While on the one hand, the transformation of the party gave the moderate wing more scope, on the other, the main strategy of the radical wing sorely tested the combined presence of these two elements within what had always presented itself as a mainstream party. Unsurprisingly, the name of the 'old' party – that of a party that had been in government for decades – had never been challenged by the new leadership. However, factionalism grew above all with the increasing centralisation of the party, which peaked when the leader was in government and there was a drive to impose greater discipline on the parliamentary group.[3] This also explains an increasing factionalism and the moderate wing's alliance with centre-right and left-wing representatives in order to expel Blocher from the government in 2007.

Also in terms of legislative behaviour, it appears far from realistic to define the SVP simply as a protest or outsider party, since its behaviour also avoids policy purism. Even though the SVP chooses to stand out markedly from the other parties in government on various issues, it also converges with the other parties on many others, especially with the centre-right-wing parties on economic issues, but also on those issues closest to its own agenda, such as Swiss membership of international organisations (such as Bretton Woods institutions, or the WTO), avoiding any policy purity. In other words, the differences of opinion between the SVP and the other main parties about Europe and immigration are offset by similar stances on other issues. While in some cases, it focused on keeping faith with its manifesto, sacrificing a number of policy-seeking goals, this did not mean that it was incapable of forming alliances with other parties, or accepting convergence on other issues. All of the other parties therefore continue to profit from the SVP's votes in parliament, in an approach based on reciprocal exchanges and influence.

Another dilemma is represented by the limits imposed on the vote-seeking strategy by the electoral system. The electoral advance of the SVP is much more evident in elections based on proportional representation, where it is the number one party nationally, namely in the elections for the lower chamber of the Federal Assembly and for the cantonal parliaments. In multiple-winner, two-round elections decided on a first-past-the-post basis, on the other hand – namely those for the upper chamber of the Federal Assembly and the cantonal governments – the SVP is generally in third or even fourth place. In 2011, the national party's strategy revolved around attempting to win in both chambers, but the decision to further its agenda and pursue a vote-seeking strategy led to failure in the upper chamber, where the party should have sought to create electoral coalitions with the centre-right parties and to focus more on office-seeking goals. What makes this dilemma difficult to resolve is the fact that the two elections took place at the same time, making it hard to campaign effectively for both. The result of this was that in 2011, the SVP lost votes in the election for the lower chamber, and did not even win a single additional seat in the upper chamber.

Organisational, institutional and inter-party conditions

However, to the extent that the SVP has been able to maintain a radicalised posture over the 2000s and 2010s, the party leadership has exploited a mix of organisational, government and inter-party conditions.

First, it is important to underline that the ideological transformation of the 'new' SVP has been consolidated by a profound organisational change within the party. Despite the attempt to maintain an internal equilibrium with the moderate wing, under Blocher's leadership the party became more professionalised and vertically integrated (Mazzoleni and Rossini 2014b). In contrast to the amateurish and light model of organisation that it had hitherto shared in common with the other Swiss parties, the SVP strengthened its national organisation and resource availability, enhancing both capital-intensive and labour-intensive campaign mobilisation (Mazzoleni and Skenderovic 2007; Skenderovic 2009b). One of the main consequences of these organisational changes was a greater autonomy from the government rules through an empowerment of its extra-parliamentary face, allowing a more coherent collective and ideological identity (Panebianco 1988: Chapter 4), which provided a durable contrast, also in terms of policy purism, to the cooperative and power-sharing rules prevailing in Swiss politics.

Second, the radicalised and anti-establishment strategy of the SVP benefits greatly from the fact that all parties are recognised as independent forces in respect to the government. Swiss democracy represents a rare example of a regime without alternating governments, in which one or more parties retain exclusive control over the government for a lengthy period, without any swapping around (Mair 1997: 207–208). Since the mid-nineteenth century, the seven members of the Swiss government have been elected by the federal parliament, using a first-past-the-post system for each individual member. There is no real president or prime minister, just the mainly ceremonial position of president, which is occupied by one of the seven councillors every year. There is no vote of confidence mechanism, in the sense that parliament cannot oblige any member of the executive to step down. Since the coalition has never been based on a common legislature programme, each party member is in principle free to take an independent stance on different issues. This widely acknowledged principle was a cornerstone of the Swiss government legacy enabling the parties to enjoy a considerable level of autonomy with respect to their representatives in government and vice versa (Burgos *et al.* 2011).

Third, the strategy formulated by the SVP, underlying its strength as the leading electoral party across the country, is enhanced by challenging the traditional rules of the game, namely the pact of 'desistance' between the main parties. The institutionalisation of the government coalition implied a limited level of electoral competition, reducing any incentive to invest in professional and capital-intensive campaigns during the era of the 'magic formula' (Kirchheimer 1966: 188). In other words, within Strøm's conceptual frame (1990: 593), namely that of a low-competition multiparty system, all the main parties first prioritised office-seeking strategies, and then policy-seeking strategies, with vote-seeking decidedly tertiary, a tactic generally left to the weaker parties not represented in government. When it comes to elections, the main goal of vote-seeking is melded with that of office-seeking. In contrast to the stability of the past and in the wake of its repeated electoral successes in parliamentary elections, the SVP began, as of 1999, to demand an increasing presence in the federal government, which it temporarily obtained in 2003. This situation challenged an unwritten rule that had been in place for decades, namely that an outgoing candidate had the right to stand again for the Council and was usually re-elected. After 40 years of observance, a second unwritten rule was also overturned in 2003, meaning that the distribution of seats was no longer automatic. On two consecutive occasions, in 2003 and 2007, the Council excluded a member standing for election for a second time – including Blocher himself in 2007 – showing that parties were responding to the rising level of competition by increasingly employing vote-seeking strategies. Since 2008, the four main parties have been joined by the Conservative Democratic Party (BDP), a spin-off from the SVP founded that same year by the moderate wing headed by Widmer-Schlumpf.

Fourth, as the power-sharing rule has not substantially changed and the SVP has continued to be represented as a minority party in the executive, this paradoxically helps the SVP's protest strategy itself. On the one hand, the party provides a recurrent claim for increased representation within the government, denying the popular legitimacy of the CDP and the majority of the parties supporting its participation; on the other, its minority participation (as an 'underrepresented' party) and the absence of a common government platform allow the party to avoid any government responsibility. According to Schlesinger (1968: 434):

> Parties which govern in coalitions ... can more easily develop a refined ideological position than can parties which must govern alone. The extent to which a party can be held responsible for government affects its ability to retain or to define a stand independent of the government. In coalitions where the governing responsibility is shared or obscure, parties can govern and retain a doctrine which has little relation to the governing experience.

Last but not least, it would have been difficult for a party like the SVP to continue to be part of a coalition government with simply a radicalised and antiestablishment strategy alone. However, there are at least three reasons to help explain why the SVP has continued to endure: the first is that the SVP has continued to enjoy the legitimacy that comes with being a long-term government party. In Switzerland, the SVP is only publicly attacked for being a 'populist' party by a limited number of voices from the right-wing and left-wing fringes. There has never been any kind of *cordon sanitaire* or attempt to discredit its institutional and governmental role. The second reason has to do with its ideological affinities with centre-right parties and its respectability among them, especially when it comes to the economy, and in particular in terms of a liberal and pro-market orientation (Mazzoleni and Rossini 2014a). The third reason is that all the other parties, including the Social Democrats, have always believed that the 'strongest' party cannot be excluded from a broad coalition government, which is held to be the supreme guarantee of the country's social, cultural, and political diversity, and the SVP's popularity lends it the power of veto in referendums and popular initiatives. Moreover, given the fact that any law passed by parliament in Switzerland can be challenged by a referendum, excluding the SVP from government would risk compromising effective policy-making.

Direct democracy as a protest institutional arena

From the SVP's perspective, its vote-seeking strategy – based on a more professionalised party organisation, with some policy pragmatism, tactical coalitions in the parliamentary arena, and minority government participation – benefits from an additional condition, favouring its niche issues (immigration and EU) and its anti-establishment style. Without the opportunities offered by Swiss direct democracy, it would be virtually impossible for the SVP to consolidate its radicalisation over time. In the 1990s, but also in the 2000s, the SVP presented itself as a party of 'protest and government' – using an expression that has often been employed in the past to describe the role of left-wing parties in European democracies – and it has repeatedly been extremely active in the referendum arena, which includes both legislative referendums and popular initiatives permitting change to the federal constitution (Mazzoleni 2008; Skenderovic 2009a).

Switzerland is the only country in the world where national politics is shaped to so great an extent by the direct democracy, in particular the use of legislative referendums and popular initiatives able to change the federal constitution (see, for example, Kobach 1993; Linder 2010). Used as far back as the nineteenth century, referendums are applicable to virtually all laws passed by parliament. Though they may differ in terms of approach and consequences, on a federal level, both referendums and popular initiatives strongly influence the scope of action of parliament and government. Through popular initiatives, even minority players and movements can use them to bring up new issues that the political institutions and government are then forced to place on the agenda. While referendums are like a kind of sword of Damocles that hangs over the laws passed by parliament and government (only 50,000 signatures are needed to call for a nationwide vote), popular initiatives are a way to put forward proposals, or sometimes protests, that the political establishment is obliged to take into account, which is also due to the fact that if the initiative is accepted in a popular vote – after gathering the signatures of at least 100,000 Swiss voters – it changes the federal constitution.

The tools of direct democracy are used by all the Swiss parties and have to date been broadly legitimated. For the SVP, the referendum arena is the crucial sphere for its radicalised stances, and it has made continuous use of referendums throughout the 1990s and 2000s, with particular regard to Europe and immigration. Boosting the de-mainstreaming transformation of the SVP, direct democracy gives the SVP the scope for lasting autonomy as an anti-establishment party and opens opportunities to shape the political agenda and its power of veto on its niche issues. As referendums and initiatives are a key opportunity to mobilise activists and gain media attention, with the rise of the 'new' SVP these issues acquired increasing importance on the Swiss political agenda. Given its widespread legitimacy, direct democracy also permits the regular challenging of the government majority. This phase began in 1992. In December of that year, the Swiss were called to vote in the referendum on the European Economic Area, wherein the Swiss government ended up in a minority. This referendum campaign and its result opened a new window of opportunity for the new generation of politicians gravitating around the leader of the Canton Zurich branch of the SVP, which was opposed to the government (Mazzoleni 2008). Given that the Swiss were the people who were called upon most often in Europe to express their vote during the 1990s and 2000s, and in almost all these cases the SVP went against the position of the government (see, for example, Church 2006), the party has also made pivotal use of referendums and initiatives for electoral purposes, to the point of achieving a voting majority to change the federal constitution.

Considering its increasing success in the referendum arena, it is not surprising to observe how the SVP strategy has radicalised further on immigration since 2003 (see Appendix). In the 2000s, it contributed to the launch of the first popular initiative aiming to introduce a ban on the construction of new minarets (a ban that would later be approved in 2009, see Rayner and Voutat 2004), the call for the expulsion of foreign criminals (2010), and a limit on the flux of immigrants (2014). In the latter initiative, the Swiss people were invited to vote in a popular initiative entitled 'against mass immigration', which was a call to limit the free circulation of people from the EU and to restrict the flow of asylum-seekers. In this case, the SVP once again managed to win a majority in terms of votes and cantons, forcing the Swiss government and parliament to re-think relations with the EU. In other words, the use of popular initiatives and referendums has not lessened over time: on the contrary, with the increase in grass roots support between the 1990s and the 2000s, it became even more effective, consolidating the opponent strategy of the party.

Conclusion

As such, the SVP appears to be a stable party of government that is avoiding being converted by (re-)mainstreaming. By pursuing a challenger strategy since the 1990s, the 'new' SVP has provided an example of de-mainstreaming transformation, developing from a small and moderate government party towards a strong, radicalised and anti-establishment party. Meanwhile, the SVP has continuously been represented in the federal government, maintaining an ambivalent position as a government and oppositional party. Party manifestos and legislative behaviour show its radicalisation and its anti-establishment stances have also been consistent through the 2000s and 2010s.

By providing strong entrepreneurial leadership and strengthened party organisation, and by becoming the strongest party in the federal parliament, the SVP has developed the ability to exploit and shape several political opportunities. The party has been able to benefit from some government rules, including the recognised legitimacy of the relative independence of government members from their own party. The SVP is also able to exploit its minority participation in the large coalition government, which avoids a common policy platform shared by all representatives. The mainstream (and government) parties have also acknowledged, albeit critically, that the SVP had the 'right' to participate in government for a number of reasons, first and foremost because of its reputation as a 'government party' with which long standing relations were already in place. Its old reputation as a government party, never denied by the new leadership of the SVP, but also some persistent accommodative behaviour in the legislative arena, were essential factors in the political legitimation of the SVP in the Swiss political system. Despite its prevalent vote-seeking strategy, the SVP also managed not to be excluded from government and was even able to return to it after a brief interlude in 2008. Moreover, the mainstream parties also believe that if a party as strong as the SVP were to be excluded from the government, it might develop an increasing power of veto through referendums. Alongside its higher capacity to mobilise in the electoral arena and the prevailing government rules, the referendum arena represents the other crucial factor allowing the party to maintain its protest profile over time. Over the course of the last two decades, it is by also being able to achieve greater capacities for mobilisation in the referendum arena that the SVP has been able to shape the national agenda around its own issues, namely those of Europe and immigration.

More generally, through its increasingly organisational and electoral strength, and its role in the government and in the referendum arena, the SVP has contributed to changes that have occurred in some traditional rules and equilibriums, namely an increasing level of competition and uncertainty in various arenas, which have progressively allowed opportunities to pursue their own vote-seeking goals. In light of this, the SVP has in no way changed its strategy, although it has had to deal with a number of strategic dilemmas which caused a split and led to it losing ground in the most recent federal elections in the autumn of 2011.

Notes

1 Here we follow the results arising from the code scheme adopting quasi-sentence units as part of the international project 'Left of the radical right' (version 3.0), headed by Simon Otjes at the University of Groningen and Sarah De Lange at the University of Amsterdam.
2 In order to measure the salience of socioeconomic issues we count the number of quasi-sentences relating to the respective issues. The CMP Manifesto project database places the SVP's 2011 federal platform in the centre of the left-right spectrum. This outcome could be due to the inclusion of non-economic items (like military issues) in the CMP coding, which we avoided in our own scale.
3 Controversies within the SVP about MPs' discipline also arose in the public sphere (see, for instance, *Neue Zürcher Zeitung*, 19 April 2003 and 12 August 2004; *Thurgauer Zeitung*, 16 August 2004).

References

Adams, J., Clark, M., Ezrow, L. and Glasgow, G. (2006) 'Are niche parties fundamentally different from mainstream parties? The causes and the electoral consequences of Western European parties' policy shifts. 1976–1998', *American Journal of Political Science* 50, 3: 513–529.
Afonso, A. (2013) 'Whose interests do radical right parties really represent? The Migration policy agenda of the Swiss People's Party between nativism and neoliberalism', in Korkut, U., Bucken-Knapp, G., McGarry, A., Hinnfors, J. and Drake, H. (eds) *The Discourses of Politics of Migration in Europe*, New York and Basingstoke: Palgrave Macmillan, pp. 17–36.
Albertazzi, D. (2007) 'Switzerland: Yet another populist paradise', in Albertazzi, D. and McDonnell, D. (eds) *Twenty-First Century Populism: The Spectre of Western European Democracy*, New York and Basingstoke: Palgrave Macmillan, pp. 10–118.

Albertazzi, D. and McDonnell, D. (2015) *Populist Parties in Power: Italian and Swiss Success Stories*, London and New York: Routledge.

Altermatt, U. and Kriesi, H. (1994) *Rechte und Linke Fundamentalposition. Studien zur Schweizerpolitik, 1965–1990*, Basel: Helbing & Lichtenhahn.

Betz, Hans-Georg (2005) 'Mobilising resentment in the Alps. The Swiss SVP, the Italian Lega Nord, and the Austrian FPÖ', in Caramani, D. and Mény, Y. (eds) *Challenges to Consensual Politics. Democracy, Identity, and Populist Protest in the Alpine Region*, Brussels: Peter Lang, pp. 147–166.

Blanchard, P., Mach, A., Mazzoleni, O. and Pilotti, A. (2009) 'La double loyauté des députés suisses: Cohésion partisane et liens d'intérêt au sein du Conseil national', in Mazzoleni, O. and Rayner, H. (eds) *Les Partis Politiques en Suisse: Traditions et Renouvellements*, Paris: Houdiard, pp. 208–247.

Burgos, E., Mazzoleni, O. and Rayner, H. (2011) *La Formule Magique. Conflit et Consensus dans l'Élection du Conseil Federal*, Lausanne: Presses Polytechniques et universitaires romandes.

Church, C. H. (ed.) (2006) *Switzerland and the European Union: A Close Contradictory and Misunderstood Relationship*, London: Routledge.

De Lange, S. L. (2007) 'From pariah to power broker. The radical right-wing and government in Western Europe', in Delwit, P. and Poirier, P. (eds) *The New Right-Wing Parties and Power in Europe*, Brussels: Editions de l'Université de Bruxelles, pp. 21–40.

Deschouwer, K. (2001) 'Freezing pillars and frozen cleavages. Party systems and voter alignments in the consociational democracies', in Karvonen, L. and Kuhnle, S. (eds) *Party Systems and Voter Alignments Revisited*, London: Routledge, pp. 205–221.

Downs, A. (1957) *An Economic Theory of Democracy*, New York: Harper & Row.

Giugni, M. and Passy, F. (2001) 'La politique contestataire de l'immigration. Modèles de citoyenneté, opportunités politiques et les débats publics autour des relations ethniques en France et en Suisse, 1990–1998', Research Report, Bern: Swiss National Science Foundation.

Hertig, H. (1978) 'Party cohesion in the Swiss parliament', *Legislative Studies Quarterly* 3, 1: 63–81.

Kerr, H. (1987) 'The Swiss party system: Steadfast and changing', in Daalder, H. (ed.) *Party Systems in Denmark, Austria, Switzerland, the Netherlands, and Belgium*, London: Frances Pinter, pp. 107–192.

Kirchheimer, O. (1966) 'The transformation of the Western European party system', in LaPalombara, J. and Weiner, M. (eds) *Political Parties and Political Development*, Princeton, NJ: Princeton University Press, pp. 177–200.

Kitschelt, H. (in collaboration with McGann, A. J.) (1995) *The Radical Right in Western Europe. A Comparative Analysis*, Ann Arbor, MI: Michigan University Press.

Kobach, K. W. (1993) *The Referendum: Direct Democracy in Switzerland*, Aldershot: Dartmouth.

Kuisma, M. (2013) '"Good" and "bad" immigrants: The economic nationalism of the True Finns' immigration discourse', in Korkut, U., Bucken-Knapp, G., McGarry, A., Hinnfors, J. and Drake, H. (eds) *The Discourses of Politics of Migration in Europe*, New York: Palgrave Macmillan, pp. 93–108.

Lanfranchi, P. and Lüthi, R. (1999) 'Cohesion of party groups and interparty conflict in the Swiss parliament: Roll call voting in the national council', in Shaun, B., Farrel, D. M. and Katz, R. S. (eds) *Party Discipline and Parliamentary Government*, Columbus, OH: Ohio State University Press, 99–120.

Linder, W. (2010) *Swiss Democracy Possible Solutions to Conflict in Multicultural Societies*, Basingstoke: Palgrave Macmillan.

Lutz, G. (2012) *Elections Fédérales 2011. Participation et Choix Électoral*, Lausanne: Selects – FORS.

Mair, P. (1997) *Party System Change. Approaches and Interpretations*, Oxford: Clarendon Press.

Mazzoleni, O. (2008 [2003]) *Nationalisme et Populisme en Suisse. La Radicalisation de la "Nouvelle" UDC*, 1st edn, Lausanne: Presses Polytechniques et universitaires romandes.

Mazzoleni, O. (2009) 'Des partis gouvernentaux face à la "crise": Les cas du Parti libéral-radical et du Parti démocrate-chrétien', in Mazzoleni, O. and Rayner, H. (eds) *Les Partis Politiques en Suisse: Traditions et Renouvellements*, Paris: Houdiard Editeur, pp. 410–442.

Mazzoleni, O. (2013a) 'Government and opposition. The case of the Swiss People's party', in Hartleb, F. and Grabow, K. (eds) *Exposing the Demagogues. Right-wing and National Populists in Europe*, Brussels and Berlin: KAS-CES, pp. 237–260.

Mazzoleni, O. (2013b) 'Des convergences inhabituelles: l'Union démocratique du centre et le Parti socialiste dans l'arène parlementaire fédérale', in Mazzoleni, O. and Meuwly, O. (eds) *Les Partis Suisses Entre Coopération et Compétition*, Geneva: Slatkine, pp. 89–108.

Mazzoleni, O. and Rayner, H. (2009) 'Une coalition gouvernementale "immuable"? Emergence et institutionnalisation de la "formule magique"', in Mazzoleni, O. and Rayner, H. (eds) *Les Partis Politiques en Suisse: Traditions et Renouvellements*, Paris: Houdiard Editeur, pp. 127–168.

Mazzoleni, O. and Rossini, C. (2014a) 'Salience, orientation and content of socio-economic issues: The electoral manifesto of the Swiss People's Party (1995–2011)', paper presented at the ECPR General Conference, Glasgow, 3–6 September.

Mazzoleni, O. and Rossini, C. (2014b) 'Party organization and populist stances. The case of the Swiss People's Party', paper presented at the Workshop Toward a Core Model of Populist Party Organization, University of Salzburg, 14–15 March.

Mazzoleni, O. and Skenderovic, D. (2007) 'The rise and impact of the Swiss People's Party: Challenging the rules of governance in Switzerland', in Delwit, P. and Poirier, P. (eds) *The New Right-Wing Parties and Power in Europe*, Brussels: Les Éditions de l'Université de Bruxelles, pp. 85–116.

Mény, Y. and Surel, Y. (2000) *Par le Peuple, Pour le Peuple. Le Populisme et les Démocraties*, Paris: Fayard.

Müller, W. C. and Strøm, K. (eds) (1999) *Policy, Office, or Votes? How Political Parties in Western Europe Make Hard Decisions*, Cambridge: Cambridge University Press.

Neue Zürcher Zeitung (19-04-2003) 'Ausschluss von SVP-Nationalratsliste. Nationalrätin Lisbeth Fehr hält SVP Spitze für 'totalitär''.

Neue Zürcher Zeitung (12-08-2004) 'SVP-Nationalrat Siegrist droht Kommissionsausschluss'.

Niggli, P. and Frischknecht, J. (1998) *Rechte Seilschaften. Wie die 'Unheimlichen Patrioten' den Zusammenbruch des Kommunismus meisterten*, Zurich: WoZ im Rotpunktverlag.

Panebianco, A. (1988) *Political Parties: Organization and Power*, Cambridge: Cambridge University Press.

Rayner, H. and Voutat, B. (2014) 'La judiciarisation à l'épreuve de la démocratie directe. L'interdiction de construire des minarets en Suisse', *Revue Française de Science Politique* 64, 4: 689–709.

Schedler, A. (1996) 'Anti-political-establishment parties', *Party Politics* 3, 2: 291–312.

Schlesinger, A. J. (1968) 'Party Units', in *International Encyclopedia of Social Sciences*, www. encyclopedia.com (accessed 20-04-2015).

Schwarz, D. and Linder, W. (2006) *Mehrheits- und Koalitionsbildung im Schweizerischen Nationalrat. 1996–2006. Studie im Auftrag der Parlamentsdienste der Schweizerischen Bundesversammlung*, Bern: University of Bern.

Skenderovic, D. (2009a) *The Radical Right in Switzerland. Continuity and Change. 1945–2000*, New York: Berghahn.

Skenderovic, D. (2009b) 'Campagnes et agenda politiques. La transformation de l'Union démocratique du centre', in Mazzoleni, O. and Rayner, H. (eds) *Les Partis Politiques en Suisse. Traditions et Renouvellements*, Paris: Michel Houdiard Editeur, pp. 378–409.

Strøm, K. (1990) 'A behavioral theory of competitive political parties', *American Journal of Political Science* 34, 2: 565–598.

SVP (1991) 'Programme du Parti '91 de l'Union Démocratique du Centre', Bern: Swiss People's Party.

SVP (1995) 'Programme des Priorités Politiques '95 de l'Union Démocratique du Centre', Bern: Swiss People's Party.

SVP (1999) 'Wahlplattform 1999', Bern: Swiss People's Party.

SVP (2015a) 'Party Programme 2015–2019. The SVP, The party for Switzerland', Bern: Swiss People's Party.

SVP (2015b) 'Extrablatt März 2015 der Schweizer Volkspartei. Schweizer Recht Statt Fremde Richter!', www.svp.ch, Bern.

Thurgauer Zeitung (16-08-2004) 'Ist die SVP eine Sekte, Caspar Baader'.

Wagner, M. (2012) 'Defining and measuring niche parties', *Party Politics* 18, 6: 845–864.

Wolinetz, S. B. (2002) 'Beyond the catch-all party: Approaches to the study of parties and party organization in contemporary democracies', in Gunther, R., Ramón-Montero, J. and Linz, J. (eds) *Political Parties. Old Concepts and New Challenges*, Oxford: Oxford University Press, pp. 136–165.

10 It is still a long way from Madou Square to Law Street

The evolution of the Flemish Bloc

Paul Lucardie, Tjitske Akkerman and Teun Pauwels

Introduction

Madou Square (Place Madou, Madou Plein) is the location of the headquarters of the Flemish Interest (Vlaams Belang, VB), the only significant radical right-wing or national-populist party in Belgium since the Second World War. The Flemish party has survived external pressures, electoral ups and downs and internal strife since its foundation in 1978/1979. In spite of a fairly sizeable electorate and a strong party organisation, the party seems as far removed from governmental power today as it was 35 years ago. Geographically, its headquarters are not at all far from the government buildings at Law Street (Rue de la Loi, Wetstraat), but politically the distance is considerable. Mainstream parties – in Belgium: the Social Democrats, Liberals and Christian Democrats – together with the Greens imposed a *cordon sanitaire* in 1989 which has been maintained effectively until the present. Lack of opportunities for office and a *cordon sanitaire* have been identified by scholars as negative conditions for mainstreaming (Minkenberg 2013; Van der Brug and Fennema 2004; Van Spanje and Van der Brug 2007). Others, however, have demonstrated that ostracised parties have not frozen their programmatic development, and are very well able to move into the mainstream (Akkerman and Rooduijn 2014). Moreover, the effects of the *cordon sanitaire* on the positions of the VB are highly contested (Breuning and Ishiyama 1998; Coffé 2005; Damen 2001; Swyngedouw and Van Craen 2001). Adding to the dissensus is that different conceptualisations of mainstreaming which been used. We therefore use a broad concept of mainstreaming which covers different dimensions (see Introduction). Moreover, we not only look at external or internal conditions like office opportunities, *cordon sanitaire* and party organisation, but also take account of the goals and strategies of the VB.

Flemish Interest has its roots in the Flemish nationalist movement. When the party emerged in 1978 under the name Flemish Bloc (Vlaams Blok, VB), a large part of its activists and candidates came from Flemish nationalist organisations (Swyngedouw 1998: 61; Art 2011: 111–115). In 1940 a large part of the Flemish nationalist movement embraced national-socialism and began to collaborate with the German occupation. After 1945 many of its cadres were arrested and sent to prison. In 1954 it re-emerged as a political party, the Flemish

People's Union (Vlaamse Volksunie, VU). The VU was a broad coalition of 'hardcore' and authoritarian nationalists with more moderate autonomists, including even a small but growing left wing with social-democratic ideas (Gijsels and Van der Velpen 1989: 39–55; Matheve 2014: 97–98). When the moderate majority decided to cooperate with the mainstream parties in a grand coalition and agree to a constitutional reform aimed at regional autonomy, the hardcore nationalists bolted the VU (Van Haute 2005: 247). Two new parties emerged, one led by Karel Dillen, the other by Senator Lode Claes. The two parties participated in the 1978 parliamentary elections as a cartel (alliance) under the name 'Flemish Bloc'. Yet only Dillen managed to win a seat in the Antwerp district, where a fertile soil for hardcore nationalism existed as many former nationalists who had collaborated with the German occupation had settled in this city (Art 2008: 427).

Initially, the VB advocated above all an independent and authoritarian Flemish state. The leader of the party, Dillen, referred often to 'elites' and 'aristocratic ideals' (Gijsels and Van der Velpen 1989: 34, 64; see also *Volkskrant* 04-02-1992). Many leading members of the party had direct or indirect connections with the quasi-fascist movement of the 1930s or mentioned a father, uncle or grandfather who had fought in the Second World War on the German side (Art 2008: 427–428; Van den Brink 1999: 55–56, 98–99, 112, 187–188, 203). The historical origins of the party and its embeddedness in a hardcore Flemish nationalist subculture incited public questioning of its legitimacy from the beginning. A *cordon sanitaire* by mainstream parties was imposed in 1989 and has been maintained until today, with very few exceptions.

In 1989 the leaders of all major parties in Flanders – Christian Democrats, Social Democrats, Liberals, Greens and the Flemish nationalist People's Union (VolksUnie, VU) – signed an agreement that they would refrain from any cooperation with the VB at any level (Damen 2001: 92–93). Though the agreement has been interpreted differently by the signing parties and was even formally cancelled by the president of the VU, it has been respected in practice. The VB has been excluded from government and from electoral alliances at the federal, regional and local level. In the Belgian as well as the Flemish parliament, it has been isolated very effectively (Damen 2001: 103–104). A few cracks in the *cordon* have appeared in some municipalities, when members of VU and its successor the New-Flemish Alliance (Nieuw-Vlaamse Alliantie, N-VA) or the Christian Democrats were elected in local government with support from the VB (Damen 2001: 101–103; Buelens and Deschouwer 2003: 33–34; *Het Belang van Limburg* 2013).

The legitimacy of the VB was also denied in court in 2004. Three organisations affiliated with the VB were considered 'racist' and consequently banned by the Supreme Court (Court of Cassation). Immediately the party decided to adopt a new name – Flemish Interest instead of Flemish Bloc – and a new, somewhat more moderate programme (Erk 2005; see also below).

For the first ten years of its existence, the VB was probably too small to be taken very seriously by the established parties. In terms of votes, the VB had a modest start: after 1.4 per cent of the vote in 1978 it obtained only 1.1 per cent (and again one seat) in 1981 (see Table 10.1). During the early 1980s it gradually shifted its emphasis from Flemish independence to the immigration issue (see also below). That programmatic change, combined with an organisational strengthening, appeared to be electorally rewarding. In the late 1980s the party managed to gain electoral influence around Antwerp, and after 1991 also in other areas (Van Craen and Swyngedouw 2002). At the municipal elections of 1988 the party made a breakthrough in Antwerp (almost 18 per cent of the vote) and could no longer be ignored (Van Eycken and Schoeters 1988: 22–25). The VB made its first impressive national breakthrough in the 1991 general elections, gaining 6.6 per cent of the popular vote. Electoral growth culminated in 11.6 per cent of the national vote and 17.9 per cent in the regional elections in Flanders in 2003. As the VB does not present lists in the unilingual French-speaking constituencies, its share of the Flemish target electorate represents a more exact image of its electoral performance (see Table 10.1). The electoral growth slowed down after 2000 and turned into decline after 2007. The party lost voters to the N-VA. Led by the popular Bart De Wever, the N-VA also promoted a tough Flemish nationalism combined with an anti-establishment discourse, but without xenophobia. The N-VA was quite successful at the elections in 2007 and even more in 2010 and 2014 – at the expense of the VB (Matheve 2014; Pauwels 2013: 85–86).

The declining electoral results and continuing isolation of the VB may have exacerbated internal tensions. In the 1980s and 1990s, disagreements about strategy and personal tensions between Antwerp-based 'activists' around Filip Dewinter and 'parliamentarists' around Gerolf Annemans and Frank Vanhecke could still be managed and reconciled (Van den Brink 1999: 118–119, 180). Vanhecke was appointed party president in 1996, succeeding the leader of the first hour Dillen. He resigned in 2008 and left the party in 2011 when he felt that the Antwerp-faction had gained complete control and did not tolerate divergent views any more (*Het Laatste Nieuws* 2011; *Trouw* 08-12-2009; Vanhecke 2011). Annemans was elected party president in 2012 and promised renewal, but could not stop the exodus of prominent party members, many of whom joined the N-VA (Knack.be 29-01-2014; Pauwels 2013: 94–95). At the elections of May 2014 the VB lost again many voters to the N-VA and achieved its worst result since 1987: 3.7 per cent (see Table 10.1). Five months later, the 28-year-old and relatively unknown Tom Van Grieken succeeded Annemans to become the youngest party president ever in Belgium.

Ideological development: mainstreaming, but not enough

Nationalism is the core ideology of the VB. In its first declaration of principles the party mentioned three notions that defined its ideology: ethnic nationalism (*volksnationalisme*), solidarism and conservative ethical values and traditions such as family, authority and private property (Vlaams Blok n.d.; see also Mudde 2000: 96–115; Spruyt 1995). When Vlaams Belang adopted a new declaration of principles and a new constitution in 2004, it referred again to nationalism, solidarity and to conservative ethical values (Vlaams Belang 2004b; Vlaams Belang n.d.).

Nationalism has an internal and an external side: on the one hand the promotion of internal unity and homogeneity, on the other hand the pursuit of independence or autonomy vis-à-vis other states.

The VB began as a regionalist party pursuing autonomy and independence for Flanders, but soon began to emphasise internal homogeneity as well. In its first declaration of principles the party already had defined the nation as an organic community and called for the return of 'the overwhelming majority of non-European guest workers to their home country' without elaborating or explaining this position (Vlaams Blok n.d.: 1–2, 7). During the 1980s, immigration gained importance as an issue in election campaigns – and contributed substantially to the electoral growth of the party.[1]

In 1992 the VB published a '70-point programme' with proposals to 'solve the foreigner problem' (Vlaams Blok 1992). An adapted version was published in 1996 (Vlaams Blok 1996) and was meant to demonstrate that repatriation of immigrants, including those of the second and third generations, was a realistic option. The plan was highly contested, as it was widely regarded as conflicting with the European Declaration of Human Rights. Integration of non-European immigrants was rejected on the ground of cultural incompatibility with specific references to Islamic 'culture'. The principle of 'our own people first' ('eigen volk eerst') was to be applied by giving priority to natives in the public housing domain, on the labour market, in public service etc. The party's migration

Table 10.1 Votes and seats of the VB in the Belgian Kamer van Afgevaardigden (House of Representatives) 1978–2014

Year	Votes (%)	Seats
1978	1.9	1
1981	1.1	1
1985	1.4	1
1987	1.9	2
1991	6.6	12
1995	7.8	11*
1999	9.9	15
2003	11.6	18
2007	12.0	17
2010	7.8	12
2014	3.7	3

Note: * The VB participated only in Flanders, like other Flemish parties.
Sources: Belgische verkiezingsuitslagen (Belgian election results) (2014) online: www.ibzdgip.fgov.be/result/nl/main.html (accessed 06-05-2014); www.verkiezingen2007.belgium.be/nl/cha/results/results_tab_etop.html (accessed 29-05-2014); www.verkiezingen2010.belgium.be/nl/cha/results/results_tab_CKR00000.html (accessed 25-05-2014); http://verkiezingen2014.belgium.be/nl/cha/results/results_tab_CKR00000.html (accessed 27-05-2014).

programme has been considered by its opponents as the clearest proof of the racist nature of the VB. Under the threat of possible conviction for racism, the most extreme features were removed from the Vlaams Blok's programme in 2003. The principle that immigrants should not integrate but repatriate was now replaced by the basic line that they should fully assimilate or otherwise leave the host country ('aanpassen of opkrassen') (Vlaams Blok 2003: 15–20).

In response to the legal complaints against the party, the VB aimed to get rid of its racist reputation more generally after the turn of the century. The party instructed local branches how to avoid violations of the law against racism in 2000 (Buelens and Deschouwer 2003). In 2004, Vlaams Blok was renamed Vlaams Belang after the ruling of the Court of Cassation, a ruling that could lead to prosecution of individual members and withdrawing of governmental subsidy. Yet, there were on and off incidents that threw doubt on the ability or the willingness of the VB to shed its extremist reputation. Dewinter often demonstrated an ambivalent position. He distanced himself warily from his 70-points plan, arguing that it was no longer realistic in the current context (Coffé 2005: 210). Yet, when the VB was renamed, Dewinter made clear that this change was merely a veneer. He said: 'The Flemish Bloc is dead, long live the Flemish Bloc'. He added that the 70-point plan had been useful and that it was to be saved for the future (Boeckz 2004). With respect to disreputable members, the leadership of the party also acted sometimes half-heartedly. Although the revisionist Roeland Raes, who in an interview on Dutch TV in 2001 cast doubt on the scale and the extent of the Holocaust, was forced to resign from his senior post in the party and as senator, Raes remained active within the VB even when he was convicted in 2008 and 2010. The tensions behind the ambivalent course of the VB came into the open after the electoral downturn in 2009 and 2010. A radical course promoted by the Antwerp faction of Dewinter became more prominent again. An early campaign for the local elections in 2012 gave rise to accusations of racism, because it featured pictures of criminals which linked immigration and criminality. Dewinter also supported a contentious statement of Geert Wilders against Moroccans (see Chapter 7). 'Just as in The Netherlands, there should be fewer Moroccans in Antwerp and fewer Roma in Gent', Dewinter said (*Elsevier* 20-03-2014). An online game designed by the VB called 'fewer, fewer, fewer' that enabled players to kill Islamic terrorists and criminals, was banned as racist in 2015 (*Telegraaf* 11-02-2015). The shimmering tensions within the party about a strategy to detoxify the party became clearly manifest after 2010.

The strategy to detoxify the party implied an important step towards mainstreaming after the turn of the century. Replacing the general demand for repatriation of immigrants with a conditional one not only was a matter of reputation management, but also implied a moderation of policy with respect to the core issue of immigration.

However, the further working-out of immigration and integration policy proposals in the 70-point plan had been rather modest. An analysis of concrete policy proposals in election manifestos with respect to immigration and integration makes clear that in this respect a trend towards mainstreaming cannot be observed (see Appendix). A highly restrictive and assimilationist policy programme was adopted again in 2003, demanding full assimilation and a citizen's test as condition for a residence permit, an effective immigration stop, active tracing of illegal immigrants, restrictions of family reunification, no recognition of Islam, and removal of the option of dual citizenship (Vlaams Blok 2003). These policy proposals even became more extensive and restrictive over time, with increasing restrictions for family reunification and asylum, more stringent demands for citizens' tests, recurring proposals to re-establish the principle of citizenship based on Flemish origins (*ius sanguinis*), and proliferating restrictions with respect to Islam. The VB had targeted Islam already in the 70-point plan as a culture that was incompatible with the Flemish way of life, and proposed to withdraw recognition of Islam as official religion and the closing of mosques in which hate was preached 'against Western civilisation'. A ban on wearing headscarves in public service was added in 2007 and a halt to building new mosques in 2014.

With respect to law and order issues the VB did not change its course very much (see Appendix). An authoritarian programme, demanding zero tolerance, stricter punishment, and more police remained intact over the years. This chimes in with the conservative worldview of the party and its pessimistic or 'realistic' view of human nature – man has to be recognised as he is, and cannot be changed (Vlaams Belang n.d.: 2). Law and order issues were often linked to immigration as in the controversial election campaign of 2012.

Flemish independence has always been an important purpose of the Flemish Bloc as well as the Flemish Interest (Vlaams Blok n.d.: 1; Vlaams Blok 2003: 2; Vlaams Belang n.d.: 1; Vlaams Belang 2014; see also Spruyt 1995: 86–97).[2] The nationalism of the VB was initially not translated into a Eurosceptic position. The VB used to favour European integration, mainly to protect the continent against Russian and American imperialism, provided the EU would respect the identity of the different ethnic communities (*volksgemeenschappen*) (Vlaams Blok n.d.: 3). After 1992, as European integration proceeded, the VB has become more critical of the European Union: it preferred a confederal Europe based on cooperation between sovereign nation-states to a 'superstate' (Vlaams Blok 2003: 51–52; see also Spruyt 1995: 236). Moreover, the ethnic nationalism of the party increasingly influenced its position with respect to European integration. In 2013, the anti-immigration agenda of the VB was translated into a demand to discard the principle of free movement of European citizens (Vandecasteele 2013). In 2014 it considered itself 'the only EU-critical party' in Belgium: still 'pro-Europe' but opposed to the 'multi-headed bureaucratic monster of the European Union which rules over our money, our prosperity and welfare, without any input from the people' (Vlaams Belang 2014; see also Vlaams Belang 2012: 138–151).

Sociocultural issues were important for the VB from the beginning. Flemish independence was initially the main goal of the party, soon to be complemented by immigration issues. Party leaders identified Flemish independence, immigration and law and order as core issues, and these issues also central in election campaigns and to voters. As Dewinter said in an interview in 2003:

We will round off any sharp edges, and slide somewhat to the centre-right. But not too much, since our unique selling proposition remains a clear position on immigration, security and Flemish independence.

(Cited in Coffé 2005: 210)

Immigration and law and order were the main issues that voters mentioned as their motives to vote for the VB (Abts, Swyngedouw and Billiet 2010: 38; Swyngedouw 2001; Van Eycken and Schoeters 1988). Even though the party initially devoted quantitatively more attention to socioeconomic issues in its election manifestos, sociocultural issues gained salience over time and became dominant in 2007. Even after the financial crisis in Europe had broken out in 2008 sociocultural issues remained very dominant in the manifestos of the VB (see Appendix). However, the activities of the party demonstrated that economic issues regained some relevance recently; the VB organised conferences on socioeconomic policy in March 2012 and June 2013 (see Vlaams Belang 2012, 2013). Overall, one cannot conclude that the VB fundamentally adjusted the niche character of the party. Dewinter said that with the campaign of 2012 the VB returned to the roots of the party: 'Immigration, illegality, Islamization' (Knack.be 29-01-2014). In this respect, the party did not convincingly mainstream its programme.

The anti-establishment position of the VB became somewhat more moderate around the turn of the century, but was emphasised again after 2007. Originally, the ideology of the VB was rather elitist. During the 1980s, aristocratic elitism gave way to democratic populism (Mudde 2000: 113; Spruyt 2000: 77–128). In 1996 the VB embraced explicitly parliamentary democracy, combined with elements of direct democracy: a binding referendum, and direct elections of the head of state and mayors (Vlaams Blok 2003: 8–10; see also Vlaams Belang 2004a: 10–15). Like other populist parties, it argued that democracy had been undermined and diluted by the elites, and that 'real power is no longer in the hands of the elected representatives of the people' (Vlaams Belang 2004a: 10).[3] However, the party has also moderated its populist references to the people and its critique of elites somewhat since 1995 (see Appendix (Belgium). Pauwels and Rooduijn (forthcoming) analysed whether the recent economic and political crises in Belgium had led to an increase of populist rhetoric. They found that immediately after the political crisis, which started at the end of 2007, populist elements were found more often in the ideology of the VB. In 2009 and 2010 populism decreased again to pre-crisis levels in spite of these being election years.

The VB also packed its messages in a populist style. In public debates and election campaigns the VB used somewhat stronger language than other parties in its attacks on 'the political caste': 'political mafia', 'thieves, liars, incompetents', 'traitors of the people', 'corrupt scoundrels', 'pigs and perverts' (Spruyt 2000: 93). In parliament, several verbal confrontations – once even culminating in a fight with the military police and a conditional suspension of Dewinter and Annemans – occurred in the 1990s (Van den Brink 1994: 141). The VB moderated its campaign style at the turn of the century (see also Erk 2005). While the party originally campaigned with anti-establishment symbols like boxing gloves in 1991, a broom in 1994 (to bring about a 'clean sweep' in politics) and a fist in 1995, a softer style emerged in 1999 with the depictions of a family or a child (Bosseman 2000). Yet after 2007, the style of the VB became harder again. Dewinter said 'I admit that we have become more assertive in order to improve our profile' (Knack.be 06-07-2012). Dewinter had always been in favour of a confrontational style, although he made an exception for Antwerp where the VB might gain a majority and therefore should demonstrate a more respectable style. He already stated in the beginning of the 1990s that the party needed polarisation in order to draw media attention and to get the sympathy of the man in the street, who also felt like an underdog *vis-á-vis* the government (Van den Brink 1994: 158). A recent example of the return to a confrontational style is the establishment of an online site in 2012 where one could report complaints about illegal immigrants (Knack.be 10-04-2012). As described above, some recent confrontational events that Dewinter promoted were inspired by the ways in which Geert Wilders, leader of the Dutch Party for Freedom (Partij voor de Vrijheid, PVV), managed to draw media attention and voters by making controversial statements about Moroccans or taking controversial initiatives like a website where complaints about immigrants could be reported.

The fundamental ideological features of the VB have changed in other respects as well. The VB has adapted its conservative ideology with respect to moral issues and economic solidarism. Although these are important changes for the VB, it is difficult to capture them under the definition of mainstreaming that is used in the Introduction to this volume. Therefore, we discuss them briefly as case-specific changes. The party was outspokenly conservative in the 1980s and 1990s, highlighting the importance of tradition and family, endorsing support for large families, and opposing abortion. Although the VB moderated its views over time, it has recently turned back to a more conservative stance. Yet, a remarkable change is that the salience of family relations has decreased substantially and consistently over time. Its conservative profile has turned rather pale in this respect (Akkerman 2015: 49; De Lange and Mügge 2015).

The socioeconomic ideology of the VB also has been modernised. Originally, the ideology of solidarism was highly influential. Solidarism was conceived as a 'Third Way' beyond liberal capitalism and Marxist socialism, inspired by Catholic ideas about reconciliation and cooperation between classes in society (Vlaams Blok n.d.: 4; see also Spruyt 1995: 180). In election manifestos of the 1980s and 1990s solidarism gradually and implicitly gave way to liberalism, however.[4] Solidarity has not completely given way to liberalism though and perhaps regained importance in recent years – due to competition with the neoliberal N-VA (Knack.be 29-01-2014).[5] It can be concluded that the VB has moderated its conservative views after the turn of the century, but this trend does not seem to persevere.

Summing up, we might conclude that the VB has only gone into the mainstream by moderating its reputation as a racist party after the turn of the century. However, its radical niche profile as an anti-immigration and law and order party has not been moderated. The party emphasised these issues more over time and radicalised its positions with respect to immigration and integration again after 2007. The VB shifted early on to democratic populism in its ideas about the state and its institutions and continued to display anti-establishment attitudes, with some softening of its populist style between 2000 and 2010. The conservative outlook of the party became more modern over time with respect to family and gender relations, but recently the party tends to be moving away from the centre again. The VB has modernised its economic conservatism, mixing it with economic liberalism.

Goals and strategy: why the VB has remained a niche party outside the mainstream

The VB started as an uncompromising 'radical combat party' (*radicale strijdpartij*) and 'the voice of radical Flemish nationalism' (Vlaams Blok n.d.: 1). Its founding members might have been motivated by ideological and identity incentives, rather than expectations of a political career (see Lange 1977). If we use the trichotomy of Strøm (1990), the party's strategy was policy- and vote-seeking more than office-seeking. Office-seeking was mainly a long-term perspective based on a majority strategy (Buelens and Deschouwer 2003). An exception may have been the campaign to get Dewinter elected as mayor in Antwerp in 2006, but it remained unclear whether the party was willing to let go of the majority strategy in this case (ibid.). As long as an electoral majority was not accomplished and access to office was barred, vote-seeking was important to increase policy influence indirectly through the 'whip' function of the party, which means that the party exerts influence on governing parties and the political agenda while remaining in the opposition. Indirect influence through electoral pressure and a majority strategy allowed the VB to aim for policy purity rather than policy influence (see Chapter 1). These goals were perhaps exacted by the *cordon sanitaire*, as the *cordon* barred the VB from coalitions in office and cooperation in parliament, and left the party little choice. However, Dillen and other hardliners also welcomed the *cordon sanitaire* and the isolation of the party as it would ensure its purity and prevent it from compromising its principles (Buelens and Deschouwer 2003: 35). At any rate, the VB made the best of its pariah position, positioning the VB as a martyr of the fight for freedom of expression and a victim of established politics. Vote-seeking incited the party to upgrade the issue of immigration in 1984. This change was inspired by the electoral success of the French National Front (Front National, FN) and the Dutch Centre Party (Centrumpartij, CP) at the time (Mudde 1995: 11). Vote-seeking also was a motive to accept the *cordon sanitaire*; the 'victimisation' of the VB seems to have contributed to its electoral success. According to Van Spanje and Van der Brug (2009: 372, 376), the VB benefited electorally from being ostracised in the 1990s, probably because ostracism reinforced its distinctiveness and facilitated 'victimisation'. While the *cordon sanitaire* was used to utmost advantage, juridical threats were more difficult to cope with. Dewinter emphasised that the high costs of convictions for racism overruled electoral gains in this case; the financial costs of a trial and the fundamental threat of a ban on the party were decisive for the party to avoid further juridical actions and to adapt its profile (Knack.be 06-07-2012).

Even though the *cordon sanitaire* was welcomed as an electoral opportunity, not everyone within the VB embraced wholeheartedly the role of opposition party. The local elections in Antwerp on and off brought up the question of how to pursue an office strategy. This was the case in 1994 and again in the run up to the elections of 2000 (De Winter 2004). The party moderated its confrontational style in the latter elections to show that it was willing to give up its protest role. However, leaders of the party also made clear that they were not up to make programmatic compromises or to enter a coalition. Annemans emphasised the importance of maintaining a pure programme, even if the electoral results required the VB to accept office (Van den Brink 1994: 161–162). Dewinter wanted to woo voters away from the Christian Democrats and Social Democrats and to win office, as well as voice protest (Van den Brink 1999: 182–183). It was not clear though whether he was willing to join a coalition, and at what costs (Buelens and Deschouwer 2003: 31). The perspective of a local majority in Antwerp and the office of mayor came into view after the electoral triumph in 2004. Dewinter used a great deal of party resources and mobilised party activists to reach this goal in 2006, but did not succeed (Cochez 2010). Vanhecke, party president since 1996, seemed willing to join a coalition. Yet Vanhecke also saw the VB as a 'whip party' (Van den Brink 1999: 207–209). The VB apparently was reluctant to pursue an office strategy that required willingness to compromise. A coalition strategy was barred by the *cordon sanitaire*, but neither was the VB much inclined to publicly incite other parties to reconsider their options for coalition partners. Policy influence through the whip function of the party and a majority strategy was unanimously supported as long as the party booked electoral successes, but this was no longer the case when the VB gradually began to lose voters, particularly to its new rival, the N-VA.

The electoral decline was probably a consequence of the *cordon sanitaire* and the subsequent exclusion from office, which made the VB look less relevant to voters, as Pauwels (2011) argues. The idea that the party could influence policy through its whip function was only credible as long as the VB built up electoral pressure. Electoral decline opened up diverging views within the party about its priorities. The radical strategy of Dewinter which remained intact after the electoral losses has clearly alienated part of the VB members and main figureheads. Several well-known figures of the party, including Vanhecke, Jurgen Verstrepen, Koen Dillen and Karim Van Overmeiren, have consequently left the VB. Politicians such as Vanhecke and Van Overmeiren have stated clearly that they can no longer identify with the radical strategy that is maintained by the VB. On his website, Van Overmeiren stated that he wanted to leave the strategy of the whip party and participate in government in order to realise a stricter immigration policy. When it became clear that this would not happen, he became first an independent MP and currently he is an N-VA MP.[6] The recent conflict where the regional party executive of Ghent (second largest Flemish city) opposed the national party executive and was expelled is another illustration of these tensions (Pauwels and Van Haute 2013).[7] Remaining figureheads, however, have also opened up the possibility of sharing office in a coalition. Annemans, elected party president in 2012, expressed his willingness to share office responsibility in a coalition in an interview in 2014.[8] Yet, in the election campaign of 2014 the VB still defined itself as 'stick behind the door' – an image similar to the whip.

In sum, we can conclude that mainstreaming in terms of detoxifying a racist reputation has been important for the VB, but apart from that few strategies of mainstreaming have been undertaken. As long as vote-seeking was successful, the VB prioritised policy purity and indirect influence through the 'whip' function of the party. There were little incentives for further mainstreaming as long as a radical niche profile appeared to be electorally rewarding. Whether its strategy of a 'whip-party' has been effective, is debatable. In a quantitative comparative analysis of immigration and integration policies in nine countries, Akkerman (2012: 519, 528–529) finds that immigration and integration policies became more rather than less liberal in Belgium between 1999 and 2010, regardless of growth or decline of the VB. Only after 2010 did mainstream parties begin to move towards a more restrictive immigration policy, but this was due to the electoral success of the N-VA (Davis 2012). One of the main reasons for this lack of influence is the lack of cooperation with other parties in the parliamentary arena.[9] The VB has not been able to realise many of its policy proposals as an opposition party (De Lange and Akkerman 2012). Between 2009 and 2013, the VB initiated 112 motions in the Flemish Parliament, more than any other party; none of them received any support from any other party, while the VB was never involved in joint motions of other parties (Vlaams Parlement 2014: 14–21).[10] The *cordon sanitaire* made it difficult for the VB to exert influence as an opposition party; parties sometimes interpreted the *cordon* broadly and accordingly dismissed all proposals of the VB (Buelens and Deschouwer 2003).

One might argue that the VB had few incentives to moderate as long as a *cordon sanitaire* restricted its opportunities. However, a *cordon sanitaire* does not necessarily 'freeze' the programmatic course of a party. A freezing effect may occur when social and political isolation affects the internal organisation of the party and furthers the ideological rigidity of its members and thus enhances the influence of *fundi*'s within the party. However, there is no evidence that VB members suffered social stigma (Art 2011: 144). The political isolation due to the *cordon sanitaire* was effective, but right-wing mainstream parties displayed an ambivalent stance towards the VB. According to Mudde, they combined a great deal of anti-VB rhetoric with conciliatory gestures (Mudde 2000: 89). Moreover, as Akkerman and Rooduijn (2014) have demonstrated, ostracised parties can be quite flexible programmatically. They can try to become acceptable coalition partners by mainstreaming their policy programmes. The VB apparently did not choose to pursue this option. The predominant strategy was aimed at vote-seeking by maintaining a radical niche profile. The party often walked a thin line in order to avoid a racist reputation and legal actions while at the same time cultivating its profile as anti-immigration, law and order and anti-establishment party. The increased competition from the N-VA on issues such as Flemish nationalism might even make the VB focus more on its unique selling proposition: a radical view on immigration. In this respect, it is telling that the VB – or at least Dewinter – now seems to draw inspiration from the way Geert Wilders manages to gain media attention and, according to the polls, to book electoral successes. The PVV of Wilders has become politically almost as isolated as the VB (see Chapter 7). Both parties seem to welcome their political isolation as an opportunity to heighten their profile as radical, anti-establishment and niche parties.

External pressure clearly was the main incitement to amend the racist reputation of the party. The VB took care to avoid racist statements or actions under pressure of pending convictions. Yet, hardcore activists in the party were appeased as far as possible. Dewinter, with his base in Antwerp where a hardcore nationalist culture existed, sometimes signalled to hardcore nationalists in and outside the party that mainstreaming was in this respect merely a veneer. The external pressure to moderate apparently did not lead to an internally supported change of strategy.

After 2010, the choice between mainstreaming or remaining a radical niche party became a serious source of conflict inside the party. The classical dilemma of radical right populist parties between a group of *realo*'s that wanted a more moderate course and a group of *fundi*'s that held on to a radical course became apparent (De Lange and Akkerman 2012). Particularly in the last few years important members of the VB have defected (mostly to the N-VA). While the reasons to do so vary, the radical strategy (and consequently permanent exclusion) that is particularly symbolised by Dewinter is often mentioned as the main reason why some can no longer identify with the VB. At any rate, the exodus of experienced and moderate politicians does not augur well for the future of the party.

Conclusion and prospect

The VB has mainstreamed in a highly important way by its endeavour to detoxify its reputation as a racist and extremist party. The party did not always succeed in doing so convincingly. The VB gave the impression that it only avoided racism in anticipation of juridical actions, and sometimes party leaders demonstrated an ambivalent stance about the new course. The party moderated its xenophobic rhetoric, but maintained and cultivated a radical profile as an anti-immigration and law and order party. Together with the issue of Flemish independence, these core issues gained importance over time. There were only incidental efforts to broaden the agenda to social-economic issues, but the VB did not substantially amend its niche character. The party also cultivated a populist ideology and style in order to draw media attention and as a vote-seeking strategy. Periodically, between 2000 and 2007, the anti-establishment style was softened to demonstrate that the VB was willing and able to bear office responsibility. After electoral decline became apparent in 2009 and 2010, moderates left the party and the VB tended to radicalise on core issues and to revert to an anti-establishment style. Dewinter possibly hopes that by imitating the radical strategy of the Dutch PVV, voters may be regained. Yet, the VB is still far away from the strong position of the PVV in recent elections and polls. As the VB has more hurdles to overcome than the PVV, such as serious competition on nationalist issues and a *cordon sanitaire*, it is unlikely that it will soon be able to equal the PVV in this respect.

Vote-seeking in order to realise a majority had been a predominant goal over time, partly because the options were restricted due to a *cordon sanitaire*. As long as the VB was electorally successful, the *cordon* could be embraced as an electoral opportunity, and the goal of policy influence could be maintained by exploiting the whip function of the party. In reality, however, the whip function of the party was not very effective. When electoral decline set in, these goals lost credibility. Internal tensions about the strategy came into the open, and moderates left the party. With the exit of moderates, the party has radicalised again in some respects. Although the VB reverted to a fierce anti-establishment and anti-immigration course, sometimes risking renewed legal actions based on anti-racism legislation, the party also appears to be less confident about its solitary strategy. There are some signs that the party is more open to enter into coalition government. As the electoral decline continues, the VB tends to lose even its (modest) blackmail potential and its whip function might not frighten anyone any more. Its prospects seem far from bright. It might hope to win back some voters from the N-VA now that the latter takes part in a (federal) government and inevitably will dilute its demands for Flemish independence. Yet the N-VA is not the VU: it is probably less heterogeneous and – more importantly – a lot bigger. History will not repeat itself in exactly the same way.[11] No matter how close Madou Square is to Law Street, the distance may be unbridgeable in the end.

Notes

1 In a survey held in Antwerp in 1988 about 80 per cent of the VB-voters referred to this issue ('immigrants', 'guest workers', etc.) when asked to explain their vote, whereas only 12 per cent mentioned Flemish independence or Flemish nationalism (Van Eycken and Schoeters 1988: 30–32; see also Swyngedouw 2001).

2 'Als nationalistische partij komt het Vlaams Blok op voor onafhankelijkheid van Vlaanderen' (Vlaams Blok n.d.: 1); 'een onafhankelijk Vlaanderen is en blijft dan ook het eerste programmapunt van het Vlaams Blok' (Vlaams Blok 2003: 2); 'de partij strijdt voor een onafhankelijk Vlaanderen' (Vlaams Belang n.d.: 1) 'wij willen dat Vlaanderen resoluut kiest voor zijn onafhankelijkheid' (Vlaams Belang 2014).

3 In 1995 the total number of seats of the House was reduced from 212 to 150.

4 In 2002 the VB advocated a 'corrected free market economy', 'depoliticised unions', more transparent social security and a reduction of taxes and labour costs for employers (Vlaams Blok 2003: 34, 41–45). In its 2004 declaration of principles Vlaams Belang refers to solidarity within the ethnic community in rather vague terms, but not to solidarism (Vlaams Belang n.d.: 3). It called for an open but (again) 'corrected market economy', reduction of taxes and state subsidies but also protection of Flemish industry and agriculture (Vlaams Belang 2004a: 38–42). Protection of key sectors of the economy and of public utilities are recurrent issues (Vlaams Belang 2012: 18–19).

5 President Annemans, for instance, claimed that the VB was more leftist than the N-VA, as the VB opposed the reduction of unemployment benefits (Knack.be 29-01-2014).

6 www.karimvanovermeire.be/.

7 In 2011, a regional executive was appointed with the support of the party leadership, but the local office holders disagreed and even established the dissident 'Belfort
group'. The leader of this group argued that the appointment of the regional
executive was a problem, but that there is also a deeper underlying reason of dissatisfaction: 'We are dissatisfied because the party leadership clings to its style and
methods of 20, 25 years ago. We think that the party's message should be translated into
the 21st century with less provocation. But the style of Filip Dewinter still dominates,
you might say the style of the Antwerp municipal council.' (Knack be 11-07-2011).
8 When interviewed on Flemish television during the 2014 election campaign,
Annemans repeatedly said the VB could still influence the political agenda as
opposition party, yet he and Barbara Pas, who had succeeded him as leader of the
parliamentary party, also expressed willingness to share responsibility in a coalition
government, at least in Flanders (*Canvas* 14-05-2014).
9 With respect to Flemish independence, however, the whip function of the VB may
have had some success (see Erk 2005).
10 It does show that the VB was very active in parliament; since 1995 it has also
interpellated ministers more often than any other party (Vlaams Parlement 2014: 8–10).
11 An opinion poll in October 2014 indicated a very slight and hardly significant
increase in support for the VB: from 5.9 to 6.5 per cent of the vote in Flanders
(www.deredactie.be/cm/vrtnieuws/politiek/23604, accessed 02-03-2015).

References

Abts, K., Swyngedouw, M., and Billiet, J. (2010) 'De structurele en culturele kenmer-
ken van het stemgedrag in Vlaanderen: Analyse obv postelectorale verkiezingsonderzoek',
Instituut voor Sociaal en Politiek Opinieonderzoek (ISPO), https://soc.kuleuven.be/
web/files/6/34/Structurele_en_culturele_determinanten_van_stemgedrag_in_Vlaand
eren2010.pdf (accessed 08-06-2015).
Akkerman, T. (2012) 'Comparing radical right parties in government: Immigration and
integration policies in nine countries (1996–2010)', *West European Politics* 35, 3: 511–529.
Akkerman, T. (2015) 'Gender and the radical right in Western Europe: A comparative
analysis of policy agendas', *Patterns of Prejudice* 49: 1–24.
Akkerman, T. and Rooduijn, M. (2014) 'Pariahs or partners? Inclusion and exclusion of
radical right parties and the effects on their policy positions', *Political Studies* 62: 1–18.
Art, D. (2008) 'The organizational origins of the contemporary radical right: The case of
Belgium', *Comparative Politics* 40, 4: 421–440.
Art, D. (2011) *Inside the Radical Right. The Development of Anti-Immigrant Parties in
Western Europe*, Cambridge: Cambridge University Press.
Boeckz, P. (2004) 'Vlaamse choc', www.dailymotion.com/video/xk32p_vlaamse-choc
_news (accessed 08-06-2015).
Bosseman, V. (2000) 'De Communicatiestrategie van het Vlaams Blok: Evolutie van
positionering, Doelgroep en Boodschap', Master thesis, University of Gent, www.
ethesis.net/vlaams_blok_communicatie/vb_communicatie.pdf (accessed 08-06-2015).
Breuning, M. and Ishiyama, J. T. (1998) 'The rhetoric of nationalism: Rhetorical strategies
of the Volksunie and Vlaams Blok in Belgium, 1991–1995', *Political Communication*
15, 5: 5–26.
Buelens, J. and Deschouwer, K. (2003) *De Verboden Vleespotten. De Partijorganisatie van
het Vlaams Blok tussen Oppositie en Machtsdeelname*, Brussels: Vrije Universiteit, http://
aivpc41.vub.ac.be/standpunten/uploads/Rapport%20Organisatie%20Vlaams%20Blok.pdf
(accessed 27-02-2014).

Canvas (14-05-2014) 'Interview with Annemans in "Terzake"'.

Cochez, T. (2010) *Eigen Belang Eerst*, Leuven: Van Halewyck.

Coffé, H. (2005) 'The adaption of the extreme right's discourse: The case of the Vlaams Blok', *Ethical Perspectives* 12, 2: 205–230.

Damen, S. (2001) 'Strategieën tegen extreem-rechts. Het cordon sanitaire onder de loep', *Tijdschrift voor Sociologie* 22, 1: 89–110.

Davis, A. J. (2012) 'The impact of anti-immigration parties on mainstream parties' immigration positions in the Netherlands, Flanders and the UK 1987–2010: Divided electorates, left-right politics and the pull towards restrictionism', Doctoral Thesis, European University Institute.

De Lange, S. L. and Akkerman, T. (2012) 'Populist parties in Belgium: A case of hegemonic liberal democracy?', in Mudde, C., and Kaltwasser, C. R. (eds) *Populism in Europe and the Americas: Threat or Corrective for Democracy?* Cambridge: Cambridge University Press, pp. 27–46.

De Lange, S. L. and Mügge, L. M. (2015) 'Gender and right-wing populism in the low countries: Ideological variations across parties and time', *Patterns of Prejudice* 49, 1–2: 61–80.

De Winter, L. (2004) 'The Vlaams Blok and the heritage of extreme-right Flemish-nationalism', Paper prepared for presentation at the seminar 'The extreme right in Europe, a many faceted reality', coordinated by Dr Xavier Casals, 5–6 July at the Sabadell Universitat.

Elsevier (20-03-2014), 'Filip Dewinter: Ook minder Marokkanen in Antwerpen', www.elsevier.nl/Buitenland/nieuws/2014/3/Filip-Dewinter-ook-minder-Marokkanen-in-Antwerpen-1486725W/ (accessed 08-06-2015).

Erk, J. (2005) 'From Vlaams Blok to Vlaams Belang: The Belgian far right renames itself', *West European Politics* 28, 3: 493–502.

Gijsels, H. and van der Velpen, J. (1989) *Het Vlaams Blok: Het Verdriet van Vlaanderen*, Berchem: EPO.

Het Belang van Limburg (2013) 'Vlaams Belang doorbreekt cordon sanitair in Dender-leeuw', www.hbvl.be/nieuws/binnenland/aid1310195/vlaams-belang-doorbreekt-cordon-sanitair-in-denderleeuw.aspx (accessed 25-02-2014).

Het Laatste Nieuws (2011) 'Frank Vanhecke stapt uit Vlaams Belang', www.hln.be/hln/nl/957/Binnenland/article/detail/1290803/2011/07/11/Frank-Vanhecke-stapt-uit-Vlaams-Belang.dhtml (accessed 07-05-2015).

Knack.be (11-07-2011) 'Gentse Belfortploeg breidt uit naar andere provincies', www.knack.be/nieuws/belgie/gentse-belfortploeg-breidt-uit-naar-andere-provincies/article-normal-23984.html (accessed 23-10-2015).

Knack.be (10-04-2012) 'Vlaams Belang lanceert meldpunt voor illegaliteit', www.knack.be/nieuws/belgie/vlaams-belang-lanceert-meldpunt-voor-illegaliteit/article-normal-53618.html (accessed 07-05-2015).

Knack.be (06-07-2012) 'Filip Dewinter hoopt dat klacht wegens racisme extra kiezers oplevert', www.knack.be/nieuws/belgie/filip-dewinter-hoopt-dat-klacht-wegens-racisme-extra-kiezers-oplevert/article-normal-60481.html (accessed 11-05-2015).

Knack.be (29-01-2014), 'Le nouveau Vlaams Belang van Gerolf Annemans: warme erwten-soep met varkensspek', www.knack.be/nieuws/belgie/le-nouveau-vlaams-belang-van-gerolf-annemans-warme-erwtensoep-met-varkensspek/article-normal-126265.html (accessed 23-10-2015).

Lange, P. (1977) 'La teoria degli incentivi e l'analisi dei partiti politici', *Rassegna Italiana di Sociologia* 18, 4: 501–526.

Matheve, N. (2014) 'Nihil novi sub sole? De historische wortels van het naoorlogse Vlaams-nationalisme en hun invloed op de hedendaagse politiek', *Res Publica* 56, 1: 95–110.

Minkenberg, M. (2013) 'From pariah to policy-maker? The radical right in Europe, West and East: Between margin and mainstream', *Journal of Contemporary European Studies* 21, 1: 5–24.

Mudde, C. (1995) 'One against all, all against one! A portrait of the Vlaams Blok', *Patterns of Prejudice* 29, 1: 5–28.

Mudde, C. (2000) *The Ideology of the Extreme Right*, Manchester: Manchester University Press.

Pauwels, T. (2011) 'Explaining the strange decline of the populist radical right Vlaams Belang in Belgium: The impact of permanent opposition', *Acta Politica* 46, 1: 60–82.

Pauwels, T. (2013) 'Belgium: Decline of national populism?', in Grabow, K. and Hartleb, F. (eds) *Exposing the Demagogues: Right-wing and National Populist Parties in Europe*, Brussels and Berlin: Centre for European Studies and Konrad Adenauer Stiftung, pp. 81–104.

Pauwels, T. and Rooduijn, M. (forthcoming) 'Populism in Belgium in times of crisis: Intensification of discourse, decline in electoral support', in Kriesi, H. and Pappas, T. (eds) *Populism in the Shadow of the Great Recession*, London: ECPR Press.

Pauwels, T. and Van Haute, E. (2013) 'The party organization of the Vlaams Belang', paper prepared for the 2013 CES Conference, Amsterdam, 25–27 June, http://difu sion.ulb.ac.be/vufind/Record/ULB-DIPOT:oai:dipot.ulb.ac.be:2013/144843/Holdings (accessed 23-10-2015).

Spruyt, M. (1995) *Grove Borstels: Stel dat het Vlaams Blok Morgen zijn Programma Realiseert, Hoe Zou Vlaanderen er dan Uitzien?* Leuven: Van Halewyck.

Spruyt, M. (2000) *Wat het Vlaams Blok Verzwijgt*, Leuven: Van Halewyck.

Strøm, K. (1990) 'A behavioral theory of competitive political parties', *American Journal of Political Science* 34: 535–598.

Swyngedouw, M. (1998) 'The extreme right in Belgium: Of a non-existent Front National and an omnipresent Vlaams Blok', in Betz, H.-G. and Immerfall, S. (eds) *The New Politics of the Right: Neo-Populist Parties and Movements in Established Democracies*, New York: St. Martin's Press, pp. 59–75.

Swyngedouw, M. (2001) 'The subjective cognitive and affective map of extreme right voters: Using open-ended questions in exit polls', *Electoral Studies* 20, 2: 217–241.

Swyngedouw, M. and Van Craen, M. (2001) 'Vlaams Blok en de natiestaat: Het rechts-radicale Vlaams-nationalisme onder de loep', *Fédéralisme Régionalisme* 2, n.p.

Telegraaf (11-02-2015) 'Spel Filip Dewinter offline gehaald', www.telegraaf.nl/digitaal/games/ 23669372/__Spel_Filip_Dewinter_offline_gehaald__.html (accessed 08-06-2015).

Trouw (08-12-2009) 'Heeft het Vlaams Belang nog toekomst?'.

Van Craen, M. and Swyngedouw, M. (2002) 'Het Vlaams Blok doorgelicht.20 jaar extreem-rechts in Vlaanderen', Leuven: ISPO KUL.

Vandecasteele, N. (2013) 'Kwalitatief Empirisch Onderzoek naar de Positie van Vlaams Belang en N-VA tov de Europese Integratie', Masterthesis, Ghent University, http:// buck.ugent.be/fulltxt/RUG01/002/064/225/RUG01-002064225_2013_0001_AC. pdf (accessed 08-06-2015).

Vanhecke, F. (2011) 'Voorzitter FDW? Enkele beschouwingen', www.frankvanheck evb.skynetblogs.be (accessed 11-05-2014).

Van den Brink, R. (1994) *De Internationale van de Haat. Extreem-Rechts in West-Europa*, Amsterdam: Sua.

Van den Brink, R. (1999) *De Jonge Turken van het Vlaams Blok: Extreem-rechts tussen Uniform en Maatpak*, Ghent and Amsterdam: Scoop and Jan Mets.

Van der Brug, W. and Fennema, M. (2004) 'Est-ce que le cordon sanitaire est salutaire?', in Van Broeck, B. and Foblets, M.-C. (eds) *La Faillité de l'Intégration: Le Débat Multicultural en Flandre*, Louvain-la-Neuve: Bruylant-Academia, pp. 199–203.

Van Eycken, F. and Schoeters, S. (1988) *Het Vlaams Blok Marcheert*, Deurne: Imprint.

Van Haute, E. (2005) 'La Volksunie (VU): Triomphe des idées, defaite du parti', in Delwit, P. (ed.) *Les Partis Régionalistes en Europe: Des Acteurs en Développement?*, Brussels: Éditions de l'université de Bruxelles, pp. 243–264.

Van Spanje, J. and Van der Brug, W. (2007) 'The party as pariah: The exclusion of anti–immigration parties and its effect on their ideological positions', *West European Politics* 30, 5: 1022–1040.

Van Spanje, J. and Van der Brug, W. (2009) 'Being intolerant of the intolerant: The exclusion of Western European anti–immigration parties and its consequences for party choice', *Acta Politica* 44, 4: 353–384.

Vlaams Belang (n.d.) 'Beginselverklaring Vlaams Belang', www.vlaamsbelang.org/pdf/beginselverklaring.pdf (accessed 04-02-2014).

Vlaams Belang (2004a) 'Programmaboek 2004', www.vlaamsbelang.org/files/200412 12_programma.pdf (accessed 28-01-2005).

Vlaams Belang (2004b) 'Statuten', Brussels: Vlaams Belang.

Vlaams Belang (2012) 'Sociaaleconomisch Programma: "Een Beter Vlaanderen voor een Lagere Prijs!"', Brussels: Vlaams Belang Studiedienst.

Vlaams Belang (2013) *Sociale Volkspartij*, Brussels: Vlaams Belang Studiecentrum.

Vlaams Belang (2014) 'Uw stok achter de deur', http://vlaamsbelang.org/pdf/20140 128/uwstokachterdedeur.pdf (accessed 04-02-2014).

Vlaams Blok (n.d.) 'Ten geleide: Waarom het Vlaams Blok?', http://users.telenet.be/supportfiles/grondbeginselen.htm (accessed 23-10-2009).

Vlaams Blok (1992) 'Immigratie: de oplossingen. 70 voorstellen ter oplossing van het vreem-delingenprobleem', http://web.archive.org/web/20070927172805/http://www.blokwa tch.be/content/view/62/39/lang,nl/.

Vlaams Blok (1996) 'Immigratie: de tijdbom tikt. Het 70 punten plan', http://web.archive.org/web/20070927172949/http://www.blokwatch.be/content/view/86/50/lang,nl/.

Vlaams Blok (2003) 'Een Toekomst voor Vlaanderen. Programma en Sstandpunten van het Vlaams Blok', Brussel: Vlaams Blok.

Vlaams Parlement (2014) 'Statistisch overzicht van de parlementaire activiteiten (April) Interpellaties en moties', www.vlaamsparlement.be/vp/informatie/overhetvlaa mspa rlement/jaarverslagen/interpellaties_en_moties_201404.pdf (accessed 27-05-2014).

Volkskrant (04-02-1992) 'Vergeleken met het Vlaams Blok is Janmaat liberaal'.

11 A new course for the French radical right?

The Front National and 'de-demonisation'

Gilles Ivaldi

Introduction

The French National Front (Front National, FN) is commonly considered a model for the West European radical right (Kitschelt 1995: 19; Mudde 2007: 41). The party was formed in 1972 as an attempt to bring together various extreme right groups, which originated from neo-fascist and pro-French Algerian sub-cultures. The FN remained irrelevant throughout the 1970s and early 1980s, however, experiencing its first electoral breakthrough in the 1984 European elections with 11 per cent of the vote.

Since the mid-1980s, the FN has established itself as a major actor in the party system. Its electoral development has been symptomatic of the political mobilisation strategy of the pan-European radical right. The FN has pioneered a new potent 'master frame', which combines ethno-nationalist xenophobia with anti-political-establishment populism (Rydgren 2005). Its politicisation of cultural issues of immigration and law-and-order has created a niche in the electoral arena, giving the FN levels of electoral support between 10 per cent and 18 per cent in French legislative and presidential elections. During the 1990s, the FN reinforced its status as principal anti-globalisation and Eurosceptic force in French politics (Zaslove 2008). Following the outbreak of the global financial crisis, the party has emerged as a strong opponent of the EU, endorsing economic nationalism (Ivaldi 2015).

Because of its historical legacy of far right extremism, the FN represents the archetypal 'political pariah' isolated by a *cordon sanitaire*. The party has never achieved coalition potential at the national level and only on rare occasions has it shared power in local or regional governments. This has been the result of its political ostracisation by parties of the mainstream, but mostly it has been contingent on the structure of political opportunities produced by the institutional framework of the Fifth Republic and the FN's inability to gain parliamentary representation under France's majoritarian system. With the exception of the 1986 legislative elections,[1] the FN has been either excluded from national parliament or it has had only a marginal presence.

In 2011, Marine Le Pen replaced Jean-Marie Le Pen, her father, as party leader, setting a new trajectory for the FN away from its extreme right status. Changes in party strategy have been embedded in the so-called rhetoric of de-demonisation (*dédiabolisation*), of which the main goal is to detoxify the party's reputation. The recent electoral revitalisation of the FN suggests that de-demonisation may have allowed the French radical right to broaden its support base. The party set new historical records in the 2012 presidential and 2014 European elections with 17.9 and 25 per cent of the vote, respectively. This success was reiterated in the 2015 departmental elections where the FN received 25.2 per cent of the national vote.

However successful electorally, de-demonisation is still a contentious issue. Looking at party change, Harmel *et al.* (1995) argue that it is somewhat easier for political actors to alter the packaging rather than the core of their ideological positions. Most accounts of FN modernisation focus on changes in the party's narratives and communication style. Whilst Marine Le Pen has undeniably succeeded in presenting a more amenable face and a softer 'packaging' for her party in the media, there is little evidence of more substantial changes to the FN's ideology, culture and party system status (Crépon *et al.* 2015; Shields 2013).

This chapter examines the development of the FN in the French party system since the early 2000s and asks whether the party is moving into the mainstream. It looks first at the extent to which the party has changed as a radical, niche, and anti-establishment party, and examines the extent to which it has shed its extremist reputation. It then turns to party goals and strategies of de-demonisation, considering also internal and contextual stimuli for the current transformation of the FN, and its consequences. This chapter concludes that the FN has not yet shed its radical right-wing populist profile despite the moderation of its rhetoric and policies. De-demonisation is primarily a short-term vote-maximising strategy, which seeks to address important institutional and party system challenges. It aims to change the FN's reputation as an extreme right party to improve its credibility, while simultaneously preserving its radical right-wing populist potential for voter mobilisation. Current de-demonisation replicates also previous strategic readjustments conducted by pragmatic modernist factions in the FN during the 1990s.

Continuity and change in non-mainstream features

In recent years, the FN has striven to address issues of credibility, cooperation and identity. Whether the current transformation of the FN reflects a process of mainstreaming is debatable however. Most efforts concern the strategic policy packaging of the party and severing its ties to the neo-fascist milieu in France. Changes are less perceptible across core constitutive features of radical right-wing populism, such as the radicalness, nicheness and anti-establishment character of the party.

Persistence of core radical policies

The French FN exemplifies the radical right agenda, which according to Mudde (2007) combines nativism, authoritarianism and populism. The analysis of the FN in the comparative chapters of this volume confirms that the party has been consistently located at the right end of the cultural dimension of competition since the late 1990s. Eurosceptic positions are also characteristic of the FN and populism increased significantly in its 2012 manifesto (see definitions and data in Chapter 1 and Chapter 2).

Because of the historical connection of the FN with neo-fascism, however, radicalism should not only be taken here in terms of spatial location – i.e. is the party more radical in stances than its mainstream competitors? In the case of the FN, radicalism refers also to a set of illiberal policies, which pose a viable challenge to fundamental democratic values and practices. One crucial issue, therefore, is to evaluate the extent to which the FN has distanced itself from those radical policies.

In addition to the comparative analysis of party positions, this section examines the content of FN presidential manifestos from 2002 to 2012. Party programmes are analysed exhaustively in order to extract all policy pledges that form part of the FN's radical agenda. Pledges are valid and substantive indicators of the policy positions taken by parties.[2] They reflect 'the specific policy commitments that parties make in their election manifestos' (Akkerman 2015: 59). The dataset concerns all policies which can be assigned to one of the following categories: nativism, authoritarianism or populism.

Although nativist, authoritarian and populist policies are radical 'in essence', they may vary according to their formulation and the degree to which they challenge constitutional rules or universalist values. Pledges are therefore coded on a 3-point scale to differentiate between extreme (+1), moderate (+0.5) and status quo (0) positions. To improve coding consistency, a unique ID is attributed to each individual policy pledge, which allows also the tracing of changes in specific issue positions over time. Let us note here that no liberal, cosmopolitan or progressive policies were found that would require us to consider opposite scores such as those used by Akkerman (2015). Pledges to maintain the existing status quo were also almost non-existent.

Figure 11.1 below has the salience and structure of the FN's radical agenda in presidential elections between 2002 and 2012. The overall size of the FN's radical platform shows a significant decrease in salience in 2007, when the total number of radical policy pledges was halved from 106 in 2002 down to 58, followed by an augmentation up to a total of 80 proposals in 2012. The 2002 manifesto stands out also as significantly more radical with regards to the way in which nativist, authoritarian and populist policies are formulated. Policies formulated in an extreme form – i.e. policies posing the most serious hurdle to universalist values and human right standards – are over-represented in the 2002 manifesto (62 as opposed to 21 and 32 in 2007 and 2012, respectively). The data indicate that the FN has de-radicalised in 2007, only to radicalise again in 2012 after Marine Le Pen took over the party.

The use of unique policy pledge IDs over time allows the tracking of changes in the policy profile of the FN. We distinguish between three main groups of policies. The first group concerns the stable radical right core of the FN, i.e. policies that can be found across the whole 2002–2012 period. The second group

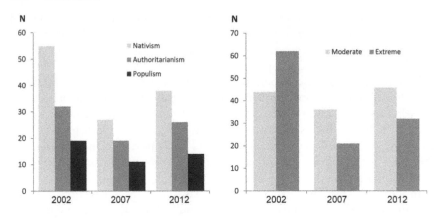

Figure 11.1 Salience and degree of extremeness of the FN's radical agenda★ 2002–2012
Note: ★ Number of radical policy pledges in presidential manifestos.

refers to new radical policies which emerged in 2012 and that can be deemed representative of Marine Le Pen's modernisation agenda. Finally, the third group concerns the FN's old radical right policies, which were abandoned after 2002. We briefly examine each of these groups in turn.

The stable radical right core of the FN consists of a total of 59 policies that can be found across the whole 2002–2012 period. More than half (54.2 per cent) of those are nativist policies, while authoritarian and populist policies account for another quarter (25.4 per cent) and a fifth (20.3 per cent), respectively. Of the 59 policies in the radical core, 38 are present in all three manifestos, while another 21 are only common to the 2002 and 2012 programmes, reflecting the short-lived period of FN de-radicalisation which occurred in 2007, whereby the FN abandoned some of its previous radical policies.

This stable radical right core includes some of the FN's historical policies such as the repatriation of all illegal immigrants and foreign offenders, the end of legal immigration, a drastic reduction in asylum, enforcing 'national preference', opposition to the building of mosques, reintroducing the death penalty and a more severe punishment for offenders and criminals including minors aged 13+, the suppression of family reunion rights for migrants, more powers to the police, the fight against anti-French racism (*racisme anti-Français*), an exit from Schengen and ultimately from the EU, a call for discipline and authority in schools, the fight against trade union monopolies and against the politicisation of civil servants, or the greater use of the referendum and proportional representation. All policies in this first group exhibit stability and show also little variation with regard to their formulation: cases where the FN has adopted a more moderate policy formulation in 2012 compared with ten years earlier represent about a fifth (22 per cent) of all 59 policies in this first group. The most notable change is the party's official position now acknowledging abortion rights and civil union contracts. In 2002, Jean-Marie Le Pen strongly opposed abortion rights, stigmatising abortion as the 'symbol of the culture of death into which

European leaders have settled' (Front National 2002: 11). The FN 2002 presidential manifesto called for the abrogation of both abortion laws and the civil union contract (*pacte civil de solidarité*, PACS) enacted by the socialist government in 1999.

The second group refers to new radical right policies, which have emerged in the 2012 party manifesto. These can be regarded as representative of Marine Le Pen's personal input. This second group has a total of 21 policy pledges of which more than half (57.1 per cent) have a focus on law and order issues – in particular repression against violent behaviour in schools, more rights for victims in courts, citizen supervision of criminal trials or the suppression of social welfare for repeat offenders. Another third (33.3 per cent) concern nativist policies, mostly articulated around the new secular agenda and the fight against communitarism (*communautarisme*),[3] as well as anti-immigration measures such as a legal ban on undocumented migrant regularisation. The introduction by Marine Le Pen of this new set of policies reflects the need for her party to re-establish ownership over its traditional cultural issues. As will be discussed, this can be deemed a response to the policy positions taken by the centre-right UMP and the increasing appropriation by the latter of the FN's immigration and law-and-order agenda since the early 2000s (Marthaler 2008).

Finally, the third group contains the FN's old radical right policies abandoned after 2002. The reasons behind the decision by the party to scrap those policies are unclear. It is reasonable to assume that some of those policies were deemed too radical, possibly undermining the efforts by the FN to present its anti-immigration platform in a more 'acceptable' form. In about half (48.9 per cent) of the cases, these concern nativist policies, in particular proposals such as national preference in company layoffs, the dismantling of emergency homes for migrants, sanitary controls at France's borders to fight AIDS, a safety deposit for tourists, the control of naturalisation of migrants by municipal councils, extended powers to the police to check migrants or a compulsory medical examination for visa applicants. For another third (34 per cent), these old policies refer to law-and-order issues such as police checks in schools, forced labour camps for offenders and criminals, or restoring high-security quarters in prisons.

These results suggest that the FN has somewhat de-radicalised over the past ten years, albeit not in a linear fashion. The party has shed a number of its former extreme nativist and authoritarian policies while simultaneously moderating its social conservative views on issues such as abortion and civil union. De-radicalisation occurred primarily in 2007, but the party returned to a more radical agenda in 2012. The data reveal nevertheless the persistence over time of a substantial and stable nativist, authoritarian and populist ideology characteristic of radical right-wing populism. Moreover, the new cultural policies adopted by the FN in 2012 show no significant departure from the more established radical right-wing populist core.

Still a niche party

A second dimension of mainstreaming concerns the niche profile of the FN. It can be measured by the salience attached by the party to socioeconomic and sociocultural policy domains, relative to the other parties in the system. Compared with their more established competitors, niche parties pay less attention to socioeconomic issues and compete primarily on issues that belong to the sociocultural dimension, such as immigration or crime. A greater emphasis by the FN on socioeconomic issues can be therefore considered an indicator of mainstreaming.

The French data presented in the cross-national analysis in this volume reveal that the FN has indeed broadened its programme over time to include a larger set of socioeconomic issues. The latter made up 37 per cent of its 2012 manifesto as opposed to 15 per cent in the mid-1990s, exceeding in size the party's traditional sociocultural agenda. The FN data suggest also a decrease in sociocultural salience from 44 per cent in 1997 down to 28 per cent in 2002. A significant drop occurred in the early 2000s and sociocultural salience has remained more or less constant ever since. This recalibration of the FN's policy agenda, albeit partial, suggests mainstreaming of the French radical right since the late 1990s. It corroborates the programmatic and strategic priorities set by Marine Le Pen in the 2012 elections:

> I am standing on my own two legs, she said. On the one hand, unemployment, public debt and purchasing power. On the other hand, immigration and insecurity.
>
> (Marine Le Pen, Interview, TF1, 6 March 2012)[4]

The FN continues, however, to differentiate its policy agenda from other competitors on the sociocultural dimension. The gap between the FN and the mainstream has remained constant since the early 2000s. Despite significant changes in salience profile, the FN maintains a distinctive niche status on sociocultural issues compared with the other French parties.[5] The above analysis of policy pledges confirms that the FN has not yet shifted entirely from niche to mainstream status. In 2012, radical policies made up more than half (53 per cent) of all pledges in Marine Le Pen's presidential manifesto, as opposed to 34 and 17 per cent in 2002 and 2007 respectively. Whilst there has been a substantial decrease in the overall size of FN electoral platforms between 2002 and 2012, the relative salience of radical policies has indeed augmented.[6]

Continuation of anti-establishment populism

For over four decades, the French FN has relied on anti-political-establishment mobilisation. The FN discourse has traditionally exhibited strong characteristics of populism, vilipending 'decadent' and 'corrupt' elites, opposing the 'gang of four' – in reference to France's major parties during the 1980s and the 1990s – while simultaneously claiming to speak for the people.

Anti-establishment rhetoric was temporarily toned down in 2007, with Jean-Marie Le Pen claiming to be 'centre-right' and explicitly calling for cooperation with the UMP. Since Marine Le Pen's accession, however, the FN has returned to anti-establishment strategies. The FN continues to claim that it represents a third competitive bloc and a political alternative to France's bipolar polity, while simultaneously ruling out cooperation with other actors in the system. It persists also in its violent attacks against mainstream parties and the so-called 'UMPS caste' – the conflation of the acronyms of the two main parties of the right and the left in France, the UMP and the PS.

As revealed in the FN data in the comparative chapter, populism was central to Marine Le Pen's presidential bid in 2012, which campaigned for the votes of the 'invisible majority', making a vibrant call to all the 'forgotten ones' in French politics:

> Farmers, workers, job seekers, young people, craftsmen, shopkeepers, employees, civil servants, pensioners, people in rural areas, you are the forgotten ones, you are the invisible majority ... crushed by the madness of the financial system which has become the sole horizon for the ruling political caste. For them and their God, the triple A, you are triple nothings.
>
> (Marine Le Pen, Speech in Metz, 10 December 2011)[7]

The FN continued also to exert its power of nuisance in the 2012 legislative and 2015 local elections where it ran in all possible second round runoffs. In the 2012 presidential runoff, Marine Le Pen refused to endorse either contender, calling herself the 'anti-system candidate'.[8] As she explained:

> The FN is against the system, the whole system is against us ... . The elite doesn't want us. The oligarchy doesn't want us ... . De-demonization is not meant for the elite, it's meant for the people.
>
> (Marine Le Pen, interview, *Le Monde*, 12 April 2012)[9]

The FN undermines the existing political status quo – as revealed for instance in its opposition to EU membership. The anti-liberal culture of the FN is exemplified by its critique of international laws, intermediary bodies, constitutional courts, checks and balances, parliamentarianism and trade unions. Aggressive anti-establishment populism was corroborated by the FN manifesto in the 2014 EP elections. The party reiterated its attacks against the 'UMPS', depicting them as 'serial liars' in its election material.[10] It continued Marine Le Pen's virulent campaign against the so-called 'globalist' (*mondialiste*) ideology. In her book *Pour que vive la France*, Marine Le Pen wrote:

> The ruling political caste ... shares a similar globalist ideology which is born from ultraliberal capitalism, and which serves the interests of an oligarchy.
>
> (Le Pen 2012: 12)

The perpetuation of anti-establishment politics has been counterbalanced with a relative opening up of the party locally. At sub-national level, the FN seeks to reduce its political isolation (*désenclavement*). The party adopted a more conciliatory tone in the 2012 legislatives, calling for local pacts with the mainstream right. This vertical approach to inter-party cooperation, which differentiates between the local and national arenas of competition, resembles the 'two-tier' strategy, which had been briefly endorsed by the FN in the late 1990s (Ivaldi 2007). In 2012, this position was formalised by the founding of the Marine Blue Rally (*Rassemblement Bleu Marine*, RBM) electoral umbrella. It was reiterated in the 2014 municipal and 2015 departmental elections, whereby co-operation was conditioned upon agreement with key FN local immigration and tax-cut policies. Actual alliances between the FN and the centre-right occurred in a very small number of cases, however.

Shedding the extremist reputation

One last dimension of mainstreaming relates to FN's reputation as an extreme right party. Current national leaders of the FN are incontestably seeking to get away from the historical legacy of the French extreme right, avoiding in particular explicit references to anti-Semitism or Holocaust denial, which have been the principal causes for demonisation in the past. Before becoming party leader, Marine Le Pen had already distanced herself from extreme right themes. In October 2004, for instance, she had publicly 'unambiguously and sincerely disapproved' of Bruno Gollnisch after he had called into question the number of Jews killed during the war.[11] In February 2012, as party leader, she condemned solemnly 'Nazism as an abomination and the height of barbarism'.[12] In June 2014, following new anti-Semitic comments by her father, she said she was 'given the opportunity to remind people that the Front National condemns firmly any form of anti-Semitism'.[13] The change in party line was further evidenced by the internal crisis caused by Jean-Marie Le Pen, after he reiterated his controversial comments about Nazi gas chambers being a 'detail of the second world war',[14] ultimately leading to his disciplinary suspension in May 2015, and his expulsion from the FN in August 2015.

Additionally, there seem to be efforts to break ties to the nationalist milieu and extreme right groups. During the 2011 leadership race, Marine Le Pen had publicly indicated that she would distance the FN from neo-fascist groups.[15] She said in December 2010:

I don't want radical groups, which are a political caricature and an anachronism, to return to the FN. Between traditionalist Catholics, pétainists and those obsessed with the Holocaust, it doesn't seem coherent to me. The FN will not serve as an echo chamber for their obsessions.

(Marine Le Pen, Interview, Canal +, 4 December 2010)[16]

The 2011 leadership election altered profoundly the internal balance of power. Marine Le Pen took clear advantage of her position of strength in the polls and won 67.7 per cent of the members' vote in the party congress in Tours. This revealed the decline of the orthodox factions led by her rival, Bruno Gollnisch, while new *mariniste* elites rose to all top-level positions, taking about 70 per cent of the seats in the political bureau. The readjustment of the internal balance of power was confirmed by the central committee election at the 2011 congress, which gave the *mariniste* camp 57 per cent of the seats, resulting in Gollnisch's supporters stepping down from all official posts.

Recent political controversies surrounding racist or homophobic statements by FN representatives indicate, however, continuation of the cultural traits of the extreme right within the party's rank-and-file. The 2015 departmental election campaign of the party was hampered by revelations of racist, anti-Islam and homophobic social media postings, which concerned about 100 FN candidates locally.[17] Additionally, a growing connection between the FN and Russia was exposed by revelations of a loan to the party from a bank with links with the Kremlin, showing FN ideological support to Putin's autocratic regime.[18]

In conclusion, looking at the extent to which the FN has changed as a radical, niche, and anti-establishment party, there is little evidence of party mainstreaming. Despite the recalibration of its salience profile and moderation of some of its policies, the FN retains core features of the populist radical right party. As will be discussed in the next section, the shedding by the FN of its extremist reputation forms part of a broader attempt to soften its public image, while preserving its radical right-wing populist potential for voter mobilisation.

Goals, strategies and public impact of de-demonisation

Since the mid-1980s, the FN's strategies have been aimed at two somewhat contradictory political objectives.[19] On the one hand, the party has confronted the need to shed its original extreme right status to grow its representation and to escape the margins of the French party system. On the other hand, electoral demand for radical right-wing populist politics in France has produced strong incentives for ideological and political differentiation by the FN, often resulting in the accentuation of its radical right-wing populist profile. De-demonisation refers to the search for a point of equilibrium. The interplay between normalisation and radicalisation has varied over time, reflecting changes in the internal balance of power, as well as in the external conditions of the party.

De-demonisation as vote-maximisation strategy

Whilst closely associated in the public's eye with Marine Le Pen's leadership, de-demonisation has its roots in the opening of the party to former members of the mainstream right in the mid-1980s.[20] In the 1986 legislative elections, this strategy materialised in the National Rally (Rassemblement National, RN), which attracted right-wing defectors such as Bruno Mégret, Yvan Blot or Jean-Yves Le Gallou. The period following his appointment as Delegate General in October 1988 saw Mégret play a crucial role in enacting substantive changes to FN strategies, whilst showing no significant departure, however, from the FN ideological core (Birenbaum and François 1989: 93). Tactical disagreements and a personal rift between Mégret and Jean-Marie Le Pen led to Mégret and his faction leaving the FN in 1999, which put an abrupt end to the first period of FN de-demonisation (Ivaldi 2003).

Current de-demonisation replicates largely Mégret's strategy of the 1990s, reflecting also the presence of former supporters of Mégret – e.g. Bruno Bilde, Steeve Briois and Nicolas Bay – in Marine Le Pen's entourage. In the true sense of the word, de-demonisation is the strategy through which the FN seeks to achieve governmental credibility and political respectability, while simultaneously preserving its radical right-wing populist potential for voter mobilisation. Based on the framework by Strøm (1990), de-demonisation can be disaggregated further into vote, policy and office-seeking forms of behaviour across the electoral, legislative and executive arenas of competition, according to political goals and also to the time frame for the realisation of those goals – i.e. short-term interests versus long-term objectives (see Table 11.1).

De-demonisation prioritises short-term maximisation of votes. The twin processes of FN normalisation and mainstreaming of its ideas seeks primarily to augment electoral support. It must be situated within the party's political development and the external electorally related 'shocks' experienced by the FN in 2002 and 2007. In 2002, Jean-Marie Le Pen's progression to the presidential runoff was the paroxysm of the FN as electoral nuisance. Mass anti-FN mobilisation between the two rounds demonstrated, however, strong resistance, which helped contain the growth in support for Le Pen in the decisive round. This (mis)performance was bitterly disappointing to the party's rank and file, and it acted as a powerful catalyst for party change, creating opportunities for Marine Le Pen's faction. The 2007 elections saw on the other hand the failure of the first attempt by the FN to de-radicalise its policies, while the mainstream right successfully appropriated immigration and criminality issues (Mayer 2007; Marthaler 2008). Jean-Marie Le Pen received 10.4 per cent of the presidential vote and his party polled a mere 4.3 per cent in the legislatives. The 2007 debacle incentivised the FN to re-emphasise its radical cultural positions, resulting in Marine Le Pen's repositioning of her party on immigration and law-and-order issues (Evans and Ivaldi 2013: 107).

The prioritisation of votes stems from the FN's status as political outsider. Its strategies are largely contingent on the incentives generated by the electoral

Table 11.1 FN de-demonisation goals and strategies

Party goals	– Augment electoral support – Shift the party balance on the right of the party system – Create coalition opportunities	– Influence public discourses of immigration and law-and-order – Produce mainstreaming of FN ideas and policies – Create policy convergence from the mainstream right	– Achieve governmental credibility – Enhance valence and competence
Form of behaviour	Vote-seeking	Policy-seeking	Office-seeking
Arena of competition	Electoral	Legislative	Executive
Goal status	Primary	Secondary	Secondary
Time frame	Short-term	Long-term	Long-term
Strategies	– Populist radical right anti-establishment mobilisation – Reformulation of ethno-pluralist policies – Detoxification of FN extremist reputation	– Agenda-setting – 'Taboo breaking' – Social exposure and 'noise' though mass media	– Recalibration of salience profile – Increasing presence in sub-national executives – Expanding the party's local power base

Source: Adapted from Strøm (1990).

system. The majoritarian rule, which forms the electoral backbone of the Fifth Republic, is detrimental to the FN. French legislative elections are characterised by high levels of disproportionality, which account for the FN's inability to win enough seats to acquire coalition potential. Secondly, France's majoritarianism tends to a clustered multiparty system, with two separate party subsystems of the left and the right, which have been dominated by the PS and the UMP respectively since the early 2000s (Brouard *et al.* 2009). To win a majority, parties within each bloc must co-operate to build competitive alliances. The FN represents the archetypical 'outsider' party, kept out of mainstream politics by a *cordon sanitaire*. Because of its continuing political ostracisation by mainstream parties, the FN has been deprived of any coalition opportunity. Ultimately, therefore, vote-seeking behaviour by the FN seeks to replace the UMP as dominant actor in the party subsystem of the right.

FN short-term vote-maximising goals are combined with long-term policy and office-seeking objectives. As regards policy goals, the polarisation of immigration, identity and law-and-order issues by the FN aims mainly to influence public discourses and party narratives. This goal is a crucial aspect of de-demonisation and it is satisfied through strategies of social exposure, 'taboo breaking' and noise in mass media. Mainstreaming the FN's ideas is instrumental to producing policy convergence with proximal parties of the conservative right in order to increase the potential for future coalitions. Because the FN has been constantly excluded from the legislative arena since the late 1980s, it has had very little or no impact on the parliamentary game and the determination of government policy, therefore it does not fit the exact definition of a policy-seeking party. Its position as outsider has allowed the FN to avoid policy compromises, which are generally associated with government participation or coalition agreements, thereby preserving ideological 'purity'.

Finally, since Marine Le Pen's accession, office-seeking has been brought to the forefront of the FN's strategic goals. As had already been the case in the 1990s, the aim is to present the FN as a responsible actor of government. The 2002 elections in particular had revealed the persistent status of the FN as protest party. In the first round of the presidential ballot, only 41 per cent of Jean-Marie Le Pen voters said they wanted him to win the election, compared with over 90 per cent among those supporting major mainstream candidates. Additionally, just over half of Le Pen second-round supporters (56 per cent) said he had presidential stature, as opposed to 85 per cent of Chirac voters.[21]

As party leader, Marine Le Pen has been seeking to address the FN's credibility deficit. In her inaugural speech of January 2011, she claimed that her party was getting ready to assume the mantle of power:

> The FN that I will preside, she said, will be a renewed, open and more efficient party. With your help, my own self-requirement is to turn our party into the most powerful, efficient and performant instrument for our strategy of conquering power.
>
> (Marine Le Pen, inaugural speech, party congress in Tours, 16 January 2011)[22]

The FN's long-term ambitions of assuming power have been repeatedly reiterated since 2011. After her party's success in the 2014 EP elections, Marine Le Pen called for the dissolution of the National Assembly and expressed her willingness to lead a government of cohabitation with Socialist president François Hollande.[23]

Strategies of de-demonisation: political communication and agency credibility

De-demonisation rests on three main strategies. As discussed earlier in this chapter, a first strategy is the filtering of political communication in order to dissociate the FN from classic extreme right subjects. The new party leadership pays incontestably closer attention to avoiding Holocaust denial and overtly racist statements, which have led to the prosecution of FN officials in the past. This adaptation of the FN discourse reflects also the generational replacement which has occurred among top party leaders and which has led to the relative waning of Second World War memories and controversies. The party congress in Lyons in November 2014 confirmed the rise of a younger and more pragmatic cohort of FN elites such as Marion Maréchal-Le Pen, Florian Philippot, David Rachline,

Stéphane Ravier, Nicolas Bay or Julien Rochedy. In May 2015, two prominent members of the 'old' guard – Gollnisch and Marie-Christine Arnautu – were shunted aside by Marine Le Pen after they had expressed their support to Jean-Marie Le Pen in the conflict between him and his daughter.

A second strategy concerns the reformulation by the FN of its traditional ethno-pluralist platform. In 2002, the FN's immigration policies were still dictated by the core features of the party's ethno-cultural agenda. Immigration was for instance considered a 'deadly threat to France's identity [which] profoundly altered the very substance of the French people' (Front National 2002: 22). Since 2007, the FN has been downplaying national identity issues. Immigration issues have been reinterpreted within a 'civic' repertoire related to the values of secularism (*laïcité*), which are pivotal to the French Republican model of assimilation. The 'Republican' turn of the FN was inaugurated in Jean-Marie Le Pen's highly symbolic speech in Valmy in September 2006, which was orchestrated by Marine Le Pen and Alain Soral, a former member of the French left. Le Pen called for:

> French people of foreign origins to join together on our values ... and to immerse themselves in the national and republican melting-pot, sharing the same rights but also the same duties ... . Yes, all of us, he added, not only native-born French ... we can assemble around the idea of the Republic, which is one and indivisible, proud of its history ... around our Constitution which is secular, democratic and social.
> (Jean-Marie Le Pen, speech in Valmy, 20 September 2006)[24]

The republican framing of immigration and identity narratives is key to the FN's act of balancing party normalisation and ideological purity, whilst producing little change to substantive policies. As explained by Marine Le Pen herself in 2010:

> my positions with regards to immigration are not seriously different from those of my father ... I am carrying out a lot of pedagogic work within the party. I above all defend republican values.
> (Marine Le Pen, interview, *Le Nouvel Observateur*, 6 December 2010)[25]

The party now emphasises the alleged standoff between Islam and secularism. This strategic appropriation of secularism helps the party evade accusations of racism or xenophobia, while instrumentalising Islam as an embodied threat to liberal democratic values. The 2012 campaign referred for instance to the so-called menaces of 'islamisation' and 'green fascism' in French society, a strategy which is similar to that employed by other radical right-wing populist parties in Western Europe (Betz and Meret 2009).

The third and last strategic dimension of de-demonisation is governmental credibility. As emphasised by Van Kessel (2015), party agency and credibility factors are of vital importance to radical right-wing populist party electoral consolidation. The search for a credible executive alternative to mainstream parties was already central to Mégret's strategy during the 1990s. In 1989, it had led to the creation of a Scientific Council, an expert panel whose purpose was to provide a wider range of credible socioeconomic policies. Similar 'valence' issues were put at the forefront of the FN's summer university in Avignon in September 2006, where sectoral committees (*Commissions d'Action présidentielle*, CAP) were set up to enhance the FN's expertise. In recent years, the 'technocratisation' of the FN has been central to Marine Le Pen's agenda of party modernisation. During the 2012 presidential campaign, the FN made every effort to present a credible costing for its programme, while simultaneously seeking independent expert advice on its most controversial plan to abolish the Euro.

The greater emphasis put on governmental credibility was revealed for instance by the appointment of a former high ranking administrative civil servant, Florian Philippot, as strategic campaign director in October 2011. This had been preceded by the creation by Louis Aliot of the *Idées Nation* think thank in 2010, which aimed to provide a centre of exchanges and meetings with experts outside the FN. The 1990s had seen the proliferation of FN-related societies (*Cercles*) (Ivaldi 1998). Similar attempts were made recently through the founding of several flanking organisations (*Collectifs*) to target specific socioeconomic groups. These include *Racine* (for teachers), *Nouvelle Ecologie* (for the environment), *Audace* (for young actives and entrepreneurs), *Culture-Libertés* (for arts and culture), *Marianne* (for students) and *Mer et Francophonie* (for overseas territories and the French-speaking community). As explained by Philippot:

> We have an objective of 51 per cent [in the 2017 presidential election]. This goal guides everybody. And this is why we must send a message to all socio-professional milieus.
> (Florian Philippot, interview, Slate.fr, 7 September 2014)[26]

Finally, the focus on credibility and competence has been accompanied by the expansion of the FN's power base and the revitalisation of its pool of local candidates. These go hand in hand with the technical professionalisation of its personnel and grassroots. Art (2011) suggests that the political persistence of radical right-wing populist actors is contingent on their ability to recruit experienced and moderate activists. The FN has made significant gains in elections where it had been notoriously weak in the past. In the 2014 municipal elections, the FN won 11 cities with more than 1,000 inhabitants and 1,544 councillors. Success at the local level allowed the party to take two seats in the Senate in the September 2014 elections. With an estimated membership of about 51,000 in July 2015 and a growing sub-national middle-level elite, the party is also gradually rebuilding the local base, which had been severely damaged by the *mégrétiste* split of the late 1990s. In March 2015, the FN had the strongest presence of all French parties in the departmental elections, running candidates in more than 90 per cent of the 2,054 cantons.

Impact of de-demonisation

The FN seems to be reaping the fruits of de-demonisation. The party has reached new electoral heights in recent elections. One of the most remarkable recent changes in the FN's support is the disappearance of the electoral gender gap, which was characteristic of the French radical right (Mayer 2013). The FN is drawing also greater support from younger voters (Stockemer and Amengay 2015) and it continues to attract left-wing working and lower middle-class voters (Gougou and Mayer 2013). Since 2012, the FN has augmented its potential reservoir of voters in decisive runoffs, challenging the traditional bipolar format of French politics.

Polls show high levels of support for the FN's cultural views (see Table 11.2 below). French voters remain highly concerned about immigration, national identity and crime. Immigration topped the 2014 European Parliament election agenda and was the most salient issue for 31 per cent of voters.[27] A majority of the French hold negative opinions of Islam, while over two thirds (67 per cent) adhere to the FN's claim that there are too many foreigners in the country. More than half of the French (52 per cent) agree also that death penalty should be reinstated.

Since 2008, the ramifications of the global economic crisis in France have also created a more favourable environment for the FN. The deterioration in the economic situation has amplified public discontent with mainstream parties, providing strong incentives for the FN to prioritise populist strategies of voter mobilisation. Anti-establishment attitudes have become pervasive in French society: over 85 per cent of the French think that 'politicians don't really care about people like them' and say they want a 'strong leader in France to put everything in order'. Euroscepticism and anti-globalisation sentiments are also now more widespread. More than half of the French (56 per cent) see globalisation as a threat, while another 72 per cent agree that more power should be given to the country instead of the EU (see Table 11.2).

Public opinion data point to the increasing, albeit slow, normalisation of the FN in the public's eye (see Table 11.3). In February 2015, 54 per cent of the French said that 'the FN was a threat to democracy' compared with 75 per cent in the mid-1990s. Other indicators of de-demonisation include popularity ratings for both the FN and its leader, which have almost doubled since Marine Le Pen's accession, as well as public support for the FN's ideas, which are now shared by a third (33 per cent) of the French. With all evident necessary methodological precautions, presidential voting intention polls published in April 2015 suggested that Marine Le Pen could win about 30 per cent of the first-round vote and up to 45 per cent in the runoff.[28]

Significant changes have occurred in the FN's political environment. The electoral revival and softening of the FN's image are certainly putting the *cordon sanitaire* under greater strain. Since 2002, the UMP has maintained a strict

Table 11.2 Salience of the FN agenda

Item (% agree)	2014	2015
There are too many foreigners in France	66	67
Islam is not compatible with the values of French society	63	54
In France, things were better in the past	74	70
In general, foreigners don't make much of an effort to assimilate in French society	59	56
We should give more power to our country even if this limits that of the EU	70	72
France's economic power has declined over the past ten years	90	—
Economic globalisation is a threat to France	61	56
We need a strong leader in France to put everything in order	84	85
Death penalty should be reinstated	45	52
Politicians don't really care about people like us	88	—
The French democratic system is not working very well and my ideas are not represented	78	76
Most men and women in French politics are corrupt	65	66

Source: IPSOS-CEVIPOF survey. Les Nouvelles fractures françaises, Wave 2 and 3, January 2014 and May 2015, www.ipsos.fr/ipsos-public-affairs/actualites/2014-01-21-nouvelles-fractures-francaises-re sultats-et-analyse-l-enquete-ipsos-steria (accessed 07-06-2014); www.jean-jaures.org/content/down load/21024/218010/file/Fractures_Franc%CC%A7aise_2015_DEF%20v2.pdf (accessed 12-05-2015).

Table 11.3 Public opinion indicators of de-demonisation 1997–2015

	1997	2002	2007	2011	2014	2015
Average % FN popularity[1]	13	11	12	16	23	21
Average % leader popularity[1]	15	13	13	23	27	26
Is a threat to democracy (%)	75	70	60	56	50	54
Agreement with FN ideas (%)	20	28	26	22	34	33

Note: [1] Annual average of monthly (Le Pen) and quarterly (FN) popularity ratings.
Source: TNS-SOFRES popularities and annual barometer surveys.

demarcation from the FN. In 2012, however, Sarkozy pushed the political legit-imation of the FN one step further by acknowledging the 'democratic nature' of Marine Le Pen's party and its 'compatibility with Republican values'. More recently, the controversy surrounding the possibility that Marine Le Pen would take part in the national march organised after the *Charlie Hebdo* terrorist attacks of January 2015 revealed the ambiguity in the exclusionary stance by mainstream leaders vis-à-vis a supposedly 'de-demonised' FN.

National coalitions between the FN and the UMP are a very remote possibility, but the normalisation of the FN in the eyes of voters makes it increasingly difficult for the UMP to legitimate political exclusion of their radical challenger. Moreover, the radicalisation of the mainstream right since 2007 has further decreased the attitudinal distance between the core supporters of both the conservative UMP and FN with regard to immigration and law and order issues. The study by Fourquet and Gariazzo (2013) confirms that both the UMP and the FN electorates have undergone a marked attitudinal shift in their cultural positions in the 2012 elections, which facilitates electoral swings between the mainstream and radical poles of the right.

Finally, recent years have seen the deterioration of the Republican Front (*Front Républicain*). The Republican Front consists traditionally of ad hoc local alliances of parties across the spectrum wherever and whenever a radical right candidate is likely to win a decisive round. Since 2011, however, the mainstream right UMP has adopted a 'neither, nor' strategy of maintaining its candidates in all three-way contests, urging voters to reject both the FN and the left. This has created a more favourable opportunity structure in constituencies with strong FN presence, particularly in the Southern regions. The deterioration of the Republican Front has important electoral implications. Runoffs with three or more candidates promote the viability of middle-sized parties and the possibility that the FN will win seats without a clear majority of the votes.

De-demonisation has as yet failed to alter public perceptions of the FN as a credible party of government, however: less than a third of the French (31 per cent) believe that the FN is capable of taking responsibility in office, while another 78 per cent see the FN as an extreme right party. The FN's economic strategy lacks credibility. Its Euro-exit platform is currently rejected by the vast majority of the French, with only 25 per cent in favour of returning to the national currency, down from 34 per cent in January 2011. Similarly, the 'national preference' scheme, which is the cornerstone to FN socioeconomic policies, is supported by just over a fifth (22 per cent) of the French.[29] Moreover, the perpetuation of populist anti-establishment mobilisation strategies by the FN continues to interfere with the realisation of office-seeking objectives, undermining Marine Le Pen's claim that the FN is changing from opposition to power.

Conclusion

This chapter offers an account of the current transformation of the French FN. Since her accession in 2011, Marine Le Pen has been advancing a line of party change. In March 2015, she gave herself full marks on 'fulfilling [her] objectives [of] local entrenchment, professionalization and normalization, which', she said, 'formed the triptych of [her] mandate' when taking over as FN leader four years earlier.[30] As Harmel and Janda (1994: 262) suggest: 'party change is normally a result of leadership change, a change of dominant faction within the party and/or an external stimulus for change'. The FN has been seeking a new strategic equilibrium between 'normalisation' and 'differentiation'. The search for this dual political objective originated in the electoral 'shocks' experienced in 2002 and 2007. Both elections acted as strong stimuli for change and paved the way for the new party leader in 2011, resulting in a new factional balance and the strategic recalibration of the FN through 'de-demonisation'.

Replicating previous attempts by the party to modify its strategies, de-demonisation aims to shed the FN's pariah profile, while simultaneously maximising electoral opportunities for radical right-wing populist politics. Despite repeated claims that it is preparing itself to assume power, the current FN follows primarily short-term vote-maximising strategies. De-demonisation aims to enlarge its pool of voters to challenge the UMP as dominant actor on the party subsystem of the right. To do so, the FN must change its longstanding reputation as extreme right party and enhance its credibility, while simultaneously preserving its potential for radical right-wing populist mobilisation of votes. Therefore, de-demonisation concerns mostly the strategic policy packaging of the party and the softening of its tone, and it has not substantially altered the main traditional features of the FN. The latter has not yet shifted from niche to mainstream status. It has accentuated economic nationalism and anti-EU stances, while endorsing also social populism in the domestic arena (Ivaldi 2015). Moreover, de-demonisation has produced only limited amounts of change to the party's anti-liberal culture. The FN has filtered its political rhetoric, but core radical immigration and law and order policies have remained. Finally, its current competitive strategies are dominated by anti-political-establishment populism, juxtaposed with timid efforts of opening the party locally.

The prioritisation of vote-maximisation is largely a consequence of the political isolation of the FN, and of its lack of coalition potential. The FN continues to be politically ostracised by its neighbouring competitors of the conservative right. As suggested elsewhere in this volume, a vote-seeking strategy is the most realistic option for radical right-wing populist parties when they are ostracised and stigmatised by mainstream competitors. The French case corroborates therefore the assumption that majority systems and a *cordon sanitaire* tend to impede radical right-wing populist parties to choose an office-seeking strategy. De-demonisation is increasing the pressure on the *cordon sanitaire*, however, as the FN is gradually gaining more political legitimacy, producing strategic shifts by other actors. In particular, the waning of the Republican Front might create new opportunities for party competition in the future.

The FN is now at a political crossroads ahead of the 2017 presidential election. De-demonisation has allowed the party to broaden its electoral support and tap into new social groups, such as women or younger voters. Presidential polls promise Marine Le Pen new electoral heights in the 2017 elections. Public opinion polls suggest that the FN's negative views of immigration, Islam or the EU are currently shared by a large proportion of the French, showing also wide popular support for the party's authoritarian and populist agenda. Changes in the electoral market include also growing attitudinal convergence between the conservative and the radical right poles of the French electorate, which augments the potential for future coalitions. The FN seems to be gradually normalising in

French politics, although a majority of the French still regard it as an extremist party with little governmental credibility.

The FN will continue therefore to face a trade-off between radical right-wing populist politics and normalisation. Normalisation strategies may be costly in terms of votes. Niche parties risk losing their distinctiveness and support if they move too far beyond their core issues or moderate their policy positions (Adams *et al.* 2006). Additionally, the current economic crisis produces strong centrifugal incentives for the FN to sustain its populist anti-establishment appeal to all non-centrist, disenfranchised and protest voters, which interfere clearly with its long-term ambition of assuming power. As argued by Harmel and Svåsand (1993), however, the final stage of radical right-wing populist party institutionalisation targets credibility and cooperation, and it requires a more pragmatic and 'power-seeking' leader. The FN must enhance credibility and shed its radical right profile to grow its representation or it will otherwise continue to alienate the moderate sectors of the electorate. Most importantly, whether it succeeds or fails to achieve electoral supremacy, the FN will continue to confront institutional constraints arising from the majoritarian system. It will need to address political cooperation with the mainstream right and, thereby, resolve its position within France's bipolar system of competition.

Notes

1 The exceptional reintroduction of proportional representation in the 1986 legislatives by the socialist government allowed the FN to win 35 seats in the National Assembly, which were lost in 1988 after the new right-wing government returned to the majority system.

2 The basic coding unit is the individual policy proposal or pledge. The analysis is restricted to 'hard pledges' and ignores soft pledges or more general policy statements.

3 The word 'communautarisme' refers to alleged religious and community splits in French society, and what is described as a drift by French Muslims towards cultural isolationism and sectarianism.

4 Interview, TF1, 06-03-2012, http://elections.lefigaro.fr/presidentielle-2012/2012/03/06/01039-20120306ARTFIG00317-marine-le-pen-a-l-aise-face-aux-vraies-gens.php.

5 According to Meyer and Wagner (2013), a party de/emphasises an issue more than its competitors if its salience is at least one standard deviation below/above the mean party system salience. In 2012, the FN difference from the mean party system was of about two standard deviations.

6 In 2012, there were 150 policy pledges in Marine Le Pen's presidential programme, compared with 310 and 342 in 2002 and 2007 respectively.

7 www.frontnational.com/videos/meeting-a-metz-discours-de-cloture-de-marine-le-pen/.

8 www.ledauphine.com/politique/2012/04/04/je-suis-la-candidate-anti-systeme/.

9 www.lemonde.fr/election-presidentielle-2012/article/2012/04/12/mon-objectif-c-est-d-arriver-au-second-tour_1684440_1471069.html/.

10 www.fn31.fr/wp-content/uploads/2014/05/profession-de-foi-de-louis-aliot-candidat-de-leuro-circonscription-sud-ouest-europeennes-france-mai-2014.pdf/.

11 Gollnisch had declared: 'historians have the right to discuss the number of deaths and the way that they died. Fifty years after the facts, we can discuss the real number

of deaths (…). The existence of the gas chambers is for historians to discuss.' Gollnisch had received official support from the political bureau of the FN which had denounced a 'political and media witch-hunt' (www.liberation.fr/politiques/2004/10/19/le-fn-absout -gollnisch-et-desavoue-marine-le-pen_496452 (accessed 03-04-2015).

12 www.lemonde.fr/election-presidentielle-2012/article/2012/02/01/pour-marine-le-pen-le-nazisme-fut-une-abomination_1637416_1471069.html (accessed 03-04-2015.

13 In a video posted on the FN website, Jean-Marie Le Pen lashed out at Jewish singer Patrick Bruel, saying 'we'll do up a batch next time', using the word fournée (ovenful) (www.lefigaro.fr/politique/2014/06/08/01002-20140608ARTFIG00158-marine-le-pen-condamne-la-faute-politique-de-son-pere.php (accessed 03-04- 2015).

14 During an interview on BFM-TV on 2 April 2015, Jean-Marie Le Pen repeated his incendiary comments of September 1987: 'what I said corresponds to what I think. The gas chambers were a detail of the war, unless we admit that the war was a detail of the gas chambers' (www.bfmtv.com/politique/jean-marie-le-pen-persiste-sur-les-chambres-a-gaz-873716.html).

15 In order to avoid political entryism, section 6 of the FN statutes prohibits dual membership, stipulating that 'membership of the FN is not compatible with membership of any other party or political movement'.

16 'Pétainists' refers here to supporters of Marshal Philippe Pétain, leader of the collaborationist Vichy regime in 1940 (www.lefigaro.fr/flash-actu/2010/12/07/97001 -20101207FILWWW00388-fn-gollnish-s-en-prend-a-marin-le-pen.php, accessed 6 June 2014).

17 An exhaustive list can be found at www.huffingtonpost.fr/2015/03/23/resulta ts-departementales-2015-derapages-candidats-fn-pas-penalises_n_6921814.html/.

18 See www.washingtonpost.com/blogs/worldviews/wp/2015/02/18/europes-far-rig ht-still-loves-putin, (accessed 20-03-2015).

19 The data in this second section come from public discourses and interviews given by FN leaders to French media, as well as secondary literature.

20 The term 'de-demonisation' was first coined in the FN Summer University in La Baule in September 1989 (www.lemonde.fr/archives/article/1989/09/02/reuni-a-la -baule-le-front-national-met-en-forme-sa-reflexion-sur-les-avantages-de-l-exclusion_ 4135802_1819218.html (accessed 25-05-2015).

21 Source: CEVIPOF 2002 Electoral Panel Surveys (http://cdsp.sciences-po.fr/enquet es.php?lang=FR&idRubrique=enquetesFR&idTheme=35).

22 www.frontnational.com/videos/congres-du-fn-a-tours-discours-d%E2%80%99inves titure-de-marine-le-pen/ (accessed 25-05-2015).

23 www.lemonde.fr/politique/article/2014/09/05/marine-le-pen-prete-a-devenir-pre miere-ministre-avec-francois-hollande_4482614_823448.html (accessed 25-05-2015.

24 www.egaliteetreconciliation.fr/Discours-de-Valmy-2974.html (accessed 25-05-2015).

25 http://tempsreel.nouvelobs.com/politique/20101206.OBS4257/interview-marine-le-pen-le-sursaut-vital-face-au-mondialisme.html (accessed 15-05-2015.

26 www.slate.fr/story/91839/fn-collectifs (accessed 03-05-2015).

27 Source: IPSOS survey, www.ipsos.fr/sites/default/files/attachments/europeennes_ipsos_ -_comprendre_le_vote_des_francais_-_25_mai_2014_-_20h.pdf (accessed 20-03-2015).

28 www.leparisien.fr/politique/presidentielle-2017-pour-70-des-sondes-valls-ferait-un-meilleur-candidat-que-hollande-04-05-2015-4745305.php (accessed 20-05-2015.

29 Sources: IFOP, Fractures françaises 2015; www.jean-jaures.org/content/download/ 21024/218010/file/Fractures_Franc%CC%A7aise_2015_DEF%20v2.pdf (accessed 12-05-2015; TNS-SOFRES Baromètre 2015 d'image du Front national (February 2015) (www.tns-sofres.com/sites/default/files/2015.02.16-baro-fn.pdf (accessed 19-03-2015).

30 www.lemonde.fr/politique/article/2015/03/29/marine-le-pen-toutes-les-cartes-son t-rebattues_4605113_823448.html/.

References

Adams, J., Clark, M., Ezrow, L. and Glasgow, G. (2006) 'Are niche parties fundamentally different from mainstream parties? The causes and the electoral consequences of Western European parties' policy shifts, 1976–1998', *American Journal of Political Science* 50, 3: 513–529.

Akkerman, T. (2015) 'Immigration policy and electoral competition in Western Europe. A fine-grained analysis of party positions over the past two decades', *Party Politics* 21, 1: 54–67.

Art, D. (2011) *Inside the Radical Right: The Development of Anti-Immigrant Parties in Western Europe*, Cambridge: Cambridge University Press.

Betz, H. G. and Meret, S. (2009) 'Revisiting Lepanto: The political mobilization against Islam in contemporary Western Europe', *Patterns of Prejudice* 43, 3-4: 313–334.

Birenbaum, G. and François, B. (1989) 'Unité et diversité des dirigeants frontistes', in Mayer, N. and Perrineau, P. (eds) *Le Front National à Découvert*, Paris: Presses de la FNSP, pp. 83–106.

Brouard, S., Appleton, A. and Mazur, A. (eds) (2009) *The French Fifth Republic at Fifty. Beyond Stereotypes*, Basingstoke: Palgrave Macmillan.

Crépon, S., Dézé, A. and Mayer, N. (eds) (2015) *Les Faux Semblants du Front National. Sociologie d'un Parti Politique*, Paris: Presses de Sciences-Po.

Evans, J. and Ivaldi, G. (2013) *The 2012 French Presidential Elections. The Inevitable Alternation*, Basingstoke: Palgrave Macmillan.

Ezrow, L. (2008) 'Research note: On the inverse relationship between votes and proximity for niche parties', *European Journal of Political Research*, 47, 2: 206–220.

Fourquet, J. and Gariazzo, M. (2013) *FN et UMP: Electorats en Fusion?* Paris: Fondation Jean Jaurès.

Front National (2002) 'Pour un avenir français: Programme du Front National', http://h16free.com/wp-content/uploads/2011/11/prg-fn-2002.pdf (accessed 30-06-2015).

Gougou, F. and Mayer, N. (2013) 'The class basis of extreme right voting in France: Generational replacement and the rise of new cultural issues (1984–2007)', in Rydgren, J. (ed.) *Class Politics and the Radical Right*, London: Routledge, pp. 156–172.

Harmel, R. and Janda, K. (1994) 'An integrated theory of party goals and party change', *Journal of Theoretical Politics* 6, 3: 259–287.

Harmel, R. and Svåsand, L. (1993) 'Party leadership and party institutionalization: Three phases of development', *West European Politics* 16, 2: 67–88.

Harmel, R., Tan, A. C., Janda, K. and Smith, J. M. (1995) 'Substance vs. packaging: An empirical analysis of parties' issue profiles', paper delivered at the 1995 Annual Meeting of the American Political Science Association, Chicago, 1 September.

Ivaldi, G. (1998) 'The National Front: The making of an authoritarian party', in Ignazi, P. and Ysmal, C. (eds) *The Organization of Political Parties in Southern Europe*, Westport, CT: Greenwood-Praeger, pp. 43–69.

Ivaldi, G. (2003) 'The Front National split: Party system change and electoral prospects', in Evans, J. A. J. (ed.) *The French Party System: Continuity and Change*, Manchester: Manchester University Press, pp. 137–154.

Ivaldi, G. (2007) 'The Front national vis-à-vis power in France: Factors of political isolation and performance assessment of the extreme right in municipal office', in Delwit, P. and Poirier, Ph. (eds) *The Extreme Right Parties and Power in Europe*, Bruxelles: Editions de l'Université de Bruxelles, pp. 167–186.

Ivaldi, G. (2015) 'Towards the median economic crisis voter? The new leftist economic agenda of the Front National in France', *French Politics* 13, 4: 346–369.

Kitschelt, H. (in collaboration with McGann, A. J.) (1995) *The Radical Right in Western Europe: A Comparative Analysis*, Ann Arbor, MI: University of Michigan Press.

Le Pen, M. (2012) *Pour que Vive la France*, Paris: Jacques Granchet.

Marthaler, S. (2008) 'Nicolas Sarkozy and the politics of French immigration policy', *Journal of European Public Policy*, 15, 3: 382–397

Mayer, N. (2007) 'Comment Nicolas Sarkozy a rétréci l'électorat Le Pen', *Revue Française de Science Politique* 57, 3–4: 429–445.

Mayer, N. (2013) 'From Jean-Marie to Marine Le Pen: Electoral change on the far right', *Parliamentary Affairs* 66, 1: 160–178.

Meyer, T. M. and Wagner, M. (2013) 'Mainstream or niche? Vote-seeking incentives and the programmatic strategies of political parties', *Comparative Political Studies* 46, 10: 1246–1272.

Mudde, C. (2007) *Populist Radical Right Parties in Europe*, Cambridge: Cambridge University Press.

Rydgren, J. (2005) 'Is extreme right-wing populism contagious? Explaining the emergence of a new party family', *European Journal of Political Research* 44: 413–437.

Shields, J. (2013) 'Marine Le Pen and the "new" FN: A change of style or of substance?', *Parliamentary Affairs* 66, 1: 179–196.

Stockemer, D. and Amengay, A. (2015) 'The voters of the FN under Jean-Marie Le Pen and Marine Le Pen: Continuity or change?', *French Politics* 13, 4: 370–390.

Strøm, K. (1990) 'A behavioral theory of competitive political parties', *American Journal of Political Science* 34, 2: 565–598.

Van Kessel, S. (2015) *Populist Parties in Europe. Agents of Discontent?* Basingstoke: Palgrave Macmillan.

Zaslove, A. (2008) 'Exclusion, community, and a populist political economy: The radical right as an anti-globalization movement', *Comparative European Politics* 6, 2: 169–189.

12 The UK Independence Party

The dimensions of mainstreaming

Simon Usherwood

Introduction

The UK Independence Party (UKIP) represents something of an outlier in a number of aspects. In contrast to the other cases presented in this collection, it developed from a very specific and focused opposition to the European Union (EU) in the early 1990s, gradually growing into a more broadly based party since the 2000s. As a result, its existence and operation pre-date any notion of a party ideology, which remains a deeply questionable proposition, given the way in which UKIP has grown to date by drawing in activists (and voters) from across the British political spectrum. As such, it is much more negatively defined – marked by what it does not like – than a classic radical right-wing populist party, even if we might consider the latter's nativism as being informed by dislike (Mudde 2010).

At the same time, there is much that suggests the party should be considered alongside its continental counterparts. The dominance of anti-establishment policies, most notably around controlling immigration, and of soft populist appeals to 'common sense politics' make it easy to draw comparisons with the logics of groups such as the Dutch Party for Freedom (Partij voor de Vrijheid, PVV) or even the Finns Party (Perussuomalaiset, PS), albeit without the explicit xenophobia of either. That UKIP sits with some of these parties in the European Parliament (EP) reinforces the point. Similarly, the personal domination of UKIP by Nigel Farage highlights the similarities to the French National Front (Front National, FN) or the Danish People's Party (Dansk Folkeparti, DF).

While it is tempting to attribute some of this to a sociocultural argument about the UK and its 'otherness' in Europe, this is not a particularly helpful approach, especially since the processes of mainstreaming UKIP look to be very similar to those found in other countries. In this chapter, I will argue that the key differential at play is that of opportunity structures that both privilege and hinder particular courses of action. In particular, the closed nature of Parliament – with its first-past-the-post electoral system and tendency towards single party government – has meant the party has been pushed towards exploiting other sites of political activity, such as the EP and the media. As the 2015 general election amply demonstrated, the British political system does not favour challenger parties, leading them to pursue adaptive behaviours. These points are developed in the final section of this chapter.

A brief recapitulation of the party's development would be in order here, especially since its origins remain largely ignored by most analysts. The party was set up in 1993 by a professor at the London School of Economics, Alan Sked, who had become progressively more disillusioned with the development of European integration since the late 1980s: he had been a key figure in the (initially) cross-party Bruges Group, created after Margaret Thatcher's famous Bruges speech, but as that group had become aligned with the Conservative party, he had left to pursue a purer form of Euroscepticism. The new party's sole policy was to provoke a British exit from the EU, by winning seats in the EP and then refusing to take them, so causing a constitutional crisis.

Such a position didn't result in any seats in the 1994 EP elections and the period up to the next EP elections saw the party struggle to survive, between a mix of far-right groups trying to gain influence, a strong challenge on its policy from James Goldsmith's Referendum Party, and a set of deeply divisive internal differences. These last produced several major schisms in the senior leadership, although always with a strong reaction against any association with the far right, either in membership or policy. Ironically, the saving factor for the party was probably the Labour party's decision to switch to a list system for the 1999 elections, which allowed three Members of the European Parliament (MEPs) to be returned for the party, including Farage: by this point, UKIP had decided it would take up seats, to gain better knowledge of the system and to expose that to voters.

While the European issue was very important at this stage in British politics – focused on the question of British participation in the Euro – UKIP was unable to translate their European success into other arenas, either national or local, so the large majority of its efforts went into the EP cycle of elections. 2004 saw a major breakthrough, with a propitious set of circumstances moving it to 12 MEPs and fourth place in votes. Importantly, this election marked the start of efforts to campaign on a broader basis than just 'Europe', with a strong theme of anti-establishmentism. This success laid much of the groundwork for subsequent EP elections, building up to 2014, where the party came first in votes and MEPs (see Table 12.1).

During this decade, the party has developed a fuller set of policy positions, the most important of which has been on immigration, where use has been made of its withdrawalist stance to highlight the impact of intra-EU migration. Likewise, the party has been able to develop a more substantial organisational structure, particularly at local level, which has in turn enabled it to start to build representation in local government. Finally, the almost-continuous efforts to gain representation in Westminster since the party's formation moved into a new stage in late 2014: previously, defectors to the party had not been strengthened by a re-election, but the two by-elections in that year for former Conservatives Douglas Carswell and Mark Reckless marked a high level of confidence in the momentum that the party took into the 2015 general election.

Table 12.1 UKIP's performance in European Parliament elections 1994–2014

Year	Number of votes	% of votes	Seats
1994	150,251	1.0	0
1999	696,057	7.0	3
2004	2,650,768	16.0	12
2009	2,498,226	17.0	13
2014	4,352,251	27.0	24

Source: UK Parliament.

That election demonstrated the potential and the limits of the party. Despite the strongest showing by a third party (in votes) since the rise of the Labour party a century ago, UKIP only secured one seat – Carswell's – and was immediately plunged into internal tensions over the continuing leadership of Farage (whose resignation had been rejected by the National Executive). While the referendum on British membership of the EU in 2016 or 2017 might provide a focus for activities, the party remains without a meaningful presence in the House of Commons and the scope for maintaining momentum looks somewhat limited.

Mainstreaming

The question of mainstreaming is a central one for UKIP, not least because of its very particular origins. In contrast to other parties considered in this collection, UKIP is the only one to have originated as a truly single-issue party and, moreover, that issue to have been withdrawal from the EU. As the introductory comments have indicated, the party's development has necessarily implied a broadening of both its aims and its practice, which in turn could be argued to be some kind of mainstreaming, at least in the sense that the party has had to cleave to the environment in which it operates. Aside from this somewhat semantic aspect, it is clear that there has been a process of mainstreaming within the party, albeit one that presents a degree of complexity that is not immediately apparent.

This mainstreaming is evident at a number of levels. Most obviously, the initial focus on the EU has been broadened into a much wider package of policies, albeit one still dominated by the twin issues of immigration and 'Europe'. Similarly, there has been an increased effort by the party to weed out both extremist and extreme voices: in its pursuit of electoral respectability, the party has strived to show itself as not only credible but also competent. This is reflected in the following exploration of the different aspects of mainstreaming.

Policy mainstreaming: moving away from a single issue

Positioning and salience are deeply intertwined issues for UKIP. Given its roots as a single-issue party, in contrast to the other examples in this collection, there has necessarily been a reduction in the salience of its original anti-EU position, purely as a function of developing other policies. That the party was established on this single-issue basis was also a reflection of the particular structure of political debate in the UK in the early 1990s.

During the 1990s and 2000s, 'Europe' ranked high as an issue for many in the UK, reflecting the importance accorded to the various treaty revisions and the discussions about Euro membership. However, that interest has fallen sharply, with less than 10 per cent of people rating it 'an important issue' since 2005, mainly due to a lack of structural developments in the EU itself and the continued unwillingness of Labour and Conservative parties to invest political capital in debating it (Ipsos-Mori n.d.). By contrast, the economy is scored as important by at least 50 per cent of people and immigration has progressively climbed in importance, especially since the 2004 EU enlargement to Central and Eastern Europe. One could argue that the economic crisis since 2007 has actually worked against UKIP, by exposing the weakness of European regulation of economic activity, and underlining the continued dominance of national governments in managing financial and economic affairs, so challenging the notion of 'Brussels' as an all-pervasive controller. Certainly, the structure of political debate does not lend itself as conveniently as it did in the 1990s to a single-issue anti-EU party. Notwithstanding the strong performance in the 2009 and 2014 European elections, this has only gradually translated into an ability to shape debate outside of the European issue.

UKIP appears to have understood this problem, for it has progressively broadened itself out from its initial, highly principled origins under Sked. This was most apparent in the run-up to the 2004 European elections, with the development of an immigration and asylum policy modelling in part on ideas of Pim Fortuyn in the Netherlands: the problem was not immigrants *per se*, but the ability of the UK to handle them (with health, welfare or education pro-vision) and the consequent costs to others (i.e. UK nationals). This broadening of UKIP's activities was not without difficulty. Most notably, one senior member invested much time in fighting what he perceived to be a shift in the core policy of the party: in 2003, election leaflets were drawn up with the slogan 'No to European Union', which seemed to imply something different to the 'No to the European Union' that had been used before, the former implying a dislike of any form of European integration, rather than the specific form of the latter (*Ukipuncovered* 2004). Likewise, under Farage's leadership there has been a similar broadening of action, both in his willingness to convey a position on most matters of political debate and to commit party resources to those; for example in the 2009 Irish referendum on the Lisbon treaty or the 2011 referendum on electoral reform (Tonra 2009; BBC News 28-03-2011). This approach is now generally accepted, at least amongst the party's official candidates, both as a maturation of UKIP's policies and as a means to increase pressure on the Con-servative party towards greater Euroscepticism (Lynch *et al.* 2010). It is also reflected in the manifesto data presented in this collection's introduction, with a distinct shift towards more populist positions, especially on immigration (see Appendix).

The party's European policy has clearly softened over time. Sked's initial policy of refusing to take up seats had already been amended by the time of the 1999 European elections, with its three MEPs taking up seats to secure funding, gain 'inside knowledge' of the EU and to then use it to expose the flaws to voters. This has remained the party's position towards the EP ever since. In addition, UKIP has also modified its stance on British membership of the EU. Whereas it originally used to consider that the election of a UKIP government was a *de facto* decision by the British people to leave the EU (Gardner 2006), this became muddied by the debate about a referendum. This debate has some very long roots, but had come to prominence at the time of the Constitutional Treaty debates in the early 2000s (Closa 2007), when the main British parties conceded that any new treaty would have to be submitted to a popular vote. UKIP was one of the key voices in pushing this position further to become a vote on membership *per se*, regardless of treaty reform. This position, while not adopted directly by other parties, is now (in 2015) the party's official policy: its 2015 general election manifesto stated that UKIP will hold an immediate referendum on membership and would campaign for withdrawal (UKIP 2015). As is discussed later, this is partly a reflection of the changed political landscape in the UK, but it is a striking modification (and retreat) from the party's original position.

If European policy has changed, then this also needs to be understood in the context of the development of a wider set of policy positions. Again, there is a contrast here between UKIP and Continental radical right-wing populist parties: the latter have always held a portfolio of policy positions, based around an underlying ideology. UKIP has never had (and does not have) an ideology – radical right or otherwise – and has developed organically from its single-issue starting point. This is not to say that there are not ideologues in the party, nor to deny a constant struggle by the leadership with entryist elements (Tournier-Sol 2015), but rather to point to a different dynamic of policy development. Thus while immigration control has become a central part of UKIP's political identity (to use the most pertinent example), it does not stem from the same roots as in other parties. Instead it is used as a means of maintaining political relevance in an opportunistic manner, rather than representing the confirmed will of the party in an institutionalised form.

When immigration first became part of the party's policy platform in the early 2000s, it was largely as a function of EU membership: the free movement of people from other member states meant that British governments could not really control who entered the UK. With the unexpectedly large inflows from Central and Eastern Europe after 2004, particularly into areas that had previously not encountered immigrant populations, UKIP moved immigration into a more central position (Bakker *et al.* 2015). It was an early adopter of the calls for the introduction of a points-based immigration system, as used in Australia, and for the withholding of benefits to EU migrants for a period of years, both policy points that have been picked up by other parties. However, the party has also been very consistent in trying to frame the policy as a need for controlled immigration, rather than as being anti-immigration *per se*. In this, the key driver has been the deep unwillingness to be tarred with the brush of xenophobia and racism used against the British National Party (BNP) and its predecessors: this clearly echoes the reputational dimension of mainstreaming discussed in Chapter 1. Indeed, given the very broad range of political views contained within the party, it is more useful to consider this policy development as an example of populist 'common sense' than as racism in another form. It is not coincidental that the most constant feature of the party since its foundation has been a rejection of any overt radical right infiltration. This infiltration has taken the form of former and current members of the BNP and other racist groups trying to join the party and secure positions of influence; in all cases that have come to light, UKIP has been swift to expel those individuals, just as it has taken prompt disciplinary action against any member who expresses discriminatory views. The most prominent recent example was the 2013 expulsion of Godfrey Bloom, MEP and close confidante of Farage, for remarks about women.

As a result, immigration policy has actually hardened and become more central over time, rather than less, which would suggest radicalisation in the framework of this collection. However, this needs to be contextualised in Farage's wider repositioning of the party. Farage has long understood that UKIP has the potential to be a touchstone for voters' discontents, not only on European integration, but also more widely. Immigration represented the simplest and most cogent area into which to develop, but with the rapid hardening of political debate in this field during the 2000s (Bale and Partos 2014), there was a need to consider all fields of public policy. While UKIP did have some (very basic) policies aside from EU withdrawal when contesting the 1997 general election and the 1999 European election, these where neither much advanced by the party, nor noticed by the electorate or media (Pennings 2002). The major turning point came in 2004, when a new campaign management team decided to articulate a message of broad-based rejection of 'politics as usual' and to play up the party's anti-politics (Daniel 2005; Gardner 2006). From this point onwards, party manifestos grew considerably in content and scope.

While this did give the party the potential to become involved in more political debates, this potential was not always realised in practice. In part, this was due to the almost total lack of venues in which to operationalise such positions: UKIP MEPs have an almost perfect record in not voting in the EP, while they have not had any local or national bodies. In part, this was also due to the continuing lack of ideological coherence of the party and a dearth of competent senior party figures (a longstanding issue, see Usherwood 2008). The resultant profusion (and confusion) of policies reached an apogee in 2010, with a manifesto that even the party leader admitted he had not read and that Farage was to dismiss as 'drivel' in 2014 (BBC News 24-01-2014). The upshot was a very brief document in 2014 and a more concentrated and developed manifesto for 2015 (including an independent financial analysis). While this more recent work has tried to pull together policy into a more coherent whole, it remains largely predicated on substantial financial benefits from EU withdrawal being used to support increased spending on defence, health, education and tax cuts. Even as spokesmen for different policy areas have been foregrounded by the party (see www.ukip.org/news) in recent years to demonstrate the wider relevance of the party's agenda, there remains a strong emphasis on the core messages around immigration and the EU. Where there is profiling of other issues, these are primarily opportunistic forays into those topics where there is some localised impact on potential voters. The pressing of veterans' rights and opposition to a high-speed railway line are cases in point.

UKIP's changing reputation

The final area of mainstreaming to be addressed is that of the party's changing reputation. As has been noted above, UKIP has moved from being a single-issue party into one that claims to speak on a much wider range of issues. This shift has necessitated adaptations by other political parties and a change in public attitudes.

Until recent years, the main thrust of other parties to UKIP was one of ignoring them. The ability to characterise them as single-issue and amateurish provided an obvious path, best characterised by Conservative party leader David Cameron's comments in 2006, where he described the party as comprising 'fruitcakes, loonies and closet racists' (BBC News 04-04-2006). In more practical terms, this meant an unwillingness to enter into debate with UKIP and a closing down of policy spaces on the EU and immigration. On this latter point, it should be observed that this was driven more by the internal struggles of the Conservative party than by fear of a challenge from UKIP (Bale and Partos 2014). Such attitudes were also mirrored in the public, which would turn to voting for the party at European elections – given its distinctive stance – but without a broader engagement with the party's agenda (see Figure 12.1). Any electoral legitimacy that UKIP might have built in European elections did not translate into support for the party in the national arena.

This picture began to change during the 2010–2015 Parliament. The broadening of UKIP's messaging has made it harder for competitors to ignore it, especially as levels of trust in politicians have fallen even lower (British Social Attitudes n.d.). One marker of this was the offer by the Liberal Democrat leader, Nick Clegg, to hold televised debates on European integration with Nigel Farage in 2014. While UKIP has continued to maintain a central position for immigration and EU membership in its rhetoric, its ability to tap into the discontents of the 'left-behinds' (those who have not benefited from economic and social modernisation) identified by Ford and Goodwin (2014) have progressively embedded the party into the political landscape, picking up on themes of political and social marginalisation. As Figure 12.1 shows, since 2012 the party has been able to build a popular following far beyond what it has previously achieved, breaking out of the European election cycle that it has previously occupied. In part, it has been one of the key beneficiaries of the Liberal Democrats' entry into government in 2010: whereas that party has long occupied the position of the protest vote in British politics, its participation in the coalition has left the way open for UKIP (and others) to pick up those who feel unserved by the system. As Ford and Goodwin (2014) point out,

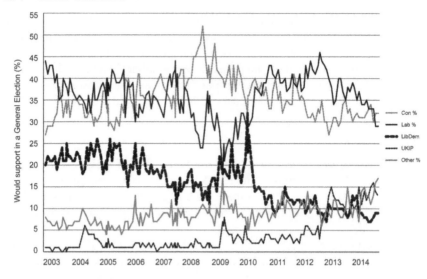

Figure 12.1 General election voting intentions, UK, 2003–2014

membership for the party draws not only from former Tories, but voters from all parties, as well as a significant number of previous non-voters (see Table 12.2). With a membership now in excess of 40,000 (UK Parliament 2015), the party is now in a position where it is treated by broadcast media as a 'major party' (OFCOM 2015), which will further serve to maintain its public profile.

As Table 12.2 highlights, UKIP voters tend to be older, less educated, of lower social class and more male than the average. Even if this does still constitute something of a niche – and one that we might have expected would be squeezed over time by both demographics and economic modernisation – it still represents a much less specialised and particular position than the party occupied in its earlier incarnation. Indeed, it could be argued that as the party has captured much of the electoral market for those disaffected by both political and economic change, there is considerable potential for medium-term success, even if it would require further steps to translate into substantive power.

Goals and strategies

As will be clear from the evidence above, UKIP has changed considerably, both since its foundation in the early 1990s and more recently since 2012. In this section, I will assess why this has occurred. In particular, the tensions between the four goals – office, policy purity, policy influence and votes – set out in the introduction will be explored.

The securing of *office* remains the most distant of the party's objectives. The focus in earlier years on the EP and the nature of the British political system have meant that office-seeking is rather necessarily aspirational. Indeed, it explains why British Euroscepticism has very largely avoided office-seeking as a strategy,

Table 12.2 Breakdown of UKIP voter characteristics

	All voters (%)	UKIP voters, Oct. 2014 (%)
2010 Vote:		
Conservative	37	48
Labour	30	15
Lib Dem	24	17
Other	9	20
Gender:		
Male	49	57
Female	52	43
Age:		
Under 40	37	19
40–59	35	40
60+	29	41
Social Grade:		
ABC1	57	44
C2DE	43	56
Highest Educational Level:		
GCSE or lower	34	52
A-level	16	12
University	27	14
Other	19	18
Home Ownership:		
Own outright	33	40
Mortgage	34	31
All homeowners	67	71
Social Housing	12	15
Private rented	16	12
All renting	28	27

Source: YouGov.

in comparison to other countries where barriers to entry are considerable lower (see Usherwood 2002, 2004). Even where electoral success has been more forthcoming, as in the EP, the decision to not participate in the institution's structures suggests that office is not a priority: instead it is a combination of platform and of funding for other activities. While the apparent breakdown of the two-and-a-half party system in the Commons since 2010 continues, and the possibility of ever-more frequent coalition governments increases, until such time as the party can secure a more substantial number of seats it will continue to pursue other goals.

If office-seeking is not a priority, then *policy purity* is much more important. As was outlined above, while both EU withdrawal and immigration control – the two key policy positions of the party – have been adapted, their core intent remains the same. The shifts in packaging can be understood primarily as responses to the evolving political debate in the UK. For EU policy, that meant an accommodation of the referendum debate since the mid-2000s, while for immigration it was more a case of developing from the core idea that uncontrolled immigration was undesirable. If this latter sounds somewhat vague, then it is another reflection of the absence of ideological underpinning to the party: until the 2010s, the party was largely free to critique other parties' policies, without having to set out alternatives. Even on EU withdrawal, the party has never committed to a particular mechanism for that withdrawal nor to a particular set of new arrangements for relations with the EU and its member states.

Thus the lack of ideology must be seen as a double-edged sword. On the one hand, it allows the party to tack around the changing shoals of contemporary political debate at relatively low cost. On the other, it means that the party does not stand *for* anything, but rather *against* what it doesn't like, which makes for a more difficult pitch to voters. Even the use of classic anti-politics packaging of 'common-sense' and 'changing the system' suffer from the intrinsic limitation that they must ultimately be tested as the party moves more into the mainstream. While this has not reached the point of office-holding, there has certainly been a normalisation of the party into political debate and when Farage does step down as party leader the focus will necessarily fall all the more on the policies.

All of this then sets up a discussion of *policy influence*. With office-holding a very distant prospect, influence becomes a much more central objective, even as the scope of what UKIP would influence has changed. Again, there is a confounding of factors here, since UKIP's primary thrust – on EU membership – has taken place simultaneously with the progressive capture of the Tories by Eurosceptic voices: the pro-integrationists are largely retired or marginalised, while the pragmatists have found it ever harder to contain the critics (Bale 2011). In part, those Tory Eurosceptics have used UKIP as leverage in moving their own party towards a more critical policy position, notwithstanding the increasing evidence that UKIP draws support from across the political spectrum. Certainly, former Tories still represent a very substantial block of UKIP and many commentators still see Farage as the epitome of small-c conservative thinking (Evans and Mellon 2015; Webb and Bale 2014). However, this all remains influence on policy at one remove, since UKIP itself has developed a broader strategy.

In some respects, the party has not so much influenced policy as used its position to exploit the gaps in other parties' approaches. Thus, on immigration, UKIP never really had a clear field to critique policy, but has been able to use its desire to leave the EU to open up an area of immigration control that no other party is willing to use. Similarly, EU withdrawal itself has not had to be hedged about with rhetoric about trying first for reform of the Union, which lets the party cast doubt on the true intentions of others. And beyond this, the policy portfolio is relatively flexible – again in part because of the lack of ideology – which permits opportunistic attacks on policy failures, often refracted through the prism of immigration or the EU. Such an approach echoes the anti-politics, outsider message that the party has cultivated. Policy influence is then partly about securing the two main goals on the EU and immigration, but it is also about a brand management that aims to secure votes.

UKIP has long considered *votes* to be central to its developmental path. At its origin, its single-issue nature made the European elections the obvious focus, and with each passing cycle the growth in success has supported the party's development, both politically and financially. However, since 2004 it has been evident that there would be falling returns from further European success, given the proportional representation electoral system and decline in public interest in European integration. Therefore, attention moved increasingly towards national elections. The local election, 'Liberal Democrat', strategy of building strong local associations has already been discussed, as has the increasing professionalisation of by-election campaigns (with their relatively low cost and high media profile). General elections have been treated somewhat differently, but the increasing vote secured has been used repeatedly by the party to validate its wider relevance in political debate (Tournier-Sol 2015). Ford and Goodwin (2014) talk of a '2020' strategy, whereby the 2015 general election will be used to secure some limited number of MPs, as well as a large number of second places in constituencies, in order to make a much more significant advance in the next general election.

From this overview of the four factors, it is also possible to draw out some wider lessons.

The trend towards a more pragmatic politics within UKIP is evident on several fronts. Most noticeable has been the progressive shift in its rhetoric on the EU itself. This shift has been examined elsewhere (Usherwood 2008), but in essence there has been a development from the initial visceral nature of Euro-scepticism into something wider and more diffuse. This development can be seen as a progression from principled non-engagement, to pragmatic engagement, to developing new policy lines and arenas of activity, to recontextualising the entire opposition to the EU in a wide-ranging notion of 'Independence' (see Gardner 2006 for further discussion). Put differently, the EU is no longer the sole problem, but rather a part of a wider range of challenges that UKIP talks about having to confront: withdrawal from the EU would not bring about the end of the party. As much as the party has pursued a line of withdrawal since its foundation, it has been prepared to buy into a system that gives it some legitimacy through its MEPs, as well as funding. Without doubt, this shift has been in part due to the intrinsic ambiguity of UKIP's 'ideology': built as it is around a negative, the party has always struggled to agree even on the reasons for its opposition, let alone the solutions beyond withdrawal.

The reasons for that lack of ideology are readily apparent. By its exceptionally limited initial goal, the party attracted support from across the political spectrum (Sked himself was a former member of the Liberal party) and even during the late 1990s and early 2000s it retained much of that culture, even as former Conservatives came to predominate. By the time that the party was able to begin raising its profile more – first in European elections and then in national ones – it had broadened its policy base, but in such a way as to leave political space for all comers. The rejection of radical right-wing populist framings of immigration ensured that UKIP did not become trapped into that corner of the political debate – at least in its own perspective: in short, the opposite situation from other radical right-wing populist parties that have tried to escape from that pigeonhole. At the point of the party's acceleration from 2012, the ideological mismatch persists. The core of the leadership, including Farage, can be said to hold libertarian views, something that was an important factor in bringing over Carswell and Reckless in 2014 (certainly more than any consideration of vote-seeking). This includes a strong belief in small government and a wholesale reaffirmation of citizens' rights (see Carswell 2012 for a good overview). However, voters for the party are typically those in relatively precarious economic and social situations – Ford and Goodwin's 'left-behinds' (2014) – who might have been traditional Labour supporters: their interests in preserving an effective and extensive welfare system do not easily marry to those of the core leadership, or even to the more conservative approach of the rest of the party organisation. The result has been an on-going fudging on the underlying values of the party, even in the most cogent (and recent) manifesto produced for the 2015 general election (UKIP 2015). Using the language of populism, the manifesto talks of putting power 'back in the hands of the people' and 'believing in Britain', but frames matters in terms of problems to be solved, rather than values to be achieved.

All of this raises the question of whether UKIP is a populist party. Whether we use the definition given in the first chapter or Albertazzi and McDonnell's (2015) version, there is certainly some sense of 'the people' being held back by assorted 'others': the political system, the media, the EU, and so on. However, it is also important to recognise that both 'the people' and the 'others' are subject to constant change in the party's eyes. In particular, the values ascribed to the people are typically ones that are not exclusive: 'hard-working', 'fair', 'wanting to be free of imposition', for example. Likewise, the others are approached very conditionally: the political system is broken, but it only needs UKIP to gain power to be mended; foreigners are a burden, unless they contribute to the economy and society; and so on. Moreover, while such modulation is to be expected, the rhetoric of populism is not predominant across the party, not least because of its continuing ideological disparity: populism becomes a support to the different currents present, rather than a replacement. Thus Carswell is able to promote his libertarian agenda of political reform alongside spokesmen who talk of expanding the welfare state with the savings from EU withdrawal. While this is not without problems, it does highlight the accommodative nature of the party as a refuge for a wide group of people.

Of course, it is also apparent that the shifting rhetoric has also allowed the party to negotiate and maximise its appeal to voters, not least in opening up new policy areas to its attention: a classic problem for single-issue parties (e.g., Mudde 1999). Bearing in mind the changing profile of popular interests – and more particularly the decline in interest in European integration and the rise of immigration during the 2000s – the development of new strands of political discourse and action gave the party more flexibility than would have been possible under the initial set-up. However, it also has to be recognised that by moving more clearly into the debate on immigration, UKIP continued to expose itself to the problems it has long faced of entryism on the part of the radical right. This exposure is brought up very regularly – particularly around elections – both by other parties and by disillusioned former members. While the party has been able to resist any significant penetration (as discussed above), the fact that such efforts still persist in being made demonstrates the perceived contingency of UKIP's position and the weakness of its internal organisation in forestalling them (Tournier-Sol 2015).

There is a second dimension to this diversification of UKIP's interests. A key frame in the party's discourse has always been one of being an anti-politics actor. However, while that frame has produced certain benefits in EP elections, it does not appear to have paid off in the first-order arena of Westminster. Even when presented with a political expenses scandal that tarred all the major parties and raised very significant debate about the shortcomings of Parliament, UKIP was unable to make a clear advance on its performance in the 2010 general election. In that contest, the Speaker of the Commons, John Bercow, came under much scrutiny and opprobrium for his part in the scandal. With his seat (Buckingham) traditionally not being contested by other parties, this presented an excellent opportunity for UKIP to present itself as an anti-system alternative (in line with Abedi and Lundberg's 2009 model). However, Farage's extensive campaigning was still only able to take third place behind Bercow and a local independent candidate. Across the rest of the country any advance was incremental, rather than revolutionary. It could be argued that this was in part due to a perception of UKIP as a party that did not have the necessary credibility to enter into office.

The 2015 general election reinforced this point. Even with Farage's increased political profile and a more advanced campaigning system, he was unable to secure his target seat of Thanet South, as the other candidates coordinated activity against him, encouraging potential voters for smaller parties to vote tactically against him. Even Carswell's re-election in Clacton came with a considerable reduction in his majority from his by-election eight months earlier. While the securing of almost 120 second places in constituencies across the country does give the party a degree of legitimacy that it could have barely dreamt of a few years previously, it still means that UKIP has to maintain its efforts until the next general election in 2020 before it has any chance of making the next major step towards more institutionalised credibility.

Pragmatism is evident in other areas too. In a very limited sense, there has been some socialisation of MEPs into the EP. As Brack (2013) has shown, while some of UKIP's MEPs avoid the Parliament as much as possible, others have conceived of their role as one of representation, even if that representation is primarily about rejecting the authority of the Parliament. Likewise, they have become much cannier about using the Parliament's rules of procedure to maximise both funding (by forming a political group) and speaking time (both by maximising the number of MEPs in the group and by leading it) in order to further their objectives, especially those of raising their national profile. The archetype in this is Nigel Farage himself, who has made an impact across Europe with his plenary speeches, which are crafted for YouTube viewers and broadcast media rather than for those in the room.

Ultimately, UKIP finds itself in a bind. On the one hand, it could stick to its core policy positions, but at the risk of losing out on the pragmatic possibilities offered by expanding its key messages outside of Euroscepticism. The additional danger here is that scepticism lacks a coherent ideological background – it is a negative dislike of the EU, rather than a positive set of values – and appears to be an ever more marginal concern for most voters. On the other hand, the party could continue to attempt to make the most of the political opportunity structure and adapt itself to push through into a new stage of political profile and impact. While this has been the dominant approach of the past few years, it does come at a price, namely that in the absence of a positive ideological or programmatic worldview, the party is in danger of losing the very qualities that have secured its successes to date. In particular, as Abedi and Lundberg (2009) have noted, if we do treat UKIP as an anti-political establishment party, then the structural difficulties in engineering a step-change in British politics mean that a longer-term approach of gradual normalisation and legitimisation put that anti-system identity in question.

Contextual factors: the political opportunity structure and leadership politics

Throughout this chapter, it has been argued that UKIP is bound by a number of factors that largely sit outside its control. This can be read as a version of Kitschelt's (1986) notion of political opportunity structures, whereby both internal and external factors shape, constrain and encourage practical courses of action by an actor. As a heuristic, such an approach is helpful in understanding UKIP's development as it tries to become a more mainstream actor. In particular, we might consider the impact of the UK's political opportunity structure, as manifested in its electoral systems, and the role of leadership politics, especially under Farage. These two factors have been perhaps the most important in shaping the path that UKIP has taken.

The electoral opportunity structure

UKIP has been adept at exploiting the opportunity structure created by the various electoral systems at play in the UK. From its very foundation, UKIP's leadership recognised that securing House of Commons representation (and ultimately control of a majority) was small enough to be negligible. Sked's academic background and the involvement of a broad church of activists (former Conservative voters only predominated from the late 1990s onwards) at the point of UKIP's foundation meant that there was substantial disagreement about wider political ideology. This in turn put the focus on the EP; even with its first-past-the-post electoral system pre-1999, this was seen to be less important by national parties, allowing protest votes to carry more weight (Rief and Schmidt 1980). The initial aim was to create pressure on the British government of the day by not taking up any seats it might win: 'there is no case in principle or practice for taking up seats in Strasbourg' (*Sunday Telegraph* 24-04-1994). With the introduction of the party list system in 1999, that potential for representation could be taken much further, not least given the unwillingness of Labour and the Conservatives to make much of an issue of European integration at all in subsequent elections (e.g. Rallings and Thrasher 2005). By this point, the party's line had changed, so that any MEPs elected would take their seats, in order to gain a public platform, expose fraud and mismanagement and report on the EU's activities (against the perceived 'conspiracy of silence' of British media unwilling to draw attention to the UK's relationship with the EU, for both political and commercial reasons) (Gardner 2006: 115); a set of objectives somewhat under-mined by the generally very low levels of attendance by most UKIP MEPs through to the present day (see Brack 2013).

The major breakthrough came in 2004, through a very unusual and favourable conjunction of events. From 2003 Dick Morris, previously Bill Clinton's cam-paign manager, worked on the development of a strategy for the 2004 elections of making 'UKIP and "no" synonymous' (Gardner 2006: 174), a much broader and more ambiguous platform than simply withdrawal. This was reinforced by the engagement of two other key individuals. First, publicist Max Clifford, a Euro-sceptic Labour supporter, was contracted for six months to help manage the party's media image. Second, and ultimately more consequentially for the party's public profile, Robert Kilroy-Silk joined the party in April 2004. Kilroy-Silk had been a Labour MP in the 1970s and 1980s, before pursuing a new career as a television presenter. His recruitment to UKIP provoked massive media interest and he was quickly placed at the top of the party list for the Midlands, mixing UKIP policy with his general political message of distrust in 'metropolitan, political-correct elites' (Gardner 2006: 189). The subsequent snowballing of the campaign was apparent in the increased demand for UKIP representatives in the national media (helped by Clifford's contacts) and the massive investment the party poured into campaigning (funded in large part by key individuals such as Paul Sykes and Alan Brown).

The success of the 2004 elections opened up an increasingly strong presence at a European level (see Table 12.1), culminating in the 2014 elections, where the party polled more votes than any other party and won seats in all of the UK's electoral regions. This has also allowed it to take more control of its situation within the Parliament. In 1999, it was a relatively small part of the Europe of Democracies and Diversities (EDD) group, with little voice, but by 2009 it led the formation of the Europe of Freedom and Democracy (EFD) grouping, something it repeated with the Europe of Freedom and Direct Democracy (EFDD) group in 2014. Thus UKIP has been able to reach a point of confirming its structural role in the British EP party political system (Hayton 2010).

However, UKIP has increasingly sought to secure representation in national arenas. This first began at the sub-national level, in local councils, under the leadership of Roger Knapman from 2002, working on the basis that this was how the Liberal Democrats and Green had built up their support base (Gardner 2006: 175). The party's ideological flexibility and the second-orderness of local elections allowed an opportunity to apply the party's populism and pragmatic politics to local issues. This comes even without a strongly defined ideological agenda for local government or its policy competences (cf. UKIP 2010). Thus, the major breakthrough of the 2014 local elections, where the party moved from 2 to 163 local councillors (UK Parliament 2014a), owes at least as much to the simultaneous European elections as to the development of stronger constituency associations.

However, it is the national parliament that has become the prime target for UKIP, not only in the sense of campaigning but also for its continued development and mainstreaming. Regardless of the historical ambivalence towards the EP, there has been ever more recognition that the party can never achieve substantial influence on EU policy in that institution, much less secure British withdrawal from the system. Thus, for both its European ambitions and the rest of its programme, UKIP has turned back to the national arena to secure its objectives. While the party has contested general elections since its foundation (see Table 12.3), it was very much a secondary activity to European elections until at least the late 2000s. Particularly since 2010, when the Conservatives brought in a substantial cohort of new MPs who were much more viscerally anti-EU and less beholden to the party leadership (Bale 2011), UKIP has sought to secure defections, as well as focusing on by-election campaigns. This twin-track strategy, alongside the increasing volume of resource being put into general election campaigning (Electoral Commission n.d.) has provided a mixed picture.

Most successfully, the defection strategy has produced representatives in both the House of Lords and (more recently) the House of Commons, in all cases from former Conservative party members. However, it was only with the Carswell/ Reckless defections in late 2014 that this was underpinned by their re-election by voters: the 2015 general election will thus be an important event for the party in determining how solid that local support might be. Likewise, the progressive improvement in by-elections, especially since 2012 (UK Parliament 2014b), reflects much improved resource management and mobilisation, but it remains to be seen whether this can be replicated in a general election.

General elections remain the most problematic area for the party, despite its improving trajectory. With relatively small amounts of funding available – compared either to other parties or to UKIP's own spending in European elections – the party has not been able to make a breakthrough. The 2015 election marked the

Table 12.3 UKIP's performance in general elections 1997–2015

Year	Candidates fielded (of possible seats)	Number of votes	Deposits saved* (% of candidates)	Seats	% of votes
1997	194 (659)	106,028	1 (0%)	0	0.34
2001	428 (659)	390,575	6 (1%)	0	1.48
2005	496 (646)	603,298	38 (8%)	0	2.20
2010	572 (650)	919,546	99 (17%)	0	3.10
2015	624 (650)	3,888,099	545 (87%)	1	12.80

Note: * Requires at least 5% of vote in constituency.
Source: UK Parliament.

emergence of a somewhat different approach, which was much more focused, driven by increased capacity for campaign management and by a much better understanding of the party's voters, but it still did not translate into seats in the Commons, not least because of the equally targeted efforts of other parties to block UKIP. In the matter of improved profiling of voters, it is important to note the impact of academic research: Ford and Goodwin's *Revolt on the Right* (2014) was the first large-scale analysis of UKIP voters and also produced a list of 'most UKIP-friendly' constituencies, which the UKIP has since used to inform its resource allocation.

Leadership politics under Farage

Nigel Farage has undoubtedly been a transformational leader for UKIP. Even prior to his taking up office in 2006, it could be argued that he had been highly influential in earlier years, not least as one of the party's first MEPs. Since 2006, he has secured a very dominant position in the party structure, which has come with many benefits, but also some costs.

The continuing organisational weakness of the party, coupled to a dearth of experienced party officials to fill posts (cf. Abedi and Lundberg 2009), has made it simple for Farage to build a tight group around himself and Steve Crowther, the party's chairman, which can control policy and resources. Those willing to support this arrangement are brought in, but none is allowed to rise to a position of influence or prominence that might impinge on Farage himself. As the 2015 'unresignation' of Farage demonstrated, there might be substantial discontent with this arrangement, but it can still be contained.

The benefits are clear. As the party's most valuable media (and public) asset, Farage is a key means for UKIP to mobilise voters: even as there has been a move to diversify communications across a large number of people in recent years, Farage remains clearly dominant. While it is also partly a consequence of Farage's tight hold on the party leadership (Usherwood 2008), that is also validated by the strong personal resonance he is able to generate. Moreover, his clear hold on policy has provided a way for the party to overcome the internal divisions of interests mentioned above. Even if this is done more through charismatic staging than through a rigorous and coherent ideological framework, that it has reaped such extensive electoral gains is good enough for most party members.

The downsides are equally clear. The continual marginalisation of other party figures makes any eventual succession much more difficult, especially if Farage intends to retain some role in the party. The events surrounding his aborted resignation in May 2015 highlighted these problems: his perceived value to UKIP, especially in the run-up to a referendum on British membership of the EU, seemed to weigh heavily on many and the thought of replacing him with a lesser figure clearly contributed to enabling his step back from leaving. Even if that choice is vindicated in the referendum, then the manner in which it happened will have called into question whether he is so different from other politicians. Charisma and personalisation are good while they work, but they also tend to come with a hefty price-tag, further down the line (Bynander and 't Hart 2006). As to what Farage's personal motivations and goals might be, these remain rather unclear: in neither of his books (Farage 2010, 2015) does he articulate much more than dissatisfaction with the way politics is done by others and there is a certain sense that he enjoys his work and campaigning for itself, rather than for a higher purpose. His alacrity in stepping back from the party leadership in 2010 to fight the general election is a case in point.

Conclusion

This chapter has argued that UKIP differs from other parties in this collection. While it espouses policy positions that are very close to radical right-wing populist parties in other countries, its ideological trajectory and its position within the national political opportunity structure are fundamentally different. For this reason, it is important that there is not a simple cross-labelling from one to the other: it is very hard indeed to position it on the radical right and there remain questions about its populism.

The ideological vacuum at the centre of UKIP is driven by its particular origins as a cross-party pressure group (in effect) and by its strong determination to resist entry from the radical right during its early phase, when it was most vulnerable. While the party has become a natural for radical right voters, especially with the collapse of the BNP in the 2010s, it has maintained a strict line on this. Certainly it contributed to the unwillingness to join forces with the French FN in the EP in 2014, despite the obvious advantages in financing, speaking time and influence it would have brought the party (Treib 2014): for a party trying to make a break-through in national politics, such an association would have caused too many problems for UKIP. This is also reflected in the evidence that the party appeals not only to those on the right, but across the spectrum, including a substantial minority who think that EU membership is a good thing (Ipsos-Mori 2014).

This last point also highlights the degree to which the party has mobilised support on the basis of an attitude, rather than on specific policies. The 'left-behinds' are motivated less by Euroscepticism than by concerns about the eco-nomic situation since the great recession and by the state of politics in general (Ford and Goodwin 2014). Their worldview is more restricted and parochial than for the population at large, their concerns more focused upon securing their personal needs: consequently, socioeconomic issues tend to play a more domi-nant role, even if it is the rhetorical framing that draws them in. Farage's role as a communicator of that discontent and of a 'return to common sense politics' is central in this, as evidenced by his willingness to make policy decisions on the move and to cast aside those within the party who might jeopardise its profile. With the collapse in the Liberal Democrats' support since 2010, UKIP has been well-placed to pick the votes of those who feel that a change is needed. Indeed, it might be argued that the very opacity of the party's stance on conventionally important matters – most notably, the economy – allow voters to imagine that UKIP would not disrupt those areas, but would simply tidy up around the edges and deal with the annoying things that other parties ignore. Even if the party does not have a coherent approach in those areas, it does still have ideas that – when coupled to EU withdrawal and controls on immigration – would presage major socioeconomic change: it is a mark of the party's success in its rhetorical packaging that this has not been picked up.

If UKIP is rather typical in its opportunistic populism, then it is also striking that this takes place in a political system that is designed to be very unaccommodating of newcomers. The prevalence of first-past-the-post electoral systems and the weakness of sub-national government means that without representation in the Commons there is a constant struggle to secure media coverage. Indeed, one might also observe that even when parties do secure an MP, that does not automatically improve things: this is certainly true of the Green party since 2010, and also arguably of UKIP itself since the 2014 defections, which came at the end of the parliamentary term and were intended to give a boost to the general election campaign in the following spring. Tellingly, neither Carswell nor Reckless were brought into the centre of the party after their defections and re-elections, despite their strong totemic value.

If UKIP has become more mainstream, then it remains only a conditional acceptance. The unexpected election of a majority Conservative government in May 2015 has opened up a referendum on EU membership by the end of 2017. UKIP's (and Farage's) role in that campaign will be highly contested, given the mutual antagonism between the party and other Eurosceptics (both in other parties and more generally in civil society). Moreover, the extended disruption surrounding Farage's 'unresignation' after the 2015 election hints at the difficulties that the party will face in any eventual leadership succession.

While the conditionality of the situation has to be acknowledged, so too must the resilience of the party. Since its foundation in 1992 it has undergone several major internal conflicts and splits. Even the breakthrough success of the 2004 European elections was followed almost immediately by a leadership challenge and a collapse in support and financing (see Gardner 2006 for a potted history). As much as the party remains reliant on a small number of major financial donors and a limited group of professional managers, it has persisted through these set-backs. Whether the '2020' strategy can be brought to fruition remains to be seen, but the party looks set to continue to have an impact on British politics for some time yet.

References

Abedi, A. and Lundberg, T. C. (2009) 'Doomed to failure? UKIP and the organisational challenges facing right-wing populist anti-political establishment parties', *Parliamentary Affairs* 62, 1: 72–87.

Albertazzi, D. and McDonnell, D. (2015) *Populists in Power*, London: Routledge.

Bakker, R., de Vries, C., Edwards, E., Hooghe, L., Jolly, S., Marks, G., Polk, J., Rovny, J., Steenbergen, M. and Vachudova, M.A. (2015) 'Measuring party positions in Europe: The Chapel Hill expert survey trend file, 1999–2010', *Party Politics* 21, 1: 143–152.

Bale, T. (2011) *The Conservative Party: From Thatcher to Cameron*, Cambridge: Polity Press.

Bale, T. and Partos, R. (2014) 'Why mainstream parties change policy on migration: A UK case study–The Conservative Party, immigration and asylum, 1960–2010', *Comparative European Politics* 12, 6: 603–619.

BBC News (04-04-2006) 'UKIP and Cameron's war of words', http://news.bbc.co.uk/1/hi/uk_politics/4875502.stm (accessed 22-10-2015).

BBC News (28-03-2011) 'Voting referendum: William Dartmouth's view', www.bbc.co.uk/news/uk-politics-12606881 (accessed 22-10-2015).

BBC News (24-01-2014) 'Nigel Farage: 2010 UKIP manifesto was "drivel"', www.bbc.co.uk/news/uk-politics-25879302 (accessed 22-10-2015).

Brack, N. (2013) 'Euroscepticism at the supranational level: The case of the "untidy right" in the European Parliament', *JCMS: Journal of Common Market Studies* 51, 1: 85–104.

British Social Attitudes (n.d.) 'British Social Attitudes 2015 edition', www.bsa-data.natcen.ac.uk/ (accessed 27-04-2015).

Bynander, F. and 't Hart, P. (2006) 'When power changes hands: The political psychology of leadership succession in democracies', *Political Psychology* 27, 5: 707–730.

Carswell, D. (2012) *The End of Politics and the Birth of iDemocracy*, London: Biteback Publishing.

Closa, C. (2007) 'Why convene referendums? Explaining choices in EU constitutional politics', *Journal of European Public Policy* 14, 8: 1311–1332.

Daniel, M. (2005) *Cranks and Gadflies: The Story of UKIP*, London: Timewell Press.

Electoral Commission (n.d.) 'Political party spending at previous elections', www.electoralcommission.org.uk/find-information-by-subject/political-parties-campaigning-and-donations/political-party-spending-at-elections/details-of-party-spending-at-previous-elections? (accessed 27-04-2015).

Evans, G. and Mellon, J. (2015) 'Working class votes and Conservative losses: Solving the UKIP puzzle', *Parliamentary Affairs*, doi: 10.1093/pa/gsv005.

Farage, N. (2010) *Fighting Bull*, London: Bite Back.

Farage, N. (2015) *The Purple Revolution*, London: Biteback.

Ford, R. and Goodwin, M. J. (2014) *Revolt on the Right: Explaining Support for the Radical Right in Britain*, London: Routledge.

Gardner, P. (2006) *Hard Pounding: The Story of the UK Independence Party*, Totnes: June Press.

Hayton, R. (2010) 'Towards the mainstream? UKIP and the 2009 elections to the European Parliament', *Politics* 30, 1: 26–35.

Ipsos-Mori (2014) 'Support for EU membership highest for 23 years, even as UKIP rises in the polls', www.ipsos-mori.com/researchpublications/researcharchive/3463/Support-for-EU-membership-highest-for-23-years-even-as-UKIP-rises-in-the-polls.aspx (accessed 27-04-2015).

Ipsos-Mori (n.d.) 'The most important issues facing Britain today', www.ipsos-mori.com/researchpublications/ (accessed 05-08-2011).

Kitschelt, H. (1986) 'Political opportunity structures and political protest: Anti-nuclear movements in four democracies', *British Journal of Political Science* 16, 1: 57–85.

Lynch, P., Whitaker, R. and Loomes, G. (2010) 'The UK Independence Party: A portrait of its candidates and supporters', Briefing Paper No. 2, Competing on the Centre Right series, University of Leicester, www.le.ac.uk/po/centrerightbriefingpapers.html (accessed 19-09-2012).

Mudde, C. (1999) 'The single-issue party thesis: Extreme right parties and the immigration issue', *West European Politics* 22, 3: 182–197.

Mudde, C. (2010) 'The populist radical right: A pathological normalcy', *West European Politics* 33, 6: 1167–1186.

OFCOM (2015) 'Ofcom list of major parties', http://stakeholders.ofcom.org.uk/broadcast/guidance/major-parties-mar14.pdf (accessed 27-04-2015).

Pennings, P. (2002) 'The dimensionality of the EU policy space: The European elections of 1999', *European Union Politics* 3, 1: 59–80.

Rallings, C. and Thrasher, M. (2005) 'Not all "second-order" contests are the same: Turnout and party choice at the concurrent 2004 local and European Parliament elections in England', *British Journal of Politics & International Relations* 7, 4: 584–597.

Rief, K. and Schmidt, H. (1980) 'Nine second-order national elections: A conceptual framework for the analysis of European election results', *European Journal of Political Research* 8, 1: 3–44.

Sunday Telegraph (24-04-1994) 'Sunday Comment: Dear Tory, don't vote Tory on Europe'.

Tonra, B. (2009) 'The 2009 Irish referendum on the Lisbon Treaty', *Journal of Contemporary European Research* 5, 3: 472–479.

Tournier-Sol, K. (2015) 'Reworking the Eurosceptic and Conservative traditions into a populist narrative: UKIP's winning formula?', *Journal of Common Market Studies* 53, 1: 140–156.

Treib, O. (2014) 'The voter says no, but nobody listens: Causes and consequences of the Eurosceptic vote in the 2014 European elections', *Journal of European Public Policy* 21, 10: 1541–1554.

UKIP (2010) 'Empowering the people: 2010 General Election Manifesto', www.ukip.org/page/ukip-manifesto (accessed 19-09-2012).

UKIP (2015) 'The UKIP Manifesto 2015', www.ukip.org/manifesto2015 (accessed 27-04-2015).

Ukipuncovered (2004) 'Damian Hockney statement on party election leaflet', 14 October, http://ukipuncovered.blogspot.com/ (accessed 19-09-2012).

UK Parliament (2014a) 'Local elections 2014', Research papers RP14/33, www.parliament.uk/business/publications/research/briefing-papers/RP14-33/local-elections-2014 (accessed 27-04-2015).

UK Parliament (2014b) 'By-elections since 2010 General Election', Standard notes SN05833, www.parliament.uk/briefing-papers/SN05833/byelections-since-2010-general-election (accessed 27-04-2015).

UK Parliament (2015) 'Membership of UK political parties', Standard notes SN05125, www.parliament.uk/briefing-papers/SN05125/membership-of-uk-political-parties (accessed 27-04-2015).

Usherwood, S. (2002) 'Opposition to the European Union in the UK: The dilemma of public opinion and party management', *Government and Opposition* 37, 2: 211–230.

Usherwood, S. (2004) 'Beyond party politics: Opposition to the European Union in France and the UK, 1985–1999', Doctoral Thesis, London School of Economics.

Usherwood, S. (2008) 'The dilemmas of a single-issue party: The UK Independence Party', *Representation* 44, 3: 255–264.

Webb, P., and Bale, T. (2014) 'Why do Tories defect to UKIP? Conservative Party members and the temptations of the populist radical right', *Political Studies* 62, 4: 961–970.

Conclusions

Tjitske Akkerman

Have radical right-wing populist parties moved from the margins into the mainstream, and why have they (not) done so? An important theoretical framework to explain 'mainstreaming' is provided by the inclusion-moderation thesis, which holds that participation in democratic institutions and procedures will amend the radical nature and ideology of political parties. The inclusion-moderation focuses on electoral competition and office participation, an argument that has been elaborated and qualified in the theoretical framework outlined in Chapter 1 (see Table 1.1). We emphasised that parties do not automatically adapt their behaviour or ideology to changing circumstances. One has to take account of the interaction between environmental changes and the strategies of radical right-wing parties: what goals did radical right-wing populist parties prioritise and what choices did they make when faced with the trade-offs that new opportunities such as office or constraints such as a *cordon sanitaire* implied?

Understanding the concept of moderation as a multi-dimensional concept is key to our approach in this book. We have adopted the term 'mainstreaming' rather than moderation to underline the relative meaning of radicalness. Mainstreaming means that radical parties change to become more like mainstream parties. We have distinguished four dimensions: (1) changes with respect to radical positions on core issues like immigration, EU or authoritarianism; (2) changes from a niche party to a party with a broad policy agenda that equally emphasises sociocultural and socioeconomic issues; (3) changes in anti-establishment profile; and (4) changes with respect to an extremist reputation.

Comparative analyses

Our comparative and quantitative analyses (see Chapter 2) indicate that on the dimensions of radicalness and anti-establishment positions, the trend is not into the mainstream. Radical right-wing populist parties tend, on average, to remain radical. Their positions on immigration and integration and on authoritarianism have moved further away from average mainstream positions since the turn of the millennium. Only with respect to European integration there has been some mainstreaming. Neither have the parties moderated their anti-establishment ideology. On average, radical right-wing populist parties have become more populist after the turn of the millennium. Only with respect to 'nicheness' is there some evidence for mainstreaming. Although the emphasis on socio-cultural issues has on average increased, there has also been more attention for socioeconomic issues during the past decade.

All parties included in the comparative analyses have participated in democratic, electoral competition, and they have often done so successfully. Nevertheless, our comparative analyses make clear that inclusion into electoral competition is not an incentive for radical right-wing populist parties to become less radical or populist. The Downsian logic does not seem to apply in these respects. Downs argued that electoral competition will incite parties to appeal to the median voter in order to attract a majority of voters. Over time, this vote-seeking logic will force parties to amend their narrow and sectarian appeals. The electoral strategies of most radical right-wing parties, however, are not aiming at the median voter, but at a niche of the electoral market.

The analysis of voter profiles (see Chapter 3) confirms that radical right-wing populist parties do not appeal to the median voter. The gap between the profiles of voters of radical right-wing populist parties and those of mainstream parties has remained relatively stable between 2002 and 2012. Regarding socioeconomic status, differences between these two groups of voters have not diminished: voters for radical right-wing populist parties are lower educated and their positions on the labour market tend to be more characterised by unskilled or manual work. In other words, the distinct profiles of voters for radical right-wing populist parties and for mainstream parties as 'losers' or 'winners' of globalisation have not changed. The attitudes of radical right-wing populist voters are also distinct from those of mainstream parties. Radical right-wing populist voters hold strong and negative attitudes towards immigration, and they tend to be more negative about European integration. The differences with mainstream voters in policy pre-ferences have not decreased with respect to immigration in the period 2002–2012, but the gap has narrowed with respect to European integration. However, this is not due to the mainstreaming of radical right-wing populist voters, but inversely to the radicalisation of mainstream voters. Only on one indicator do we find evidence for mainstreaming. On average, voters for radical right-wing populist parties tend to be more dissatisfied with politics than voters from main-stream parties. In some cases we observe temporary mainstreaming, with radical right-wing populist voters becoming somewhat more satisfied with politics, also compared to mainstream voters. However, the gap with mainstream voters appears to have been re-established in recent years. Overall, since the beginning of this millennium there is a distinct gap between voters of main-stream parties and radical right-wing populist voters, and the latter have not mainstreamed.

Inclusion into office may have incited some parties to moderate their radical positions or broaden their policy agendas to socioeconomic issues (see Chapter 2). It should be noted though that other factors could also have played a role. For instance, changes in the salience of issues in the manifestos of radical right-wing populist parties correspond to general shifts in salience in the party system during the past decade. The financial and economic crisis that broke out in 2008 could therefore also be an important incentive for radical right-wing populist parties to pay more attention to socioeconomic issues. The case studies in this volume assess in depth whether, how and why radical right-wing populist parties have mainstreamed.

Case studies

In the case studies, mainstreaming has been assessed with the help of contextual, quantitative as well as qualitative data, and strategic choices and opportunities have been analysed to explain why particular parties have (de-)mainstreamed.

All Western European radical right-wing populist parties that have been selected for the case-studies in this book – DF, FN, FPÖ, FrP, PS, PVV, SVP, VB and UKIP – are parties that fully participate in democratic elections. Most parties, apart from VB, FN and UKIP, also have had opportunities to enter national office. Various parties are still young with a relative short socialisation in democratic electoral competitions, representation or office. The SVP and the FPÖ were already vested parties before they renewed their ideological profile and joined the radical right populist party family. The PS did not have to start from scratch either, but were formed as a successor party to an agrarian populist party in 1995. The others are new parties that emerged in the 1970s or later, but not all of them started out as radical right-wing populist parties. As the case studies in this volume show, the specific historical trajectories and origins of radical right-wing populist parties are important for their later development.

All these parties have managed electoral breakthroughs at one time or another, and gathered sufficient electoral strength and issue attention through media coverage to be able to put pressure on the policy agendas of political competitors. They also have blackmail potential in the sense that they have been able to politicise issues like immigration, European integration or law and order issues, which forced other parties to amend their policy agendas. Some of the parties, however, have a hard time to execute their blackmail potential through representation in parliament. Majority systems make it hard for FN and UKIP to gain access to parliament. These parties also have great difficulty in gaining coalition potential. While FN and UKIP face an electoral system that raises high hurdles for new parties, VB lacks coalition potential mainly because it has been subjected to a *cordon sanitaire* by other parties. The other radical right-wing populist parties described in this book – DF, FPÖ, FrP, PS, PVV, SVP – all have at one time or another managed to gain coalition potential. DF and SVP have participated in national office more than once, FPÖ, FrP, PS and PVV have a one-time experience. It should be noted that coalition potential can be gained but also can be lost again. The PVV, for instance, has squandered a great deal of its coalition potential in 2012, when it withdrew its support and caused the fall of the then reigning cabinet.

On the inclusion-exclusion continuum we can range the parties as follows:

- SVP, DF: parties with the longest history of (semi-) inclusion into national office and continuous blackmail and coalition potential;
- FrP, PS, FPÖ, PVV: parties with incidental or recent (semi-)inclusion into national office, substantial blackmail potential, but varying coalition potential;
- UKIP, FN, VB: parties with blackmail potential, but excluded from national office and lacking coalition potential.

SVP

The SVP is an exceptional case, as it has, in contrast to all other radical right-wing populist parties, never lacked coalition potential. When the SVP was constituted in 1971 it became, like its agrarian conservative predecessor, a fully-fledged member of government. The party underwent a profound ideological transformation in the 1990s from a conservative right-wing party to a radical right-wing populist party as part of a vote-seeking strategy. The declared aim to become the leading right-wing party in Switzerland – in the proportional elections for the lower chamber of the Federal Assembly – was realised in 1999, and the party has preserved this leading position over time. Vote-seeking has incited the party to maintain and even increase its radical profile, especially with respect to immigration. The party cultivated an anti-establishment profile as well, reverting to uncompromising parliamentary behaviour and emphasising the illegitimacy of the Swiss government and the Swiss 'political class'. The SVP succeeded in doing so while in office, thanks to favourable organisational, institutional and inter-party opportunities. Swiss federal government is a rare example of a regime without alternating governments and without a common legislature programme, enabling the parties to enjoy a considerable level of autonomy with respect to their representatives in government and vice versa. Moreover, without the opportunities offered by Swiss direct democracy, it would be virtually impossible for the SVP to consolidate its radicalisation over time. However, the SVP never was transformed into a pure anti-establishment and radical niche party. The old wing within the SVP and its representative in government remained moderate and cooperative. The right-wing socioeconomic agenda of the SVP also often enables the party to logroll. Nor did the SVP have to fear 'demonisation' as a party with impeccable origins and being a long-term government party. Its coalition potential has been unquestioned. There has never been any kind of *cordon sanitaire* or attempt to discredit its institutional and governmental role.

DF

The DF is also a party with a long and successful office trajectory, be it as a support party rather than a full-blown governing party. The DF was a semi-office party from 2001 till 2011 and has regained this position in 2015.

Notwithstanding this long association with office, the DF has only partially mainstreamed with respect to core issues such as immigration, EU and law and order issues. DF managed sometimes to logroll on its core issues when entering government. Yet, the party has also somewhat moderated its radical profile during its (semi-) office position. DF also has been successful in maintaining its niche profile, although the party recently has extended its attention to socioeconomic issues and has begun to support leftist welfare positions. The party has most clearly mainstreamed in the sense that it proved itself to be a loyal support party which conformed to the political rules and mores. Even in opposition DF has mainly behaved as a 'housetrained' party. The party did not have to cope with a history that evoked associations with or accusations of classic extremism. Yet, the anti-immigration profile of DF attracted hardcore members, and high-ranking members sometimes overstepped boundaries regarding racism or discrimination. While the party leadership has been careful to discipline and expel racist lower-ranking members, high-ranking members have been afforded more leeway in this respect. DF has overall been fairly successful in maintaining a radical niche profile, but the party has more difficulty in combining its increasing commitment to leftist welfare issues with office aspirations. DF has not yet managed to become acceptable as a full-blown government party, but also seems unwilling to pursue such a position.

FrP

The FrP has a relatively moderate ideological profile, and the party has further mainstreamed since the beginning of the new millennium. The programmatic appeal was further expanded and the party was no longer campaigning exclusively on anti-immigration. Prior to the national election in 2001, it was decided to focus less on the immigration issue. FrP moderated its anti-immigration rhetoric, but the actual anti-immigration policies remained equally radical. FrP also mainstreamed its reputation. With its respectable origins and pro-Israel position, the FrP has not been associated with classic extremism, even though the party has attracted right-wing extremists. Office-seeking induced the party leadership to improve its reputation and to distance itself clearly by expelling extremist members in the late 1990s. At that time, the party was widely perceived by the public as racist. In parliament, however, the relationship with other parties continued to be characterised by ambivalence and lack of mutual trust. The gradual transformation toward the mainstream was fortified after Siv Jensen replaced the longstanding chairman, Carl I. Hagen, in 2006. Since then, the anti-establishment behaviour in parliament diminished and FrP gradually moved in the direction of the other parties. The gradual transformation towards a mainstream party has been reinforced after the party entered office in 2013. Before entering government in 2013, the FrP had already been a reliable support party of two cabinets. While the party began with mainstreaming its reputation, its niche profile and radical anti-immigration rhetoric, office-seeking induced the party to further mainstream. The FrP has more recently also tempered its anti-establishment profile and has become less radical with respect to core issues. This has created tension within the party and a division has begun to emerge between the party in government and the party in parliament.

PS

PS is an offspring from an agrarian populist party, and since its formation in 1995 the party's reputation has not seriously been questioned. To gain coalition potential, however, legitimacy is not sufficient. Blackmail potential through electoral power is also required. PS reached this stage when it spectacularly increased its vote share in 2009 and 2011. Its radicalisation with respect to immigration and European integration and its anti-establishment appeals contributed largely to these results. Although the radicalisation on immigration has brought about accusations of racism, PS faces a relatively comfortable situation. Media and most mainstream parties have defended the reputation of the party, and only some minor Finnish parties have questioned its reputation. Yet, the PS has not put much effort into disciplining representatives or members who were accused of or sentenced in court for racism. Soon after its electoral breakthrough the party was invited to take part in government negotiations, but a vote-seeking strategy and organisational reasons withheld the leadership from accepting the offer. In 2015, PS became member of a centre-right government. The main policy costs that PS fears are with respect to European integration and socio-economic policy. PS has from the beginning combined its radical and populist profile with a centrist position on socioeconomic issues. The latter has given PS an advantage as a median legislator party that includes the mainstream left in its range of potential coalition partners. This centrist position also requires compromise, though, now that PS has entered a centre-right coalition.

FPÖ

The FPÖ has been more successful than the PVV (see below) in regaining its coalition potential, even though the party also gave up office and broke away from a coalition with the ÖVP in 2005. The FPÖ was organisationally not well prepared for office, but in contrast to the PVV, the party had followed an office-seeking strategy by mainstreaming on all dimensions before entering a coalition government in 2000. The FPÖ did not have a strong reputational shield, but had been pressed to distance itself unambiguously from Nazism in the late 1990s in order to become coalitionable. In office, the party did not manage to keep up a radical policy profile, and it also lost electoral support due to its commitment to social insurance reform and welfare state restructuring. After office, the FPÖ reverted to an unambiguous vote-seeking strategy by emphasising and radicalising its positions on immigration and European integration again. After its success in the national elections of 2013, the FPÖ is contemplating public office again and adopting a more moderate tone with respect to Islam and immigration. More recently the party also has begun distancing itself again from associations with classic extremism in order to capitalise on its coalition potential. The FPÖ thus mainstreamed when participating in office and again recently as part of a renewed office-seeking strategy, but it is questionable whether this is an enduring effect. The party reverted to a radical vote-seeking strategy when in opposition.

PVV

The PVV has a strong reputational shield as it not only descends from a respectable mainstream party, but also is protected against accusations of anti-Semitism through its pro-Israel profile. This reputational shield together with electoral success made the party very soon after its foundation coalitionable. The PVV did not seek office, however, but stumbled into it in 2010. As a formal support party of a minority government, the party mainstreamed with respect to its anti-establishment behaviour and to some extent on immigration policies, but the PVV also fully used the free room left in the coalition agreement with respect to Islam. Although the PVV had managed to logroll, its leftist positions on care and social security made it difficult for the party to commit itself to the stepping up of austerity policies along the way. Most importantly, however, the party was not ready organisationally for semi-office. After the PVV brought about a premature ending of the minority government in 2012, the coalition potential of the PVV dwindled. Mainstream right parties excluded the option of governing with the PVV again. Political isolation has incited the PVV to boost electoral pressure in order to strengthen its blackmail potential and to regain coalition potential. Party leader Wilders tried to enhance the anti-immigration and anti-establishment profile of the party by provocative statements which attracted media-attention and electoral support. Accusations of racism and pending court cases have been the result, which in case of conviction may affect the legitimacy of the party negatively and secure its political isolation.

FN

The French FN is a party that still lacks opportunities for office. A small number of alliances between FN and the mainstream right have recently occurred, but only on the local level. The party has only incidentally mainstreamed its radical and populist agenda. The FN experienced a short-lived period of de-radicalisation with respect to core issues such as immigration and with respect to its anti-establishment rhetoric, primarily around 2007. External electorally related shocks in 2002 and 2007 explain this temporary mainstreaming. Under Marine Le Pen, however, radical and populist appeals have made a full comeback. Only on the local level, where FN seeks strategic alliances, has the party moderated its anti-establishment behaviour. The party has changed in other respects though. The FN has broadened the scope of its agenda and increasingly emphasised socioeconomic issues like unemployment and purchasing power. Yet, the party has maintained a distinctive niche profile in comparison to mainstream parties. The only evident mainstreaming can be observed with respect to its extremist reputation. Under Marine Le Pen efforts have been made to 'de-demonise' the party. The FN leadership is seeking to get away from the legacy of the French extreme right by publicly rebuking members who vented anti-Semitic or racist opinions and by making efforts to break the ties to hardcore nationalist and extreme right groups. This partial mainstreaming is incited by vote-seeking. The majority system in France with its high levels of disproportionality and the necessity to build competitive alliances forces the FN to enhance optimal electoral pressure in order to break the *cordon sanitaire* and to gain office.

UKIP

UKIP also lacks coalition potential due to the British plurality voting system. Like the FN it has great difficulty in gaining representation in parliament notwithstanding substantive electoral support. Both parties, therefore, follow a two-tier strategy by pursuing coalition potential through local alliances while maintaining an anti-establishment profile on the national level. In contrast to the FN, however, UKIP has respectable origins as a single-issue party led by intellectuals who distanced themselves from any association with the far right. The party lacks a strong nativist ideology and has been careful to distance itself from the far right. Its messages about immigration are relatively moderate and the leadership has rejected the infiltration of members of the BNP or other racist parties or groups and has been swift to expel them in cases that have come to light. Yet, when UKIP began to compete on immigration issues it became more difficult to keep up its respectable reputation. The party can be characterised as a populist and nationalist niche party, campaigning mainly on immigration and European integration, but with a relatively strong mainstream orientation. UKIP is therefore a party that contradicts our expectation that parties with little or no coalition potential will mainstream less than parties with such potential. Office has remained a very distant goal for the party. Like the FN, UKIP faces a political system that requires a broad vote-seeking strategy in order to gain representation and to acquire coalition potential in the long run. In contrast to FN, however, the origins of UKIP as a non-ideological party still linger on in a pragmatic and relatively moderate profile.

VB

The VB also has not managed to acquire coalition potential due to a *cordon sanitaire*. The party mainstreamed to some extent under pressure of the courts by changing its name and programme in 2004. However, internal tensions about a detoxification strategy remained; the leadership sometimes demonstrated an ambivalent position and seemed willing to install a firm and unambiguous discipline vis-à-vis individual members. Although the VB moderated its xenophobic rhetoric, the party maintained a radical programme with respect to immigration, law and order issues and Flemish independence. These issues remained highly salient, although there were incidental efforts to reach out to voters who were most concerned about socioeconomic issues. The party temporarily moderated its anti-establishment style as part of its reputation management and as part of a local office-seeking strategy. However, the VB lacked a clear strategy with respect to gaining coalition potential. The leadership sometimes embraced the *cordon sanitaire* as an electoral opportunity, using its exclusion by established parties to appeal to dissatisfied voters. The leadership seemed unwilling to make a choice between a long-term majority strategy that required little ideological compromise on the one hand and a coalition strategy on the other hand. After the electoral decline of the VB became apparent in 2009 and 2010, tensions came into the open and moderates left the party. Political isolation and electoral loss incited VB foreman Dewinter to step up anti-immigration messages again. This renewed radicalisation, copied in part from the PVV – its Dutch ally in the European Parliament – has incited new complaints of racism. The party, or at least Dewinter, seems to accept a lack of coalition potential and to choose 'splendid isolation'. He also seems willing to test legal boundaries and bear the costs of reputation damage in exchange for a clearly differentiated and strong ideological profile.

Partial mainstreaming

The case studies as well as the comparative analyses confirm that it is important to distinguish multiple dimensions of mainstreaming. While there has been relatively little mainstreaming on the dimensions of radicalness, there has been partial or substantial mainstreaming on the other three dimensions.[1]

Radicalness

The case studies confirm that radical right-wing populist parties have overall remained radical in their positions on issues related to their nationalist ideology such as immigration, authoritarianism and European integration. Exceptions are the FrP and to some extent the DF and FN.[2] FN has incidentally moderated, but has resumed its radical course again recently. While the FN moderated incidentally as part of a vote-seeking strategy, the FrP and to some extent the DF have mellowed their radical positions due to office-seeking and participation in office. PS moderated its positions on European integration when entering office. However, office is not an effective pressure to mainstream. When in office, some parties manage to prevent or soften compromises with regard to their core issues; logrolling on immigration versus socioeconomic issues (DF, PVV), agreements to disagree on Islam (PVV), initiating referendums about immigration or Islam (SVP); these are ways out of coalition pressure to mainstream. The FPÖ and PVV mainstreamed only to some extent when in office, and reverted to a radical vote-seeking strategy again when in opposition. The SVP did not mainstream at all.

Anti-establishment ideology and behaviour

The most sustainable change is apparent with respect to anti-establishment profiles. This conclusion may seem somewhat surprising when one sticks to the comparative analysis in Chapter 2, which showed that almost all parties had become increasingly populist since the turn of the millennium. The comparative analysis, however, was restricted to populist ideas. Although radical right-wing populist parties do not soften their populist *ideology*, the case studies make clear that their anti-establishment *behaviour* clearly changes when pursuing office or when participating in government. In many cases, office-seeking or participation induces the parties to adapt their role in parliament. They moderate their lone opposition and increasingly cooperate with other parties in parliament. Various parties have acted as trustworthy coalition partners and demonstrated the ability to conform to political rules and mores. The DF, FrP, and PS all have built up a solid reputation of 'housetrained' parties. The FPÖ and PVV also acted as trustworthy parties when in office. At first sight, the SVP is an exceptionable party as it became more radical and anti-establishment while in office. However, the SVP also has remained in many respects a housetrained party when its behaviour in the executive and in parliament is considered. The expectation that office-seeking and participation will compel radical right-wing populist parties to mainstream is confirmed in this respect. However, inclusion into office also implies an increasing gap between the rhetoric and the behaviour of radical right-wing populist parties.

Niche profiles

With respect to niche profiles, radical right-wing populist parties appear to be rather flexible. Especially when pursuing office they tend to broaden their attention to socioeconomic issues. It is interesting to note that various radical right-wing populist parties have shifted to the left with respect to welfare state restructuring. This tends to be a complication and sometimes a hurdle in their office-seeking strategies insofar as radical right-wing populist parties are mainly dependent on right-wing parties as coalition partners. The more they commit themselves to leftist socioeconomic promises on welfare state issues, the more they are bound to disappoint voters in government coalitions with right-wing parties and the more difficult it will be to compromise with mainstream right-wing coalition partners. For the PVV and the FPÖ this contributed to a premature ending of office participation. The DF also faced these difficulties incidentally when supporting a centre-right minority government in the past, and will increasingly do so now that it has begun to emphasise a leftist position more. On the other hand, the PS has a long centre-left position on socioeconomic issues and the party keeps its options open with regard to left-wing or right-wing partners. The FPÖ also has recently hinted at a coalition with the SPÖ. The more radical right-wing populist parties are emphasising their socioeconomic centrist positions – left-wing with regard to welfare state restructuring but right-wing with

278   *Tjitske Akkerman*

respect to other socioeconomic issues such as taxes – the more they will risk disappointing a part of their voters during incumbency. On the other hand, the increased emphasis on a centrist socioeconomic position brings the advantage of a median legislator party with extended coalition options.

Extreme right reputation

Finally, an extreme right reputation appears to be a highly important issue for almost all radical right-wing populist parties. Classic extremism – that is anti-Semitism, classic racism and/or positive references to Nazism or Fascism – is mostly associated with the FN, FPÖ and VB, because these parties have origins in extreme right and hardcore nationalist subcultures. However, radical right-wing populist parties generally risk being branded as racist due to their nativist ideology and anti-immigration positions. Competing for media attention and electoral support on this niche segment requires radical right-wing populist parties to balance between becoming respectable and legitimate, on the one hand, and maintaining a clear and differentiated ideological profile as a nationalist party, on the other hand. Overall, radical right-wing populist parties tend to avoid a classic extremist reputation, partly out of fear of legal repercussions, but also for office-seeking and vote-seeking reasons. Office-seeking is an important incentive in the case of the FPÖ, but the 'de-demonisation' strategy of the FN shows that vote-seeking can also incite parties to mainstream in this respect. That is not to say that radical right-wing populist parties will refrain from testing the boundaries with respect to new cultural and nationalist conflicts such as those related to immigration of Muslims and anti-Islam positions in order to enhance an ideological profile. Especially when office becomes a distant goal, due to political isolation or substantial electoral loss, parties may seek to enhance their ideological profile. The VB and PVV, for instance, have lately reverted to de-mainstreaming their reputation. Other parties on and off display an ambivalent attitude towards disciplining individual members. The FPÖ, for example, is not consistently mainstreaming its reputation, but becomes stricter when office-seeking. The PS does not discipline individual members even when it is office-seeking or in office. The party does not face much 'demonisation' by other parties and can afford to remain ambivalent. The DF has mainstreamed, but still refrains from disciplining members belonging to the party elite. UKIP has been comparably strict in protecting its reputation. The party was swift to expel individuals or to take disciplinary action against any member who expressed discriminatory views. The SVP has not suffered 'demonisation' either due to its impeccable origins and its ongoing government status.

The inclusion–moderation thesis revisited

The trajectories of radical right-wing parties appear to be quite diverse. The inclusion-moderation thesis is a good starting point to explain why radical right-wing parties have (not) mainstreamed, but the comparative analyses and case studies make clear that it needs to be amended in some fundamental respects.

Inclusion into what?

First, the inclusion-moderation thesis is partially inadequate in the case of radical right-wing populist parties. Electoral competition generally does not pressure radical right-wing parties to moderate, because the Downsian logic hardly applies. These parties do not tend to aim at the median voter. Exceptions to this finding, however, are FN and UKIP. These parties have to compete in electoral systems that give them little choice but to aim at a majority of voters. Only electoral systems, therefore, that require a plurality or majority will have a moderating effect on the inclusion of radical right-wing populist parties.

The inclusion-moderation thesis is more relevant with respect to inclusion into office. This is an important incentive for mainstreaming, but office also needs to be qualified. The cases of DF and SVP demonstrate that office is a term that refers to highly diverse pressures. While the semi-office role of DF has provided the party opportunities to partially hold up its radical profile, the full participation in office of the SVP has implied even less pressure to mainstream. The Swiss political system is exceptional as it has no alternating governments and governments lack a common legislature programme. Direct democracy also enables the SVP to participate in office and to still maintain a radical and anti-establishment profile.

Environmental changes

Second, inclusion or exclusion are not sufficient to explain (non-)mainstreaming. There are other environmental changes that need to be included. First, external shocks play an important role in party change (Harmel and Janda 1994). External shocks that figure largely in the literature about policy or party change are economic and financial crises and sudden electoral losses/success (Abedi and Lundberg 2009; Bale and Partos 2014; Burchell 2001; Duncan 2007; Müller 1997; Nohrstedt 2005). The case studies confirm that sudden electoral losses pressure parties to change, but that it is an open question in which direction. FN, for instance, was shocked by the disappointing election results in 2002 and 2007, but the two events had opposite results. FN began to moderate after 2002, but when the elections of 2007 were also disappointing, the party de-mainstreamed again. VB was also shocked by electoral losses in 2009 and 2010, and the subsequent conflict within the party and the exit of moderates pressured the party to radicalise rather than to mainstream. Sudden electoral success also is an important factor. The PVV reverted to office-seeking under pressure of its electoral success in 2010.

Socioeconomic shocks should also be taken into account. The financial and economic crisis that broke out in 2008 has pressured radical right-wing parties to pay more attention to socioeconomic issues. Long-term social changes can be important with respect to the internal composition of radical right-wing parties. Especially parties with origins in extreme right and xenophobic nationalist subcultures face internal constraints when they moderate their ideological profiles.

Demographic changes in party composition may soften these constraints. A change of generation among leading elites is, for instance, apparent in the FN. Origins are more generally important for the internal constraints and opportunities of parties. UKIP, for instance, still maintains features of its original character as an intellectual and pragmatic party.

Strategies and goals

Third, the inclusion-moderation thesis focuses on opportunities and constraints. The role of parties as actors that make decisive choices when facing environmental changes is not sufficiently taken into account in this thesis. In contrast, theories of party change derived from the framework elaborated by Harmel and Janda and their co-authors (Harmel and Janda 1994; Harmel and Tan 2003; Harmel *et al.* 1995; Janda *et al.* 1995) have the advantage that they give a central role to parties as actors. The case studies confirm this crucial role. Whether parties mainstream not only depends on their inclusion or exclusion, but also on the choices they make. FN, UKIP and VB lack coalition potential due to the political system in which they have to operate and/or a *cordon sanitaire* installed by other parties. Yet, strategic choices are important. As the case studies make clear, VB has sometimes embraced the *cordon sanitaire* as an electoral opportunity – using its exclusion by established parties to appeal to dissatisfied voters – rather than trying to weaken it by displaying its willingness to cooperate with other parties. FN, in contrast, has set out a 'de-demonisation' course that makes it increasingly difficult for mainstream parties to keep up the *cordon sanitaire*, and the party has also waged a cooperative strategy at the local level. It is therefore important to look both at strategic goals and at opportunities to understand the different trajectories of radical right-wing populist parties.

Parties with office opportunities have a strong incentive to move into the mainstream, but they are not always willing or able to do so. Parties generally, and radical right-wing populist parties in particular, have good reasons to be wary of changing an ideological profile that has brought them electoral advantages. Changes in ideology and policy may cost voters or raise internal tensions. Radical right-wing populist parties tend to face relatively hard trade-offs between office, policy and votes. Vote-seeking is highly important for these parties, because voters and activists supporting these parties tend to value policy purity and the parties are often strongly bound to their electoral promises. Moreover, they need electoral pressure to improve their relatively weak positions in coalition negotiations. Yet, they seldom refuse participation in office when the opportunity arises, and they seldom voluntarily leave office. Of the parties included in the case studies, only PS declined to govern after the 2011 elections, and the PVV actively brought down the government which it supported in 2012. The FPÖ split during incumbency in 2005; the BZÖ remained in government, the rest of the party left government under the name of the FPÖ. Overall, however, radical right-wing populist parties find it hard to resist office opportunities. The opportunity of national office sometimes takes them by surprise as in the case of the FPÖ and the PVV. Even though these parties were not prepared for office they did not decline. Rather than denying the opportunity of office, most radical right-wing populist parties seek to amend hard trade-offs by limiting the necessity to soften their radical and anti-establishment profiles.

Radical right-wing populist parties are sometimes characterised as short-term vote-seekers and long-term office- and policy-seekers. That is only true for those radical right-wing populist parties with little or no coalition potential. Parties like the FN and UKIP that face a political system with high hurdles for newcomers will have to rely on a long-term strategy for office-seeking. They are necessarily short-term vote-seekers. Ostracised parties like the VB or politically isolated parties like the PVV also will be tempted to rely primarily on vote-seeking. Radical right-wing populist parties that have coalition potential will seek to capitalise on it. As office-seekers and once in office, however, they will try to limit ideological change in order to confine incumbency costs. As their main vote-seeking strategy is to compete on niche segments of the electoral market, this requires them to keep up a differentiated and strong ideological profile on core issues like immigration, authoritarianism or European integration.

Notes

1 It should be noted though that the parties included in the comparative analyses (see Chapter 2) vary due to the different datasets used for the dimensions of radicalness, nicheness and populism. Moreover, quantitative and comparative data of the parties were not (fully) available for all the parties central to the case studies. With these restrictions in mind, though, we can conclude that the case studies confirm to a large extent the results of the comparative analyses.
2 Some case studies qualify the results of the comparative analyses slightly. While DF and FN were identified as the only parties that were mainstreaming with respect to immigration/integration in the comparative analyses (see Chapter 2 and Appendix), the case study about the FN (see Chapter 11) underlines the incidental character of this aspect of mainstreaming. The case study of DF only partially confirms that DF has moderated its policy programme with respect to immigration (see Chapter 5). The case study of the VB confirms that the party maintained its radical programme with respect to immigration and authoritarianism, but underlined that the VB moderated its xenophobic rhetoric.

References

Abedi, A. and Lundberg, T. C. (2009) 'Doomed to failure? UKIP and the organisational challenges facing right-wing populist anti-political establishment parties', *Parliamentary Affairs*, 62, 1: 72–87

Bale, T. and Partos, R. (2014) 'Why mainstream parties change policy on migration: A UK case study – The Conservative Party, immigration and asylum, 1960–2010', *Comparative European Politics*, 12, 6: 603–619.

Burchell, J. (2001) 'Evolving or conforming? Assessing organisational reform within European green parties', *West European Politics*, 24, 3: 113–134.

Duncan, F. (2007) '"Lately, things just don't seem the same": External shocks, party change and the adaptation of the Dutch Christian Democrats during "Purple Hague" 1994–1998', *Party Politics*, 13, 1: 69–87.

Harmel, R. and Janda, K. (1994) 'An integrated theory of party goals and party change', *Journal of Theoretical Politics* 63, 3: 259–287.

Harmel, R. and Tan, A. (2003) 'Party actors and party change: Does factional dominance matter?', *European Journal of Political Research* 42, 3: 409–424.

Harmel, R., Heo, U., Tan, A. and Janda, K. (1995) 'Performance, leadership, factions and party change: An empirical analysis', *West European Politics* 18, 1: 1–33.

Janda, K., Harmel, R., Edens, C. and Goff, P. (1995) 'Changes in party identity: Evidence from party manifestos', *Party Politics* 1, 2: 171–196.

Müller, W. C. (1997) 'Inside the black box: A confrontation of party executive behaviour and theories of party organizational change', *Party Politics* 3, 3: 293–313.

Nohrstedt, D. (2005) 'External shocks and policy change: Three Mile Island and Swedish nuclear energy policy', *Journal of European Public Policy* 12, 6: 1041–1059.

Appendix

Position and salience scores of radical right-wing populist parties and average scores of other/centre parties per country.

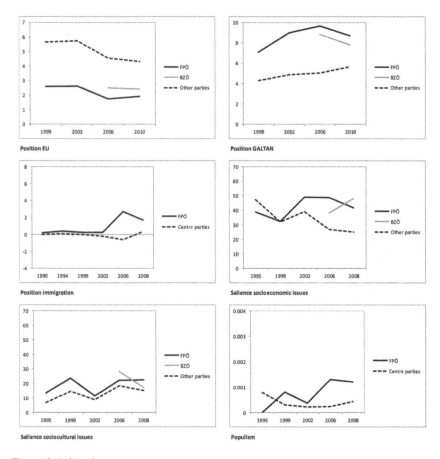

Figure A.1 Austria

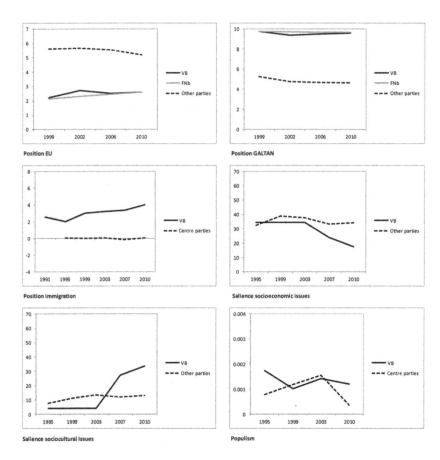

Figure A.2 Belgium

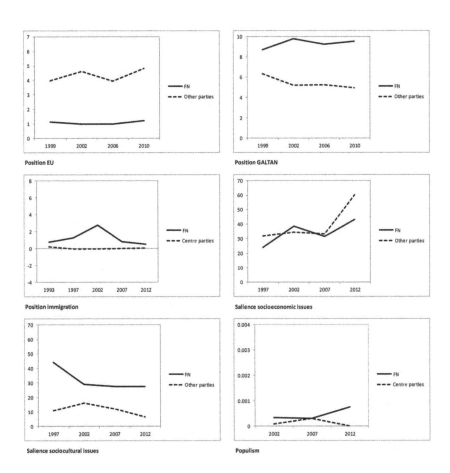

Figure A.3 France

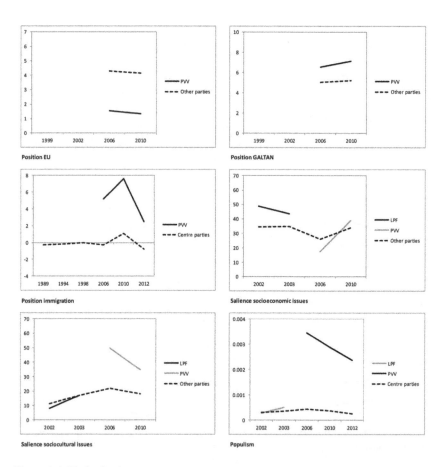

Figure A.4 Netherlands

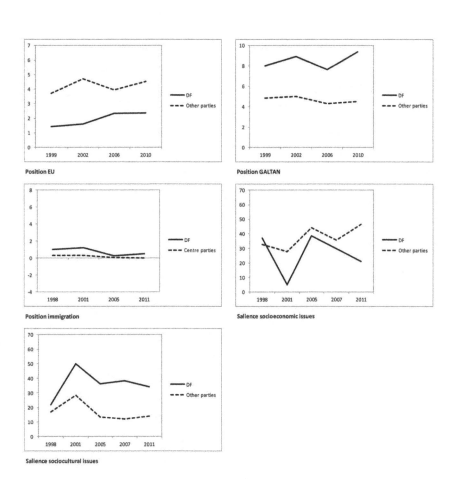

Figure A.5 Denmark

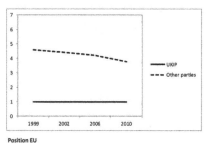

Position EU

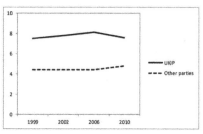

Position GALTAN

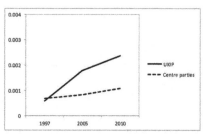

Populism

Figure A.6 UK

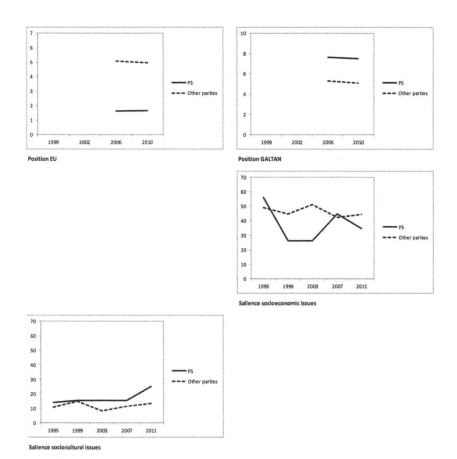

Figure A.7 Finland

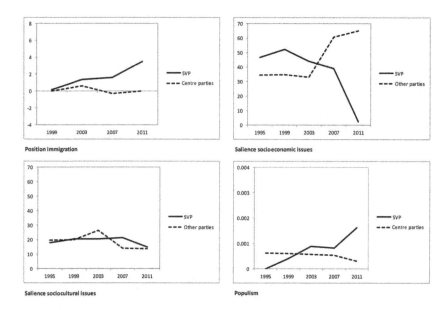

Figure A.8 Switzerland

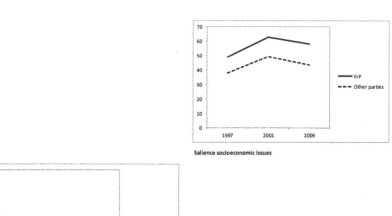

Figure A.9 Norway

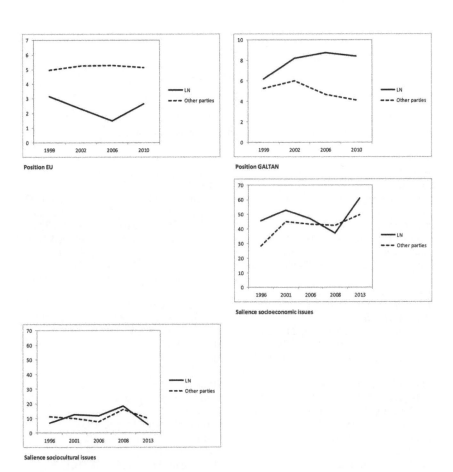

Figure A.10 Italy

Index

Note: Individual parties are shown under their respective countries